Praise for
A Generation of Sociopaths

"Informative, provocative, and entertaining reading for those interested in political economy and U.S. social and economic history."   —*Booklist*

"Gibney lays into the 'Me' generation for cashing out their children's future and leaving the planet looking like a rock star's hotel room...Timely."
—*Esquire*

"*A Generation of Sociopaths* is a polemic, but what a polemic: filled with data, rich in anecdote, deadly serious yet wickedly funny."
—Alexandra Wolfe, author of *Valley of the Gods:*
A Silicon Valley Story

"The core of Gibney's argument, that the boomers are guilty of 'generational plunder,' is spot-on. He accuses them of 'the mass, democratically sanctioned transfer of wealth away from the young and toward the Boomers,' and he's right."   —Dana Milbank, *Washington Post*

"Remarkable...Impressively weighted with hard numbers and specifics, the volume serves as both an indictment of and rebuttal to a Woodstock Generation that has gleefully celebrated themselves for decades while gradually running the country into the ground...Gibney paints a persuasive and frequently hilarious portrait of the Me Generation."   —*Men's Journal*

"Like Thomas Piketty's *Capital in the Twenty-First Century*, Bruce Cannon Gibney's *A Generation of Sociopaths* proceeds from a deceptively simple premise: that the gains made by the American middle class in the period after the world wars of the previous century were a fluke...A damning, searingly relevant indictment."   —*The Globe and Mail* (Canada)

"[Gibney] maintains that the Boomer Generation, privilege incarnate, exhibit all the traits associated with that clinical pathology: 'deceit, selfishness, imprudence, remorselessness, hostility, the works.' He argues the case well."
—*Toronto Star*

A Generation of
Sociopaths

How the Baby Boomers Betrayed America

Bruce Cannon Gibney

New York   Boston

Hachette Books
Hachette Book Group
1290 Avenue of the Americas
New York, NY 10104
hachettebookgroup.com
twitter.com/hachettebooks

Originally published as a hardcover and ebook in 2017 by Hachette Books, Inc.

First trade paperback edition: March 2018

Hachette Books is a division of Hachette Book Group, Inc.

The Hachette Books name and logo are trademarks of Hachette Book Group, Inc.

The publisher is not responsible for websites (or their content) that are not owned by the publisher.

The Hachette Speakers Bureau provides a wide range of authors for speaking events. To find out more, go to www.hachettespeakersbureau.com or call (866) 376-6591.

LCCN: 2016046022
ISBN: 978-0-316-39579-3 (pbk.)

Printed in the United States of America

LSC-C

10 9 8 7 6 5 4 3 2 1

To my parents, Jeb and Ling-yee Gibney

CONTENTS

CONTENTS

Society is no comfort
To one not sociable.
—William Shakespeare, *Cymbeline*, Act 4, Scene 2

Great Kronos kept swallowing them as each arrived at
his mother's knees from her sacred womb, intending
that no other one of the illustrious children of Ouranos
hold the kingly province among the immortals.
—Hesiod, *Theogony*

FOREWORD

What happens if society is run by people who are, to a large degree, antisocial? I don't mean people who are "antisocial" in the general sense, the sort who avoid parties and hide from the neighbors. I mean people who are antisocial in the *clinical* sense: sociopaths. Could a sociopathic society function? Unfortunately, this is not a thought experiment or an investigation into some ramshackle dictatorship in a distant land; it is America's lived experience. For the past several decades, the nation has been run by people who present, personally and politically, the full sociopathic pathology: deceit, selfishness, imprudence, remorselessness, hostility, the works. Those people are the Baby Boomers, that vast and strange generation born between 1940 and 1964, and the society they created does not work very well.

Some of the sociopathic society's malfunctions appear in the daily headlines: collapsing bridges, fresh deficits, poisoned water, collapsing ice sheets, financial catastrophes, and an economy lurching from one disaster to another, with only the most anemic recoveries in between. Other disturbances lurk out of the spotlight, in the back pages of the business section, dense academic literature, and complicated government spreadsheets: pension systems now trillions of dollars underfunded, a Social Security system destined (by the government's own admission) to falter, a corrections system that presides over nearly seven million people, and a political culture so warped that the Supreme Court recently found itself unable to distinguish between gross corruption and business as usual. Individually, these items are tragic vignettes. Stitched together, they produce a cohesive and unsettling narrative of a generation that—in the many decades it has dominated political and corporate America—squandered its enormous inheritance, abused its power, and subsidized its binges with loans collateralized by its children.

The premise of a stagnating and dysfunctional America is not particularly controversial. Blaming the Boomers might be more provocative, but after decades of dysfunction under Boomer leaders and the grotesque spectacle of recent elections, which force us to endure more of the same, provocation may be necessary. For those readers who are Boomers, or have parents or grandparents who are Boomers, it may be of small comfort that this book does not argue that *all* Baby Boomers are sociopaths. Rather, the argument is that an unusually large number of Boomers have behaved antisocially, skewing outcomes in ways deeply unfavorable to the nation, especially its younger citizens. The challenge is to prove it, not merely by pointing out the (by now fairly clear) correlation between American underperformance and Boomer tenure, but by establishing causal links between Boomer misbehavior and national stagnation. There is, as it happens, a diverse and large body of evidence to support the case.

It didn't have to be this way, and for a long time, nothing like America's present dilemma seemed remotely probable. In 1946, the United States was unquestionably the richest, most dynamic country the world had seen, a nation that overcame the tragedies of the Great Depression and two World Wars to achieve remarkable gains in prosperity and freedom. Success built on success, and while there had been occasional setbacks like the Korean War, the assassinations of John F. Kennedy and Martin Luther King, the Vietnam debacle, and the stagflation of the 1970s, America just kept leaping ahead until, one day, it didn't. This is odd, because by historical standards, every challenge after 1946 was minor compared to what had come before; all should have been easily surmounted, and, for a time, most were. But the fact is that American dynamism did peter out, no later than the 1990s. The question that originally perplexed me wasn't the semi-academic paradox of the antisocial society; it was something more direct: why isn't twenty-first-century America doing vastly better? Readers under forty might pose the question a little differently, not as "Have we been screwed?"—they already sense the answer to that—but "How badly?" and "By whom?"

The various and dispiriting candidates of recent years have offered their own explanations for the mystery of American underperformance, though being mainly Boomers themselves and dependent on Boomer votes, they have relocated blame to other suspects: unfair trade, rapacious immigrants, vicious superPACs, greedy corporations, hyperpartisanship, foreign terrorism, a predatory 1 percent or a lazy 99 percent, too much federal government or too little, not enough Trumpism and altogether too much. Yet, the most compelling answers are not found in candidates' position papers, but in the facts of the elections themselves. Not only have we heard these explanations before, in many cases we have heard them from *these very same candidates*, forever peddling the same magic beans of fantasy and excuse. Even the presidential election of 2016, despite its superficial weirdness—a contest between two desperately unpopular nominees winnowed out of an inventory of even less appealing also-rans—was really notable only for the sheer staleness of the leftovers.

This political recycling, right down to the surnames, should have been a sufficient reminder that the candidates had themselves been the authors and practitioners of the nation's despoliation. Many candidates were incumbents or had served in other offices, and essentially all of them were members of the political and business establishment that created the mess in the first place. The only real development was that the excuses were getting more baroque as the facts got worse; the practitioners and their dogma remained the same, as they have for decades. More middle-class tax cuts, more perorations on the sacral nature of Social Security, more promises of change without any real plans for achieving it, more blame located everywhere except the obvious places. Boomer politics are like Ptolemy's astronomy, where new and inconvenient evidence is explained by increasingly complicated epicycles and exceptions; the system itself is never fundamentally questioned. At some point, implausible systems have to be jettisoned in the face of overwhelming evidence, in favor of simpler and better explanations.

This book's explanation is straightforward: America suffers from its present predicament because a large group of small-minded people *chose* the leaders and actions that led to our present degraded state. Combing over the data, a picture emerges, one of bad behaviors and unchecked self-interest, occurring at the individual level and recapitulated, via the voting booth, by the state. No Ptolemaic epicycles, Rube Goldberg political machinery, or Koch/Voldemorts need be invoked. The only requirement was the exercise of the vote by a huge group, united by short-sightedness and self-interest: the Boomers.

Can the case be made: Can an entire generation be described as sociopathic? Long after I started this book, people took to diagnosing presidential candidates (one in particular) and a debate ensued about psychological labeling—not so much about whether the labels were accurate as much as whether they could be properly justified. It may seem even trickier to describe a generation than an individual—but if anything, it's easier. There is a huge amount of proxy data—a truly depressing and varied amount—collected over long periods, all of which serve as evidence. The Boomers' disinclination to save maps to a key sociopathic characteristic, improvidence. Data on sexual behavior, drug use, and divorce correspond to sociopathic characteristics like risk seeking and an inability to form lasting relationships. We can populate the entire clinical checklist this way, a vast tasting menu of dysfunction, no substitutions allowed. Our results correspond to one of the few major studies of mental health issues in the United States, the ECAS, which found significantly higher levels of sociopathy in Boomer-age populations in the 1980s relative to other groups.[1] There is something wrong with the Boomers and there has been for a long time.

If the Boomers' status as sociopaths is of great, if abstract, interest, the effects of their sociopathy are matters of undeniable and tangible consequence. The more power Boomers accumulated, the more self-serving and destructive their policies became. For purely selfish reasons, the Boomers unraveled the social fabric woven by previous generations. We can match the sociopathic checklist to Boomer behaviors, Boomer behaviors to social policies, and social policies to the nation's present difficulties, tracing causation. Because this is a book and not an address to Congress, it enjoys privileges denied even to presidents: it can argue that the state of the union is *not* good, that Congress is at fault, and that a plurality of the people who voted for Congress and its warped policies are to blame.

For some time, no president has dared to defy the Boomers, a generation whose enormous size always meant they would be powerful and who started making that power felt from the 1970s on. Eventually, Boomers displaced other generations almost entirely, and Boomerism reached its peak (or nadir) under generational representatives like Bill Clinton, Newt Gingrich, George W. Bush, Donald Trump, and Dennis Hastert—a stew of philanderers, draft dodgers, tax avoiders, incompetents, hypocrites, holders of high office censured for ethical violations, a sociopathic sundae whose squalid cherry was provided in 2016 by Hastert's admission of child molestation, itself a grotesque metaphor for Boomer policies. *Someone* had to elect these tornadoes of vice and it was, of course, Boomers who were content, often enthusiastic, to vote for people who looked like them and showered them with improvident goodies, whose failures were often overlooked and forgiven because they seemed so familiar.

In Silicon Valley, where I spent most of my career, it's standard to ask what constitutes a given project's "value proposition," B-school jargon that reduces in this case to: What are you getting for the cover price? Above all, this book's goal is to collect in one place and under one narrative the diverse and distressing stories glancingly treated in the media churn, and to trace their origin. Younger readers wishing to induce apoplexy at the next family reunion will find additional utility in these pages—Uncle Jim may think kids these days are terrible (Snapchat! Tattoos! Jeans in the office!), but when confronted with the evidence of what *actually* happened in the Sixties, he might fall refreshingly silent, especially when you explain exactly how many of your tax dollars subsidize his health care. The nonsociopathic wing of the Boomer generation may also find value in seeing the acts of their contemporaries in a different light and be persuaded to stand against a sociopathic agenda that serves them at the expense of their children.

The subject may be grave, but this book has its optimistic moments. America is not on a death march from which the only escape is a razor and a warm bath, or the often-promised-never-practiced emigration to Canada. Although the Boomers will not relinquish their grip on power for some time—2016 proved that—demographic changes will eventually end Boomer dominance. While it is too soon to know how subsequent generations will perform when they finally take control, we have early indications that they will be better stewards than the Boomers, who appear to be a sociopathic anomaly. And America, whatever Donald Trump or any of his avatars say, is still great, still rich and powerful; it's just operating well below potential. Even a plague of generational locusts like the Boomers can do only so much damage in a lifetime, however unduly prolonged that lifetime may be courtesy of benefits funded by the young. These facts are what permit optimism and also a little gallows humor; the noose may be on, but it's not inescapably tight. It helps that the Boomers are often ridiculous, and this book supplies ridicule accordingly, not for spite (or at least, not for spite alone). All tin-pot expropriators have fragile egos, and if sarcasm helps ease the Boomers out of office, let there be sarcasm.

For now, the Boomers are in power; as 2017 began, they again controlled every branch of government. And this is despite the Boomers disgorging the most revolting example of electoral politics since the Gilded Age, a spectacle whose angry, populist results were (perversely) guaranteed by the social and economic dilemmas bequeathed by earlier Boomer policies. That Boomers would sweep government in the 2016 elections was never in doubt, even if the identity of the new president surprised many. The choices, as often noted, were less than ideal. Hillary Clinton, the longtime fixture of the Boomer establishment, viewed her nomination in the same way that seniors view Social Security, as an entitlement to be realized whatever the risk. Donald Trump, the Section 8 scion, a bully whose quantum of thought is no greater than a tweet, decided to prove that the lowest common denominator could be found further down than anyone in the commentariat thought possible. That Clinton and Trump were the two most unpopular presidential candidates in decades, if not since the Civil War, deterred the Boomer machine not a whit, because they all agreed on what mattered.

Thus, while there were very real differences between Clinton and Trump, many pundits did not fully appreciate what the candidates had in common, starting with an unshakeable commitment to senior benefits—which should have been sufficient notice of which group would decide the election and what other generations would pay the inevitable bill. It would be ridiculous to argue that the candidates (or many of their Mini-Mes down ballot) were equivalent, but neither were they different enough. The choices in November 2016 were only about how bad the following years would be. Would the already sizeable debt balloon by another $3–5 trillion or by $5–15 trillion, the proceeds expended on projects either somewhat dubious or mostly self-defeating; would the disabling legal scandal emerge as civil litigation over prior frauds or as a ginned-up impeachment by a Boomer Congress; would the cronyism be only significant or completely outrageous; would the earth simmer or would it roast; and in what ways would the rule of law be undermined by presidential arrogance? In the week this book went to press, the electorate decided and Boomers provided the critical votes. But essentially nothing already written here had to change—the sheer inertia of Boomerism guaranteed some sort of fiasco would unfold at every level, whether it was Madam or Mister President on January 20th. It's true that voting participation by youth could have been more vigorous, but we should not blame the victims too much. In an election between Boomers, mostly moderated by Boomers, and heavily covered by Boomers, a process in which the issues of greatest moment to the young—climate change, education policy, the debt—took a backseat or were simply not mentioned at all during debates, it's understandable that many young people declined to participate in the Hobson's Choice offered to them; they had no good option. However infeasible his policies were, Bernie Sanders was the only candidate to give the needs of the young real priority, and he was dispatched by a Democratic Boomer machine busily giving Mrs. Clinton her "due." If young people were cynical and disengaged, they were not without partial justification.

The final exit polls were sliced and diced into the rich, the poor, the educated, the not, the rural and the urban, white and non-white, but in important ways, it was always going to be Boomer versus not-Boomer. (I generally define the Boomers as the eroding middle-class white cohort born 1940 to 1964 for reasons we will shortly take up, and in the states where such people predominate, the pivots of the election could be found.) In the end, the country broke Boomerish and Boomers broke the country, yet again. It would be a mistake to view the events of 2016, however startling, as a total outlier or to ascribe overmuch to the personal infirmities of the candidates; the candidates did not, after all, emerge from nowhere. They and their many companions in business and politics were merely vessels for the Boomer id.

Still, the country remixes the legislature every two years and resets the presidency every four. The opportunities of the coming years should be seized; for issues like climate and debt, the elections of the coming years may be the last stops before irreversible catastrophe. Unless younger generations remove the Boomers from power *soon*, the next quarter century will be even worse than the last one—a parade of missed opportunities and bad choices. The poor choices the Boomers have already made and the results they engendered are reflected in this book's charts, snapshots of the decades of Boomer power. In the charts, lines that should have been going steadily up (like median income) have flattened and sometimes plunged, while lines that should be going down (like debt and obesity rates) have been going up, trends that will continue absent dramatic change. There aren't many excuses for these failures, only explanations, and they all point the same way, as they have for years.

What qualifies me to write this book? I hope the evidence ultimately speaks for itself, rendering biographical details of only passing interest. Since we're at the beginning, here's my backstory: I spent most of my career in finance, first at a hedge fund and then at a venture capital firm.* Both jobs required me to think about where the markets would go, what companies might succeed, and by necessity, about the American future and the forces shaping it. About half my career was spent during some kind of recession, crisis, or pseudorecovery, which is odd enough when you think about it, a reason in itself to explore American stagnation. If half of all American history had been as mediocre as the past few decades, there would be a lot fewer stars on the flag, and no American flags on the moon.

Still, years of economic mediocrity notwithstanding, there always seemed to be a few good things to invest in, *if* you were in the right place at the right time. For me, in 1998, that thing was PayPal (my college roommate cofounded the company, and I bought some early shares); in 2004, it was Facebook (my then boss made the first outside investment in the social network, and I worked as a junior associate on part of that deal). Later, I made personal investments in SpaceX, Lyft, Palantir, and DeepMind, which are not all household names, though they have succeeded well enough. But

---

* For the constructivists, that history probably establishes me as a free-market capitalist, albeit one who will argue for higher taxes and more (and more competent) regulation.

these companies were exceptions, very rare ones. I mention them less to establish my credibility as a prognosticator than to show the value of socially funded innovation (every company I mentioned was built on technologies pioneered by government grants or research) and, most important, to show the overwhelming importance of luck in a stagnating economy. Sharing a dorm with the next Mark Zuckerberg is a boon not to be denied, but in the luck department, it really should be enough to be born American. And so it was, before the Boomers took over. Most Americans with moderate talent and ambition could find a good job, buy a home, and invest their savings in the Standard & Poor's 500, and in doing so, accumulate enough for a comfortable retirement. But proper jobs are increasingly hard to find, and buying and holding the S&P 500 *today* (which is to say, making a long-term bet on America) doesn't seem like a sure path to Happily Ever After. Thanks to perpetual financial crisis, you can't even expect a real, positive return on cash in the bank. Again, why?

My first attempt to answer these sorts of questions came in a 2011 essay, "What Happened to the Future?" which worried about deceleration in technological progress. (That essay's tagline—"We wanted flying cars, instead we got 140 characters"—is recycled by the media whenever it wants to passingly indict technological failure.) While I think that essay was correct on its own, narrow terms, the dynamics of national stagnation transcend Silicon Valley specifically and technology generally. This book is my attempt to present a comprehensive explanation, and research led to the Boomers. What happened to the future? The Boomers did; they sold it off piece by piece.

And so let us begin with one more question. If the nation had been unblighted by Boomer sociopathy, how well could we have been doing? Shockingly well, as it turns out.

INTRODUCTION

The difference between an American and any other kind
of person is that an American lives in anticipation of
the future because he knows it will be a great place.
—Ronald Reagan (1979)[1]

The Gipper believed many silly things—in voodoo economics and, in the case of his White House astrologer, just plain voodoo—but one thing Reagan truly *knew* was that the Americans he would lead were optimistic people, and that their optimism made an otherwise disparate and divided land a functional and thriving nation. In 1979, Reagan was right; he was still right when he left office in 1989. By 2002, Reagan would have been wrong: A majority of Americans no longer believed their children would live better lives than their parents—and that was *before* the crash of 2008 and eight years of lackluster recovery.[2] By 2016, American optimism had shrunk into the form of a tacky hat ("Make America Great Again!") peddled by a serial corporate bankrupt who could not manage to make his shambolic empire great even once, let alone "again."[3] That was not how it was supposed to be.

The goal of American politics has been, until the advent of the Boomers, the creation of a "more perfect Union" and the promotion of the "general Welfare" to "secure the Blessings of Liberty to ourselves and our Posterity."[4] The Constitution promises as much, and over time America generally made good on that promise, first to a few, then to many. By the twentieth century, constitutional abstractions had taken concrete form, and "Blessings" in the modern vernacular were understood to mean the creation of an ever larger and more affluent middle class. If the middle was not doing well, neither was America. James Carville, the operative who brought Bill Clinton to power as the first Boomer president, understood that modern politics boiled down to "It's the economy, stupid." And the Council of Economic Advisers (CEA) has made clear how to evaluate that economy: the "well-being of the middle class and those working to get into the middle class…is the ultimate test of an economy's performance."[5] Measured against the Constitution's noble imperatives or the more prosaic words of Carville and the CEA, America generally made a great success of things for two centuries. Since the Boomers' ascension to power, America has accomplished far too little, and in many important ways, has slid backward.

A "more perfect Union" is hard to measure, but the economy and the well-being of the middle class are not. These latter items can be reduced to numbers, and what the numbers show is not reassuring. A family with a statistically middling income can no longer afford the trappings of an actual middle-class life: the nice house, college tuition, decent cars, the annual vacation, appropriate health care, some prudent savings, and perhaps a little left over to pass as a legacy. That life would require something like $100,000–150,000 in annual family income, depending on geography and taste, but actual family income was just $70,697 in 2015.[6] As for the "Posterity" that obsessed the Founders, it may do considerably worse.

The difference between what is and what could have been is substantially the product of Boomer mismanagement and selfishness. Had America pursued more reasonable policies, it might have continued the pattern of growth of the golden years after World War II and before the arrival of Boomer power. Family income in 2015 could have been around $106,000 to $122,000 (or $113,425 to be misleadingly precise). In other words, the actual middle class could afford genuinely middle-class lives. Editorialists would never have had to switch adjectives from "comfortable" to "struggling" when discussing the midriff of the income distribution.

Family Income—What Is and What Could Have Been

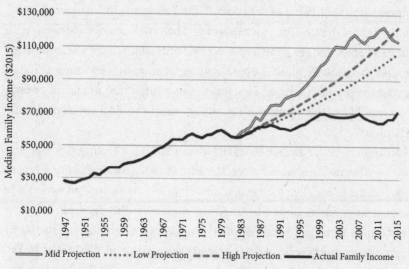

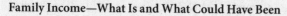

What's going on here? This is a "counterfactual"—the path American family incomes would have taken if they had kept growing at pre-Boomer rates. Under all projections incomes would have been substantially higher than they are today. The "mid" estimate projects incomes as if they had grown in exactly the same way, year by year, with all the ups and downs, as they had in the pre-Boomer period through the 1981–1982 recession. The "low" and "high" estimates construct smooth averages, respectively including and excluding the early Eighties recession. In every scenario, there have been substantial lost opportunities, with gaps really widening as Boomer power and policies took hold. None of this is to say that America hasn't grown, it just hasn't grown as fast or equally as it could have or once did.[7]

The numerical gap is compelling in an abstract way, but the loss can be felt most viscerally in, of all places, Flushing Meadows, Queens. People passing from JFK to Manhattan, or watching aerial shots of the US Open, may have noticed saucer-topped towers and a strange steel globe, artifacts left by aliens with a *Mad Men* aesthetic, right in the Meadows. These oddities are the neglected remnants of the 1964 World's Fair, which promised a world of flying cars, undersea colonies, clean energy, mass prosperity, cities on the moon, and more. *That* was what the early twenty-first century was supposed to be like. The Fair's promotional video promised, in full mid-century sincerity, a time when the "science of plenty" delivered a "city of tomorrow," with humanity charting "a course...that frees the mind and spirit and improves the well-being of mankind."[8] The Fair has vanished and so, eventually, did the dream. The Fair's neighbor, Shea Stadium, opened along with the Fair; Shea, too, is gone, replaced by Citi Field, which was completed around the time its giant corporate namesake nearly went under. Today, against the rust, cobwebs, and a stadium named after the paradox of a nearly bankrupt bank, the whole rah-rah optimism of the '64 Fair seems faintly ridiculous.

No one in 1964, however, would have seen the Fair's Technicolor fantasias as naïve. Twenty-five years before, the Fair of 1939, also in Flushing Meadows, had made equally ambitious claims. The '39 Fair foresaw an America of convenient suburbs, linked by interstate highways, ending at plush homes from which want had been banished, predictions offered at the distinctly unpromising juncture between the Great Depression and World War II. Yet, by 1964, *it had all come true*. With the promises of the '39 Fair (centerpiece: Futurama) already fulfilled, Americans of 1964 saw no reason why they would not soon enjoy the dreams of their own Fair (featuring: Futurama II). By the 2010s, Americans were supposed to be living richly, attended by a robotic staff, with the occasional vacation to the Lunar Hilton. Obviously, none of that came to be: There is no Pan Am flight to the moon; there isn't even a Pan Am anymore. What actually happened was that in 1969 Neil Armstrong stepped onto the moon and in 1972 Gene Cernan stepped off, and that was it. The future slipped away and the timing was not coincidental. By the late 1960s, the earnest and industrious old regime was fading. The future would soon be reposed in the hands of a group altogether less competent and well-meaning.

———

Like all chronicles of a big country over a long period, this book faces the same dilemma as Jorge Luis Borges's imperial mapmakers: to be entirely precise would require creating a map as big as the subject itself. One of the virtues of data is that it resolves at least some of the mapmakers' problem, reducing the 324-odd million stories of the American people into comprehensible summaries and simple charts.[9] What these data show is what those millions of citizens sense: The country is off course. Median income growth has been slow, then stagnant, and at times in the recent past, outright negative. America's other vital signs are producing similarly ominous bleeps.

America is not, however, poor. In fact, America is substantially richer in the twenty-first century than it was in the twentieth, and the rise in *average*, rather than median, incomes reflects that. The divergence between mean and median reflects gains by the top end of the distribution. The Constitution's pursuit of "general welfare" has turned into a very specific kind of welfare. It isn't quite as simple as the 99 percent versus the 1 percent. Rather, it is the mass, democratically sanctioned transfer of wealth away from the young and toward the Boomers, the latter having adjusted tax and fiscal policies to favor the accumulation of wealth during their lives, at the expense of the future—a future whose course is of little concern, because whatever failures it holds will be cushioned by the tens of trillions of entitlement dollars Boomers will receive. Whatever you think about the 1 percent (and many of them are Boomers), their accumulations pale in comparison to the generational plunder of the Boomers overall.

A casual stroll through average neighborhoods would not reveal any major signs of decline; there would be few hints of even the gross divergence between the reality of middle-class incomes and middle-class expenses. Living standards still seem relatively good, and there is a simple explanation: People tread water by borrowing. As a fraction of gross domestic product (GDP), debt owed by American families has roughly doubled since 1980, and in nominal terms is over $14 trillion. Government has done the same—indeed, this is a primary Boomer tactic to ensure their benefits flow while expenses pass to others. The national debt has almost tripled as a fraction of GDP since the mid-1970s, so that the nation's debt is now slightly larger than the nation's total annual product, approaching $19 trillion by the end of 2015, and that figure is set to grow ~3 percent annually, more or less indefinitely. The proceeds from that expanding pile of debt have been used to consume, not to invest, and so growth, already slow, will get slower still. Eventually, it will become impossible to sustain living standards by borrowing. And at some roughly coterminous point, the Boomers will be dead and the problem will belong to someone else.

That someone else, of course, is statistically likely to be: *you*.

The central theme of this book is that America's present dilemma resulted substantially and directly from choices made by the Baby Boomers. Their collective, pathological self-interest derailed a long train of progress, while exacerbating and ignoring existential threats like climate change. The Boomers' sociopathic need for instant gratification pushed them to equally sociopathic policies, causing them to fritter away an enormous inheritance, and when that was exhausted, to mortgage the future. When the consequences became troubling, Boomer leadership engaged in concealment and deception in a desperate effort to hold the system together just long enough for their generational constituencies to pass from the scene. The story of the Boomers is, in other words, the story of a generation of sociopaths running amok.*

Sociopathy is characterized by self-interested actions unburdened by conscience and unresponsive to consequence, mostly arising from non-genetic, contextual causes. The current professional standard, the fifth edition of *The Diagnostic and Statistical Manual of Mental Disorders* (the DSM-V), focuses on the following criteria, which our Boomer subjects must display relatively constantly across time and context, including "moderate or greater impairments in personality function" due to:

1. ego-centrism; self-esteem derived from personal gain, power or pleasure; goal-setting based on personal gratification; absence of prosocial internal standards and associated failure to conform to lawful or culturally normative ethical behavior;
2. lack of concern for the feelings, needs or suffering of others...incapacity for mutually intimate relationships, as exploitation is a primary means of relating to others; and,
3. disinhibition [irresponsibility, impulsivity, risk taking] and antagonism [manipulativeness, deceitfulness, callousness, hostility].[10]

---

* For this book, I treat the Boomers as generally white and always native-born, for reasons that will become clear in Chapter 1, and also because the lives of certain minorities, especially of blacks, were significantly different from those of whites, who formed the vast majority of the Boom. From time to time, minorities do make an appearance in the book, because how the Boomers treated their minority cogenerationalists often fell well below stated ideals, but to do justice to the minority experience requires an entirely separate book.

In other words, sociopaths are selfish, imprudent, remorseless, and relentless. "Me first and damn the consequences"—that's the sociopathic motto.

As individuals, Boomers are a mixed bag of good and bad. But *as a generation*, the Boomers present as distinctly sociopathic, displaying antisocial tendencies to a greater extent than their parents and their children. As policy, these behaviors manifest in subtle ways. The AARP has unleashed no hordes of scooter-powered geriatrics to lash Millennials to the train tracks. Instead, villainy expresses itself through the mundane depredations of tax policy and technical revisions to the bankruptcy code. These and other adjustments are insidious, all the more effective for being harder to see.

The first two chapters of this book begin by identifying the "nongenetic, contextual" causes of Boomer sociopathy and the first expression of its symptoms, which began as personal and would end as political. While the Boomers' childhoods are long past, they remain relevant, that we might see what the Boomers had, what they wasted, and what methods of child rearing never to repeat. For readers born after the 1960s, these chapters are revealing excursions into a totally unfamiliar society, one that despite its many imperfections was decidedly nonsociopathic and not coincidentally politically functional, fast growing, and rich with advances in everything from medicine to civil justice. Because we cannot run a controlled experiment—we can tap no alternate universe of an America without the Boomers—the period between the 1940s and the Boomer ascendancy is as close as we can come to seeing the benefits of a prosocial agenda. And the benefits were considerable; America is in many ways still living off that legacy.

Chapter 3 witnesses the rise of Boomer sociopathy, when Vietnam emerged as the defining experience of early Boomer adulthood. An age-based draft forced mainstream Boomers to cohere, rather uniquely, on generational lines. Vietnam provided an early stage for sociopathic behaviors, as young people were simultaneously the most hawkish about the war and also busily evading the draft, by means whose legality varied, but whose net effect was to shift burdens to America's most disadvantaged communities. Boomers may now remember Vietnam otherwise, just as in 1945 every Frenchman claimed that he had been a resistance fighter all along. But we need not rely on convenient memories. We have the data, and they paint a less flattering picture.

Chapter 4 follows the Boomers' downward slide, showing the development of other sociopathic behaviors—deceit, empathy deficits, relationship failures, self-indulgence, and financial mismanagement. Boomers divorced, borrowed, ate, and spent improvidently, relative to their parents and their children at comparable ages. Disabled by sociopathy, Boomers also began abandoning reason itself. The sociopaths would be governed by feelings (though never ones of empathy), which liberated Boomers from considering tiresome evidence suggesting their practices might be destructive.

Eventually, private behaviors congealed into a debased neoliberalism, the sociopathic operating system that has dominated Boomer politics, Right and Left, for more than three decades. The Boomers' ersatz neoliberalism emphasizes consumption over production, dogmatic deregulation instead of thoughtful oversight, permanent deficits instead of fiscal prudence, and capitalism liberated from the bounds of the state, though always free to replenish itself at the federal trough in the event "sub-prime mortgages," "junk bonds," or "collateralized debt obligations" somehow lived up to their names.

The heart of the book then details the implementation of the Boomers' sociopathic agenda and its consequences. It starts with the wholly democratic means by which the revolution was achieved, courtesy of the Boomers' vast numbers, which made the generation an outright majority of the electorate by the early 1980s. Long influential as voters, Boomers had by the early 1990s achieved full institutional power, starting with control of the White House in 1993, half of the House the following term, and by 1995 holding the nation's top three offices, with colonization of courts and governors' mansions proceeding apace.* Their hold on all three branches

---

* One can question whether Barack Obama, a chronological Boomer, is really a cogenerationalist. Half black, raised in a distant part of the United States and then Indonesia, Obama comes from a very different background than mainline Boomers, and this may explain why his White House was comparatively moderate and scandal free. Nevertheless, until his last feverish year of executive orders, Obama was routinely hemmed in by a distinctly Boomerish Congress, and he was not without his own Boomerish tendencies. His presidency compares favorably with what came before and what will probably follow, but it is not marked by the sorts of accomplishments seen under Dwight Eisenhower or Lyndon Johnson.

of government reached its peak in the mid-2000s, when Boomers made up 79 percent of the House, and they still retained a supermajority a decade later, when I was finishing this book. Even the occasional deposition by a younger officer—like Speaker John Boehner by Paul Ryan—could be off-set in other areas, as with the succession of Boomer John Roberts to William Rehnquist's seat at the top of the federal judiciary, or directly, as with Trump's emasculation of Ryan.

With government at their disposal, the Boomers could fully realize their sociopathic goals. The popular story of recent years is that government is dysfunctional. Viewed through the red-and-blue lenses of pundits, that may seem to be the case, and in many places there is some truth to this account. But through *generational* lenses, one sees a smoothly functioning system, consistently delivering benefits to its most powerful constituents. And it is benefits—economic benefits—that serve as the abiding interest of the Boomers and represent their antisocial endgame. The parts of government that serve the Boomers must work, and do.

Nowhere did sociopathic avarice, deceit, imprudence, and political power combine more powerfully than in tax policy, which allowed the Boomers to reshuffle in their favor the benefits and obligations of an entire economy. The impact on the total tax take, while problematic, was surprisingly modest; the generational burden shifting and unrestrained, underfunded spending, however, were breathtaking. Whatever the economic climate, whichever the party, tax policy evolved in ways that favored Boomers and their (perceived) interests.

These chapters also examine (again, in varied and wide contexts) the Boomers' sociopathic "improvidence"—a word Boomer behavior forces me to use frequently—a trait manifesting notably in Boomer disdain toward investing for the Posterity cherished by an increasingly obsolete Constitution. The sociopaths' goal is to wring every last dollar from the system, and any investment that could not be fully realized within Boomer lifetimes was to be avoided. Therefore, the nation's infrastructure, built by the Boomers' parents and once the world's finest, was allowed to decay. Henceforth, state-sponsored research would be radically curtailed. Higher education was neglected; the Boomers had their cost-free diplomas in hand, so meaningful reform and costly subsidies were no longer relevant. Public tuition, formerly zero, could rise dramatically. Even better, the loans taken out to meet those new educational bills, including those produced by the Boomer-created plague of for-profit colleges, could be converted into today's $1.3 trillion of student loans, profits on which the Boomers harvest and shall so forever, thanks to a modification of the bankruptcy code in 2005 that makes student debt nearly impossible to discharge. The Flower Child of Berkeley would become the Merchant of Midtown.

Just as sociopathy limits the horizons of planning to the Boomers' lifetimes in matters of investment, so it does for existential crises whose arrivals Boomers expect to be postmortem. Future generations being Not-Self are of minimal concern to the sociopath. Unlike acid rain, which had immediate impacts on Boomers' quality of life and was therefore swiftly addressed, climate change is a problem whose consequences will fall most heavily on other generations, so far too little has been done. Other existential crises have been equally ignored, like the risks posed by artificial intelligence. But sentient machines being at least twenty-five years away, so long as Amazon's neural networks continue to improve on the timely delivery of Depends, AI may be treated with malignant neglect.

Given the unpalatable scale of the Boomers' expropriations, political power sometimes required garnishment with pleasing untruths. Fortunately, "manipulativeness," "deceit," and "hostility" are something of a sociopathic forte. Concealment and pacification were deployed as necessary to keep the machine operating at maximum antisocial efficiency; examples appear throughout the book. The mechanisms of finance have proved especially useful. Economic decline has been papered over by debt and chicanery, especially on matters of pensions and entitlements.

When problems could no longer be hidden, there was always the expedient of the bald-faced lie. Sometimes the lies work and even when they don't, they provide helpful distractions from the real issues. Consider that the most powerful people in the world spent months in 1998–1999 parsing whether the insertion of a cigar into a vagina or the receipt of fellatio counted as sex, instead of, say, addressing the known and looming crisis of Social Security. Consider also Bill Clinton's treatment of language in his subsequent perjury scandal, which is worth quoting for its entertaining and generationally representative dishonesty:

> It depends on what the meaning of the word "is" is. If the—if he—if "is" means is and never has been, that is not—that is one thing. If it means there is none, that was a completely true statement...Now, if someone had asked me on that day, are you having any kind of sexual relations with Ms. Lewinsky, that is, asked me a question in the present tense, I would have said no. *And it would have been completely true.*[11]

The quintessential Boomer, his generation's most brilliant and influential politician, could not even manage an honest conjugation of "to be," the most fundamental verb in the language. If real issues can no longer be seriously discussed, it is because there is (or "is-is") literally no way to have the discussion—"literally," in the sense that there is no reliable language in which to conduct debate. And, from January 20, 2017, the lexical landscape will degrade further still.

What problems could not be swept into financial footnotes or lied about could always be locked away, and under the Boomers, American imprisonment rates have spiked to by far the highest rate in any major nation, a terrifying instance of sociopathic hostility. Just as the Boomer financial machine failed to plan for financial contingency, so too have Boomer politicians failed to provide a mechanism for the reintegration of this giant population. Prisoners have become the human equivalent of Wall Street's deferred liabilities, to be released at someone else's expense once Boomers safely recede into their gated retirement communities.

That the economy has failed to live up to its promise is bad enough. That the Boomers have not made investments in future prosperity is worse. That they have done so to pay their green fees is reprehensible. That they have lied about what is going on and persistently ignored threats that have a real chance of killing some of their children is sociopathy of the highest order.

———

This is a book, not a trial. It seeks to inform, persuade, and occasionally entertain; no legal code binds the discussion. Nevertheless, the law provides a convenient frame of reference, embodying socially acceptable standards of proof and fairness. (My very brief first job was as a litigator, but once a lawyer, always a lawyer.) As to proof, much of the evidence is necessarily circumstantial. Whatever defense attorneys on legal dramas say to the contrary, nothing prohibits a verdict based on circumstantial evidence. Obviously, the present case turns on nothing so convenient as the minutes of some secret Boomer conference voting to abscond with the national patrimony, though the *Congressional Record* provides considerable service in this respect. Beyond the hard facts of Boomer legislation, an enormous body of incriminating evidence exists. If the sheer size of the Boomer generation is what allows them to despoil the nation, size also permits us to trace patterns in the data.

Will that data prove the case beyond a reasonable doubt? That's the hope, but not the hurdle. This book doesn't propose to sentence Boomers to some sort of maximum-security retirement home. It seeks to promote behaviors and policies that help lay the grounds for future prosperity, and to liberate the necessary funds from Boomer wallets fattened by the profits of sociopathy. As to those reparations, the standard for money damages in a civil case is "preponderance of the evidence." If by the end of the book you think it is more likely than not that the Boomers committed generational expropriations, the standard will have been satisfied.

Whether or not a given Boomer participated directly in the plunder, all of them reaped at least some of its benefits and a great many of them behaved very badly—indeed, the electoral math means that a plurality of them often did. As a matter of fairness, the book will strive to present the evidence in context and consider what the Boomers might say in their defense; if this book is primarily an indictment, it does consider context, mitigating factors, and justifications (even if I'm supplying them, which is more than a Boomer-defunded public defense system bothers to do). In the end, the Boomers' defense is not plausible, while the case against the Boomers is strong and the evidence, compelling and varied. The only appropriate sentence is removal from office and restitution.

Once Boomers have been unseated, undoing their decades of mismanagement will require a significant social reorganization, especially of retirement and health-care benefits, and a program of reinvestment. None of the proposals offered in the book's final chapters are violently ideological or unprecedented. Though the price is measured in the trillions, it doesn't need to overwhelm, so long as the burden is shared fairly and reforms are undertaken soon. No one will be reduced to penury and no taxes will rise to confiscatory levels. The United States has faced worse than the Boomers and emerged intact.

Reform and its consequences may be intolerable for many Boomers, who resent putting others' needs ahead of their own, and prefer expedience to hard work. As sociopaths cannot be trusted to do the right thing, they must be compelled. America will shortly have the democratic means to do so and should. An antisocial society, after all, is no society at all.

CHAPTER ONE

THE VIEW FROM 1946

Happiness is like the pox. Catch it too soon,
and it wrecks your constitution.
—Gustave Flaubert[1]

Exactly when Flaubert caught the pox was unclear—he definitely had it by twenty-eight, after a sojourn to the fleshpots of Beirut—but what his biographers make abundantly clear is that his first three decades were miserable.[2] While Flaubert's youth was frustrated, it did lead to triumphs like *Madame Bovary*. Unlike Flaubert, the Boomers were happy from the start and this conditioned them to believe effortless, affluent contentment was their due, and they behaved accordingly. One might wish that the Boomers had been a little less happy then, so the rest of America could be substantially more happy today.

But happy Boomers would be; they could not be otherwise. They were, after all, the human instantiations of American optimism. Convention dates the Boom to 1946, though it started as early as 1940, when the Depression fully lifted and Americans were enthusiastic about the future. The Boom continued until the mid-1960s, delivering the largest American generation ever seen. Even under the narrowest definition, the Boom produced about seventy-five

The Boom[3]

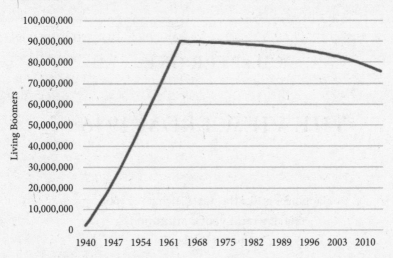

million new Americans and more than ninety million measured over the full stretch between 1940 and 1964, increasing the population by roughly half.*[4]

Boomers are products of more than mere chronology, however. They can be identified by their shared experiences, their generationally unique behaviors and beliefs, and by what they gave to America, what they took, and what they still hope to get.

The United States of the 1950s was wealthy, powerful, and expanding quickly, and if the young Boomers didn't acquaint themselves with the national income tables, they could certainly see growth all around them. They only had to look at the flags they saluted in their new classrooms, duly updated to reflect the statehoods of Alaska and Hawaii in 1959. The present

---

* The data support the start of the Boom at 1940, as birth rates recovered from the Depression-era lows and ramped up over the following years. While a slightly longer definition of the Boomer is of marginal utility to some arguments, it hurts it in others, and has the unfortunate side effect of dragging in at least one of my parents (the other was also born in 1944, but didn't come to America until the 1960s—i.e., not a Boomer). Dating the Boom to 1940 is a matter of data and interpretation, not simply a desire to expand the Boom for rhetorical convenience, and unlike conventional definitions, I exclude non-native born Americans from my calculations. As it happens, including foreign-born and reverting to the conventional date of the Boom produces numbers generally similar to those produced by my own definition.

middle age of diminishing expectations lay decades ahead—the long stagnation of the new millennium, the chronic debts and erosion of the middle class, the vanishing species and melting ice caps, the reach of terrorism into the homeland and the shambolic Middle Eastern empire it provoked—these were unimagined, indeed, unimaginable. Those disasters required a certain generation to summon them, and that generation was just rolling off the production line.

Thanks to the competent stewardship of prior generations—a mix of the Greatest Generation, the earlier Silents, and a few nineteenth-century fossils—the optimism that led to the Boom in the first place found seemingly endless confirmation in American success. In the three decades following World War II, it would have been ridiculous to pose the question, as Ronald Reagan would when seeking the presidency in 1980, "Are you better off [now] than you were four years ago?"[5] The answer was "yes," always and emphatically. The Boomers' first decades saw rapid and near-continuous gains in prosperity, education, health, technology, and civil justice, the products of revolutionary choices by earlier generations, underwritten by their saving and sacrifice.

Even the 1970s, the supposedly dismal era in which many Boomers reached adulthood, weren't that bad; in economic terms, they were better for many workers than the past decade has been. Factually, if not rhetorically, the answer to Reagan's question in 1979–1980 was no worse than "mostly better." As we'll see, a swaddled youth fostered sociopathic entitlement, and the temporary setbacks of the 1970s provoked a generational tantrum from which we have yet to recover. But that's getting ahead of the story.

Happier Days

The Boomers suffered virtually nothing of the Depression that shaped their parents and, unlike their European peers, did not have to confront the suffering and guilt that marked Europe for decades after the war. With the exception of Pearl Harbor, where 2,471 Americans died, the homeland escaped the war basically unscathed. Japanese subs blew up an oil derrick and destroyed a baseball field in Oregon, and the Empire dispossessed America of a few Alaskan islands for a time, and that was about it. A childish mind might have been inclined to view one of the greatest of wars as something of a game.

Just as the United States survived the war intact, so did most of its families. American casualties were relatively low, some 405,399 killed and 670,846 wounded out of a population in 1945 of about 140 million, a casualty rate of well under 1 percent, with few civilian deaths.[6] War deaths for Germany, Japan, the Soviet Union, and the United Kingdom stood vastly higher—at least six times higher in the case of Japan and fifty times higher in the Soviet Union, which had to battle famine, internal strife, and the Wehrmacht.[7] By V-E Day, Dresden and Hamburg had been reduced to rubble; by V-J Day, Nagasaki and Hiroshima had been wiped off the map. In 1945, ash blew off the ruined hulks on Berlin's Unter den Linden and settled on corpses. On Manhattan's Fifth Avenue, ticker tape drifted down from balconies and landed on the shoulders of soldiers kissing strangers.

If the Boomers took a different path than their American parents or their European and Asian contemporaries, a path that eschewed social solidarity in favor of personal indulgence, it was in substantial part because Boomers started from a radically different place. Boomers have always thought of themselves as Special, and nothing about their childhoods provided any evidence to the contrary. Any illusions pre-Boomers had about easy lives had been dispatched by the Depression and the actual fighting of the World Wars; the Boomers suffered none of these. The oldest Boomers might have been lightly touched by want, but American rationing was comparatively moderate and short-lived. If the greatest of wars couldn't restrain American consumption, Boomers might reason, what could? (The sociopath might add, what should?)

By contrast, the United Kingdom's restrictions on sugar and meat finally lapsed in 1953–54 and could have been only a modest consolation for the humiliating evaporation of empire then underway. The Soviet Union was afflicted by hunger, death, and tyranny for years. And the British and the Soviets were *victors*; those who lost faced even greater ruin. The destruction of Japanese cities is well known, but devastation even reached the countryside, which had been denuded of trees because the army had dug up all the pine roots to make gasoline substitute. The Germans, meanwhile, had been firebombed and were starving, reduced to eating the few zoo animals air raids hadn't killed. Even after the bodies were buried and the cities mostly rebuilt, the legacy dragged on: Non-American belligerents were still paying off some war debt and debating old claims well into the twenty-first century.

For the young Boomers, Tragedy was for Over There, privation for Others. Europe and Asia would have to work hard to overcome tragedies of epic proportions, and they built functional and caring societies—imperfect, to be sure, but radically better than what had come before. The Boomers, living a different life, took a different course.

Durable Goods

Having won the war in 1945, America had to figure out what to do with the peace, and it embarked on a course that would eventually provide tremendous direct and indirect benefits to the Boomers. The most pressing postwar question was that of a labor market swollen with newly unemployed soldiers. It was a problem after every major war, one America had not always resolved successfully. After the Civil War, benefits paperwork was wrapped in actual red tape, which probably says it all about the speed and liberality of veterans' programs in the nineteenth century.

After World War II, the United States decided on a course of generosity and foresight, one that might have served as an inspiration for later challenges, had the Boomers been apt pupils. The Servicemen's Readjustment Act of 1944 (the GI Bill) provided veterans with a range of benefits including tuition and living expenses for education, unemployment insurance, and low-cost loans for housing and to start businesses. Congress supplemented the GI Bill after the Korean War, providing further funding to the same general ends. Because the bills were not tested against class or origin, they tremendously improved economic equality, although in the early years the boons skewed overwhelmingly toward white men because of biased implementation, the lack of integrated educational institutions, and prohibitions on women's service in the armed forces. Even that would change. In the meantime, millions of (mostly white, male) people who otherwise never could have attended college did so, enjoying the benefits of education at minor personal expense. The creation of a large, well-educated, prosperous middle class, where position could be earned rather than inherited, was in large part a result of programs like the GI Bill and civilian educational grants. These helped the Boomers' parents earn and pass down wealth, and would help the Boomers themselves avoid the sort of crippling debt they forced their own children to incur.

After a brief war in Korea, peace prevailed, and in the 1950s President Dwight Eisenhower set about building much of the national infrastructure on which the United States still depends, systems the Boomers have cheerfully neglected. Eisenhower had seen the problems bad infrastructure created and what good infrastructure could do. In 1919, he led a cross-country convoy that managed a meager 6 mph across roads and bridges ranging from partially built to nonexistent. In the 1940s, Eisenhower appreciated the virtues of modern infrastructure on tour in Germany, a nation crisscrossed with the *Reichsautobahn*, where Volkswagens designed by Ferdinand Porsche (founder of the eponymous company) could trundle along with considerably greater efficiency—Adolf Hitler had mandated 100 kph, ten times faster than Eisenhower's 1919 convoy had managed.

Eisenhower demanded American *autobahnen* and got them. Construction of the Interstate Highway System (IHS) began in 1956 and concluded in 1991, fifty thousand miles in all, carrying about a third of the nation's traffic. Since then, the IHS and other midcentury infrastructure projects have been decaying, victims of Boomer neglect. But during its heyday, America had the best infrastructure in the world, especially the roads that opened up the country and made possible the Boomers' comfortable suburban childhoods.

Those childhoods, taking place in homes at the end of Eisenhower's asphalt arteries, were exceedingly comfortable. Indeed, homes were so good that when Richard Nixon unveiled a typical example at the American National Exhibition in Moscow in 1959, the Soviets refused to believe such prosperity could exist. For them it was ranch house à la Potemkin, a fraud in clapboard and shag. The Soviet propaganda arm TASS opined that there was "no more truth in showing this as the typical home of an American worker, than, say in showing the Taj Mahal as the typical home of a Bombay textile worker."[8]

TASS was wrong. The Exhibition's show home was not only realistic, it was more or less real, being a copy of 398 Townline Road of Commack, Long Island, a three-bedroom house furnished by Macy's. The original 398

Townline cost $13,000, somewhat below the average price of homes at the time, readily affordable at about 2.5 times the era's $5,400 family income.[9] (Today, Zillow values 398 Townline Road, which still stands, at about $420,000 or about six times 2015 family income.[10]) It would have been pointless to inform the Soviets that this beige box was only the smallest taste of wonders to come.

Two years before the Exhibition, the Soviets had undertaken a demonstration of their own system's merits, launching a twenty-three-inch metal ball into orbit. Generally called *Sputnik*, the satellite's proper name was Простейший Спутник, or "Elementary Satellite," and it was elementary indeed, carrying no scientific instruments, only a radio. Instruments were superfluous to the primary mission, which was to beat Americans into orbit, which *Sputnik* did.

America responded by investing heavily, creating NASA and the Advanced Research Projects Agency (now DARPA) to prepare new technological wonders to humble the Soviets. The government also quadrupled funding for the National Science Foundation, beginning a long period of sustained and lavish grants to science and technology. The National Defense Education Act of 1958 supplemented the GI Bill, pouring money into colleges, with particular emphasis on producing more scientists and engineers. The combined effect of these educational policies increased college enrollment from about 1.5 million in 1940 to over 3.6 million in 1960 and 8 million in 1970 (or in percentage terms for college-age populations, from 9.1 percent to 22.3 percent and then 32.6 percent).[11] The United States may have started slightly behind in the Space Race, but by 1958 it had satellites in orbit doing real science and handling communications traffic. America's second satellite collected geodetic data and orbits still; *Sputnik* and its Soviet creators have vanished. All of these programs would confer enormous benefits on the Boomers, at a cost disproportionately borne by their parents—a pattern the Boomers inverted and then inflicted on their own children.

These investments became the self-reinforcing engine of prosperity, and the national account books made clear the degree to which they succeeded. After a brief postwar dip, the economy grew robustly. Despite the transition to a peacetime economy, unemployment was often under 4 percent and not persistent (as unemployment is today), despite large numbers of Boomers entering the workforce.[12]

Americans under fifty might wish for the litany of midcentury accomplishments to run out, since the inescapable comparisons with the era of Boomer policies are so utterly disheartening, but the list continues—and it's just as well, because Americans still rely on the work done long ago, like the GPS developed for the military from the 1960s, the Internet developed by ARPA, and the integrated circuit from Jack Kilby's work for the Army and Texas Instruments. Even the power for these technologies depends on a grid developed from the 1930s through the 1960s, itself supplied by dams (now rotting) built during the Great Depression and reactors (now ancient) pioneered in the late 1950s, as part of Eisenhower's Atoms for Peace program. Washington's goal was "electricity too cheap to meter," provided by fission and then (hopefully) fusion, built by American ingenuity and, in the case of the versatile nuclear contractor American Machine & Foundry, the nation's leading supplier of bowling equipment (it *was* the Fifties).[13] All that relentless investment in human capital, energy, science, and infrastructure spurred growth whose gains translated into rapidly rising incomes. The Fifties are no more distant or irrelevant than your iPhone, which is charged by power distributed over a midcentury grid and depends on government-sponsored research on GPS, the Internet, and the integrated circuit.

Decay would be the Boomers' project; midcentury America had room only for progress, for more and faster. And just as the economy was modernizing, so was society. While the 1950s exist in the popular imagination as a time of stifling conformity, as static as the shellacked hairdos of its suburban matrons, they were actually a time of great social change. Legacy preferences, racial restrictions, Jewish quotas, and other systems that had perpetuated the old order began giving way to more merit-based criteria, while generous subsidies ensured that admissions offers were more than notional promises. Colleges may not have been as diverse as they are now in absolute terms, but the midcentury revolution in admissions makes today's affirmative action (partly eroded by Boomer courts and legislatures) seem timid.

Having supplied adults with college degrees, jobs, roads, and homes, all of great but sometimes indirect benefit to the Boomers, the nation began to care expressly for its newest citizens—a debt the Boomers never seriously considered repaying. The shambolic educational system that existed before the Depression was reformed and generously funded. The federal government bankrolled junior colleges and expanded vocational training from the 1940s through the 1960s, and both the states and Washington committed themselves to building world-class universities.

In 1965, the federal government decided to extend aid all the way down to primary education, supplemented by income assistance to poorer families to feed and clothe children that they might make the most of opportunities educational and otherwise. The Elementary and Secondary Education Act provided federal funds to schools serving lower-income populations, helping equalize achievement gaps.[14] It was a generous and open-hearted plan, sufficiently groundbreaking that conservatives questioned its very constitutionality.

Justice for Some Becomes Justice for Many

Before the 1940s, segregation had been an ironclad fact. After the war, Harry S. Truman integrated the army and arguments for its civilian equivalent became hard to ignore. In 1954, the Supreme Court took a chance to reverse an 1896 ruling, and found that separate was *not* equal.[15] The great revolution in rights then beggars the Boomers' achievements in this department, a subject we will resume in Chapter 16. The passage of the Voting Rights Act of 1965 also advanced equality, helping black votes, previously diminished by racial regulation, count for the same as white. The pattern of federal intervention to avoid racist abuses was therefore established early in the Boomers' childhoods. Government protection became the default; the recent rollback under Boomer Supreme Court Justices is perhaps less "conservative" than is presented.

So that was the cradle, circa 1965—free and integrating public education, good universities and substantial financial aid, decent and plentiful jobs, quality infrastructure and good homes—what about the grave? That question was addressed in the New Deal by Social Security and in the Great Society by Medicare.

At the time it was conceived in the 1930s, Social Security was a program for the relatively small number of very old retirees. The official name of the legislation was the "Old-Age, Survivors and Disability Act," which hinted at the rather limited category of people that legislators expected would collect. Life expectancy in the 1930s was just over sixty-five years and benefits kicked in, perhaps not coincidentally, around the same time.[*,16] The demographic data meant that old age benefits were originally designed for the catastrophe of extreme age, rather than nearly universal assistance to cushion years and then decades of retirement. Those who did collect were often in severe need, as elderly populations in prior decades were particularly prone to poverty (a situation that no longer applies today, when elderly poverty is quite low while youth poverty remains quite high). From the 1930s onward, the state guaranteed against disaster.

In 1966, Medicare debuted, providing funds for senior health care, so the elderly were supplied with both a modest income and a certain minimum level of medical care and insurance against catastrophic illness. As part of the Great Society and the War on Poverty, funds were also extended regardless of age to poor populations for both health care and income assistance— welfare, in short.

So, the bulk of what we think of as the social safety net was therefore in place by 1966, along with growing protections to ensure that classes of people other than comfortable whites could participate, at least in a partial way, in national prosperity and politics. For mainstream Boomers, childhood through early adult years shared the important commonality that things were both good and getting better; in the event circumstance or chance put prosperity out of reach, the state would ensure that individuals could only fall so far. This was even the case for blacks, who experienced the largest and fastest gains in equality since the Civil War and Reconstruction, though progress was uneven and often marked by violence.

---

* Social Security was partly modeled on a program established during the nineteenth century by Otto von Bismarck. Bismarck also set the retirement age at 65, though German life expectancy at birth was then only around 45. In 1930s America, those who did make it to 65 could expect to live up to thirteen to fifteen years longer, but none of these systems were designed for mass longevity of the kind we have now; less than 54 percent of males survived from 21 to 65 in 1940 (so about half would pay in but never collect), the median age of male death was under 70, and there were only 8.3 million Americans who were 65+ when Social Security began paying out.

These conditions were all provided for by the Boomers' elders, who worked and saved to ensure that the fiscal house was in reasonable order when it was passed down. Doing so required older generations to tax themselves at rates that no politician today, however far Left, would dare propose. When possible, it was pay as you go, so unlike more recent wars, the Korean War was substantially financed out of current tax receipts, as were many of the great infrastructure projects, whose costs were overwhelmingly borne by earlier generations even though later generations would reap so much of their benefit. In cases where no level of tax could balance the budget, as was the case with World War II, prior generations retired the debt as quickly as possible. Motivated by fiscal probity, Americans paid extraordinary taxes for two decades, with the highest marginal rate a downright confiscatory 94 percent in 1945 (against which today's 39.6 percent, the source of so much present angst, seems modest).[17]

The result of these sacrifices was that, by the 1960s, World War II debt had been reduced to a manageable size. Taxes could therefore be lowered, though the top rate remained a hefty 70 percent.[18] Although the Vietnam War eroded the nation's financial position, things were still in relatively good shape in 1970. As a percent of GDP, the deficit was −0.3 percent and the national debt 35.7 percent; modest, compared to −2.5 percent and 103.8 percent, respectively in 2015.*[19] Fiscal affairs were not perfect, but they were strong, especially considering the enormous investments built up after the war, and in vastly better order than they will be when the Boomers pass the books on to their children. The Boomers inherited a productive family farm with a modest mortgage; in twenty years, their children will take over a crumbling estate leveraged to the hilt.

Thus, the psychology of the Boomers formed during a period of America ascendant, master of the world and even, by 1969, of the moon. As the Boomers reached adulthood, they inherited a richly endowed and functional society, one that, despite some flaws, protected and provided for the Boomers better than it had for any preceding generation. And yet, the Boomers

---

* You'll have seen different ranges for debt, from 65 to 100+ percent in various newspapers. We'll take up the details in Chapter 8.

emerged as radicalized adults, rejecting so many of the policies that had given them so much, replacing a successful model with an antisocial failure.

Inheritances as large as those the Boomers received can have warping effects, as the unemployable trust-fund set whizzing down the slopes of St. Moritz shows. (The Boomer electorate has recently furnished a more domestic example.) Still, prosperity tends to be a boon overall, and worth risking. So what went wrong with the Boomers? Had other, less desirable factors contributed to a rising class of suburban sociopaths?

There were, because the standards by which the Boomers had been raised were, by historical standards, downright bizarre.

CHAPTER TWO

BRINGING UP BOOMER

The little, or almost insensible impressions on our tender
infancies, have very important and lasting consequences.
—John Locke, *Some Thoughts Concerning Education*[1]

As all Freudians know, analysis begins with childhood, that rich swamp
from which adulthood's good and evil spring. This is not to say that
humans are consigned to perform a deterministic play written by childhood,
only that the formative years are just so: a period in which operating assumptions and other habits of mind form. For a generation later associated with
individualism, the Boomers had surprisingly uniform childhoods, at least
in the white middle class that then accounted for the plurality of the population. Though the methods used to rear the Boomers might have been uniform *within* that generation, they were strikingly distinct *from* child rearing
practiced on other generations. The Boomers' upbringings were dominated
by a new set of influences, chiefly permissive parenting, bottle-feeding, and
television. If the Boomers grew up to be so different from any generation
before them, it was perhaps because they had been raised unlike any prior
generation; if they remain generationally unique, it is perhaps because some
aspects of their childhoods have never quite been repeated.

The popular television show *Leave It to Beaver*, which debuted in 1957, provides a fair portrait of Boomer childhood. The show's utter lack of imagination was both its artistic vice and sociological virtue. Compared to today's operatic contrivances and reality television, *Beaver* was pure anthropological rigor. The subjects of study, the Cleaver family, were studiously unremarkable: two parents (Ward and June), two kids (the Beav and Wally; presumably the statistically required fractional additional child would have been unsettling to display), plunked down in a suburban house enclosed, inevitably, by a white picket fence. Ward was a World War II veteran who had attended a state college, presumably on the GI Bill, and worked at a trust company; June ran the house. The Cleaver children were both Boomers, notionally born in 1944 and 1950, and raised in ways that would have been instantly familiar to their peers on the other side of the set—and alien to their grandparents. For above all, Ward was a soft touch, a sharp contrast to his own father, an *ancien régime* monster of discipline and corporal punishment.

Childrearing: Dawn of Time—AD 1946

If the oldest Cleaver's methods shock now, that was not the case for most of human history. Grandpa Cleaver's methods were those by which children had long been raised. The old system was not without its grim logic. Because of high infant mortality—even in the nineteenth century, it was not uncommon for 20 percent of children to die before age five—parents saw no reason to invest substantial material or emotional resources until it was clear a child would live. Should a child survive, parents would set themselves not to the arrangement of playdates and other diversions, but to the production of a miniature grown-up, conformed to adult notions of virtue and industry, ready for near-immediate employment. Dialogue with children was unnecessary and motivation best supplied by the stick.

Even more enlightened approaches, which began appearing in the seventeenth century, were unforgiving. John Locke, famous now as the expositor of the social contract (something the Boomers would gleefully rip up), was more renowned in his time as a child-care expert. Locke's *Some Thoughts Concerning Education* (1693), progressive as it was, inclined toward discipline (a word appearing an average of twice a page in my version of *Thoughts*).* Locke's goal had been to produce "virtuous, useful, and able men" by the "easiest, shortest, and likeliest means," and that certainly did not entail pampering of the kind the Boomers received.[2] The behaviorists of late-nineteenth-century America, whose thinking dominated the rearing of the Greatest Generation, shared Locke's goals. They had only to look at the country industrializing around them to know how Locke's seventeenth-century process might be improved. Locke's character-forming exercises, which depended on weird exercises involving leaky shoes and hard beds, were too haphazard for the modern world. Henceforth, good children would be manufactured by a rationalized process of positive and negative reinforcement, delivered immediately, and unburdened by Locke's philosophical meanderings about human nature. In 1899, "less sentimentality and more spanking" was the order of the day, according to G. Stanley Hall, president of Clark University, psychologist, and child-care authority. If children didn't like it, that was beside the point. One did not ask a widget whether it approved of the means of its production. Why should children be different?

Like Hall, Dr. Luther Emmett Holt of Columbia University favored the scientific rearing of children, and his views enjoyed enormous influence. Holt's *The Care and Feeding of Children* (1894) was a best seller, eventually repackaged by the Government Printing Office and widely distributed as a sort of state-sanctioned guide for child care. Like factory workers and farm animals, children were not to be indulged—they were to be managed. While the specifics of these behaviorist texts differed from prior practice, the central insights about child care remained the same until the 1940s: Children were to be formed according to their parents' wishes and society's needs, with parenting a matter of coercing useful behaviors, instead of catering to childish whims. Given the bottomless thrift, industry, and manners of the

---

* *Thoughts* went through more than fifty editions in many languages; it sold faster than *Two Treatises of Government*, and Leibniz thought it more influential than *An Essay Concerning Human Understanding*.

Greatest Generation, perhaps these ideas weren't meritless so much as victims of excessive zeal.

Dr. Spock and the Rise of Permissive Parenting

> Unstable or erratic parenting, or inconsistent parental
> discipline may increase the likelihood that [childhood] conduct
> disorder will evolve into antisocial personality disorder.
> —DSM-V[3]

Rigor was therefore the dominant practice for American children until Benjamin Spock changed things in an instant. Spock was, like Locke, a trained physician, with a specialty in pediatrics. With the assistance of his wife, he produced *The Common Sense Book of Baby and Child Care*, first published in 1946, in time to guide Boomer upbringings. A best seller of tremendous proportions, it sold five hundred thousand copies in its first six months, and in the half century following its printing, was surpassed only by the Bible in sales (or so the story goes).[4] A contemporary poll of American mothers showed that 64 percent had read Spock's book, and even those who didn't own a copy couldn't help but absorb its precepts; excerpts cropped up everywhere, with snippets even appearing on *I Love Lucy* and implicit in *Beaver*.[5] The defining text of Boomer youth came from Dr. Spock, not Jack Kerouac or Robert Pirsig.

The *Common Sense Book* treated every imaginable topic, but its core injunctions were always the same: that parents rely on their own instincts and accommodate children's needs wherever reasonable. In a radical departure, the *Common Sense Book* even strove to comprehend a child's worldview from the perspective of the child himself, a task conservatives viewed with apprehension. In the preface, Spock stated that his "main purpose in writing [his] book was to help parents get along *and understand what their children's drives are.*"[6] Older traditions could not have cared less about understanding a child's motivations.

Unlike his predecessors, Spock did have psychological training, and he disdained the old fixation on discipline and distance, instead emphasizing loving care, physical affection, and a degree of deference to a child's impulses. His attitude toward toilet training is instructive. Previously, experts advised a regimented approach, with children to be trained at three months (one wonders how) and evacuations taking place on a set schedule, Taylorism for tots. This, Spock believed, was an exercise both destined to fail and that risked the development of certain neurotic compunctions, like an anal-retentive personality overly fixated on tidiness and orderliness, though likely to be productive and deferential to authority (e.g., the Greatest Generation). Instead, Spock encouraged parents to let children set their own defecatory timetable, a system not without its own dangers. Freud had warned that indulgent toilet training could lead to an anal-expulsive personality, one that proceeded from literal to figurative incontinence, personalities of messiness, disorder, and rebelliousness (e.g., the Boomers).

Part of Spock's relative leniency came from his radically optimistic views on human nature, his belief that children would grow up well so long as their parents provided a good example. Spock wrote that "discipline, good behavior and pleasant manner... You can't drill these into a child from the outside in a hundred years. The desire to get along with other people happily and considerately develops within [the child] as part of the unfolding of his nature, provided he grows up with loving, self-respecting parents."[7] Two thousand years of parenting experts would have disagreed; parents most definitely could drill habits into a child, with the notion of relying on a child's good nature to achieve the desired results being the very definition of insanity.

Cultural conservatives predicted that America would collapse in lockstep with discipline's decline, and they were not entirely wrong. Norman Vincent Peale, a preacher famous for writing *The Power of Positive Thinking*, characterized Spock's method of child rearing as "feed 'em whatever they want, don't let them cry, instant gratification of needs."[8] Peale blamed Spock for helping create the culture of permissiveness in the Sixties, and he was not alone, though Peale and other critics failed to consider Spock's text as a whole. The *Common Sense Book* did allow for spanking as a last resort—it just preferred to deploy gentler options first. Still, in missing these nuances, the conservatives might have proved their point. Spock's book was not supposed to be read front to back like a novel, but topically, like a guidebook, consulted to resolve a particular problem on a particular day. To the extent this structure made it possible for parents to overlook a few admonitions about laxness, Peale was inadvertently correct.

The Bottle-Fed Baby Boom

There were few subjects on which Spock did not have definite opinions, many of them for the better, but on two critical subjects Spock harbored ambivalence with far-reaching and negative consequences. The first was breast-feeding, which for obvious reasons, has been the standard mode for infant nutrition for almost the entire human experience. Spock had always promoted breast-feeding, but until 1968 remained very open to using formula as an acceptable substitute. Between the convenience of formula and Spock's permission, Americans turned to the bottle in droves. So for one brief period in history, which overlapped almost perfectly with the Boomers' childhoods, bottle largely replaced breast.

By the 1970s, research emerged suggesting that breast-feeding conferred important advantages that formula did not. Studies confirm that breast-feeding positively impacts cognitive development/intelligence, significantly reduces the risk of diabetes, childhood obesity, and other illness, promotes better health in the mother, and strengthens emotional bonds between mother and child.[9] (In some of these areas, Boomers have struggled, as we will later see, though the bottle was not entirely to blame.) Influenced by these revelations, rates of breast-feeding quickly rose and now compare to those of a century ago, with only poorer, less educated, and certain minority groups still relying heavily on the bottle. But no entire generation of children before or since was so influenced by formula, and in nutrition, as they were in so many other ways, Boomers were unique.[*,10]

---

* In addition to the bottle, the Boomers were also exposed to relatively high levels of lead, which has been associated with several sociopathic indicators, like aggression and criminality, as well as lower IQ. While lead levels started declining by the mid-1960s, they remained at unacceptable levels well into the 1980s. Lead cannot be discounted as a partial explanation for the Boomers' behaviors though it did not seem to produce the same effects in, say, GenX.

From Bottle to Boob Tube

The other major area where Spock gave some very bad advice regarded that other great influence on Boomers, television. Older Americans perceive the arrival of computers and the Internet as sudden and pervasive, but these newer technologies have nothing on television, adopted at astonishing speed and scale. RCA began mass production of televisions in 1946. Before then, almost no American homes had televisions. By 1960, 90 percent had TV. In contrast, the first Internet connections were established in 1969, but access didn't become a household staple until the late 1990s, and even by 2012, more than a quarter of American households still lacked a broadband connection.[11]

Not only did television reach more homes more quickly than the Internet, use was very intense from the start. The degree of American preference for television appears most vividly measured as a percentage of leisure hours, because when given the choice, Americans greatly prefer TV. Data compiled in 2015 shows that TV consumed more than 50 percent of Americans' free time, against just 13 percent for socializing and functionally 0 percent for pleasure reading (e.g., for teenagers, 8 minutes per weekend day).[12] In a very serious way, from the Boomers' childhoods onward, TV is what Americans *do.* Leaving aside for now the considerable body of research showing that television negatively affects childhood development, reasonable people can immediately see the problem: It's just not healthy to spend the majority of one's free time immobilized in front of the box.

However, when TV first arrived, it was greeted as just another miraculous appliance, an innocuous electronic nanny. The first mass-market set arrived the same year as Spock's book, which was understandably silent on the issue. However, Spock had a generally permissive attitude toward radio, saying that children could listen to it as much as they liked, so long as it didn't detract from sleep, homework, and outside play. In later editions, Spock said the same of television, remaining unconcerned all the way through the late 1960s both about the amount of TV children consumed and its content.[13] The Boomers therefore were not only the first televisual generation, but the only one whose relationship with the box was unmediated by the cloud of expert concern, parental reservation, content chips, and so forth that later swirled around TV. Like the Windsors' mistresses, TV was a defiling enticement, one to which the Boomers were helplessly susceptible and would constantly return.

Early criticism devoted itself to TV's aesthetic deficits, but the real problem has never been one of art, but of medium. Unlike media that came before, television is at once ironic, mimetic, unidirectional, emotionally rich, informationally poor, highly habituating, and demands a certain suspension of disbelief.* These characteristics prevail regardless of whether a given show is elevating or crude, a news program or a cartoon, and the effects have not been good. While the many studies of TV have occurred over decades in which programming varied widely, the consensus has always been the same—always negative.

TV's essential characteristics make it the perfect education for sociopaths, facilitating deceit, acquisitiveness, intransigence, and validating a worldview only loosely tethered to reality. As a breeding ground for dissembling, television almost cannot help itself, because unlike older media, it inherently operates on a minimum of two levels, the visual and audio, sometimes supplemented by a third level of text. These concurrent streams make it easier to achieve multiple meanings, allowing for divergences between what is said, what is seen, and what is meant. Televisual irony trains viewers to hold otherwise inconsistent views simultaneously, and it is no coincidence that in an era where TV is the most profound cultural influence, the trend has been from earnest to ironic. It's not that television makes lying easier per se, but that television encourages a layered approach to reality in ways that other media do not. Television therefore serves as a training and reinforcement mechanism for deceit, a key trait of the sociopath. The televisual-sociopathic apex probably arrived in *Seinfeld/Curb Your Enthusiasm*, both created by Boomer Larry David. David's shows were outliers only in their brilliance; in their sociopathic aspect they were just the culmination of preexisting trends.

Television is also mimetic, spurring viewers to imitate behaviors seen

---

* It's revealing that one of TV criticism's highest compliments is to call a show "addictive," which is not generally a compliment for other products, with the pertinent exception of junk food.

on-screen, and the behaviors the industry wants to foster are consump-tive. There's plenty of dense academic literature on this subject, but noth-ing speaks louder than the enormous ad budgets devoted to TV, stoking the already robust sociopathic appetite. At least parents today understand the dynamic, and since the late 1970s, with the introduction of affordable VCRs and purchasable content like DVDs and downloads, they have been able to reduce or eliminate the number of conventional ads their children see (somewhat undone by the rise of product placement). Young Boomers could not even resort to the commercial-free uplift of public television, because PBS didn't debut until 1970, and its public predecessor offered just ten hours of weekly programming.

Given that people spend more than twice as many hours watching TV than they do socializing, TV sets the tone for all communication, and that tone is unidirectional, the conveyance of opinion rather than the mutual-ity of conversation. The box speaks one way to the audience, and the people inside the box often speak past each other; it's soliloquy, not dialogue. Though there were some early attempts at serious conversation, TV proved an infertile medium. No later than the 1960s, the modern style of televisual dialogue had been established. During the 1968 Republican National Convention, the ABC network sponsored debates between William F. Buckley and Gore Vidal, icons of the Right and Left respectively. Despite a gap of five decades, the Buckley/Vidal sessions would in their generalities be immediately familiar—two celebrities screeching at each other. Strip away the bad ties and the polysyllables (a final hangover from the empire of the written word) and the modern shouting match emerges fully formed, one that devolved into Vidal characterizing Buckley as a "crypto-Nazi" and Buckley returning the favor by calling Vidal a "queer" and threatening to "sock [Vidal] in the goddamn face."[14] These were bad debates, but "good TV." Unfortunately, the standards of television leaked out of the box and into real life, serving to dis-favor the sorts of exchanges that might promote learning and compromise, major challenges for the Boomers.

One of the redeeming features of Buckley/Vidal was that it featured two people who, however ill behaved in the moment, were intelligent expositors of genuinely different points of view on matters of substance (rather than, say, two different points of view on a starlet's outfit at the Oscars). Early in

TV's history, networks felt obliged to present controversial issues like the ones featured in Buckley/Vidal in a fair and balanced way (in the original legal sense, not the Fox News sense). The FCC enshrined this ideal in the Fairness Doctrine, enacted in 1949.[15] By 1974, the FCC found that it had never had to enforce it because broadcasters had voluntarily complied with the "spirit" of the rule; that's not to say the networks were saints, only that they made modest gestures toward balance.[16]

By the 1980s, as Boomers achieved political power, broadcasters were freed to dispense with even the modicum of balance that guilt previously induced them to provide. In 1987, FCC chairman Marc Fowler—himself a (Canadian variety) Boomer, and so oblivious that he dismissed TV as "a toaster, with pictures"—formally abolished the Fairness Doctrine.[17] The elimination of the Doctrine permitted the rise of ideologically driven channels, preaching to their respective choirs, a project completed in the 1990s when Fox News and MSNBC were disgorged by their parent companies. Dialogue became diatribe aimed at an agreeable audience in the same period that Boomers consolidated their control of governments. Boomers, who were adults by this time and also the heaviest consumers of news programming, therefore spent many hours with a device that would not challenge their worldviews.

It's not as if other media were paragons of sensible debate, but no other medium could compete with the sheer number of hours Americans spent with TV nor the box's special powers. Even if television were the acme of fairness, it would still be a uniquely limited and emotional medium, manipulating the cruder parts of the brain with musical cues so as to keep the cortex untaxed, flitting from image to image, and otherwise radically unsuited to rational thought (we will see some results in Chapter 5). Moreover, to enjoy many programs, one must literally reject reality: struggling waiters in Brooklyn do not live in giant lofts, fornicating with charming neighbors on Eames furniture. So for hours a day, people simply indulge in fantasy, forming habits that leak into other parts of life. (There's probably a doctoral dissertation in the movie *Poltergeist* alone, its vaporous antagonist manipulating a child directly through her TV.)

TV's limits pose special problems when it comes to news programming, and this is a grave problem for Boomers who, along with other (even older)

Americans, are unusually dependent on TV's witless reportage. Television operates at a distinct disadvantage to print—adults can read about twice as many words per minute as news anchors typically speak, and this does not account for the various commercials, empty banter, and other substance-free filler that consume a third or more of the average broadcast. Television isn't kind to facts and even less so to nuance. Causation may run both ways, but the fact is that people who watch commercial broadcast TV news are significantly unrepresented in the category of people highly knowledgeable on matters of current events, the mechanics of government, etc.[18]

The warping effects of all these problems, from the collapse of the Fairness Doctrine to the limitations of TV and its presentation of the news, could be seen in the Boomers' avatar Donald Trump. Like many of his generation, Trump relies heavily on TV news, and expects his preferred channels to cater to him first and reality second (if at all). When even the hermetic world of Fox proved insufficiently fawning, Trump tried with some success to conform the news to his preexisting conceits. The spectacle of The Donald bullying Fox in the crudest terms alarmed certain audiences, but after the Fairness Doctrine collapsed, that event was exceptional only in that an individual informed a network of his preferences directly, rather than the network divining those preferences through the inexact map of ratings.

Television, therefore, is a disastrous influence in purely theoretical terms; what about in practice? As an empirical matter, it's hard to evaluate the full consequences of television, because it's now essentially impossible to run a controlled study. Such a study would require a population of TV viewers to be compared against an otherwise representative group that did not watch television, and in a country where over 90 percent of households have long had TV and watch it several hours a day, that is simply impossible. America harbors no lost tribe of appliance-less Midwesterners, watching shadow puppets on the wall and waiting for sociologists to discover them.

But, for a time, Canada did conceal its own troupe of televisual Neanderthals, and these were the subject of the only major controlled study of TV's consequences. It came about purely as the result of geographic accident. One town, whose identity was concealed behind the joking name of "Notel," nestled in a valley that mostly blocked the local broadcast transmitter. Notel therefore did not receive effective TV coverage until years after surrounding communities did; Notel was otherwise similar to the two control towns, which did have TV.[19]

Adjusting for other variables like IQ, researchers found that Notel's younger children scored higher on various tests, including reading comprehension and creativity.[20] After TV arrived in Notel, scores declined to levels of other TV communities and researchers concluded, among other things, that "the weight of our evidence indicates there is a significant negative relationship between reading achievement and amount of television watched, even after IQ is controlled."[21] Notel's children also became more aggressive after TV arrived, and TV might have exacerbated performance differences between more intelligent students and richer students and those who were less so.[22] Effects in some categories were weak, and in other areas strong, but the overall effect of TV was decidedly disturbing. Eventually, children tended to converge toward the same levels of performance as they got older, but TV seemed to slow acquisition of important skills and have some hangover effects, and of course once children were older, the "No" had vanished from "Notel."[23]

Even if we can no longer study large communities without TV, it is still at least possible to study differences between light and heavy viewers. These tests reveal a similar dynamic, "relatively strong negative correlations between viewing and achievement."[24] Reading comprehension and math performance all suffer when TV viewing is relatively heavy; children who watch a lot of TV are also more aggressive than light watchers (regardless of whether the programs themselves are especially violent).[25] In 1980, newspapers widely circulated the conclusion of the California Superintendent of Schools: "Television is not an asset and ought to be turned off."[26]

Needless to say, the superintendent has never gotten his wish—TV use remains high, and the greatest consumers of TV remain the Boomers, the generation most inclined to view TV as a "necessity" (a status ascribed to TV by about two-thirds of Boomers and their elders and by less than half for younger cohorts).[27] It's not that other generations don't have their own issues with television, and the effects of newer media like immersive video games, smartphones, and Facebook will not be clear for some time. They are also beside the point for now, because it will be years before younger generations run the country. The unavoidable fact is that the nation is currently run by people who have a deep and unshakable relationship with TV, entranced from their beginnings by a medium with unambiguously negative effects on personality and accomplishment.

All of these factors, the shift to more progressive parenting, baby formula, and television, had effects that manifested by the mid-1960s. Studies repeatedly show that more permissive parenting styles produce lower performance in schools, make children more susceptible to peer pressure, and more likely to exhibit problem behaviors, though permissively raised children do have notably higher self-esteem than those raised in stricter households—a description that by now may sound familiar. That's not to say authoritarian parenting avoids problems, as it produces, inter alia, higher levels of depression in girls and greater aggression in boys, but stricter parenting helps children achieve better self-regulation and higher achievement in schools.[28]

It is perhaps not surprising that Boomers' test scores began sliding. Before they were even adults, Boomers were already failing. Constant SAT scores in both verbal and math categories slipped from 478 to 424 between 1964 and 1980; i.e., when the Boomers were taking these tests; once the Boomers graduated, test scores stabilized. We will take up this disturbing slide in Chapter 14. Boomers may have been wealthier and more secure than many test takers before or since, but they were less disciplined and had been raised in distinctly odd and unhelpful ways.

So that was the Boomers' upbringing—televisual, formula fed, and above all, influenced by Dr. Spock and his new style of parenting. Those factors, along with the feelings of entitlement that postwar prosperity kindled, affected the entire generation, and the subset born between 1946 and 1955 perhaps most of all—and some of the Boom's worst examples do seem to have been born in those years, as we'll see. Nevertheless, these were only *influences*, not instructions. Some were negative and others were outright advantages. And however odd their upbringings, the Boomers were always free to choose—as they spent many years reminding the nation.

Many Boomers chose poorly, and those critics, like Norman Vincent Peale, who warned that the Boomers' novel upbringings would lead to calamity, did not have to wait long for proof. It arrived the moment the Boomers became adults amid the turmoil of Vietnam. Unlike their parents, who faced a great challenge and left the world better for their participation, the Boomers confronted a minor conflict and found ways to make it substantially worse. The proof of Boomer sociopathy begins there and continues for the rest of the book.

CHAPTER THREE

VIETNAM AND THE EMERGING
BOOMER IDENTITY

Among the calamities of war, may be justly numbered
the diminution of the love of truth, by the falsehoods
which interest dictates, and credulity encourages.
—Samuel Johnson[1]

No survey of the Boomers can be complete without revisiting the Vietnam War and its upheavals, which defined early adulthood for all save the youngest Boomers. The war began as a modest foreign intrigue in the Fifties, when the Boomers were children, and escalated into a genuine war from the mid-Sixties, just as older Boomers were becoming draft eligible. America withdrew in 1973 and South Vietnam collapsed in 1975, ending the war. America was desperate to move on, and President Jimmy Carter offered a wide pardon to draft avoiders in an attempt to close the book. Carter's gambit failed to clear away the stench of strategic failure and domestic strife, and Vietnam still influences national life. Boomer Washington still strives to avoid "another Vietnam" even as it embroils itself in new quagmires. The politicians themselves cannot help but exhume Vietnam's traumas. Anytime a man born in the 1940s or 1950s runs for office (Clinton, Kerry,

McCain, Bush II, Bush-not-quite-III, Trump, etc.), the electorate must endure another parade of yellow draft documents and misinformation. Given Boomer longevity, Vietnam may linger for many years yet. Because of this, and the centrality of Vietnam to Boomer identity, it is important to understand Vietnam for what it actually was, rather than what the Boomers would have it be.

The Boomers are right about one thing: Vietnam was remarkable, though in unusual ways. In the *usual* ways, Vietnam was just a middling proxy war of middling strategic importance, of less consequence, and prosecuted with less mendacity and cruelty than other wars that are either forgotten or provoke no real anxiety. The Spanish-American, Mexican-American, and Native American wars were as bad as or worse than Vietnam, ranging from the fraudulent to the borderline genocidal. Status: forgotten. The Civil War, an existential crisis with horrific moral and constitutional dimensions, generates no mass hand-wringing; it's even easy to drum up Confederate reenactors (try imagining Vietcong reenactors). World War II, of course, is generally seen as a "good war," despite its considerable moral compromises, ranging from the indiscriminate bombing of civilian centers to the reduction of American citizens to internment camps. The Korean War, which was the closest analogue to Vietnam (Cold War proxy fight in Asia, indifferent conclusion, roughly similar fatality rates), lives on only in anodyne reruns of *M*A*S*H*. Even the conflicts in Iraq and Afghanistan, which have dragged on even longer than Vietnam and for purposes no more certain, occasion nothing like the angst of America's Indochinese adventure. These latterly conflicts largely disappeared from the news even as they ground on; it's easy to forget the United States remains involved. Why then all the strife about Vietnam—was it not, by war's grim standards, nothing special?

The answer derives not from Vietnam's strategic importance, which was never overwhelming; rather, Vietnam's poisonous longevity arises in substantial part from the war's entanglement with the other debates in the 1960s about civil rights, economic justice, personal freedoms and, more than anything, Boomer hypocrisy. Hindsight now allows many Boomers to recall an antiwar prescience they never actually possessed, of an unjust war prosecuted by old men over the objections of the young. A willful blindness about the mechanics of draft avoidance completes the whitewash, allowing many Boomers to characterize their escape from Vietnam as the mere exercise of an inconsequential administrative prerogative. Whether they see themselves as heroes or merely bystanders, the Boomers do not conceive of themselves as the authors of many of Vietnam's misfortunes. The evidence shows something altogether less convenient for the Boomers, and therein lie the engines of Vietnam's divisiveness. Vietnam triggers unease in America for the same reasons the Empire remains an uneasy subject for Britons: The moral failures of each stretched well beyond the Pentagon and Whitehall.

Guerrillas in the Mist

It's been over forty years since the last American troops left Vietnam, and while the war continues to make itself felt as part of the dark matter of the American political universe, details have gotten fuzzy. For Americans who did live through the war, including all the Boomers, time erodes many details. Others facts have mutated or vanished entirely (e.g., the confusion surrounding the sincerity of B. Sanders' application for conscientious objector status), lost to assiduous mythologizing like whitewashed draft histories (B. Clinton, D. Trump), misrepresentations by political opportunists (the Swift Boat ads that helped kill Kerry's presidential bid); plain weirdness (Trump's statements about John McCain being a loser for being captured); or in some cases, a simple refusal to discuss.[2] For the rest, there are no memories to distort; over half of all Americans were born after the war and have no direct experience of it.[3] The American history curriculum at public schools does little to inform these younger generations, and they know accordingly little about the conflict, though this doesn't stop anyone from having feelings about Vietnam.[*,4] So a brief recap seems in order.

While the Vietnam War is a remarkable and important part of American

---

* Historian James Loewe, a professor at the University of Vermont, examined a dozen textbooks and found that Vietnam received about the same (brief) coverage as the War of 1812, and even these treatments were uninformative. He also recounts a dispiriting survey of his students, one that posed the question "Who fought the war in Vietnam?," to which one quarter responded North and South Korea, which demonstrates

history, for the Vietnamese it was just another iteration of a two-millennia-long struggle for independence (a history not dissimilar from those of Iraq or Afghanistan). Vietnam was a palimpsest onto which various empires wrote their own stories, all of which the Vietnamese struggled mightily to erase. The Chinese had the longest tenure and designated Vietnam "Annam," or "pacified south." The official name was more revealing—"The Protectorate General *to Pacify* the South"; the present participle hints that even the most enduring hegemons had difficulty keeping hold of a region that wanted no foreign masters. This history did not deter the French, who arrived as China collapsed in the nineteenth century, any more than it dissuaded the Axis Japanese who booted the French. When it was Axis Japan's turn for defeat, the Americans expressed understandable misgivings about French reoccupation of Vietnam. But the French returned, flailed against the guerrillas for a time, and then evacuated, leaving behind a nation partitioned between a communist junta in the North and an ugly military dictatorship in the South, whose only redeeming quality for the West was its notional capitalism.

In a different era, Vietnam could have been left to its own devices, but the Cold War was raging through proxy fights the Communists seemed to be winning in the Fifties. Communists had established control of Eastern Europe in 1945, China in 1949, and North Korea by 1953, and they were making advances in Latin America. South Vietnam looked vulnerable, and President Eisenhower worried that new victories would embolden other communist revolutionaries. Given events, the "domino theory" was not entirely ludicrous, nor were the atrocities of communism fictional or wholly unknown (though the young Boomers often ignored them).

However, Eisenhower had been elected to stop one proxy fight against communism and had little personal or political appetite for another war. Instead of combat troops, Eisenhower dispatched a handful of advisers and special operatives in the 1950s. His successor, John F. Kennedy, amplified these efforts, but also refused formal combat. While the United States had

---

a surprising level of specific ignorance about the war, to say nothing of the questions it raises about Lowe's students—the survey *did* mention *Vietnam*.

a meaningful presence in Vietnam, it had not committed to full war, and there were even signs (albeit highly inconclusive) that Kennedy considered abandoning Vietnam outright.

The election of 1964, however, made a wider conflict inevitable, and this poor decision can be placed almost entirely at the feet of other generations. But the wider war finally dragged Boomers into the mix, because the two contestants in 1964 agreed that a real war was in the offing. Senator Barry Goldwater, the Republican from Arizona, was pitted against JFK's successor, Lyndon Johnson, and the two clashed dramatically over domestic policies in ways that defined the following decades; we'll return to those issues in Chapter 6. However, both candidates agreed on a full war in Vietnam. Goldwater was an anticommunist hawk, and his motivations were straightforward. Johnson was also anticommunist, and proving it overseas was helpful to offset criticisms that his social programs at home veered uncomfortably toward socialism. Militarism was not expected to be overly costly, because while paddy-peasants might defy the pusillanimous French, they would be crushed by mighty America. The difficulty was that the war would require American bodies, and at the time, those bodies belonged to the Boomers.

Vietnam: The Unremarkable War

Nothing about the statistics suggested that Vietnam-qua-war would be the catalyst for the dramatic social struggles it ultimately provoked. Vietnam was a moderate war and somewhat collateral to core American interests. One would never know this from tapping Boomer memories, but what the numbers show is a mid-grade proxy war, and it's helpful to review them so as not to be trapped by the idea that Vietnam was a struggle of world-historical importance to be resisted by whatever means Boomers found convenient.

In blood and money, Vietnam was modest for America. There were 58,307 dead and 303,644 wounded, death rates about half those of World War I and less than one-seventh of World War II.* American losses were

---

* I don't mean to downplay death and sacrifice, only to provide context. My own namesake, a soldier named Bruce Cannon, died in the war, and my father fought in it, for what it's worth.

much closer to those experienced in the Korean War (36,000) and lower than those borne by France during its own twentieth-century conflict in Southeast Asia (90,000 lost across the French Empire). Though roughly as deadly, neither the America-Korean nor French-Vietnamese wars sparked major domestic upheavals. Vietnam wasn't even particularly expensive. Measured as a fraction of annual GDP, combat operations in Vietnam cost 2.3 percent at its peak, substantially less than Korea at its height, somewhat more than the War on Terror, and an order of magnitude less than World War II.[5]

As for Vietnam's supposedly unique length, it was long but not always intense. For most of the period 1955–1964, personnel numbered in the hundreds and were not involved in formal combat. Many Americans were not even aware that the United States had a presence in Vietnam, nor did they care, with almost two-thirds of Americans saying as late as 1964 that they paid "little or no attention to developments in South Vietnam."[6] On the ground, only five years saw elevated troop levels and the total number of person-years was notably lower than for other major conflicts. (The recent wars in Iraq and Afghanistan on this metric have been about as long a slog.) Vietnam dragged on, but it commanded intense attention for only a few years, ones that happened to overlap with the draft of the Boomers.

As for Vietnam's reputation as a dirty, an immoral, and, above all, an unsuccessful war, it was again, by history's depressing standards, unremarkable. The justifications were neither new nor entirely unreasonable. The Korean War set a precedent for communist containment, and the domino theory wasn't divorced from reality. If anything, the argument had gotten stronger since Korea, given new repressions in the Eastern Bloc. It's true Johnson's excuse for the war—a supposedly outrageous attack on an American ship in the Gulf of Tonkin (which led to the eponymous resolution authorizing force)—depended on flexibility with the truth. President Johnson's mendacity about Tonkin emerged later and, regrettably, represented no departure from the sorts of embroidery used to justify America's often-dubious foreign policy. Indeed, it was no different from the sorts of dissimulation the Boomers themselves used for their own wars, as the most recent war against Iraq showed. While Vietnam was a failure, that failure came *after* the domestic strife, and the loss was neither unprecedented nor a strategic catastrophe. Korea was at best a half victory, and whatever the recent operations in Iraq and Afghanistan are or might be, "unqualified success" will not be the first term reached for. The easy explanations about Vietnam as a long, dirty, expensive, unprecedented failure, cannot themselves justify Vietnam's special place in the culture.

Dodging and Its Discontents

> Failure to conform to social norms with respect to lawful
> behaviors...deceitfulness, as indicated by repeated lying,
> use of aliases or conning others for personal [gain]...
>
> Deceit and manipulation are central features
> of antisocial personality disorder...
> —DSM-V[7]

If Vietnam was a modest war, deadly and fraudulent but not especially so in its particulars, why did it prove so divisive? In a word, Boomers. As a group, the Boomers managed to be simultaneously for the war and against serving in it. Their responses to Vietnam were confused, hypocritical, exploitative, and illegal, a far cry from the unstained moral crusade produced by the laundromat of Boomer nostalgia.

Of all the war's problems, the mechanics of the draft and its evasion proved the most divisive, and the most illuminating of the Boomers' actual intentions—it was now that sociopathy really emerged. Whether or not they liked it (most did not), the male half of the Boomers had to engage with Vietnam upon adulthood, because Selective Service, aka the draft, required men to register at age 18, though they would not be eligible for induction until 18½, with primary eligibility lasting until age 26.[8] So the trick, for those disinclined to service, was to outlast the draft window. However, while the draft supplied substantial manpower, the Vietnam force was not quite what people have (re)imagined. Only a modest fraction of forces was drafted, not all of these drafted went to Vietnam, and once in the war, the likelihood of fatality was significantly lower than it had been for prior conflicts—which is not to say that the war wasn't terrifying, only that it wasn't the all-consuming monster of fatal conscription of some imaginations.

Not Quite a Draft Army

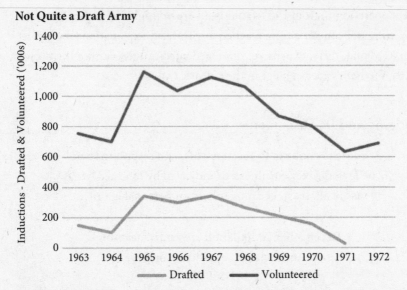

What's going on here? There is some confusion about the degree of conscription during Vietnam—the draft was more important socially than statistically—and not all military personnel served in Vietnam, and not all of those in Vietnam served in combat. The Pentagon did send a consequential number of Boomers to Vietnam against their will; just not as many as commonly imagined.[9]

Whatever the percentages, many simply did not want to serve and options were at hand: deferments and exemptions. At the beginning of the 1960s, students in college or technical school could avoid being drafted for as long as they remained enrolled. Others were rejected for obvious reasons like physical unfitness and moral turpitude. (From a brief time, marriage also provided a deferment.) The draft was modified in 1967, raising the maximum draft age to thirty-five and curtailing student deferments to the completion of a baccalaureate program or a student's twenty-fourth birthday, whichever came first.[10] Tellingly, the Boomers' reactions to the Vietnam War tended to track both the intensity of the war and the mechanics of the draft itself. It's not that creaky moral justifications for the war somehow got worse, it's that the war, specifically the draft, got worse *for the Boomers*.

Today, popular memory presents Vietnam as a story of a war opposed by the young, but that is convenient rebranding. Young people *today* tend toward the pacific. During the 1960s youthful Americans (i.e., Boomers) were the most militant cohort. Contemporary surveys routinely showed

Vietnam—The Changing Face of Deferrals

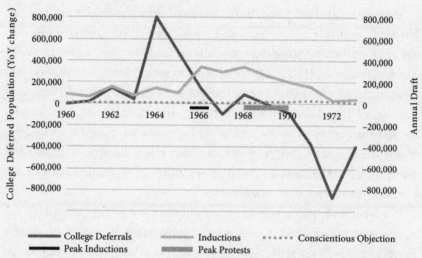

What's going on here? As the Vietnam war intensified, some deferrals became harder to get, and this contributed to the rising angst of the late 1960s. As college deferrals became less routine and the chances of mainstream Boomers serving in Vietnam increased, protests became more intense even though the morality of the war remained fairly constant. Note also that the number of conscientious objectors was never material.[11]

younger groups (generally under thirty) as the most supportive of the Vietnam War and of aggressive strategies for prosecuting it. These prowar attitudes proved stubborn, so despite accumulating news reports of reversals and abuses from 1966 onward, young people remained throughout the war the group least likely to view the engagement as an error.

From 1965 to 1971, the war's peak years, pollers at Gallup asked Americans the same question: "In view of the developments since we entered the fighting in Vietnam, do you think the US made a mistake in sending troops to fight in Vietnam?"[12] It wasn't until the second half of 1968 (we'll see why) that a majority of young Americans came to view Vietnam as a mistake and, mistake or not, youth had been stronger supporters of escalation than their elders.[13] Older Americans favored less aggressive strategies, up to and including abandonment of the Vietnam project. As late as 1965–1966, younger groups were more hawkish, and college-educated young men aged eighteen to twenty-four "tend[ed] to support the President's Vietnam policies more strongly than any other demographic group in the population" (the president's policies, at that time, being escalation).[14] Even by the war's end, when majorities in all groups harbored reservations, many young people remained aggressive, though the tenor of their opinions did evolve dramatically from mid-1968 to 1969.[15] Decades later, almost 70 percent of Americans view Vietnam as a mistake, but what matters for us is what people thought at the time, without the benefit of hindsight.[16] Therefore, the reality was the inverse of the fable, a youth hungrier for war than many older Americans. By no means were most draft dodgers hypocrites judged on their war attitudes, since many did oppose the war. But many were—and almost all dodging, regardless of ideological consistency, had sociopathic overtones, as we will see.

The other revealing surprise is the support the war enjoyed, during its inception, among the educated. A glance at the photographic record of the antiwar movement shows a sea of white college students, so it's easy to get the impression that the educated elite was against the war en masse, especially because more educated groups today trend against military interventions. But until early 1968, better educated groups skewed in favor of the war, while less educated and less affluent groups skewed against the war, not least because the disadvantaged had the highest chance of being drafted.[17] The reason there are so many old photos of college protestors is because deferments allowed so many Boomers to be in college to protest rather than in Vietnam to fight (or, in some cases, to simply and quietly pursue their studies). Only around 1968 did educational opinion gaps wither, not coincidentally as college deferments became somewhat harder to obtain.

Accounting for these demographic surprises, the unexpected belligerence of the young and the educated, and their crucial transformations from 1967 to 1969, are two factors: the progress of the war and the mechanics of the draft. In a significant sense, the war really began not in the 1950s, when the first small groups of advisers arrived in Vietnam, but in March 1965, when the first combat troops arrived to fight the ground war. At the beginning, the war was expected to be easy. General William Westmoreland's three-point plan for victory scheduled triumph within two years of initial deployments.*,[18] For a time, the American people patiently awaited success, but even as troop levels rose again and again, Westmoreland's easy win slipped further away.

---

* Westmoreland was *Time's* "Man of the Year" for 1965, followed by the Boomers in 1966.

The turning point came in early 1968. Westmoreland once again predicted imminent victory, but even as he was doing so the Vietcong (South Vietnamese communist insurgents) and the North Vietnamese were preparing a major offensive to coincide with Tet, the Vietnamese New Year. The Tet Offensive shocked the American public, not because it succeeded in the field—it did not—but because the enemy was supposed to have been so depleted as to make anything like Tet impossible. Clearly, there was some divergence between the American command's sunny reports and the reality on the ground. American public opinion quickly reversed from strong net support of the war to an even split. It would deteriorate from there, and mainstream media, including *Newsweek*, the *Wall Street Journal*, and critically, influential CBS anchorman Walter Cronkite, began to worry publicly that the war was unwinnable. However, even after the Tet Offensive, a majority of young people still did not view the war as a mistake and continued to favor belligerent policies.

What would cause young people, potential draftees, to support a war in which they presumably had the most, personally, to lose? One compelling explanation is that the young and better educated, who were most in favor of the war, *had no realistic expectation that they would be forced to serve.* This freed them to support a war most Boomers expected to be of limited personal consequence. First, only a fraction of forces were drafted; the substantial majority volunteered, though the draft did persuade some to sign up voluntarily if only to select the service they preferred, and the total number of volunteers was far smaller than the total number of deferments.[19] For many, educational deferments provided a sense of safety. Deferments, created in 1951, favored college students and those who scored well on aptitude tests, as well as those for whom war would be a "hardship" due to family or other circumstances. Until the draft picked up in 1965, deferments effectively operated as permanent exemptions from service.[20] Deferments were not some odd loophole, they were explicit social engineering designed to "channel" brighter students into useful occupations.[21] Over fifteen million Boomers in a position to do so eagerly collaborated, using various deferment options.[*,22]

---

* There is, of course, a certain irony in students protesting the injustices of a government while actively participating in its discriminatory social engineering program.

As the war intensified, so did the draft, and use and exploitation of the deferment system, and controversy over the war. By early 1966, two million men had secured college deferments. The number of students taking the (biased) Selective Service Qualification Test, success on which could either confirm or imperil deferment, rose from 2,145 in 1963 to 767,935 in 1966.*[23] Obviously, many students wanted to go to college whatever the situation overseas. However, a great many others simply wished to avoid Vietnam. This becomes evident when looking at the rates of college enrollment before and after the draft—enrollments spiked during the draft's height and tailed off as the draft and war wound down, especially for higher-status white men with bad draft numbers.[24] Even enrollment in seminaries, another source of deferral, followed the same pattern.[25] Enrollments went beyond coincidence. Statistical analysis shows that avoiding the draft was a significant causal factor in the migration of young people into education during the peak draft years.[26]

All else being roughly equal, the inescapable (statistically corroborated) conclusion is that many Boomers gamed the system to get out of the war, and they had plenty of guidance from a whole cottage industry churning out items like the popular *Handbook for Conscientious Objectors*, which went through multiple editions. Also on hand was none other than Dr. Spock, the author of the guide that had done so much to influence Boomer child rearing, who counseled his generational charges to resist the draft in the hope that "100,000, 200,000 or even 500,000 young Americans [would] either refuse to be drafted or to obey orders if in military services." Spock also encouraged resistance through refusal to pay taxes, which became a Boomer theme in other ways and contexts.[27]

Playing the system became an art, effected by means whose baroque complexity makes clear the intent of its practitioners. The form was perfected by one William Jefferson Clinton, who established an early pattern of hypertechnical compliance and regulatory manipulation, garnished

---

* The Selective Service Administration contracted with Educational Testing Service (ETS) to handle the test; ETS is still around administering things like the GRE, and TOEFL, consulting on the NAEP, and providing other analytics.

as necessary by occasional dishonesty. Like millions of Boomers, Clinton received a deferment during college and secured an additional deferment for graduate school, as was customary and legal. However, after graduate school deferments were eliminated in 1968, Clinton became eligible and received an induction notice in 1969. Facing this inconvenience, Clinton signed an agreement with the Reserve Officer Training Corp (ROTC), which lowered his chances of being immediately inducted, though it did require him to commit to a period of military service at a later date (perhaps after the war had ended, as it shortly would). The rules changed again when Nixon allowed graduate students to postpone induction until their current school year was complete. Clinton took advantage of this development, breaking his agreement with ROTC (which had a 100 percent chance of requiring service) presumably in the hope—ultimately successful—that a draft lottery would be introduced, which would by definition have better odds than ROTC's sure thing. As usual, Clinton's timing was apt: It was well understood that a draft lottery was coming, and even if Clinton drew a low number (which meant a high chance of being drafted), Nixon had been elected the prior year to bring an end to the war, which might moot the entire question. The essential thing was to continue dragging out the process, just as the Boomers are now doing with Social Security and other programs.* In the end, Clinton's gamble succeeded; he got a good draft number, and troop levels peaked in 1969, reducing draft pressures thereafter. The net effect of Clinton's several years of maneuvering meant that he was able to sit out the war.[28] (Co-Boomer Dick Cheney, meanwhile, racked up five deferments of his own—and while the number is startling, his deferments were more straightforward.[29])

The lottery worked for Clinton, but its introduction was not met with enthusiasm by younger students. When Clinton played the lottery, he was

---

* Clinton has offered several different spins to mollify critics. Since he was well understood to have opposed the war, he could have opted for CO status. He did not. Since he expressed a desire to stand in solidarity with his friends who had been shipped off to Vietnam, he could have simply turned up at a recruitment office and been done with it. He also did not. Instead, he flipped various deferment switches and then offered contradictory stories.

well out of college and had exhausted all other options (other, that is, than serving); the lottery had become his best option for avoiding the war. For students still of college age and able to attend, the innovation of the lottery was much worse than the status quo of guaranteed deferral. A 1966 survey conducted at Harvard by the Undergraduate Council showed 70 percent of students in favor of retaining the existing system of college deferments over a "more equitable" lottery system.[30] Charitably interpreted, this meant students believed that maintaining uninterrupted study was a better means of social organization than spreading the burden of the war. More realistically, it meant that they wanted to save themselves even if it meant perpetuating an unfair system that exploited groups in the worst position to defend themselves.

And the deferment system *was* exploitative. Whether one was for or against the war, whether deferment was or was not ideologically consistent, deferment by middle-class Boomers simply shifted costs to less-advantaged groups. The military requisitioned a fixed number of people every year, so each student protected by a college deferment had to be replaced by someone else—and that someone tended to be poorer and less educated. The ranks reflected this. One rough estimate of enlisted demographics put composition at "about 25 percent poor, 55 percent working class, and 20 percent middle class, with a statistically negligible number of wealthy" and other analyses showed that the likelihood of service, especially combat service, was substantially lower for middle- and high-income groups.[31] In other words, the bottom third or so provided about four-fifths of the manpower. Senator John McCain, who otherwise holds a fairly untroubled view of Vietnam, thought this was the war's true injustice: "Those who were better off economically did not carry out their obligations, so we forced the Hispanic, the ghetto black, and the Appalachian white to fight and die. That to me was the greatest crime and injustice of the Vietnam War."[32] When a revanchist Republican, one who adorned his hawkish presidential campaign with a wingnut governor of a distant province, provides voice for the "ghetto black," you know something morally troubling went down.

With deferments, it could not have been otherwise. Even though college was cheaper in the 1960s, it was not entirely free, and it required students to forgo years of full income while they studied. Students who deferred had at least some means, and richer students were better prepared for college in the first place. Therefore, the deferment system almost automatically favored people higher on the socioeconomic ladder (three of whom would be president). At least among the Boom's more middle-class members, the first signs of sociopathy begin to appear—self-service at the cost of others (the poor, minorities), a casual attitude toward the law (e.g., Clinton's representative manipulations), and actions contrary to social norms (e.g., failure to heed the nation's call, breaking the law). The deep compromises entailed in avoiding the war help explain the general fury over draft dodging that persists. Oddly, few care if a politician volunteered for, or otherwise supported, a war that everyone now hates—it's the *dodging* that rankles. People rightly sense something unsavory occurred.

Although college deferments were legal—channeling better/advantaged students into school being an explicit government aim—the Boomers abused the system generally. Some students faked an interest in college, wasting resources better spent on those who actually wanted the education. Others manufactured evidence to secure other sorts of deferments when college couldn't supply the necessary shelter. Those with access to sympathetic physicians, psychologists, and other professionals (i.e., monied Boomers) could and did present themselves as unfit for service, even when they were not. Enterprising candidates could also produce unfitness in themselves—James Fallows, who achieved fame as a journalist in later years, reportedly starved himself down to a disqualifying 120 pounds. He eventually confessed to lingering guilt for avoiding the draft while the less informed were mustered in.[33]

The most infamous tactic was outright dodging, which involved leaving the country. Dodging wasn't the act of penniless rebels, because it often required a passport (which only wealthier Americans tended to have), funds for passage, and money to live in countries that disbarred from gainful employment Boomers on the lam. Outright dodging was both completely illegal and morally problematic. It was also expensive and inconvenient, and so the numbers availing themselves of a refreshing, well-timed jaunt to Stockholm were never particularly large.

There was an honorable way to avoid the war, and that was conscientious objection, a forthright refusal to serve on moral or religious grounds, undertaken legally through the Selective Service system. Even this noble solution was not without its inequities, as securing status as a conscientious objector (or "CO") required both knowledge of the CO exemption and the rhetorical skills necessary to persuade a draft board that one's objections were sincere and divorced from mere personal self-interest, a strategy all but tailored for use by elites and not the general population. Still, for those with sincere antiwar convictions, CO would seem the most obvious and appealing route to depriving the war of bodies.* For sociopaths, however, CO was among the least desirable options, because it required sincerity, effort to secure the deferment, and some form of alternative service, usually low-paid and incommodious. It is no surprise, then, that CO was never widely used; far fewer applied for CO than for college deferment. About 175,000 were accepted (the Selective Service was not overly forthcoming about CO applications, but there were probably a few hundred thousand during the entire war, and those already in the military had their applications granted frequently—about 63 to 77 percent were approved in the war's last years).[34]

All conventional draft avoidance tactics required money and a certain knowledge and savviness about the system simply not available to less advantaged groups. The net effect was that college deferments became an exercise of class privilege, and, given the overrepresentation of minorities among the poor, of racial discrimination. It was not unlike the hiring of substitutes during the Civil War, during which a draftee could simply pay another person to take his place, but with the government itself managing the transaction in the case of the Vietnam draft. At least during the Civil War the substitute got a cash bounty from his sponsoring civilian—it was, in a sense, a cleaner transaction.

---

* Some might argue that CO was less attractive because it exposed applicants to the caprices of a government review board, and that objection has truth. But while boards frequently and arbitrarily refused to see the merits of an applicant's case, especially in the war's early phases, they did grant a substantial fraction of applications, and anyway the government could just as capriciously change the standards for other sorts of deferments, as indeed it did. The Supreme Court had also imposed some CO guidelines on the draft boards in *US v. Seeger* (1965), making things a little less arbitrary, and grants of applications became more routine.

As usual, the options for those lower on the ladder were worse and if the dilemmas of the disadvantaged demand sympathy, some of their solutions do not. For those without college deferments or the means and education to exploit alternatives like CO, only two strategies remained. If called, the first option was to serve, which most did. The second was to take advantage of a "moral disqualification," a status routinely provided to those in prison, on parole, or awaiting trial. Indeed, even if a person were presently free, a criminal record of any kind was perceived to exempt its holder from service. So while many privileged students went to college, some of their poorer counterparts turned to crime. Several studies confirm the relationship between a rise in crime in the 1960s and the draft, with avoidance as a causal explanation.[35] This was particularly the case for blacks and people of lower socioeconomic status, but not the case for wealthier whites (probably not because they were inherently more law-abiding, just that they had better options).[36] While a lack of options mitigates the offense, the simple fact is that using crime to avoid the draft is, obviously, criminal; indeed, doubly so. (One paper pertinently describes dodging down as "antisocial."[37]) Worse, crimes had to be reasonably significant to really carry weight with draft boards, and that meant inflicting some sort of harm on innocent victims, another instance of sociopathy. The perpetrators bore their own costs, as criminal records permanently reduce economic and social prospects, helping perpetuate an urban underclass.

Aside from creating lawlessness at home, draft avoidance caused serious problems in the military. Many less-privileged recruits were not qualified to serve, having failed either the physical or mental aptitude tests, usually the latter. As it became harder to satisfy recruiting demands because of the large number of students protected by deferment, the military simply admitted unqualified candidates, who predictably did not thrive in Vietnam. The four hundred thousand troops admitted under relaxed standards suffered twice the average death rate. There is, therefore, a causal connection between excess battlefield deaths and the abuse of the deferment system, although one intermediated by an implacable Defense Department.

These substandard troops also tended to be—not for reasons of inherent aptitude, but as a function in inequitable education stateside—disproportionately black. After the military waived its standards, the first major pool of substandard recruits was 41 percent black.[38] This was just another permutation of the racial skew in the military, where minorities suffered disproportionate risks. At 12–13 percent, the black fraction of the total military was roughly in line with the population, but blacks represented about a quarter of the fighting army in Vietnam and sometimes more, compensating for a white recruitment pool drained away into deferments, the officer and administrative elites, National Guard assignments (the strategy of George W. Bush), and other combat-avoiding strategies.[39]

Drunk and Disorderly: Boomers in Uniform

> Individuals with antisocial personality disorder...may
> [have] a pattern of repeated absences from work...
> These individuals may receive dishonorable
> discharges from the armed services...
> They may have associated...substance abuse disorders...
> They may repeatedly perform acts that are grounds
> for arrest...such as destroying property...
> These individuals also display a reckless disregard
> for the safety of themselves or others.
> —DSM-V[40]

Once shoved into uniform, Boomer behavior deteriorated further. The force deployed in Vietnam was perhaps the worst fielded in the modern era, plagued by indiscipline, drug abuse, insubordination, desertion, and war crimes, with occasional helpings of outright treason and murder. Draft armies tend to be less orderly than volunteer forces, but the Boomer-heavy force operating in Vietnam was vastly worse than the draft armies that fought in Korea or the World Wars, in predictably sociopathic ways. And given how widespread misconduct was—the percentage using drugs was almost certainly higher than the percentage of those drafted, for example— misconduct afflicted both draftees and volunteers.

Problems in Vietnam became so severe that Colonel Robert Heinl, a seasoned marine, lamented them in a 1971 article for the *Armed Forces Journal*, and his conclusions have been generally confirmed by other scholarly work.[41] Heinl described an army whose ordering principle, that of command, was vanishing. In Vietnam, soldiers routinely refused orders, often dramatically, as when the 196th Light Infantry Brigade "publicly sat down on the battlefield" like a group of dyspeptic school children.[42] To avoid the risks of combat, other units engaged in "search and evade" (instead of "search and destroy") missions. The Vietcong ordered its own units not to engage Americans who did not engage them, happy to exploit enemy indiscipline. Search and evade might have worked for the units doing the evading, but not for anyone else. When the enemy couldn't be avoided, another "combat refusal" entailed deliberately missing when firing at the enemy. In this case, however, the enemy was free to fire back unless it somehow divined its opponents' pacific intentions through the jungle chaos; of course, fuzzy symbolism and wishful thinking always trumped reason in the Boomer calculus. For rational people, it's hard to see how these "combat refusals" did anything but increase the risks for other soldiers.

If insubordination failed to communicate the displeasure of the rank-and-file with its orders, there was always the simple expedient of killing those doing the ordering. These murders were called "fraggings," after the fragmentation grenades whose explosions made them difficult to trace, and thus the assassin's choice. The Department of Defense recorded 96 fraggings in 1969 and 209 in 1970; in total, Vietnam witnessed at least 551 fragging incidents causing 86 deaths and over 700 injuries.[43] There are no tallies for the number of officers assassinated by other means more widely available, like guns and knives, which doubtless added to the total. A few troops even put bounties on unpopular commanders, at least one of which was advertised in an underground GI newspaper. Nothing like this had happened before and nothing like it has happened since. During the lengthy recent operations in Iraq and Afghanistan, which feature no Boomer combat troops, there have been almost no fraggings or other attempted assassinations.

The litany of indiscipline continued. Sabotage became a problem, ranging from the dynamiting of a telephone facility to, in the Navy's case alone, "almost 500 cases of arson, sabotage, or wrongful destruction on its ships."[44]

Drug use infiltrated military culture. While estimates vary, heroin affected many troops (from 4 percent to 22 percent) and use of marijuana may have exceeded 50 percent (both having significantly increased from 1967 to 1970), drinking was heavy, and soldiers routinely turned up for duty armed and intoxicated.[45] Drug discharges ramped up throughout the war until the military more or less gave up on the problem and the war. Winston Churchill used to complain that the British navy was all rum, sodomy, and the lash; the Boomer army was rum and hash, and as for sodomy, and what happened in the underage and notoriously slave-like bordellos on shore leave, is best left unimagined.

Desertions also ran rampant, with more than 507,000 instances between 1964 and 1973, committed by about 440,000 individuals.[46] Because the definition of "desertion" tightened up during the Korean War, it is hard to directly compare the experiences of the Vietnam War with earlier conflicts using drafted soldiers. But reasonable estimates place Vietnam desertion rates at more than twice those of Korea and higher than in World War II (with the exception a few months in 1945). Total desertions topped Korea, and even World War II, which involved vastly larger armies. Even in Vietnam, desertion had not been a problem as late as 1966, before Boomer draftees arrived in quantity. In the Army, the desertion rate more than tripled, from 14.7 per thousand in 1966 to 52.3 per thousand, in 1970.[47] This period coincided with the declining availability of deferments, leaving legions of entitled and resentful students stuck in the jungle. Desertion rates in Vietnam remain the highest and most sustained experienced by American forces anytime since the Civil War.

In this catalogue of dysfunction, some of the worst examples (besides the murder of American officers by their subordinates) were the crimes perpetrated against the Vietnamese. The most significant of these were the bombings of civilians orchestrated from Washington and the illegal campaigns waged in Laos and Cambodia, which collectively accounted for most unnecessary deaths. Other generations bear responsibility for those disasters. The Boomers get the blame for local, freelance disasters. Soldiers sometimes ran wild, committing atrocities in the paddies and villages, including the infamous incident at My Lai. Unfortunately, in this one respect, the Vietnam

War was undistinguished from earlier conflicts, which featured their own crimes. Fortunately, the last war to feature Boomer troops was also the last to feature widespread and deadly abuses committed at the troops' own initiative. Recent wars have featured occasional outrages like Abu Ghraib, but nothing at the scale of My Lai or, at least, nothing not ordered by senior officials (many of them Boomers).

The Legacy: All Harm, No Foul

> They generally fail to compensate or make
> amends for their behavior.
> —DSM-V

The scope of misconduct during Vietnam rules out the few-bad-apple theories; the conduct was systemic, and given the nature of the draft and the composition of those involved, it was also generational. However, it's important to note that the consequences were social, not strategic. The war was a lost cause from the beginning, as Ho Chi Minh made clear to the French in 1946, saying to them that "you can kill ten of my men for every one I kill of yours...but even at those odds you will lose and I will win."[48] As the French were dispatched, so were the Americans; there were too many Vietnamese guerrillas and not enough reasons to be in Vietnam. America's setback was not the Boomers' fault—and as we will see, neither was the peace the Boomers' victory, since their protests shriveled along with the danger of being drafted.

What is hard to doubt is that many of the strategies for avoiding the draft and the indiscipline of troops once in Vietnam made a bad war that much worse. Older civilian and military commanders bear enormous blame for presiding over a bad war and running a discriminatory draft; the Boomers must shoulder responsibility for reacting badly to an admittedly bad situation. Deferments could be legally exploited, but the fact that a system permits exploitation does not mean a person must engage in it. No one forced Boomers to opt for a deferment over CO status, any more than corporations today are forced into tax inversions to avoid paying their fair share; both are legal, neither is uncompromised. Worse still, of course, was manufacturing medical exemptions, which was fraud, and securing moral disqualification by victimizing others, which was crime. Indiscipline made the war more lethal for everyone, and fraggings were outright treason.

The various strategies of subversion are often sanitized as a noble moral protest, but it has been the case since Socrates (one of the distasteful white males then being excised from the canon) that citizens do not have the right to ignore laws because they disagree with a policy.[49] Lawlessness is lawlessness, and inherently antisocial; it can be justified only in extreme cases where no reasonable alternatives exist. (CO was one such alternative.) Anything else is society à la carte—anarchy, really.

Protests were one thing; such speech is a right and often a responsibility. Draft avoidance and insubordination were something else. Were they at least effective? That hippies must be forced to reach toward their Machiavelli says a lot itself, but did the ends at least justify the means? Not really, if for no other reason than that they were too little, too late. Ho's meat-grinder tactics rendered irrelevant all other details. All that mattered was when the American people got Ho's message, which they did. As a practical matter, the election of 1968 committed the United States to an exit and the war duly peaked in early 1969, *before* the most intense dodging and military dysfunction.

As for crafting some redeeming moral narrative around draft avoidance, doing so would require locating motives where subverting the war effort was at least as important as saving the dodger's own skin. It would have been hard for serious people to believe that dodging was an effective means of subversion, because at no point did dodging deprive the war of bodies generally, just of specific bodies, to be replaced by poorer, less qualified substitutes. And the most intense period of draft avoidance occurred after the United States began withdrawal, blunting its already small effect.

Vietnam histories tend to end around January 1973, when the Paris Peace Accords were signed, which is a mistake, because what came next sheds extra light on what really happened before. After '73, America cut and ran, leaving behind chaos that no major domestic group demanded the nation address. The first victims of America's collective hand washing were, of course, the South Vietnamese. No one seriously expected South Vietnam—an ally, remember—to survive on its own, and on April 30, 1975, Saigon fell. Though Vietnam was now geographically whole, it had been devastated by war, with several million dead and wounded, the countryside ravaged by American bombs and defoliants, and the economy in shambles—and the North eager to settle scores with America's collaborators in the South.

What about the protest movement, which had previously effected such sympathy for the Vietnamese? After all, protestors at the 1968 Democratic National Convention had waved North Vietnamese flags in support of socialist comrades, with some protestors offering to take up communist arms (unlikely), and alternative newspapers seethed against the injustices being done to Vietnam. By the end, there was no doubt America had helped to create a tremendous mess, so given all the moral outrage and the expressions of solidarity, a sustained movement for reconciliation and rebuilding would have been only natural. It never really came, nor did the once-activist Boomers dust off their protest gear and agitate for such. The closest thing Vietnam got to conciliation came from the Nixon White House, not the Haight-Ashbury, and those negotiations stalled before being rendered moot by the war between Vietnam and Cambodia.

The point is not to blame the Boomers for the failure to make amends—older generations bear responsibility—but to use Boomer passivity after the war to illuminate the generation's true motivations during the protest era.* As the threat of the draft abated, so did the Boomers' furious energy. It wasn't that the injustice in Vietnam had ended, it was that the peril visited on the Boomers had. Perhaps it had been about saving one's skin all along.†

Later, Americans, including the Boomers, resented even the smallest

---

* The Boomers can be mostly excused on this front, but only if it's conceded that the protest movement had relatively little effect on the war—because if Boomer protests *did* help end the war, subsequent protests could have influenced the peace process, especially as the Boomers had the right to vote by the war's end. Either way, the Boomers didn't acquit themselves well.

† Another option: One could have been for the war and against reparations; this might have been consistent, though not empathetic.

tokens of repentance. When the government eventually accepted about half a million Vietnamese refugees fleeing reprisals, it did so over public objection. A 1975 Gallup poll found 52 percent of Americans against Vietnamese immigration with only 36 percent in favor; roughly the same held true in 1979.[50] Jerry Brown, the governor of California and icon of the youthful Left, protested attempts at resettlement and demanded that any bill allowing it give priority to Americans seeking jobs (as, apparently, did Joe Biden). The biggest group of those seeking jobs in the 1970s were, of course, the Boomers. Boomer first, of course, has also been a hallmark of the wars run by the Boomers themselves, where they cannot even be bothered to spend a tiny amount of political capital to retrieve military allies like translators from probable assassination in Iraq and Afghanistan.[51]

Vietnam had one final lesson for the Boomers: They could get away with their misdeeds. Prosecutors had brought some high-profile cases against draft dodgers during the war, though few were convicted and sentenced. But even the hint of disapprobation was unacceptable to Boomers accustomed to unqualified praise. Almost immediately after the war ended, and with Boomer voting power on the rise, dodgers were duly forgiven. President Gerald Ford wanted forgiveness to be conditioned on community service, which was too much to ask.[52] Carter one-upped Ford during the 1977 campaign, proposing comprehensive amnesty to all civilians who had violated the draft rules (i.e., those who had dodged successfully)—a direct sop to the Boomers. In 1977, Carter fulfilled his campaign promise by issuing Executive Order 11967 granting (with very limited exceptions) a general pardon. This was a dramatic instance of the rising political power of the Boomers and a certain sociopathy—it was a pardon tailor-made for them, and of course, a pardon implies a crime. Despite the other challenges of the 1970s, Carter found the issue (and its constituency) sufficiently important that he made the pardon his first official act.

Pardons necessarily favored those who had "dodged up," who tended to be white and middle-class. People who had "dodged down" by committing crimes continued to pay the price. With the mainstream Boomers in the clear, questions about lingering domestic injustice, like questions of foreign reparations, evaporated. As for those who had served overseas, there was no warm welcome. Some were greeted by protests, and all faced a dysfunctional veterans' benefits system that, having succeeded after World War II, slowly starved as the Boomer machine prioritized other programs. But for the vast majority of Boomers who stayed home, the Vietnam era concluded in 1977. They had gotten cleanly away. The lessons of consequence-free sociopathy would not be forgotten.

CHAPTER FOUR

EMPIRE OF SELF

Individuals with antisocial personality disorder and histrionic
personality disorder share a tendency to be impulsive,
superficial, excitement seeking, reckless, seductive....
—DSM-V[1]

If you can remember anything about the
Sixties, you weren't really there.
—attributed variously

Despite rising prosperity and expanding civil rights, the Boomers found much to dislike about the America they inherited, from Vietnam to the restrictive set of cultural and social assumptions held by earlier generations. They duly attacked, using as their weapon the aptly named counterculture, which was above all a doctrine of opposition. The Leftist version is well known: antiwar, antistate, anticonformity. Rather surprisingly, the Right had its own version, a rebellion against a big government and a regulatory/welfare orthodoxy that many midcentury Republicans had helped build. The Right's counterculture gets forgotten, paradoxically because it achieved greater success becoming not so much *a* counterculture as *the* culture, and perhaps also because of its shared and inconvenient origins with the Leftist version. But before the revolution would be political, it had to be personal, fashioning a template of sociopathic improvidence that would provide the policy agenda once Boomers gained control of the state. The first agenda item would be unfettering individuals from the bonds of society, allowing the Boomers' true priorities, license and indulgence, to flourish.

The Hedonist at Home: Sex and Drugs

> [Sociopaths] may have a history of many sexual partners…
> They may have associated disorders…substance use
> disorders…and other disorders of impulse control…
> [They] also often have personality features that meet criteria
> for other personality disorders, particularly borderline,
> histrionic, and narcissistic personality disorders.
> —DSM-V[2]

As we've seen, the Boomers' engagement with Vietnam faded along with the draft. The Boomers' growing emphasis on personal satisfaction proved more enduring. As a historical moment, then, 1967 is best understood not as a summer of love or a season of protest, but as Year One of the Self.

The defining trait of all previous societies had been that they were *social*—a body of people more or less united by common goals and values. The individual was subordinated to the group or, as the other great midcentury Spock put it, "the needs of the many outweighed the needs of the few, or the one." A social imperative doesn't require socialism itself, whose practical instantiations anyway tend less toward collectivist paradise than military oligarchy. It does, however, require a broader view, in which individual liberties balance against general welfare. Unfortunately, sociopaths are antisocial by nature, and their lack of empathy and foresight consigns them to view society only as a restraint on individual freedom of action or a conduit for unearned treats, rather than a font of general betterment.

It's sometimes difficult to see the individualist current of the Sixties and Seventies because so much of the Leftist counterculture notionally embraced socialist goals, with hippie communes founded on conceptions of joint property almost tailor-made to offend the establishment's vigorous anticommunism. Offense was certainly a substantial part of the point and if *Épater le bourgeois!* was the rallying cry, then on only those grounds did communal experiments succeed. In every other way, tie-dyed, Marxist-Leninist havens were inherently dysfunctional and failed to provide the material comforts the Boomers found to be their true, long-term priority. The socialist experiment withered away. The exercises in individual license did not.

At heart, it was always and really about that license, whatever the official branding. Formally, the Love Pageant Rally of 1966 and subsequent "Human Be-In" had political goals, trying to unite in pursuit of a new age both the antiwar movement (whose elites viewed the hippies as too stoned) and the hippies (who considered the antiwar movement as too uptight and enmeshed in conventional politics). In practice, the culmination of this effort, 1967's Summer of Love, ended up less a synthesis of the various strands of Leftist political culture than a straight-up antithesis, standing against middle-class morality on matters of drugs and sex and for very little else.*

In keeping with the hedonic theme, many ostensibly political events were really more about drugs than *demos*. The Pageant's date, October 6, 1966, was not the anniversary of the Gulf of Tonkin Incident, the Emancipation Proclamation, women's suffrage, or anything too goody-goody or consistent with political platform. Rather, 10/6/66 was the day when LSD became illegal in California, an event to be protested, inevitably, by taking LSD.[3] The government somehow failed to wither in response, any more than the Pentagon levitated in response to hippie chanting a year later, though Department of Defense graciously provided the long-haired chanters with a permit to lift the building a few feet off the ground.[4]

All of it was sophomoric and ludicrous, and if it had been conceded as the (illegal) party it was that would have been one thing. Instead, many Boomers dressed up indulgence as a moral crusade, just as they had with draft dodging and would again with tax cuts and their own military adventures.

---

* My own views run libertarian on these matters, and I don't take this as a chance to do some preaching on chastity and tolerance. However, my views are irrelevant to the sociopathic diagnosis; what matters for that are society's views at the time.

(Boomers may have even believed these narratives of worthiness, a duality permitted by their training in televisual irony and suspension of disbelief.) Therefore, in the words of Sixties radical Todd Gitlin, LSD peddlers like Owsley Stanley, who "fabricated potent and pure LSD tablets in the hundreds of thousands," were, to be clear, "not just in it for the money; they kept their prices down [and] gave out plenty of free samples" in the "service of a new age"—an entirely different matter.[5] The claim was that acid and pot provided a gateway to enlightenment, intoxicating in ways more pacific and consciousness expanding than the martinis of suburban geezers (or than the street drugs that came later, which the Boomers as politically enfranchised adults violently suppressed). "It becomes necessary for us to go out of our minds in order to use our heads," per Tim Leary, the ex-Harvard lecturer and most famous advocate of LSD.[6] Leary and his followers were halfway there.[*,7]

All generations have had their affairs with substances, but few were as transgressive or widespread as the Boomers'. At the beginning of the Sixties, before the great mass of Boomers had come of drug-taking age, rates of marijuana experimentation among young people ran under 5 percent.[8] By the early Seventies, when Boomers accounted for the entirety of the teenage population, the figure was substantially larger, approaching half, and LSD and harder drugs, previously fringe substances, had become more widespread.[9]

Comparing different generations at the same point in their respective life cycles, the young Boomers had notably higher rates of drinking and illegal drug use than preceding and succeeding generations—teenagers were then (as now) the heaviest users, and use rose dramatically during the 1960s and 1970s, peaked in high school seniors of 1979–1980 (i.e., coincided with the Boomers) and fell substantially thereafter.[10] The use of alcohol, amphetamines, and cocaine by high schoolers and college-age populations began to

* The drug culture often made both sides ridiculous, with the establishment issuing hysterical prophecies ("our insane asylums are going to be filled if the young people continue to use [LSD]") and engaging in ridiculous displays, as when Richard Nixon appointed a bloated, pill-popping Elvis Presley a "federal agent at large" for the Bureau of Narcotics and Dangerous Drugs.

fall substantially in the early 1980s, as Boomers aged out of these groups.[*,11] As seniors, Boomers have pushed the rate of elder drug use substantially higher; as the government put it in 2015, "drug use is increasing among people in their fifties and early sixties. This increase is, in part, due to the aging of the baby boomers, whose rates of illicit drug use have historically been higher than previous generations."[12]

There are endless Jesuitical discussions to be had about the potency of Purple Haze in the Sixties versus Hindu Kush in the Nineties, or whether LSD then was more mind-expanding than Ecstasy is now, or if today's ADHD medication is really just yesterday's speed. To indulge in these debates is in some sense to concede the point; the Boomers did a lot of experimenting. When compiling this part of the sociopathic inventory, there's no need to get bogged down in too much detail. It's sufficient that taking drugs was dramatically against social norms—even more so forty-odd years ago than now—and required breaking laws in service of personal gratification. It was, in other words, an endeavor with sociopathic overtones, and not coincidentally, the clinical guides note that drug abuse is frequently coincident with antisocial personality disorder.

As they were with substances, the Boomers were keen experimenters on matters of sex. Given the mores of the day, this too required substantial transgression—that the terms "sexual liberation" and "sexual revolution" were essentially invented in the Sixties says a lot. The revolution was against the traditional order, one hostile to carnality outside the bounds of heterosexual marriage and, even within those unions, in favor of less adventure rather than more.

Pre-Boomer America had never been entirely a temple of chastity; nineteenth-century Oneida, New York, had a community then known for its free love, though it is famous today as the source of Oneida silverware (a thought to contemplate when next at the dinner table). Even conventional communities occasionally departed from the puritan idea, as Alfred Kinsey, William Johnson, and Virginia Masters showed from the 1940s on.

---

* Obviously, certain drugs like Fentanyl weren't available to the Boomers, so no comparisons as to those are possible.

However, that Masters and Johnson had to rely on prostitutes for some of their initial research (good Americans being too upstanding for sex studies), and that certain discoveries, like the fact that women can have multiple orgasms, came as a surprise (to men), suggest that American sexuality was not terribly advanced.

Prudishness fell away during the Boomers' adolescences. This was evident in the bookstands, which featured best sellers like *Everything You Always Wanted to Know About Sex* (*But Were Afraid to Ask)* (1969) and *The Joy of Sex* (1972) and in other media. Conventionally, Hollywood and mass media get much blame for driving a culture of sexuality, but it is at least as much the case that more sexuality in real life drove a more sexualized media. By the Sixties, it was ridiculous to pretend, as decency regulations like the Hays Code had, that a teenage population that was having more and more real-life sex would have their worlds shattered by filmic genitalia, and these limits crumbled. *The Pawnbroker*, set in the Holocaust and released in the United States in 1965, served as the unlikely vehicle for the first Code-sanctioned display of celluloid breasts, and from there matters accelerated, with the Code abolished in 1968, opening the way for semi-erotica like *I Am Curious (Yellow)* (released in the US in 1969), *Last Tango In Paris* (1972), and so on. Given what was happening in the drive-ins and theatre seats, all this was less *avant la lettre* than *après*.

However joyfully the media embraced sexuality, society remained deeply conflicted, simultaneously disapproving of casual sex while having more of it. Until about 2010, most Americans had deep reservations about premarital sex; majorities did not agree with the statement that premarital sex was "not wrong at all."[13] Nevertheless, Americans had sex earlier and earlier, even as the age of first marriage rose, suggesting that a lot of sex was premarital, if conflicted. Noticeable declines in the age at which Americans lost their virginity began with the cohorts born in the later 1940s and continued through those born in the early 1970s, almost precisely tracking the Baby Boom.[14] Generations born after 1975 were a bit more conservative, with their ages at first sex rising generally.[15]

The Boomers were also relatively promiscuous, and what is remarkable is that this is true not only in relation to earlier generations but to those born long after the sexual revolution had taken hold. In normative terms, modest promiscuity today doesn't bother most Americans now, but the Boomers' practices, evaluated in their particulars and against the prevailing social context, point to sociopathic transgression.

Promiscuity was frowned on in the midcentury, and American practices generally conformed to that view. Americans born at the beginning of the twentieth century reported one sexual partner on average (presumably, the respondent's spouse), rising to 11.68 on average for those born in the 1950s (a group composed entirely of Boomers).[16] Despite loosening mores, numbers have fallen back somewhat for those born after 1970, though it remains to be seen how online and mobile app dating sites like Tinder and Scruff ultimately influence the figures.[*,17] Confirming this, a study that controlled for other variables (including age) concluded that "the overwhelming majority of variation in number of sexual partners was generational"; in other words, a person's generation mattered more than any other factor, and Boomers led the way and in some ways remain unique.[18]

> They may engage in sexual behavior...that has
> a high risk for harmful consequences.
> —DSM-V[19]

Even though there was more sex, it was not necessarily safer sex, though Boomers had the means. The Supreme Court made prophylaxis nationally available in time to benefit most of the Boomers, and it had been widely available in many states even before the Court nationalized protection.[20] Surprisingly, even as condoms, the pill, and other prophylaxis became more accessible, levels of unwanted pregnancies increased both per capita and in total. The number of teenagers seeking abortions, for instance, increased dramatically from 1973 until the mid-1980s, a period that overlapped heavily with Boomer fertility.[21] (Just to be clear: abortion is being used as a proxy

---

* There do appear to have been very promiscuous subsets in the general population, which skews the data, but their existence underlines the general point. It also doesn't change the facts of the Boomers' generally higher levels of promiscuity, revealed in the median number of partners, a number that peaked among those born in the 1950s and 1960s—i.e., the Boomers.

for responsible sex, not for general morality.) Abortion rates for all women rose from the 1955 birth cohort (the earliest data available), peaked for the 1970 cohort (just past the Boomers), and have fallen since.[22]

It would be tidy to attribute these trends to changes in abortion regulation, but it's hard to pin everything on *Roe v. Wade*, decided in 1973. Unlike divorce, where it may take years to separate all the unhappy couples, there can only be so much backlog in the case of abortion—nine months at the outside, and, given *Roe*'s trimester framework, closer to three. Any spike due just to legal change therefore should have ended shortly after *Roe* was decided, but higher abortion rates persisted throughout the Boomers' fertile years. Rates fell thereafter, and not because abortions became illegal or vastly harder to get—to the extent that happened, it happened after a 1992 Court decision revised *Roe* to forbid "undue burdens" on abortion, which Boomer legislators took as an invitation to figure out just how much due burden they could impose.[23]

Shifts in abortion practices were predicted by changes in rates of teenage pregnancy, where the Boomers were again anomalous. Teenage pregnancy rates rose rapidly through the 1970s until 1991 (late Boomers and their immediate successors being the relevant populations) and have since been falling to well below the rates of the early 1970s, on the order of 40 percent lower.[24] Whatever the moral content of having sex early might be, modern teenagers seem to be more responsible about it than the Boomers. This is certainly due to better sex education, but neither sex ed nor contraceptives were unknown to the Boomers; how could they be, given the huge media attention given to court decisions legalizing prophylactics? If the Boomers could cook up LSD tabs by the thousands and establish "people's stores" to distribute free marijuana, the exertions and embarrassments of buying a condom were surely not beyond them. That failure wasn't just a product of the callowness of youth or the ignorance of the time. Rates of STD infection have been growing vastly faster among older (Boomer) Americans over the past several years than in the population as a whole, a fact tastefully overlooked in the pastoral commercials for Cialis.[25] If natural firmness of purpose has proved fleeting, sexual recklessness has not.

Again, the inherent morality of Boomer sexuality matters less than its transgressiveness and consequences. The simple fact is that premarital sex and numerous partners were exercises in personal gratification and, given public opinion during the Boomers' youth, distinctly against the social grain. That raises questions of sociopathy, answered by prevalence of Boomer abortion and infection. Both were easy enough to avoid. Failing to do so, as many Boomers did, indicates irresponsibility and, as to unsafe sex, a disregard for the safety of others. And the Boomers were unusually prone to these behaviors compared to their parents and children.

The Much-Married Divorcée

> Decisions are made on the spur of the moment,
> without forethought and without consideration
> for the consequences to self or others; this may
> lead to sudden changes of…relationships…
> incapacity for mutually intimate relationships…
> They may be irresponsible as parents.…
> —DSM-V[26]

Perhaps not unrelated to the sexual revolution was the growing phenomenon of divorce, whose prevalence rose rapidly from the late 1960s. Part—but only part—of this new trend was due to the liberalization of divorce laws, which had been highly restrictive. For most of its history, the Christian West made divorce exceedingly difficult, so that on the eve of Parliament's reforms in 1857, only 324 divorces had been recorded in England (Henry VIII accounted for just one of these, the rest of his marriages being curtailed by execution, natural death, or annulment).[27] Colonial America adopted the motherland's restrictions, with a given divorce often requiring specific act by a state legislature.

When jurisdiction migrated to the courts, divorces became easier but not easy, so that until the 1960s, a petitioner still had to demonstrate "fault" rather than simple incompatibility, with the bar set at abandonment, adultery, cruelty, or permanent insanity. A spouse opposing divorce could contest fault by the rather extraordinary practice of showing that the other side was equally guilty (i.e., "I did it but so did you"), which had the perverse effect of forcing couples who were mutually adulterous, cruel, and, theoretically, even completely insane, to stay together. Spouses could and did collude to work the system, with one falsely alleging cruelty and the other admitting to it, a strategy that while effective required no little perjury. The whole system was unworkable and in 1969, California pioneered "no-fault" divorces, which allowed spouses to part based solely on irreconcilable differences. This law was signed by then governor Ronald Reagan, whose own divorce had paved the way to union with Nancy (or "Mommy," as he took to calling her).[28]

Easier divorce was certainly a social good—and one pioneered by earlier generations, not the Boomers. The *frequency* with which Boomers resorted to divorce, however, proved alarming and generationally unusual. It suggested some combination of growing impulsivity about entering a union, unwillingness to expend the effort necessary to make relationships work, and perhaps a fundamental incompatibility between an antisocial Boomer culture and the state of matrimony which, after all, is a society of two. Rates of divorce increased rapidly from the late 1960s onward, reaching a peak in 1980 (22.6 per 1,000 married women annually and on a largely downward trend since).[29] Some of this was no more than the system processing the large inventory of unhappy couples who could suddenly take advantage of liberalized divorce laws. Yet some of this was a Boomer predisposition to divorce. Looking at marriages at comparable points in time, Boomers—especially older Boomers—divorced much more frequently than their parents and their children.[30]

While divorce *overall* declined and then stabilized, it has been growing rapidly among Americans over fifty, that is, heavily among Boomers, with rates doubling from 1990 to 2010.[31] Doubtless, this is a product of Americans living much longer than before—as an institution, marriage may be ancient, but before the twentieth century, its participants rarely were. Nevertheless, Boomers divorce more than their elders did at comparable ages.[32] This, too, suggests a degree of sociopathic inability to "form lasting relationships."

The consequences of divorce also point in a sociopathic direction. Divorce is expensive: It is emotionally traumatic, the proceedings are costly, and it tends to decrease economic security for everyone involved. While divorce can have real benefits, they are often not equally distributed. William Strauss and Neil Howe, writing a quarter century ago, noted that "four-fifths of...divorced adults profess[ed] to being happier afterward...but a majority of their children fe[lt] otherwise."[33] It was the perception that children paid the highest price for divorce that prompted many pre-Boomer couples to stay together "for the children," as the old cliché goes. In 1962, half of women believed parents in bad marriages should stay married for a child's benefit. By 1980, when Boomers made up a substantial part of the survey pool, only 20 percent held that view.[34] During the heyday of Boomer divorce, in the late 1970s and 1980s, there was a widespread belief that children from "broken homes" were destined to experience permanent damage. Recent research casts some doubts on that belief, even suggesting that divorce can be a net benefit for children of the most dysfunctional marriages. However, that research emerged *after* the divorce rate began to fall. And although the effects of divorce on children do not appear as bad as once thought, they still have notably negative effects in the short term, and for a minority of children these effects can be long lasting.[36] Many Boomer divorces, therefore,

Boomer vs. Boomer: The Divorce Generation

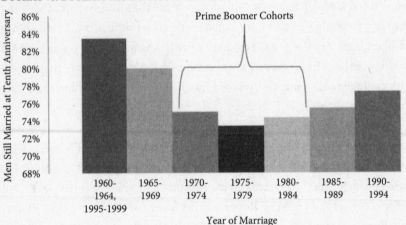

What's going on here? Divorces became more common as obtaining them became easier, but this was not a one-way trend. This chart shows the number of men who married and remained so at their tenth anniversary, and the trend for women was understandably quite similar. (The median age for marriage in this entire period was 23–26.) While the Census doesn't keep close track of marriages, the marriage success rates for the core Boomers do appear notably lower than those of generations born before and after.[35]

were examples of self-interest trumping empathy, where the interests of parents outweighed the as-then-understood needs of their children.* Moreover, divorced Boomers are four times as likely to be poor and have disabilities as married Boomers. Doubtless, causation is mixed here, though the net effect is not. Further, the gray divorcé(e) phenomenon has its own challenges. As one set of researchers put it, "the rise in later life divorce may ultimately place additional burdens on society at large, as divorced individuals will be forced to turn to institutional (i.e., government) support," and to the extent children/ex-spouses "cannot be called on to serve as caregivers," this can reduce "intergenerational" happiness.[37] Thus, even adult children whose parents are still married may, by the mechanisms of welfare and the national debt, end up suffering the consequences of Boomer broken homes. The system of Boomer marriages and divorces fits sociopathic archetypes, a pattern of relationships impulsively entered and dissolved, preference trumping duty. Not many divorcées are sociopaths, but a great many sociopaths get divorced.

Instant Gratification and Postponed Consequences

> A pattern of impulsivity may be manifested
> by a failure to plan ahead...
> —DSM-V[38]

Deficits in self-control were not limited to the sexual and marital. Perhaps the purest example of self-control and foresight is saving, the denial of pleasure now in favor of security later. This proved almost impossible for the Boomers, whose inability to save represented yet another radical break from earlier generations' practices and ultimately required them to plunder the accounts of other generations.

The Boomers' parents had been relentless savers, and as they reached their peak earning years in the early 1970s, they drove the savings rate up, briefly over 13 percent.[39] As the Boomers came to represent a larger fraction of economic activity, the savings rate slid downward from 1975 until it reached its

---

* It is unclear whether the happiness of adults who divorced persisted very long.

absolute low of 1.9 percent in July 2005. Though improved after the chaos of 2008, savings languished around 6 percent, or about half the rate of the period from 1959 to 1975. It's not that incomes were so constrained after 1975 that it became impossible to save. It's that the Boomers simply chose not to save nearly as much as their parents, as individuals or as a society.* We will delve into details and consequences in later chapters.

The Ant, the Grasshopper, and the Boomer

What's going on here? Private savings have been in decline since the Boomers entered their prime working years. Because very little cohort data exists, economists debate exactly why the savings rate has declined—questioning whether the wealth effect of stock market bubbles discouraged the rich from saving in the 1990s, the natural tendency of a modestly aging population to dissave, and so on. But during the period of steep savings decline, the Boomers had major influence on the savings rate and should have been aggressive savers, yet the inexorable direction was down, until the crash of 2008 forced people to save more. The fact that many Boomers have relatively little net worth compared to their retirement needs (data we do have on a cohort basis) also tests the idea that lower income savings could be offset by gains in homes and stocks, though these assets have been prone to bubbles the Boomers have been keen to inflate.[40]

Failures in impulse control also manifested in gluttony. As American travelers know, and Europeans delight in observing, the United States is an unusually heavy place. This is so measured against international peers and against America itself, at least the America of sixty years ago. Relatively few

---

*The Boomers' parents didn't begin retiring en masse until the 1980s, so their transition from a period of saving to spending doesn't explain away the decline. Anyway, the Boomers were a larger group than their parents, which should have more than compensated for the older group's transition from work to retirement.

adults were obese before the 1960s, about one in ten. Since then, adult obesity has been increasing, with a sharp rise from 12.7 percent in the late 1970s to 36.4 percent by 2011–2014.[41] Younger generations are also now heavy, with the shift occurring in the 1980s and 1990s, though there have been some recent improvements.

Doubtless, some thickening was just a function of age; America has been getting older and older people tend toward, in Wilkie Collins's memorable phrase, an "autumnal exuberance of figure." It's only a partial excuse. Europe and Japan have much older populations and nothing like the same level of obesity.[42] And in the period in which American obesity rose most quickly, one in which the large group of Boomers had the greatest influence on national statistics and culture, the Boomers were not autumnal, they were at most midspring, and raising the first generations of fairly heavy American children. Predictably, the Boomers' autumns are proving unusually ample, even relative to the relaxed standards of old age. From 1999 to 2002, 31.6 percent of men aged sixty-five to seventy-four (none of whom were Boomers) were obese, and by 2011–2014, when the group was essentially all Boomer, the rate was 41.5 percent; women of comparable ages increased slightly, from 39 percent to 40.3 percent, having experienced greater gains a few years earlier than men.[43] Obesity rates among eighteen-to twenty-seven-year-olds recently (non-Boomers) also rose dramatically over the past decades, though obesity figures for nonseniors have remained relatively constant since 1999.[44] Overall, the Boomers gained weight faster than prior generations and continued gaining weight, while younger generations appear to have at least stabilized at a new unhealthy normal.[45]

The Boomers did and continue to eat too much, and too poorly, and while junk food isn't blameless, it also isn't entirely to blame (this should be self-evident, though given Boomer proclivities to relocate blame, it needs discussion). Junk food has existed for a long time, in America and abroad. What did *not* exist, in America past or Europe present, was a set of consumers so susceptible to the joys of immediate gratification and so regularly seduced into its pursuit by the Boomers' other major unhealthy consumable, ad-driven television. The consequence of this indiscipline has been a tide of ill health, from diabetes to heart disease. The pleasures of overconsumption, of course, were entirely personal. The costs have been socialized in the form of rising medical expenditures borne by the state and more temperate members of the risk pool, an irritating leitmotif in the Boomers' sociopathic symphony.[46]

Me, Myself, and I

Compelling as sex, food, and spending were for the sociopath, nothing could match the pure pleasure of Self. This was only one of many generational oddities Tom Wolfe identified way back in the 1970s, in his "Me Decade" essay on the young Boomers.[47] Carried to extremes, self-obsession is inherently antisocial, as every man (*pace* John Donne) becomes his own island, indifferent to the needs and concerns of others.

Indeed, self-focus would become a primary motivation of the Boomers' neoliberal reforms after 1980, where retention of income took precedence over its partial redistribution and investment for social purposes. While there's no way to precisely measure self-obsession on a national scale, shifts in language provide a reasonable guide. As the Boomers influenced culture, the plural evolved into the singular: "We Shall Overcome" (first recorded c. 1952), the anthem of civil rights solidarity, became by 1965 "(I Can't Get No) Satisfaction," the hymn of the singular hedonist. (Let's dispense with the old saw that the latter tune critiques consumerism—the lyrics only passingly condemn ads before skipping on to the usual Boomer obsession with sex and, anyway, the Rolling Stones licensed the rights for $4 million for use in a Snickers commercial, rolling up junk food, fornication, TV, and cognitive dissonance into one perfect Boomer song/snack package.)[48]

As it was in songs, so it was in books, surveys of which show use of "we" declining somewhat since 1960, suggesting a faltering sense of community. Use of "I" has been increasing for forty years, accelerating dramatically in the late 1980s to rates in 2008 about 42 percent higher than in 1960, suggesting a rising degree of self-focus.*,[49] "You" has also enjoyed a heyday, with

---

* While the 1980s may seem relatively late for this aspect of Boomer psychology to manifest, publishing books is an enterprise of the middle-aged, a status the Boomers began to achieve coincident with the rise in the first-person pronoun. Perhaps only authors have grown more narcissistic, but it seems unlikely that writers operate totally divorced

usage tripling over the same period. The second person pronoun is a more ambiguous indicator than the first, but University of California, San Diego professor Jean Twenge, a persuasive and thorough researcher into these trends, speculates that "you" acts as a marker of individualism by separating the actor from the audience (in contrast to "we," which is strongly inclusive).[50] As the pronoun chart collapsed into the singular, so other parts of language were reoriented, powerless before the gravity of the self-hood singularity. Thus, "give" made way for "get," and so on.[51] For a sense of what effects these changes in language and conception might have on politics, one need not reach for Sapir, Whorf, and Wittgenstein. Just rewrite a Churchillian fragment in Boomerese: "*We* make a life by what *we give*" ➔ "*I* make a life by what *I get*."

Down with the Opposition!

> Individuals with antisocial personality disorder tend to
> be irritable and aggressive and may repeatedly get into
> physical fights or commit acts of physical assault.
> —DSM-V[52]

It's worth dwelling on one other feature of the individualist revolution: its reliance on illegal and often violent means. The draft avoidance of Vietnam, as we've seen, had motivations where personal benefit was at least as important as political change, and its methods ran the gamut from legal (if questionable) deferments to the patently criminal. Another illegal strategy—one whose political instantiation would form the core of Boomer neoliberal policy—was refusing to pay taxes. Some failed to remit only the temporary 10 percent tax enacted as part of war policy, which while self-serving and illegal was at least tailored to the political issue; others, like the singer Joan Baez (who provided some theme music to antiwar protests), refused to pay the majority of their bills, even though

---

from the culture if for no other reason than that they are both products of it and must sell their books to willing audiences. The war on passive-voice construction perhaps made its own contributions.

at most a quarter or so went to defense and the rest to benign enterprises like the War on Poverty (apparently, "antiwar" was a fairly expansive concept). The widespread manufacture, distribution, and use of recreational drugs was, of course, also plainly illegal, and more aggressive and less successful than the efforts of later generations to legalize marijuana through the conventional political process.

Far more troubling was the violence sometimes used by the white middle class. The Sixties riots in black neighborhoods like Watts and Compton had origins in the nation's original sins of slavery and racism; if the reactions were violent, so were the provocations. Some draft misconduct can be justified under the same logic, though only some. It is much harder to construct redeeming explanations for some of the extreme tactics and muddled motivations employed in college demonstrations, which were usually the work of privileged students distant from the chaos of the jungle and the police state of the ghettoes. Even on their own terms, these demonstrations involved a certain amount of contradiction, with violence being deployed to protest violence. Protestors might have chuckled about the infamous military statement that "it became necessary to destroy the town to save it," even as their own conduct embodied the same woolliness.

The Columbia University riots of 1968 embodied all these themes. In the riots, white students (led by the perhaps misleadingly named Students for a Democratic Society) were dismissive of the black community's specific concerns and objectives, even though a key feature of the white protest was distaste for Columbia's dismissiveness of the black community's concerns regarding development plans in Harlem. The black students disapproved of the white group's more aggressive tactics and the opportunistic use of the development issue as a springboard for a wider protest against the war. This deterred the white group not one bit. Exhibiting the same Anglo paternalism they were decrying in class (when they cared to attend), white students wanted what they wanted and would use whatever means they deemed appropriate, taking over university buildings, destroying property, taking Dean Henry Coleman as a hostage (until the black students apparently let him leave the next day) and generally escalating matters well beyond the narrow issue of Harlem development. All this was undertaken, mind you, in the name of peace and cross-racial understanding.[53]

Outside the university, political violence found greatest expression in Chicago, home of the 1968 Democratic National Convention. The Yippies, a youth party, threatened to kidnap delegates, taint the water supply with LSD, and otherwise sow chaos—the epitome of antisocial behavior.[*,54] The results were entirely predictable. The police got aggressive, the protestors reacted by throwing rocks, and the establishment went berserk. The Yippie platform stood for anarchy, and anarchy they got. Dozens on both sides were injured. The protestors got the worst of it, and not just physically— the practical result of the riots was not an anarcho-socialist utopia but a debacle that helped convince the public that law-and-order Dick Nixon was just the ticket.[55]

A cranky observation by the old about the young: They just don't make 'em like the used to. In the case of the Boomers versus their parents, the statement is depressingly true. Boomers were more promiscuous, divorced more frequently, had more abortions, saved less, ate more, had more problems with authority, and so on. The statement is true, in a more consoling way, in the case of the Boomers versus their own children. Younger generations divorce less frequently and seem to be saving more. They do have sex somewhat earlier, but they are less promiscuous overall and significantly more responsible, with rates of teenage and unwanted pregnancies declining (the exception being in some minority communities for reasons beyond this book's scope).[56]

Only on matters of narcissism and self-focus are generations younger than the Boomers noticeably worse, though the Boomers get credit for kicking off the trend. It's true that the absolute rate of some problems remains high relative to those experienced by the very oldest living generations, but as we've seen, at least younger groups are moving in encouraging directions. Even the supposed acme of youthful self-absorption, the use of electronics at the dinner table, it turns out, is more a Boomer than a Millennial habit, and

---

* Whether the Yippies were serious about any specific goal is unclear, because the movement itself was fundamentally unserious. Nevertheless, the Yippie's stated platform was anarchy, with Yippie goals captured in their flag, a black field symbolizing anarchy, with a socialist red star, overlaid by a marijuana leaf. The authorities took them at their word. Abbie Hoffman, the Yippies' leader, was pre-Boomer, but many of the Youth International Party were, obviously, youth—Boomers at the time.

if Boomers can't manage to pin dinnertime tech violations on the Millennials, maybe young people today are better than seniors think.[57]

The Boomers remained steadfast in their dysfunction. These antisocial tendencies matter, because when Boomers ascended to government, personality quirks would transmute into national policy. The phylogeny of the personal—profligate, indulgent, and irresponsible—would be recapitulated in the ontogeny of the political, as neoliberalism.

CHAPTER FIVE

SCIENCE AND SENTIMENTALITY

> All that stuff I was taught about evolution and embryology
> and the Big Bang theory, all that is lies straight from
> the pit of hell...the Bible...teaches us how to run
> our public policy and everything in society.
> —Rep. Paul Broun, MD (b. 1946), member, House
> Committee on Science, Space & Technology[1]

Before the Boomer revolt could achieve its neoliberal apotheosis, it had to dispose of the old order's remaining paladins. Of these, the most formidable and inconvenient were reality and reason. For sociopaths these virtues become vices; they could not be depended upon to supply convenient answers. Reality and reason are casualties of all sociopathic regimes, from medieval theocracies to modern dictatorships, as Galileo's house arrest or Lysenko's famine-inducing "Soviet science" attest.

The obvious place to begin the sociopathic assault on reality was on the empirical mind-set itself, the interlocutor between humans and the factual world. Whether we call it "empiricism" (which I will for lexical ease), or "reason," or "science," or "causal studies," the core principles are always the same: the collection of perceptible data and the testing of theories against them using careful thought. This way of thinking had been the dominant mode in the West since the late seventeenth century. In the philosopher Isaiah Berlin's summary, that system requires that "all statements with claims to truth must be public, communicable, testable—capable of verification or falsification by methods open to and accepted by any rational investigator."*,2 Nothing could be less helpful to the short-sighted gluttony of sociopathy than this explanatory system of evidence and causality, one that happened to undermine the deceit of which sociopaths are so fond.

Vastly better suited to the sociopathic enterprise are feelings—guaranteed to align with the needs and desires of the moment, because they supply them in the first place. As a system for organizing the sociopathic world, feelings perform beautifully, perfectly individual and exempt from debate—by nature immune to, and the inverse of, the helpful requirements that reasoning be "public," "testable," or "verifiable." Therefore, it should come as no surprise that the story of the past forty years has been the substitution of sentiment for science, of fact for feelings. That doing so deviated from centuries of practice that drove the greatest expansion of human knowledge and welfare ever seen mattered nothing to the revolutionary Boomer personality. It's not that there isn't more science today—there is—it just receives less deference.

Feelings would be the great enabler, allowing Boomers to undermine the whole edifice of fact and reason in favor of personal truth, expedient and final. Henceforth, if the science of climate change commanded reduced consumption or other sacrifices incompatible with sociopathic desires, it would be denied. If basic accounting held radical and permanent tax cuts entailed a corresponding reduction in services Boomers enjoyed, Boomers would create a parallel reality furnished with a more convenient set of books. The Boomers were the first modern generation to harbor really negative feelings about reality and science, and their success in undermining these goods has been tremendous. And by reposing ultimate truth solely in

---

* The empirical standard is not absolute proof; it is reasonable evidence for a proposition others may test themselves. Scientists furnish any number of predictions and observations with varying degrees of confidence, but this doesn't admit that their case is untrue or unproved; it is simple intellectual honesty that most things cannot be known with 100 percent certainty, however close we may get. The Boomers, however, exploit these concessions to candor in ways we will shortly take up.

feelings' subjective dominion, the Boomers were able to discount and dismiss the entire concept of expertise, scientific consensus, and elite opinion, previously a source of restraint on impulse gratification. For the Boomer, *la vérité, c'est moi.*

Trains to Tailfins: America's Former Infatuation with Science

The Boomers' anti-empiricism is recent—it is the revolution, not the tradition, certainly not in America. Notwithstanding the religious motivations of its earliest settlers, America has been for much of its history an empirical society, devoted to reason and organized around fact. In declaring independence, the Founders may have held certain "truths" to be "self-evident" (hardly scientific), but were elsewhere careful to invoke the "Laws of Nature" and to set forth their bases for rebellion in a careful appeal to logic and universal principles accessible by reason.[3] Independence was to be justified by the application of intellect to fact, not by sentiment alone—it was not "we want to be free," but "here are the reasons why we must be free." Royal ipse dixit was out, rational argument was in. If this theme had continued, there would be no need to dip into a historical digression. Because the Boomers ran the empirical project off the rails, it's worth a look at pre-Boomer America and what the combination of public opinion and resources contributed to the pursuit of private happiness.

The pre-Boomer establishment devoted itself to science and technology, eagerly importing the European Enlightenment and the scientific revolution, understood then to be the foundations of prosperity. To ensure a welcoming environment for the "Progress of Science and the useful Arts" the Framers established patent and copyright protections right at the start of the Constitution, in Article I, ahead of more quotidian matters like the courts and the Navy.[4] They also participated in the endeavor themselves, researching and designing, though Benjamin Franklin and Thomas Jefferson believed so deeply in the diffusion of knowledge that they refused to take any exclusive rights in their own inventions.

Thus came the spectacle of the great politicians of the age toiling on experiments, infinitely distant from the troglodytic science-bashing of some contemporary politicians. Almost 250 years before Senator James Inhofe brandished his snowball on the Senate floor as full and definitive proof that global warming does not exist, data be damned, the Founding Fathers were personally expanding the frontiers of science and technology.[5] Jefferson, David Rittenhouse, and Franklin were all famous inventors and discoverers; Franklin was, if anything, as famous in Europe for his scientific work as his political activities. As foreigners observed, this scientific inclination was only to be expected, because the practical and the rational were (then) the natural frame of the American mind. Writing in 1835, Alexis de Tocqueville noted American enthusiasm for the "practical applications of science."[6] De Tocqueville did muse about America's pervasive Christian dogmatism and distaste for scientific *theory*, but these worries were 150 years premature—by the mid-nineteenth century, Americans were becoming passionate about science generally.

Enthusiasm notwithstanding, it would be some time before Americans could fully compete with the European technical establishment. Europe had the money, it had the universities, and, not unrelatedly, it had almost all the great scientists and industrialists. The fruits of Europe's marriage of capital, industry, and science could be observed at London's Great Exhibition of 1851. Itself a wonder of engineering, the Exhibition's glass-and-iron "Crystal Palace" held an inventory of mechanical marvels and scientific spectacles. Visitors could see the daguerreotypes that preceded modern photography, mechanical voting machines, a predecessor to the fax, and other inventions, before unburdening themselves in another novelty, the first public toilet since the Roman Empire. In 1889, the French staged their own exhibition, crowned by a giant iron tower. La Tour Eiffel was monument with a revealing duality of purpose, at once a celebration of the French Revolution that had occurred exactly a century before and a trophy of the Industrial Revolution then under way, hinting at the connections between the two. In this, it was like the Statute of Liberty, a French gift for the American centennial, to which Gustave Eiffel also contributed.

Americans desperately wanted to join in, and that required a transformation of their scientific community, previously a loose federation of amateurs. It's worth considering these older blueprints, which contributed so successfully to American prosperity and which have been so badly neglected. The natural places to begin were the centers of learning. The original and almost exclusive focus of American universities was the production of young men for religious and legal life. Accordingly, these institutions were led by men more concerned with salvation than steam engines. Harvard's sixth president, Increase Mather, achieved enduring fame not for his (indifferent) academic administration, but for his involvement with the Salem Witch Trials. Obviously, divinity schools run by witch hunters were unsuited to the rationalist enterprise in which America hoped to compete, so new scientific curricula were imported from Europe, first to Johns Hopkins University, and then to other schools.

Merely refocusing the few existing institutions was not enough; the United States required a comprehensive network of universities, and this meant federal resources. To accomplish this, Senator Justin Morrill, a founder of the Republican Party, proposed massive federal intervention (a rather different sort of radical Republican agenda than we see today). Morrill wanted the government to contribute land whose sale would fund colleges to, "without excluding other scientific and classical studies and including military tactics... teach such branches of learning as are related to agriculture and the mechanic arts... [and] promote the liberal and practical education of the industrial classes."[7] The Morrill Act of 1862 provided over seventeen million federal acres for those purposes, an area slightly larger than the state of West Virginia. The act was successful: many state colleges like Ohio State, Rutgers, Texas A&M, and University of California, Berkeley had origins as land-grant institutions, as did some prominent private universities including Cornell and MIT.*

The first Morrill Act passed only after Southern legislators seceded; they had opposed the Act ostensibly on constitutional grounds but substantially because higher education didn't fit with their conservative, religious, anti-industrial, plantation mentality. Even after the Civil War, the South continued to resist, in part because the land-grant program required that funds also be used to provide facilities for black students. (There is some

---

* Despite their Republican origins, public universities find most of their advocates in the Leftish part of the spectrum. In the interests of balance, some red meat for the Rightish side: When governors object to spending public funds on certain disciplines, they do have the weight of history and law on their side, including the original statute that delegates specific curricular implementation to the "States."

echo of this today, in the refusal of conservative states to accept federal subsidies for health care; ideology trumps practical benefit.) The South never embraced land-grant universities, and its culture didn't value reason, science, and inquiry, or the institutions that promoted them in the same way the North's did. The trajectories of the two regions therefore provide a rough experiment in the different outcomes varying cultures can produce.*

People in the North had only to look up to see the benefits of empiricism. Skyscrapers rose, vertical emblems of progress made possible by steel and elevators and made useful by the American inventions of telephones, electric lights, and air-conditioning. Public buildings instantiated technical triumph, and the great civic structures of Industrial America were not religious institutions, but train stations, cathedrals where salvation was mediated through speed, prosperity, and change—it was an age of a Penn Station modeled on the Baths of Caracalla, rather than the dismal sewers and elevated strip malls of today's Amtrak.

Media of the age celebrated these accomplishments, in journals like *Popular Science* magazine, founded in 1872. In American cities, lectures on scientific topics, demonstrations of new inventions, and even public dissections were must-see events. The newspapers closely followed Thomas Edison, the "Wizard of Menlo Park," and Americans prided themselves on his ingenuity. The Wright brothers, who invented the heavier-than-air plane, and Charles Lindbergh, the first person to fly solo across the Atlantic, also became celebrities and heroes (in the case of Lindbergh, notwithstanding his repellent personal views). There was not one Elon Musk, there were dozens.

The stature of science and technology peaked in the two decades following World War II. In the American mind, the victories of science were literal and existential, with triumph over the Axis due in no small part to the contributions of the scientific and technical establishment, especially the Manhattan Project. Not only had science brought victory, but material plenty besides, and America returned the favor in lavish federal funding. *Sputnik* prompted the United States to redouble its efforts, enormously expanding government funding to address perceived gaps in science and technology

---

* Duke, which did not begin as a land-grant school, is the only Southern institution to regularly appear in the most elite league tables.

and strengthening relevant curricula at all levels of education. President Kennedy called on the nation to put a man on the moon, and NASA engineers and astronauts were celebrated as Lindbergh and Edison had been.

The 1930s to 1960s were, of course, also the age of the science-minded World's Fairs. The wonders of the 1939 World's Fair, with its interstate highways and suburban affluence, had come true. The 1962 World's Fair, centered on the new Space Needle, contained various wonders like cars (both emissionless and flying) and featured three fairgrounds for science and industry, against just one each for art and entertainment, a proportion inverted and then abolished by the Boomers. Futurama II in 1964 was the last of the science Fairs. By 1982, the best on offer was Knoxville's Suntower (339 feet shorter than the Space Needle) and a mechanized Rubik's cube (itself a Hungarian, not American, invention). The Space Shuttle made a desultory appearance at the 1984 Fair, but enthusiasm for this sort of display can be inferred from the fact that there has not been an American Fair since.*

In an age of endless sequels, Futurama II alone begat no grandchildren. Futurama 1964 was the end of the line, in part because of the growing skepticism of the Boomers about the merits of science and technology, whose roles in the military-industrial complex felt compromised. As usual, the Boomers' view was devastatingly unsubtle, because if technology provided the bombs, it also made modern existence possible. Average life expectancy, thanks to medicine and public health, has more than doubled over the preceding five hundred years. The tyranny of distance, which formerly confined people to a short radius around their place of birth, has been abolished by airplanes, automobiles, and the Internet. Physical toil has been replaced by mechanical power, liberating legions of Americans and their animals from drudgery (a fact some animal-loving environmentalists forget). The world's more than seven billion people are fed by scientific, high-yield agriculture and sustained in old age by modern drugs. The moral case for technology can be reduced to the simple fact that without it, billions of people would

---

* The closest thing to the gee-whiz futurism of the Fairs is Epcot Center, opened in 1982, whose Spaceship Earth featured a ride through the history of technology and communications. When I visited in 2010, the ride malfunctioned when it reached the diorama about the birth of the personal computer in the 1970s, which seems apt.

not exist in the first place, and hundreds of millions of others would die prematurely—far more than those harmed by improper uses of technology.

Science and technology also allowed many billions to achieve truly comfortable lives. From the fall of the Roman Empire until the Renaissance, a period of technological stagnation, per capita economic growth was functionally zero—economies did increase, just at a 1:1 rate with population. In other words, populations did not get richer; life was zero-sum, and wealth was reallocated by politics and violence, a condition that has reappeared in different ways. By contrast, the early Industrial Revolution drove economic growth to 1.5 percent in England, a pace that doubled output every forty-five years. By the late nineteenth century, annual expansion ran over 3 percent, cutting doubling time to under twenty-five years. The causes were many, but science, technology, and the enabling doctrines of rationalism and empiricism had the greatest effect.

One could go on, but having to justify the benefits of the empirical enterprise at all is a depressing novelty. In 1950, researchers could leave it at "science is nifty," and demand a congressional appropriation for whatever was cooking back in the lab. Over the past three decades, things have changed even as the benefits of prior work flowed into every household. Federal largesse, which once provided public colleges and space programs, has been directed to other priorities. Giant science projects like supercolliders have been put on hold or canceled while launches disappeared from television, unless they went badly, as with the *Challenger* disaster; attention focused instead on the venal doings of Princess Di, a development that would have shocked the anti-royalist Founders.

As a result, the nation that won the Space Race could, by 2011, no longer put a person in orbit. The forces of anti-empiricism, in religious, natural, and other flavors, have decisively asserted themselves, to our lasting impoverishment.

The Original Romantics: Empiricism and Its Enemies

If empiricism inclines toward the future, its opponents incline toward the past, and it was in history that Boomers located the means to overthrow the empirical order. Unsubtle, cynical minds could always exploit religion for the task, and as we'll see, many Boomers turned in this direction. Conventional religion, though, was not wholly suitable for the sociopath, given God's intolerable dictates about chastity, temperance, and so on. Less compromised (for sociopathic purposes) were the secular, sentimental movements of the eighteenth and nineteenth centuries, the ones Isaiah Berlin called a "counter-Enlightenment." These were Romantic, pastoral, and obsessed with feelings—one major branch even went under the title "Sensibility" (histrionic sensibility, that is).

The counter-Enlightenment had its beginnings in seventeenth-century England, with Protestant "Diggers" advocating communal pastoralism (they failed). The group's name was appropriated by Sixties radicals in San Francisco who practiced similar principles (failed, again). In eighteenth-century Europe, Jean-Jacques Rousseau expanded the romantic liturgy, extolling the virtues of nature and sentiment and peddling under these hazy banners thoughts on the proper and organic ordering of person and society, and more permissive and compassionate approaches to childrearing, a bewigged Dr. Spock to the Gallic masses. The American version, championed by Henry David Thoreau and Ralph Waldo Emerson, offered similar visions.

The spectacular compromises and failures of the counter-Enlightenment should have been warnings to the Boomers. For the sociopathic personality, however, Romanticism was too seductive to let details get in the way. Leave aside, then, that the Diggers achieved little, Rousseau the child expert had consigned his five children to orphanages (the better to pursue his ménage with Mme. Louise d'Epinay and her sister-in-law), and Emerson, possessed of odd racial views, also depended on money from the very industrial capitalists who were despoiling his treasured isolation—all facts which hinted at certain limitations and contradictions. Forget, also, that not all of these thinkers were against science, as with Thoreau, an avid reader of biology and geography. Remember only, as Boomers did, that they provided precedent and legitimacy for the cult of feelings.

The counter-Enlightenment fell victim to occasional incoherence, hypocrisy, and eventually, violence. In France, workers flung wooden shoes called *sabots* into the gears (sadly, this is probably not the origin of the term "sabotage") while English workers wrecked machines and rioted during their flirtation with Ludditism. Junkers, Prussia's military and agricultural aristocrats who were the implacable enemy of progress, a sort of Teutonic Old South, pursued vigorous and sometimes deadly resistance to the Enlightenment, modern government, and anything that would disrupt traditional ways of life (until Napoleon disrupted it for them at Jena; another lesson, which Junkers like Bismarck later internalized).

Against sentimentalism's emotional and physical violence, science could only point to its tangible benefits, for it had no language with which to engage the cult of feeling. For a time, tangible benefits were enough. But the appeal of sentimentalism was never far away; it just needed a body politic willing to ignore wholesale, as older generations had not, the hard evidence of reason.

The Infallible Sociopath: Antisocial and Antiscience

The Boomer revolution eventually proved more effective than its predecessors. This was nowhere more evident than in the financial priorities Boomers imposed on the nation. At some level, one has to understand and appreciate the value science creates before one can be persuaded to invest in it. Midcentury Americans clearly did and would; the Boomers didn't and wouldn't. Judged by the hard reality of the national budget, science and technology commanded much less importance for the Boomers than other twentieth-century generations. Nondefense R&D spending peaked at almost 6 percent of the budget in 1966 before declining to around 3 percent for most of the 1970s; it has never meaningfully exceeded 2 percent since 1982.[8] Public R&D in particular has fallen precipitously, and now is perhaps half to a quarter of the "socially optimal level."[9] As a percentage of GDP, government funded R&D has declined to somewhat more than a third of its 1960s highs, with total R&D investment (public and private) trending down from the late 1980s and maintained above 2.5 percent of GDP only by private investment. But private companies do not usually engage in the foundational work of basic science, on which most innovations ultimately rely.[10] Most of the pipeline of current wonders depends on work done decades ago, and the alarming decline in basic science now seems to be translating into slower innovation overall.

The decline in funding could have been predicted by looking at the

From Research to Development to ...?

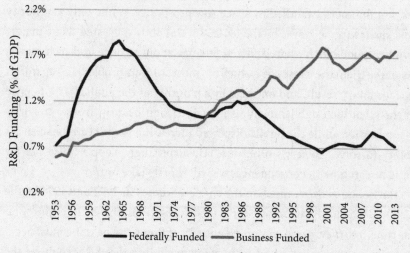

What's going on here? Although total R&D funding as a share of the economy has remained roughly stable, the composition of the funding has changed, with business picking up the slack. Business is much less inclined to do basic research and much more inclined to incremental development work. Had the lines moved upward, in tandem, there would be no problem. As they have not, it's hard to find these trends reassuring.[11]

Boomers' culture and its opinions about science, which differed importantly from those held by prior generations. During the 1950s, before Boomers were old enough to exert political control or even participate in opinion surveys, polls showed overwhelming support for science and technology.* When asked whether, "all things considered, would you say that the world is better or worse off because of science?," 83 percent of Americans answered "better." The "better percentage" dropped to around 70 percent in the 1970s, which while still high in absolute terms reflected a disturbing shift in attitudes.[12]

Notably, the percentage who believed that science had made things outright "worse" rose from 2 percent to 5–8 percent, low numbers to be sure, but alarming enough, given their embrace of a view radically contradicted

---

*In most surveys, science and technology were grouped. While there are significant differences between the two fields, the public tends to conflate science and technology, and another survey found people were, if anything, more skeptical about technology than science.

by the facts.[13] These were sentiments one might expect from popes and Junkers, not Boomers swaddled in Space Age prosperity. While only a minority held such extreme views, by the 1970s, several polls suggested that a majority of respondents harbored mixed feelings about science and technology, believing them the causes of "some" or "most" of "our problems"—again, an extraordinary result, and one held by a plurality of the public.[14] Confidence in the scientific establishment also declined significantly, from a majority to a minority, while the public displayed increasing skepticism for science's ability to solve "society's problems." Unsurprisingly, support also fell for basic research (with consequences we will shortly take up).[15]

The Boomers drove much of the change. Studies in 1972 and 1974 by the National Science Board showed that of all age groups, those under thirty (at the time, a survey group composed entirely of Boomers) held the most negative views about science and technology, including that S&T changed the world too quickly and produced outcomes that tended toward the worse.[16] (People did like some specific technologies, notably the television.) Young people also reported higher degrees of alienation from technology.[17]

Alarmed by shifts in public opinion, the NSB devoted an entire section of its 1976 annual report to the issue. Four years later, things were no better, and the president of the National Academy of Sciences warned that "there has arisen an antiscientific, antirationalist trend that should give us pause."[18] The shifts were driven in substantial part by the Boomers' sociopathic tendencies, already evident in the 1970s, and lingering today.[19] The pastoral Left, religious Right, and everywhere in between were afflicted by a resurgent sentimentality and desire for immediate gratification incompatible with the uncompromising facts and long-term investment of empiricism.

Part of the Boomers' attitudes toward science doubtless derives from their relative ignorance about it. In a 2014 survey, a majority of Boomers did not know that humans descended from earlier forms of animal. Americans also had difficulty answering how long it takes the earth to revolve around the sun, which shouldn't surprise given that around 24 to 30 percent of Americans fifty-five to sixty-four and older believed that the sun revolves around the earth, instead of the other way around—and let's not even get into their views on the origins of the universe.[20] (Heliocentrism, the Big Bang, etc., conflict with the sociopath's world-began-with-and-revolves-around-me solipsism; it's at least internally consistent.) Older Americans also have the weakest grip of the principles of scientific inquiry. Younger generations do relatively better, though the absolute level of scientific facility among all age groups dwells at unsettling lows.[21] At least majorities of younger groups are more familiar with evolution and heliocentrism.*,[22]

The problem with this ignorance, of course, is that life constantly calls upon adults to make decisions requiring at least some degree of scientific facility, like emphasizing climate change as a political priority or providing funding to the National Institutes. But Americans, especially older Americans, cannot be bothered to even learn (or anyway, remember or believe) the basics. Hence the regular spectacle of Boomer lawmakers beginning addresses on science policy with the phrase "I'm not a scientist" (which is where the speeches should end) and then proposing laws that fly in the face of scientific consensus.

The modest and static fraction of American students taking undergraduate degrees in science, technology, engineering, and math confirms the limited importance Americans repose in those fields, starting with the Boomers. The total number of STEM degrees has risen, but so has the population; as a percentage of total degrees granted STEM has at best remained fairly constant.[23] However, especially at graduate levels, the enrollment of foreign students has been an important driver of STEM education, and foreign students account for a majority of graduate students in critical programs.[24] Oddly, when they are finished, many graduates are forced back home due to bizarre immigration policies. The trend surprises all the more, because in an ever more technological world, one in which holders of technical degrees have the best economic prospects, you'd expect a considerable *rise* in such degrees by native citizens and higher funding by the American government. (Foreign students often pay more, and cash-hungry universities recruit accordingly.) What changed, then, is not the employment prospects for scientists and

---

* Americans' scientific understanding is roughly on a par with Europeans', with some specific differences—much worse knowledge of environmental matters (only the Slovaks and Russians knew—barely—less) and evolution, for example, and American policy in these areas has been unusual as well. However, Europeans tend to defer to elites somewhat more than Americans, and this neutralizes some of the effects of scientific illiteracy.

engineers, or some mass shuttering of American engineering schools; what changed was the culture.

Part of the problem was caused by the difficulty of STEM, which is more challenging for the average student than other disciplines. Difficult things do not sit well with people for whom immediate gratification and impulse control present problems, i.e., sociopaths. That the empirical disciplines are hard was bad enough, but their embrace of reality posed the greatest challenges. These—like the fact that the sun does not revolve around the earth, or less facetiously, that humans are warming the planet—can be inconvenient for people who hold opinions contrary to reality. They may require long-term planning and other behaviors incompatible with the need for immediate gratification.

Fortunately for the Boomers, the arrival of doctrines like relativism and the debasement of epistemology provided means to dispense with distasteful realities. In a crude, and for the Boomers, useful, form, relativism posits that different people can have different truths. Relativism has its uses in fields like cultural studies, but is of limited application in technical realms. Nevertheless, the Leftist Boomer academy produced different "sciences" while the Right, much as it ventilated about Leftist relativism, aped the same strategy, and manufactured confections of its own, like "Bible science" and "creation science." The defining trait of all these new sciences was that they were obligingly tailored to the specific needs of their audience, not deduced from fact. For many Boomers, science's remaining virtue was its ability to lend a patina of lexical respectability to its factual antitheses.

The profusion of sciences raised the possibility for conflict, and to evaluate competing claims, the New Left developed constructivism, which held that science was merely a social artifact like artistic merit, dependent on a given investigator's beliefs and circumstances. These new ways of thinking about science and reality proved enormously convenient to the antisocial personality, providing tools to contradict or dismiss any facts it found distasteful, as when the New Right attacked climate science, which constructivism revealed to be populated by biased tree huggers with liberal axes to grind, and therefore dismissible. If all else failed, one could invoke a fake epistemic crisis by stating—accurately, if misleadingly—that scientists are not 100 percent certain about, e.g., global warming. We cannot be 100 percent sure that we'd lose a game of Russian roulette with a fully loaded six-shooter, either, though this is largely how Boomer climate policy has operated.

Having deposed empiricism, the Boomers were free to seek new sources of truth, and these they located in feelings, a commodity not in short supply during the Age of Aquarius. The triumph of feelings shows up in the literature of the period. Usage of the word "feel," stable for decades, rose dramatically from the mid-1960s, as did the more revealing "how I feel" and "I feel that."[25] For people without sufficient access to their own thought processes, the debut of the Mood Ring in 1975—a tacky contraption designed to change colors in response to a person's mood (or body temperature, anyway)—provided a handy gauge. Concurrently, use of "true" declined, truth being a despised cudgel technocrats had employed to dispose of sociopathically destructive programs.[26]

The problem, as public policy goes, is that feelings grant each person access to purely personal truths, about which there can be no real debate and therefore no social consensus. Each person becomes an infallible pontiff on any matter that might provoke emotion. Questioning the legitimacy of those feelings is both a hopeless enterprise and bound to provoke offense, which seems to have been an increasingly common emotional state from the Boomers' college years onward. "You don't know how I feel" became a common response to authority figures from the 1960s on. It had a certain truth when uttered by black students to white professors. It was considerably less valid and relevant when spoken by an overwhelmingly white and privileged student body to its overwhelmingly white and privileged professoriate. The subtext of "You don't know how I feel" is, of course, "You cannot tell me what to do." Perfect for the ego-driven sociopath.

Delete the Elite

The Boomers' relativist and romantic agendas posed challenges to the culture of the expertise and elites generally, core functions of which are providing guidance, leadership, and the occasional restraint on mass will. The authority of such groups derives from their competence and knowledge and the social trust those abilities should create, especially regarding complicated matters beyond the scope of the average person or too time-consuming for lay study. In a complex world, deference to experts should be rising instead of, as has happened, falling. But in a system where feelings were paramount and science was diminished, why defer to experts at all? Every person, in the Boomers' Reformation of Feelings, had access to personal truth, making every man an expert, every woman an omnicompetent elite of one. The triumph of murky relativism, over universal values of the sort enshrined in the nation's founding documents and exposed by constructivism as patriarchal nonsense, exacerbated matters.

No institution suffered more than government. At least at its higher levels, government is nothing but an elite of experts, responsible for policies whose complexities were once considered beyond the ken of ordinary voters. If the Council of Economic Advisers thought the budget should be closely balanced, perhaps it should. If Federal Trade Commission models suggested a merger would produce a dangerous monopoly, then by all means forbid it. If there was something to be gained by diverting rivers of cash to NASA, do so. If the programs didn't work quite as hoped, then let the experts try again, with the benefit of new experience. Americans did just that; they trusted their government. From 1958, when consistent surveys began, until 1964, over 73 percent of Americans reported that they "trust[ed] the government in Washington to do what's right just about always/most of the time."[27]

That changed, starting with President Johnson's second term, which provided everyone with something to hate. For conservatives, the Great Society was socialist treachery. For others, Vietnam undermined the credibility of military planners and their civilian overseers. Levels of trust fell throughout Johnson's second term, though they began to stabilize after Johnson left. The release of documents like the Pentagon Papers, which revealed unseemly and undisclosed aspects of the war, raised new questions about Johnson, but by the time they were released, Nixon was in power.

Even as Nixon cruised to an easy second term and the country was recovering its footing Watergate erupted. Though Ford pardoned Nixon with the intent of putting the scandal behind the nation, he was immediately suspected of having struck a deal whereby he would offer clemency to Nixon in exchange for the White House. Trust continued sliding through Carter's indifferent presidency, which many Americans viewed as an exercise in pure incompetence. By 1979, only about a quarter of the people had much faith in government, an almost perfect inversion from the levels just two decades before.[28]

American faith in government has never really recovered. It's certainly true that political elites did themselves no favors while the Boomers were entering adulthood. The media (before the deadly "liberal" and "elite" were pinned on it) exposed political failures, and the Boomers reacted strongly and frequently correctly. They just carried the theme too widely and for too long. It was one thing not to trust Richard Nixon after Watergate; it was another thing to distrust government ever after. For one thing, the vast, largely apolitical machinery of bureaucracy—the weather service, the National Institutes, the FDA, FTC, and SEC, etc.—was never implicated in the failures of a handful of politicians. Reasonable people understand that any institution as complex as government will make mistakes on occasion, or pursue policies with which they disagree. Previously, even when the government failed, as it did in the Korean War, or when it pursued divisive policies, as was the case after *Brown v. Board of Education*, the public gave the government the benefit of the doubt. Only if the government persistently did the wrong things, over the course of decades and for no good reason (as its upper reaches have under the Boomers), would systemic distrust become appropriate.

The sociopathic personality required a new political class anyway, one that need not be trusted, because that class would not be permitted to exercise discretion on important matters, discretion that might curb the sociopathic appetite. Originally republican in the little "r" sense, a government of enlightened expert-representatives, America became more directly democratic. Politicians had less leeway to exercise discretion based on study, as groups like the National Rifle Association issued rankings that allowed politicians to be evaluated on a single and not very sensible metric.* Between

---

* Again, anti-empirical thinking. Which is more likely of a home pistol: (1) that it causes a deadly accident or (2) that it terrifies a government with nuclear weapons and Hellfire missiles into respecting the Constitution?

the pseudo-transparency these reports offered and the refusal to defer to expert opinion, representatives could no longer "vote their conscience" in favor of proposals that, however unpopular, research showed to be the prudent course. Representatives would now be mere transmission mechanisms between government and an antisocial electorate. The republican process could even be sidestepped entirely. So, the number of plebiscites rose, especially during the tax revolts of the 1970s where voters enacted tax cuts by direct referenda, electoral tools now used as weapons in the war against rights.

It was allegedly a conservative revolution, but as with neoliberalism, the name doesn't quite fit. For most of its modern history, Western conservatism followed the model of Edmund Burke, the statesman/philosopher (a category now extinct): not against liberty or the occasional revolution, but generally cautious, thoughtful, and intermediated by experts, policy divorced where possible from the passions of the uninformed masses. Revolutionary though they were, the Founding Fathers did not fashion an Athenian democracy, but a Roman republic.* The Founders did not even trust the people to elect their own senators (a situation revised only in 1913); they feared sociopathic passions should an ignorant mob be produced. As it happened, their fears were borne out.

The more intemperate the people, the more intermediation was necessary. In words of current application, ur-conservative Burke held that "men are qualified for civil liberty in exact proportion to their disposition to put moral chains on their own appetites," continuing that "society cannot exist unless a controlling power upon will and appetite be placed somewhere, and the less of it there is within, the more there must be without."[29] For the true conservative confronted with a sociopathic electorate, the correct strategy was more experts, more voting of conscience, less catering to the passions of the masses; no Boomer was putting "moral chains" on his "appetites." But contemporary neoliberal culture demands a "responsive government," greasing the skids of disaster. In the sociopathic marketplace politics has become just another service, and quality is measured by doing

---

* Not that Athens, with all those slaves and with the franchise limited to men of property, was precisely democratic anyway.

what a plurality of voters want in the moment, rather than what's best for everyone in the long run. "Your way, right away" works for Burger King, not Washington.

The great victim of sociopathic democracy was the federal government, a cancer spreading out from its marmoreal lairs on the Potomac to interfere with the lives of good people. As usual, Ronald Reagan had the best line. "The nine most terrifying words in the English language," the Gipper opined in 1986, were "I'm from the Government and I'm here to help."[30] The government went from being a benign expert to an inept, meddlesome octopus (and one with odious powers of taxation). Compare Reagan's vision with Senator George McGovern's, offered just eight years earlier: "Let us insist that Government can and must solve problems, that it can and must eliminate poverty…that it can and must set goals and define a vision for the nation."[31] (McGovern also thought Americans, who he believed were too addicted to the fleeting pleasures of saturated fat, should go on a diet.[32]) After diligent and decent service, four years in the House and eighteen in the Senate, McGovern was eliminated the same year Reagan gained the presidency. It did not stop with Reagan, who merely ventured an amusing opinion; it was Bill Clinton who formally declared that the era of big government was over.

Although the government could not be entirely abolished (it provided too many enticing benefits to the Boomers), it could at least be repopulated by a new kind of public servant, whose craven capitulation to the sociopathic electorate made prophecy of untrustworthy government self-fulfilling. For this, the essential political asset from the 1970s onward became status as an "outsider," immune to the warping forces of the bureaucrat's lifetime of issue analysis. So, Ronald Reagan: governor outsider. Bill Clinton: Rhodes scholar/governor outsider. Bush II: dynastic outsider. John McCain: maverick/senator outsider. Sarah Palin: outside outsider. Hillary Clinton: inside outsider. Bernie Sanders: senator ~~independent~~ Democrat outsider. Donald Trump: billionaire outsider. Excepting Trump, none of these people were actually "outsiders," not from government: four governors, three senators, a secretary of state, family members of presidents, etc., who collectively served lifetimes as government employees. Some might operate as outsiders to reason, but all (including Trump) are fully creatures of the establishment.

So, perversely, the key attribute of outsider candidates was not inexperience of politics or actual distance from the establishment, but hostility to the Axis of Elitism that ran from Harvard through Washington, preferably accompanied by a hearty dislike for the very entity from which they sought employment. In a wildly influential address, later simply known as "The Speech," Ronald Reagan asked voters "whether we believe in our capacity for self-government, or whether we abandon the American Revolution and confess that *a little intellectual elite* in a far-distant capitol can plan our lives for us better than we can plan them ourselves." (Whom Reagan was addressing becomes clear in Chapter 7.) Never mind that the Revolution was the product of just such a "little intellectual elite" or that it is the very function of government to plan things that voters cannot plan for themselves or, as we will see, that the Boomers manifestly cannot plan well for themselves. For Boomers, what could be worse than a group of highly intelligent people thinking about difficult subjects? Henceforth, politicians and high officials would be subject to the same standards as Hollywood celebrities, standards emerging from *People* instead of the *Post* (Washington, not New York). The highest compliment now payable is that a celebrity/politician is "one of us!"—i.e., no more knowledgeable or talented.

Even the intellectuals themselves had to sanitize their resumes. Bill Clinton's campaigns were sustained exercises in downplaying the governor's rarefied education in favor of his earthy Bubba-ness. The contrast was not only to the Rhodes-scholar-that-was (for Clinton had been just that), but also to the patrician caution of his opponent, the first Bush. These political shows, where authority turned on itself, further liberated voters from the need to consider the input of anyone who might—thanks to education, experience, and careful thought—dare to contradict or restrain.

Boomers reached beyond the government to attack the establishment wherever it could be found, never willing to defer to the experts. Campus protests erupted across the country while students shouted down professors, invaded faculty offices, and took administrators hostage. Nixon's lieutenant, Spiro Agnew, tossed off the most memorable summary: "Education is being redefined at the demand of the uneducated to suit the ideas of the uneducated. The student now goes to college to proclaim rather than to learn. The lessons of the past are ignored and obliterated [in] a contemporary antagonism known as 'The Generation Gap.'"[33] You know what generation Agnew was talking about.

John Calvin Becomes Creflo Dollar

While the experiments of the Left long monopolized the narrative, the Right also partook of its own antiestablishment revolution, especially on religious matters, with profound effects on Boomer politics. Indeed, without the anti-establishment strategies pioneered by the Left, the religious Right would be a far weaker force today, for the size and relative influence of socially conservative evangelical groups depended on defections from, and erosion within, the traditional denominations.

Though America was founded by diverse and fragmented Protestant groups, it condensed during the nineteenth century into a more limited and conventional set of churches—the "mainline" Protestant denominations of the Episcopalians, Lutherans, Presbyterians, and so on. From then until the 1960s, mainline churches accounted for a majority of American Protestants and these, along with the Catholic Church, proved reliable supporters of the establishment's political/industrial agenda.

By the 1960s, the mainline churches were collapsing, victims of the era's social strife, which left these churches in a novel and difficult position. Many mainline clergymen partook of liberalizing sentiments, marching in peace protests and expressing solidarity with the civil rights movement. Before the antiestablishment revolution, this would not have been a problem. Pastors had long been accustomed to telling their flocks how to vote and often succeeded in getting their way; certainly they did not have to fear congregants leaving in droves and tithing to the apostatic fringe. Clergy were, after all, God's representatives on earth, beacons of moral instruction and authority.

Given this, one might have expected that churches could have even served as something of a reforming force on many social matters. But congregations were restive. The members naturally disposed to liberalization drifted away as part of general secularization, which accelerated during the 1960s. Those remaining were more socially conservative, with the important exception that they were now willing to contest authority. The elite stood at odds with a flock no longer willing to take orders. It did not matter that church fathers, steeped in theology and canon law, had reached considered positions after evaluating the war and civil rights against Testamentary injunction. It did not even matter that churches had the duty and authority to instruct on moral matters (which the war and civil rights certainly were) or that convention required the laity to obey. No bookish pastor would ever more tell a Boomer congregant what to do.

Even the Catholic Church, more conservative than its Protestant peers and organized around the inviolable authority of the Pope, found itself struggling. John XXIII, a moderate, convened a council to prod the Church modestly toward the twentieth century. The result was the Second Vatican Council of 1962–1965 ("Vatican II"), which slightly liberalized the church by allowing use of the vernacular in the Mass, extending participation of laymen in the rites, and so on. It wasn't terribly radical, but conservatives came to view it as something of a Catholic Woodstock. Michael Novak characterized the American results thusly: "For the most extreme, to be a Catholic now meant to believe more or less anything one wished to believe, or at least in the sense in which one personally interpreted it."[34]

However, it wasn't Vatican II that eroded Catholic authority from above; it was the rise of sociopathic anti-elitism from the flock below. Following Vatican II, many pre-Boomer Catholics refused to indulge themselves in even the modest, optional concessions to modernity permitted by Vatican II— they would still have fish on Fridays, take Mass in Latin where available— and as to the church's firm proscriptions on matters like abortion, they toed the line. Only when the Boomers took over did that change, as they chose to believe what was personally convenient regardless of the encyclicals pouring out of St. Peter's. And so today, many American Catholics believe and behave in ways utterly contrary to official teaching; for example, 40 percent believe that abortion is acceptable (emphatically not, per *Humanae Vitae*), many believe that despoiling the environment is dandy (contra *Laudato Si'*), that divorce is acceptable, etc. American Catholics appear to operate under the impression that Francis is running some sort of Berkeley-in-the-Borgo, sanctioning whatever license one is personally disposed to.[35]

While traditional churches confronted disarray, membership bloomed in evangelical churches, which offered a more conservative tone, not so much as a matter of theology as of marketing and, occasionally, bigotry. This tactic could succeed only with the help of the antielitist, consumer-driven mentality of the Boomers. Additions to the parish rolls mixed new adherents and—this was the radical part—converts from the traditional churches. It's hard to see how this conservative transformation could have happened without the culture of self-orientation and antiauthoritarianism. Leaving a church is a deeply willful act, one of personal rebellion. So the motives may have been different, but the mechanism was pure hippie.

If anything, church defections required even more dramatic acts of personal will than firing up a joint or cohabiting, venal sins which might be remitted. For Catholics, it requires a *defectio*, "an act of apostasy, heresy, or schism" (the original text on the Vatican website is entirely in bold, just to make things clear).[36] Defections grew: Where in the 1960s and 1970s, discontented parishioners drifted away individually from the mainline churches, by the 1980s and 1990s, large chunks of the flock strayed. The trend reached a peak when the Anglican Church appointed an openly gay bishop in 2003 and congregations defected (in several cases to semischismatic "Anglican"-Nigerian church, which is decidedly less gay friendly).[37] Membership in the evangelical churches rose dramatically. The conservative evangelical revolution therefore has odd roots in the liberal counterculture it despised.

With evangelical ranks swelling, the Christian Right found itself in a position to profoundly influence political dialogue. Previously, evangelical pastors like Billy Graham had remained mostly nonpartisan (unlike, say, the Catholic Father Charles Coughlin). By the 1970s evangelical leaders had become actively involved in politics after Congress and the IRS began examining their tax-exempt status (especially regarding their unrelated operations like TV stations, bakeries, and whatnot, and also tax subsidies to religious schools that had noxious racial policies).[38] Those government actions merely expressed the Enlightenment precept that church and state must be separated and confirmed that cursory denominational affiliation did not operate as a sort of churchy tax haven. They were, however, of grievous consequence to the evangelism industry, which suddenly found an intense interest in politics. Partly, certain crude alignments existed between the conventional Right's tax wishlist and those of the churches. Just as important, a political turn became inevitable because the original appeal of evangelical churches over the mainline ones lay in hard stances on politicized issues like gay rights—they could hardly be nonpartisan while championing theological issues that were themselves political. With increasing fluidity in church membership, evangelical doctrine increasingly competed in a marketplace of ideas, Reaganism among the pews.

Many evangelical churches became less vehicles for Christian ministry than political action committees organized by political ideology. This was almost necessarily the case, because few of the new churches had the history or intellectual resources to support the scholasticism practiced by established denominations. Some perhaps lacked even the inclination, what with St. Ambrose droning on about saintly bummers like prudence, justice, temperance, and fortitude, instead of the DSM's inventory of risk seeking, lack of empathy, impulsiveness, and capitulation to short-sighted urges.

Accordingly, there would be no hour-long chat on the *700 Club* about the mistranscription of vowels in *homooúsios* and its implications for consubstantiation, but Pat Robertson fulminating about homosexuals, feminists, and praying for the deflection of hurricanes while his website minions opined on the afterlife of pets.[39] These new organizations depended on flattering the existing sentiments of their members and preying on their weaknesses. Thus, the rigor of St. Ignatius Loyola and thoughtfulness of St. Thomas Aquinas were transmuted into the gold-plated spectacle of Jim and Tammy Faye Bakker. The connection between lucre and salvation, after the long hiatus imposed by Martin Luther, reappeared in the reptilian form of Creflo Dollar and other evangelists of the "prosperity gospel," which took the metaphor of Malachi 3:10 and made it literal. Tithe a tenth of earnings, and God would "pour you out a blessing, that there shall not be room enough to receive it," a (tax-exempt) rate of return to which Goldman Sachs can only aspire.[40] This new form of worship, genuflecting to God-as-vending-machine, was all the salvation with none of the guilt, a doctrine of consumption instead of charity, individually tailored to the preexisting political beliefs of the congregation. It was perfect for Boomers (and in the case of the Bakkers and Dollar, peddled by Boomers). The growing evangelical rolls provided a ready-made mailing list, one the Right exploited even as it was co-opted by it, and paved the way for resounding conservative victories from Reagan on.

Thus, the sociopathic monster was assembled bit by bit—a population untethered by reality, unwilling to defer to experts, increasingly self-interested, with personal access to incontrovertible truth and abetted by the tax-free apparatus of a politicized evangelical movement swollen by rebellious Boomers. All that remained was the lightning strike to animate the waiting body, and this neoliberalism would provide.

CHAPTER SIX

DISCO AND THE ROOTS OF NEOLIBERALISM

We have always known that heedless self-interest was
bad morals; we know now that it is bad economics.
—Franklin Roosevelt (1937)[1]

Everybody thinks of economics whether he is aware of it or not.
In joining a political party and in casting his ballot, the citizen
implicitly takes a stand upon essential economic theories.
—Ludwig von Mises (1940)[2]

One could be forgiven for dismissing the 1970s as a best-forgotten
waiting room between the youthful rebellions of the 1960s and the
Reaganite glitz of the 1980s. The shag and the stagflation, the fleeting pres-
idencies of the crook, the bumbler, and the peanut farmer, the space station that fell out of the sky above and the mania for *Pong* down below; it's
hard to take the disco decade seriously. But lurking beneath the ephemeral
tackiness lay a profound reordering of priorities, a process that was tentative, moderate, and even reasonable at first before it became increasingly,
sociopathically unhinged in line with the Boomers' growing political power.

The faltering of an economy previously so good at delivering mass prosperity made some changes inevitable. The Seventies' combination of slow growth and high inflation were held by conventional models to be impossible, and when the impossible happened, the models were understandably at a loss. Then again, the models weren't prepared for the novel combinations of the 1970s: the new phenomena of oil crises, odd agricultural complications, sloppy monetary policy, and the sudden influx of millions of Boomers, including new "career women," all looking for jobs. Nevertheless, the old system proved fairly resilient. Though economic conditions of the Seventies may have been the worst since the Great Depression, they were not so bad in absolute terms: living standards continued to rise and performance was better, overall, than it would be in subsequent recessions.

Given that the Seventies were a time of moderate difficulty, you might have predicted an equally moderate response, and for a time, that's what the country got. Unfortunately, these conventional strategies could not bring inflation under control and the Fed, under Chairman Paul Volcker, led a dramatic and successful intervention from 1980 to 1982. Volcker hiked interest rates dramatically, prompting a sharp recession that helped tame inflation. With the inflationary threat eliminated and the old system's long and otherwise successful legacy, the natural path for further reform was incremental, not revolutionary. Even if substantial changes were on the table, they might be expected (given conventional understandings of Sixties sanctimony) to take the form of new commitments to the parts of the old program that worked well, like civil rights and environmental legislation, the reform of programs with mixed but generally positive results, like welfare, and renewed commitments to the fiscal restraint and investment priorities that had worked in the 1950s and 1960s but seemed in danger of lapsing.

The seemingly least likely choice was what actually happened, a heterodox revolution that took the worst elements of older programs and combined them into a bizarre "neoliberal" agenda that featured an economy simultaneously laissez-faire and heavily dependent on state spending and occasional federal bailouts; a conservative government, yet one with radical ideals; a rhetoric of probity, but a policy of total fiscal and other indiscipline; Republicans overseeing government bloat while Democrats promoted free trade and the "end of welfare as we know it." It was ideologically incoherent and it didn't work particularly well, not for many Americans. But—the critical "but"—it did work well for one group, and that group would be the most powerful voting constituency during neoliberalism's long reign: the Boomers.

Just as the Boomers cannot be fully understood without knowing something about Dr. Spock and Vietnam, so their policies cannot be comprehended without understanding neoliberalism. Neoliberal doctrine serves as the operating system of Boomer dominance and is so pervasive and damaging that it requires a chapter of its own. Many of the American policy calamities of the past decades have, as their animating source, some perverted fragment of neoliberal doctrine.*

Neoliberalism 1.0

A key feature of Boomer sociopathy is maximizing present consumption regardless of future costs, so reshaping the economy would be the focus of the revolutionary project. This proceeded under a set of theories, political and economic, now known as neoliberalism. Boomer neoliberalism isn't true neoliberalism (the latter is at least coherent)—the Boomer version is more free market à la carte, as we'll see.

Understanding Boomer neoliberalism requires an appreciation of the original doctrine and its flaws, in the same way that if one wants to recreate a Roman republic or Leninist paradise, it helps to know about the gladiators, slaves, gulags, and show trials. The "paleo-" liberalism that preceded the "neo-" version was classical liberalism, which dominated Anglophone policy from the Industrial Revolution to the Great Depression. Liberalism's Jurassic incarnation emphasized a "slim" state, in which individuals could do as they pleased and the government did a dead minimum,

---

* Neoliberalism did enjoy some vogue outside of America, though never to the same degree, and was most prominent in culturally similar places like Britain and Canada. Thatcher, by the way, had something more thoughtful and less sociopathic in mind when she said "there's no such thing as society" (which Labour enjoyed taking out of context since it seems so patently antisocial), but it's revealing that it became a meme for America's neoliberal cousins.

limiting itself to arbitration of disputes, national defense, and the supply of a few public works like the post. Everything else was superfluous, with Austrian-American liberal Ludwig von Mises, a later exponent, opining (in 1927, two years before the Great Crash) that the "task of the state consists solely and exclusively in guaranteeing the protection of life, health, liberty, and private property against violent attacks. Everything that goes beyond this is an evil."[3]

Liberalism viewed government as an umpire with a gun, one to be fired only in cases of the most obvious emergency. The state did not need to stimulate the economy in a depression, concern itself with the poor, establish a minimum wage, ban child labor, keep toxins out of streams, or really, much of anything. For ultraliberals, any interventions would be both immoral (von Mises wasn't just being poetic in using the term "evil") and pointless. Nothing could organize the market better than itself; any intervention, by definition, would reduce total utility.[*,4] Unfettered capitalism was Dr. Pangloss's best of all possible worlds. Liberalism in its purist form and in aspiration—though not practical instantiation—remains relevant as the capitalist utopia to which diehards desperately seek a return; it is the (ostensible) omega point of the modern neoliberal revolution. This is what the various neoliberal acolytes (the saints Paul: Ryan, Rand, Ron) are excited about, smacked on the head by *Atlas Shrugged* on their roads to Washington.

The Depression created a certain inconvenience for liberalism, since its best counsel was to stand by while quasi-Darwinian forces brought the system around. Treasury Secretary Andrew Mellon supposedly advised the government that the appropriate response to the Depression was to "liquidate labor, liquidate stocks, liquidate the farmers, liquidate real estate...it will purge the rottenness out of the system. High costs of living and high living will come down. People will work harder, live a more moral life. Values will be adjusted, and enterprising people will pick up the wrecks from less competent people."[5] This may have endeared Mellon to Ayn Rand, but not to the enfranchised multitude.

---

* Adam Smith has been co-opted by history as a pure liberal, but he was not. He endorsed some roles for government, of the sort enshrined in the body of the Constitution (but not all of its amendments).

Hoover and Mellon did more than history gives them credit for (i.e., they did more than absolutely nothing) and it's never been clear if Mellon actually called for anyone to be "liquidated." None of that mattered, because by the election of 1932, the market was clearly not healing itself. The other parts of Adam Smith's hand might have been invisible, but the position of its middle digit could be easily detected.

Americans therefore elected Franklin Roosevelt to pursue a more aggressive course. The electorate felt the poor deserved shelter, the jobless yearned for work, the bankers needed regulation, and the Hobbesian securities market needed its Leviathan; these, Roosevelt supplied. Roosevelt's policies helped, as did a monetary expansion that came from an odd combination of a falling dollar and the simultaneous flow of funds out of a destabilizing Europe and into the safety of the United States.* The economy began growing, though by the end of the 1930s it still had not reached its pre-Depression levels and unemployment remained high.

What was missing was stimulus on a truly Keynesian scale, in no small part because John Maynard Keynes himself was, for American purposes, also missing. The New Deal, which began in 1933, gets cast as a Keynesian enterprise but it was not, at least not initially or intentionally. Keynes published his first work on depressions in 1933, didn't meet Roosevelt until 1934, and didn't put out his masterwork, *The General Theory of Employment, Interest and Money*, until 1936. As it happened, FDR's policies of regulation and poor relief overlapped in substantial part with Keynesianism, even if those policies didn't quite go as far as Keynes might have liked. This disconnect meant the New Deal was not a perfect experiment and that has caused no end of political trouble. For ultra–free marketers, the New Deal was not really Keynesian (sort of true) and this was a blessing, because it meant FDR's meddling merely delayed, rather than derailed, the inevitable recovery (less true). For the Keynesians, the New Deal was a success but could have been more successful still, had FDR pushed as far as theory demanded (plausible). My own view is that the New Deal and its successors

---

* Odd, because a depreciating dollar in ordinary circumstances should have made US deposits less attractive; Europe's political misfortunes therefore became America's luck, a situation that is repeating, with China and the Gulf supplementing European money, which is also heading stateside again.

were neither Keynesian nor not-Keynesian, but rather wholly American: pragmatic responses to specific problems informed by, but never slavish to, theory.

In the twenty-first century, it may seem a bit stale to reexamine the policies of a time so distant that the champion of the masses was fond of wearing a cape and top hat, but the debate over *how* the Depression ended remains immensely relevant. After all, the Great Recession, which in many ways began in 2001, has never quite been banished, and people still argue about regulation, stimulus, bailouts, and trade. The Great Depression and Great Recession are not perfect analogues, but they are comparable. Because we cannot run controlled experiments, comprehending what got the economy moving during the 1930s and then kept it going for another four decades is one reasonable way to understand what might work now and in the future.*

Mutant Neoliberalism

Following the Great Depression, classical liberalism seemed dead: Everyone conceded a broader role for the state, and the essential question was about the right amount of intervention. Unlike the modern debate we will shortly take up, this midcentury dialogue was fruitful. The Keynesian Left argued that the modern economy was prone to problems only the state could address. The original neoliberal Right argued that too much intervention would produce a sclerotic, ever-expanding welfare state, as it indeed would in pre-Thatcher Britain. Each doctrine provided useful correction to the other. Unfortunately, neither view was sociopathically optimal. The original Keynesianism went two ways—not only did the state have a role in stimulating the economy, it also had an obligation to tamp speculation and bubbles. Since that implied occasional curbs on consumption, it was unacceptable to the sociopathic mind. As for neoliberalism, it was not only ideologically impure, which was incompatible with the sociopath's distaste for nuance,

---

* The inability to run controlled experiments is one of the many reasons macroeconomics is not a "science," though that does not mean macroeconomics has nothing to offer—even though populists are fond of deriding professional economists as irrelevant theorists.

the theory also didn't provide as many attractive social benefits and was irritatingly obsessed with fiscal restraint.

Even as the original neoliberalism developed, the purists assembled their forces. Influential thinkers like von Mises as well as Friedrich Hayek, Karl Popper, and Milton Friedman founded the Mont Pelerin Society to fight for laissez-faire.* Per its website, Society members saw—and still saw as of this book's printing—"danger in the expansion of government, not least in state welfare, in the power of trade unions and business monopoly, and in the continuing threat and reality of inflation."[6] Despite the Society's obscurity—a search of the New York Times archives produces only a handful of references, with more about the resort than the Society itself—it has nevertheless been exceedingly influential. Pelerin has included eight Nobelists in economics and in 1970 added to its rolls Charles Koch, the billionaire who has underwritten much of the conservative movement.[7] If Koch's money failed to produce results when allied to feckless nonentities like Marco Rubio, when combined with heft like Pelerin's, it produced results. After the debacle of 2008, the reason why there was any debate at all about stimulus and the risks of inflation (at a time when the country was flirting with deflation) is because of groups like Pelerin.

Obviously, given that neoliberals themselves struggle over what their doctrine means, the term has been slippery, operating as a sort of economic Rorschach blob that reveals more about its viewer than itself. For many Leftists, "neoliberal" is just a polite term for capitalism rampant, a doctrine that leads straight from Ronald Reagan to the dystopia of Blake's satanic mills, operated by enslaved child laborers and belching soot and inequality. For the Right, it is simply a label with no content, as the various subgroups prefer to organize themselves as "Austrians" (after the country that produced Hayek, von Mises, and others) or "Chicago School" (the home of Milton Friedman, et al.), etc.†

---

* Pelerin was named after the resort that hosted the Society's first meeting, just as Davos, Bretton Woods, and Bilderberg are. Not for nothing does the James Bond franchise deposit its megalomaniacal villains in lavish isolation.

† These divisions have the convenient effect of allowing any failures of the neoliberal enterprise to be pinned on a heterodox subgroup but never the core ideas themselves.

For everyone else, including the critical group of politicians that counts among its members every president since Reagan and relies on the doctrine, neoliberalism boils down to this: Individuals are best suited to take care of themselves, and therefore the default position is that government has no role. Or, anyway, as we'll see, no role until the right kind of individuals make the wrong kinds of decisions and need a little refreshment in the form of federal funds.

Regardless of the school, every variety of neoliberalism depends upon key and problematic assumptions: that individuals are rational, prudent, and informed, and that they therefore can be relied upon to meet their own needs. Most economic theories rely on these assumptions, but few to the degree that neoliberalism does. However, a large body of work, especially by Amos Tversky and Daniel Kahneman, shows that humans are not wholly rational agents, that we are susceptible to numerous cognitive biases that drive our thinking away from the rational idea. These biases lurk in normal people, but sociopaths operate at even greater remove from the rational ideal, prey to needs for immediate gratification, fond of risk, and unable to plan for the future. Neoliberalism requires Adam Smith and John Stuart Mill's *homo economicus*, the rational individual optimizing among his economic choices, but at best gets flawed *homo sapiens*, and from the 1970s on, must content itself with the Boomers' *homo sociopathicus*. The results have not been good.

The various problems of neoliberalism remained concealed for some time, because the New Deal's success mooted the doctrine. The adjustments of the New Deal set a popular baseline for government intervention. More importantly, for decades, the economy grew and delivered mass prosperity despite (for the neoliberals) or because of (for everyone else) a government that operated a social safety net, invested heavily in physical and educational infrastructure, tolerated labor organizations, intervened in trade, stimulated the economy from time to time, and maintained reasonable budget discipline including through high taxes. For years, no influential politician embraced the full neoliberal agenda, nor did citizens demand such.

Only in two areas, fiscal responsibility and a strong dollar, did conservative ideas retain any real sway, with generally good results. World War II made balanced budgets impossible, but the following twenty years saw a concerted attempt to reduce deficits and bring down debt. These efforts were not entirely successful, because of the expense of social programs, military outlays, and Eisenhower's enormous infrastructure programs. Still, the government did make substantial progress toward a balanced budget, and the federal debt became much less burdensome. Stimulus was provided (and less frequently, withdrawn) to moderate the business cycle, but any large deficits stimulus engendered were to be tolerated only in the short term, not as the permanent fixture they have become.

As for the dollar, strength was maintained by a fixed link between gold and the dollar ($35 per ounce) and between the dollar and other currencies by the Bretton Woods exchange system. In theory, if you were concerned about the value of the dollar, you could simply go up to the Gold Window and exchange $35 for one ounce of gold, though in practice only foreign governments did this and usually through the account books. These constraints kept the greenback from depreciating, preserving purchasing power. For conservatives, a balanced budget and a strong dollar were not only good economic policy, they were the instantiations of morality itself. Unfortunately, these antique notions restrained consumption and would prove an insurmountable obstacle to the adoption of neoliberal (or neo-neo-liberal) policies by the Boomers. Until the late 1960s, however, they commanded the support of the people and governments of both parties.

So liberalism, neo- and otherwise, had to bide its time as a theory waiting for an audience. Before the 1970s, there was only one credible attempt to advance anything like liberalism, and then only in its Jurassic form. The failure of that campaign suggested the future compromises necessary to get the rest of the neoliberal agenda in place. The 1964 presidential race, between Johnson and Goldwater, provided the forum. In dramatic contrast to Johnson, Goldwater had no patience for any of the government programs or fiscal indiscipline that had despoiled the capitalist landscape. He said as much in his election-year book, *The Conscience of a Conservative*. More than the standard and ephemeral election-year reminisce, *Conscience* shaped the entire conservative movement and remains sufficiently powerful that Paul Krugman, an advocate for government's ability to solve problems, Nobel Prize–winning economist, and *New York Times* columnist, titled his 2007 book *Conscience of a Liberal*, something of a riposte to a book written more than forty years before. Even the Democratic nominee of 2016, Hillary Clinton, *had been a Goldwater supporter* and as late as 1996 attributed certain of her political beliefs to those conservative early days.*,8

The third way was not Goldwater's; he hewed instead to the classical liberal position, demanding that government butt out as a matter of both sound economics and morality. In his view, the government could participate in the economy only in the exercise of its "legitimate" functions, as explicitly set forth in the Constitution.9 The Constitution, however, doesn't exactly dwell either specifically or at length about most of the activities of the modern state—which was Goldwater's point. Aside from a few things like establishing a military and post office, the Constitution spends most of its length on the mechanics of federal office holding. Crucially, however, its language is flexible to allow for a wide range of powers—as Roosevelt decisively established, albeit by coercive means, in legal cases testing the New Deal before the Supreme Court. Therefore, Goldwater would have to convince people as a political, rather than legal, matter that the nation had drifted into unconstitutional waters. His and other conservatives' failure to do so explains the hard Right's fixation since the 1980s with controlling the courts, to achieve by judicial means what politics could not.

Brandishing the Constitution, Goldwater informed the American people that programs like Social Security, farm regulation, and labor relations appear nowhere within the Constitution, and asked for a mandate to abolish them all. As for taxes, anything beyond the amounts necessary to fund "legitimate" operations were to be eliminated. What taxes did remain, Goldwater believed, should be flat instead of progressive (i.e., everyone should pay the same percentage, rather than higher earners paying a larger fraction).10 Even the infrastructure programs and modest welfare programs Eisenhower presided over were "disappointing" in their profligacy and extent, to say nothing of what Johnson proposed.11 As to that, Goldwater viewed Johnson's

---

* The voting age in 1964 was twenty-one, so the eighteen-year-old Clinton couldn't vote for Goldwater, though she did campaign for him as a "Goldwater Girl," an unappetizing anachronism that conjures up images of dubious 1960s air hostesses. In a 1996 National Public Radio interview, Clinton said "I feel like my political beliefs are rooted in the conservatism that I was raised with." Critics may despair of pinning down her political beliefs today, but we at least know some of their origins.

Great Society as an expressway to communist hell, paved with food stamps and educational subsidies. "Socialism can be achieved through Welfarism," Goldwater asserted, perhaps viewing Johnson's war in Vietnam as nothing more than a squabble among communist fellow travelers.[12]

The senator's message didn't resonate, at least, not with most of the electorate, not at the time. Johnson trounced Goldwater in 1964, with 61 percent of the popular vote to 39 percent, capturing every region of the country except Goldwater's home state and—this would be crucial—the deep South. In part, Goldwater was seen as dangerously aggressive and willing to consider tactical nuclear bombing in Vietnam. (An infamous Johnson attack ad played to these fears by cutting from a shot of a little girl picking flower petals to footage of a mushroom cloud going up.) But the senator's social and economic vision probably undid him as much as or more than the saber rattling, as Goldwater himself should have predicted when reading the book his ghostwriter had prepared, which repeatedly emphasized (and deplored) "Welfarism's strong emotional appeal to many voters."[13] Regardless, if Goldwater's views of fifty years ago seem oddly fresh, it's because they provide much of the motivating doctrine of the modern Right. Goldwater may have lost in 1964 but many of his views prevail today, with a few critical modifications.

Before the Goldwater candidacy could evolve into the Reagan presidency, it had to contend with one last champion of big government, Richard Nixon. Nixon's pro-government legacy has been obscured by Watergate and by certain Leftists' unnuanced disgust, but personal failings notwithstanding, it was the Republican Nixon who favored a government bigger than anything Clinton (either one) or Barack Obama dared propose, promoting domestic policies we would now view as unambiguously Leftist, so much so that even Noam Chomsky called him "in many respects, the last liberal president."[14]

Whether Nixon truly believed in big government, pursued it because it flattered his imperial grandiosity, or was simply engaging in political strategy, the fact remains that he hugely increased government's remit in American lives. He did so despite his loathing of the Washington bureaucracy, the poor, minorities (and really, everyone). Under Nixon, an already sizable government grew to the point where almost no aspect of American life remained untouched. Nixon helped regulate the environment through legislation and by establishing the Environmental Protection Agency. He supported safer working conditions by creating the Occupational Safety and Health Administration. He proposed health-care reform, suggesting expansion of state-administered programs to offer insurance to all Americans, which—Obamacare notwithstanding—remains a dream unfulfilled. With the Fair Labor Standards Act, he increased the minimum wage, and he supported the Equal Rights Amendment, which would have helped ensure wage parity between men and women. Even the arts, the habitat of pinko intellectuals Nixon so detested, received enormous increases in federal funding. Perhaps his boldest idea was to scrap welfare in favor of a guaranteed minimum income for all Americans, an experiment so radical that it has never been adopted by any major nation. Congress killed the idea, but it was a bold one and got surprisingly far, further than in any other until the Swiss picked up (then dropped) the idea in the twenty-first century.[15]

Nixon therefore represented the high-water mark of the big state, a world where government could solve problems rather than simply *being* the problem. But the old order soon fell, a victim of a series of crises that individually could have been absorbed but collectively proved temporarily overwhelming, opening the door for neoliberalism. The first challenge was inflation and the dollar. By the late 1960s, the economic framework that had prevailed following World War II had, like everything else, begun to fray. Though the economy continued to expand, with employment and wage growth at levels we would today consider acceptable, heavy government spending on the war and social programs created inflationary pressures whose consequences would be the defining economic experience of the young Boomers.

The Deadly Chimera

Although Johnson had imposed temporary taxes to at least partly defray the costs of Vietnam (something Bush II wouldn't repeat during Iraq II), these were too small to persuade the markets about Washington's fiscal discipline; the financial community worried that bigger deficits would lead to inflation. Today, this would simply be reflected by a falling dollar in the foreign exchange market, but that was (formally) impossible before 1971, because the dollar was pegged to gold at $35 per ounce. And before the late 1960s, it didn't need to be reflected in anything: Roughly balanced budgets created little fear of inflation, and any skeptics could simply exchange their dollars for gold, of which more than half the world's supply was held by the United States.

The gold-dollar system had been the centerpiece of the Bretton Woods agreement, which required major trading nations to adhere to the gold standard and created institutions like the International Monetary Fund and the World Bank to manage the system. Bretton Woods had successfully lubricated the postwar global economy, but the system always had weaknesses (involving problems with the American current account too technical to delve into here), and it certainly could not withstand a permanent deviation between the official price of gold and the market's views on what the real price should be. Johnson's heavy spending on the Great Society and Vietnam convinced foreign holders that the real value of the dollar was falling, and they exchanged dollars for gold at the official, and in their view, artificially high, price.

As long as the United States held enough gold, it could maintain whatever fictive gold-dollar rate it wanted, but by the late 1960s, the United States was running low on gold and the system destabilized. The prospect of letting Bretton Woods go dismayed most leaders. Various and increasingly desperate measures were taken to keep the system going, including minor adjustments to the gold-dollar rate, price controls, and cajoling members into accepting losses on their dollar holdings. None of these tactics sufficed, and in August 1971, Nixon took the United States off the gold standard.

Conservatives have fumed about this ever since, because it meant the government really could just print as much money as it wanted, eroding the value of some assets. Of course, it matters who holds those inflation-sensitive assets, and when the Boomers joined the capitalist class, they were determined to strangle inflation regardless of the price to growth. The Boomers are perhaps the savviest generation about inflation since Weimar Germans, because they lived through periods of both high and low inflation and they know whom it can help and whom it can hurt. Inflation is to the Boomers what rain is to farmers; useful when sowing, dangerous when reaping, and always a subject of preoccupation. The 1970s provided Boomers with an invaluable education, and they would manipulate inflation policy in ruthless service of their own ends. But that would come later; in the meantime, the 1970s had other inflationary lessons.

To resume, with gold convertibility gone and no effective restraints left, the value of the dollar fell and inflation accelerated. The traditional response would have been to cool demand through some combination of lower spending and higher taxes. However, the economy had dipped very slightly, and Nixon wanted strong growth ahead of the 1972 election. Though nominally a conservative Republican, Nixon embraced Keynesian mechanisms (even if he never quite said, "We are all Keynesians now"). The president cajoled the Federal Reserve and Congress and ordered agencies under his control to spend as much as they could, a mandate the Defense Department fulfilled by buying a two-year supply of toilet paper.[16] Grow the economy did, at the price of further inflation. It's not clear the economy needed much stimulating in the first place, any more than Nixon needed Watergate shenanigans to secure his 1972 landslide, but Nixon liked overkill.

Between the Nixon stimulus, the collapse of the Bretton Woods system, Vietnam spending, and natural growth, the economy overheated and inflation accelerated. Compounding the problem were new "supply shocks" in the form of sudden rises in the price of essential commodities, especially oil and food. Oil was denominated in dollars, so a weakening dollar after the collapse of Bretton Woods lowered the incomes of the oil-producing nations. OPEC subsequently repriced oil in gold terms, which effectively raised the dollar price of oil. OPEC raised prices again in response to the Yom Kippur War. Following the peace of 1974, price growth decelerated until the Iranian Revolution of 1979, which sent prices even higher than the shocks of 1973. Prices abated over time, but the legacy remains in America's enduring commitment to protecting Gulf oil supplies. It also lingers in the financialized economy the oil spikes helped produce. All those oil dollars, liberated from individual pockets, were concentrated and sent back to a limited number of American financial institutions, providing them with capital that would be deployed in the investment-banking economy that has prevailed since the 1980s.

The other major problem was unemployment, which was rising, albeit from the exceedingly low level of 3.9 percent in January 1970 to 5.1 percent just after the first oil shock, then rising substantially as recession set in. By 1979, it was back to 5.6 percent, before another oil shock wrought more havoc, but through the 1970s, conditions never quite achieved the same severity as what happened post-2008.[17] It was a fairly good result considering the oil shocks, the large numbers of veterans returning to civilian employment after Vietnam, and the hordes of Boomers entering the workforce every year. But unemployment threatened the young Boomers most of all; the economy was simply not growing fast enough for them.

Youth unemployment is often higher than the general rate, and the 1970s were no different. The problem especially affected young, blue-collar workers. The United States was substantially more unionized then than now; some 20+ percent of workers were unionized versus 11.1 percent in 2014.[*,18] The unions' seniority rules preserved old workers' jobs at the expense of the young, and this made the unemployment crisis among Boomers especially acute.

The whole mess was termed "stagflation," and it seemed intractable. The conventional tack for slower growth would be stimulus, but stimulus would provoke inflation; the traditional response to control inflation would be to suppress growth, but growth was already suppressed. This left planners in a bind. In the end, they left monetary policy loose, risking higher inflation, which they got.

To repeat, however: The 1970s weren't entirely terrible. Although the decade witnessed the (then) worst economic conditions since the Depression, things were nowhere near as bad as they were in the 1930s and not nearly as much of a lost decade for middle-income Americans as the 2000s and 2010s would be. Between 1970 and 1979, inflation and unemployment peaked at 13.5 percent and 9.0 percent, respectively.[19] The economy continued to grow, averaging 3.2 percent real growth between 1970 and 1979, and the S&P 500 rose modestly, from 85 at the beginning of 1970 to 108 at the end of 1979. Most Boomers got jobs, and most of the jobs were good. The 1970s were also the last decade in which the working class experienced meaningful wage growth.[20] While the economic dislocations of the 1970s were surely stressful and alarming, the economy's overall performance

* Public-sector workers and the Boomers remain the most heavily unionized segments.

was at worst mediocre—indeed, it was noticeably better than the period between 2000 and 2015, despite perhaps greater challenges overall, many either benign (a growing population of workers, i.e., Boomers) or exogenous (Iranian Revolution, etc.). Nevertheless, for a generation habituated to fast growth and high employment, the entire decade came as a shock.

What was to be done? As we've seen, there were three major options. Option 1: a revision of the existing Keynesian/New Deal/Great Society project—perhaps balancing budgets a bit better, making the economy less vulnerable to exogenous shocks like oil embargoes, maybe a little less regulation. Option 2: a return to the classical order that prevailed before the Depression. Option 3: neoliberal revolution. Each succeeding election provided opportunities for voters to choose a path, and every year, the Boomer component of the electorate grew and pushed politics further down the neoliberal path. In the long term, there could never have really been a question about which option would be chosen, for the only one that catered to sociopathic urges was Option 3.

The Boomers were not yet in control, and neither President Ford nor President Carter enjoyed a mandate for change. Given political stasis, the best that could be managed was a highly unconvincing Option 1. For his first year, Ford opted for a traditional economic package, trimming unnecessary spending, providing targeted stimulus, and raising taxes on corporations and higher earners to ensure some level of balance in the budget. The Republican even added a dash of New Deal, a Community Improvement Corps to hire the jobless for beautification projects if unemployment rose to over 6 percent. Ford also proposed stronger regulation, especially of antitrust laws, to avoid abusive practices.[21] The fatal mistake, however, came when he asked the American people to voluntarily reduce consumption to help ease inflationary pressures. Ford's proposals irritated an increasingly Boomerish America. Eventually, the president was forced into what his press secretary called a "179-degree turn."[22] Instead of going up, taxes were cut somewhat and spending increased. The budget did not balance, slipping in 1974–1975 from a deficit of –0.4 percent to –3.3 percent.[23] Ford pleased no one, especially not diehards in the Republican Party, who were dismayed by the president's failure to enact radical welfare cuts, his policy of détente with the Soviet Union, and his embrace of the Equal Rights Amendment.

The Rightist *National Review* even called for the creation of a third party to challenge Ford in 1976 (forty years later, they would get their wish, more and less, with Trump). In 1976, there was no need, because Ronald Reagan was leading an insurrection from within the party, though the inertia of incumbency delivered the party's nomination to Ford.

In the end Jimmy Carter narrowly prevailed, with just 50.1 percent of the vote. Carter's proposals were as modest as his victory—balancing the budget, enacting a tiny tax cut in the form of a fifty-dollar rebate, and leaving the government mostly intact. His only truly significant economic initiative was deregulation, which had long been hoped for by conservatives. This began with airlines and trucking, whose prices were constrained by federal mandate. Early deregulation was generally good, especially when accompanied by vigorous enforcement of other standards—it's one thing to deregulate the price of a plane ticket, it's another thing to abolish the Federal Aviation Administration. They were also long-term reforms, which could not reasonably be expected to bear fruit for some time.

Something more immediate was required, and here is where Waterloo came to the White House, in the form of a 1979 address known as the Malaise Speech. Preparing for reelection, Jimmy Carter decided to be frank with the American people about the problems he saw, the last effort of a decent man to cajole the American people (by then, heavily composed of Boomers) into their former probity. The Malaise Speech is worth dwelling on because it is at once so correct as a diagnosis and so feckless as a political document, and quoted are its salient points (all italics mine):

- It's clear that the true problems of our Nation are much deeper— deeper than gasoline lines or energy shortages, deeper even than inflation or recession.
- In a nation that *was* proud of hard work, strong families, close-knit communities, and our faith in God, *too many of us now tend to worship self-indulgence and consumption.*
- *Human identity is no longer defined by what one does, but by what one owns.*
- *The willingness of Americans to save for the future has fallen below that of all other people in the Western world.*

- As you know, there is a *growing disrespect for government* and for churches and for schools, the news media, and other institutions.
- These changes did not happen overnight. *They've come upon us gradually over the last generation*, years that were filled with shocks and tragedy.
- We simply must have faith in each other, faith in our ability to govern ourselves, and faith in the future of this Nation. Restoring that faith and that confidence to America is now the most important task we face. It is a true challenge of *this generation of Americans*.
- We are at a turning point in our history. There are two paths to choose. One is a path I've warned about tonight, the path that leads to fragmentation and self-interest. *Down that road lies a mistaken idea of freedom, the right to grasp for ourselves some advantage over others.* That path would be one of constant conflict between narrow interests ending in chaos and immobility. It is a certain route to failure.
- I do not promise you that this struggle for freedom will be easy. I do not promise a quick way out of our nation's problems, when the truth is that the only way out is an all-out effort.[24]

You can almost hear the wheels of the presidential Pinto squealing right before it flew off the cliff. It's not that Carter was wrong; he was simply proposing a return to the values that had worked so well before, getting at the root of a problem whose symptoms may have been stagflationary, but whose causes were behavioral and fundamental, even, Carter, hinted, "generation[al]" and maybe even the future responsibility of one generation in particular. However, while Carter was smart enough to diagnose the cause, he failed to appreciate the real implications of his message. The very people exhibiting the sociopathy he described were the ones least receptive to his prescriptions. More savings, less consumption? More trust, more family, less individualism, less self-interest? Hard work?

Carter didn't fully understand the deep changes to the American demographic the Boomers had wrought, nor did he count on the emergence as a serious political figure of Ronald Reagan, the actor whose sidekick Bubbles the Chimp had been replaced by Art Laffer and his Magic Curve. Reagan (or, at least, the public's version of him) was tailor-made for the sociopathic electorate. Never again would the Boomers be told to save, or adjust the thermostat, or define themselves other than by their material possessions, to work on their families, to trust a meddlesome government, to abandon the pursuit of unrestrained individualism, or to undertake an "all-out effort" of any kind. All problems would be resolved by neoliberalism, for once the decks had been cleared of encumbering regulation and the human bilge discharged from the holds of the welfare state, things would take care of themselves: growth, jobs, inflation, consumption, all of it.

The essence of Reagan's message was paleoliberalism, but Goldwater had shown that paleoliberalism was a hard sell. The people liked many of the benefits big government handed out, so even if doctrine required their abolition, the most that could be done was shutting off the flow to the least telegenic recipients. The second obstacle was fiscal restraint. Sociopathic consumption demanded tax cuts, but it also demanded government largesse. Liberalist orthodoxy also required tax cuts, but insisted on a balanced budget. Reducing government spending on research, development, the arts, and so on could never offset the tax cuts being proposed, and reducing middle-class benefits was out of the question. The only option, therefore, was to tolerate huge deficits, until such time as Americans were prepared to do away with the big state.

In the meantime, to cultivate a patina of fiscal responsibility, Reagan turned to a new theory that held that tax cuts would pay for themselves. (Here's where TV's suspension of disbelief became crucial, both for the actor-president and for the voters who elected him.) The government would return dollars to the people, the people would use them more productively than the government, and the economy would grow so much that even at a lower tax rate it would provide as much or more in total taxes paid. This theory, instantiated in a graph now called the "Laffer Curve" and originally inscribed on a cocktail napkin (and presumably under the influence of the cocktail that came with the napkin), was instantly ridiculed as "voodoo economics." Here's the difficulty: To halve taxes but still collect the same total dollars, the economy would have to essentially double. That outcome was plausible only over the long, long term—to achieve a doubling in the economy would require a tax-driven increase in the real growth rate of 5 percent over its base rate, and it would still take fifteen years—and in the meantime deficits would abound.

As we've seen, a combination like this had never been tried before, and many of the constituent parts had not worked very well in isolation. Low investment led to low growth, lighter taxes and less progressiveness led to greater inequality, fiscal indiscipline produced debt and could produce inflation unless growth overall was slower, and so on. The only unambiguous benefit would be a near-term increase in consumption. Therefore, the program required an electorate that cherished consumption above all, was willing to overlook long-term consequences in favor of short-term gain, had no compunctions about stripping benefits from the most vulnerable, and could tolerate the magical thinking of the Laffer Curve while discounting the large body of evidence counseling against these strategies. As it happened, just such an electorate was at hand.

CHAPTER SEVEN

THE BOOMER ASCENDANCY

The accumulation of all powers, legislative, executive, and
judiciary, in the same hands, whether of one, a few, or
many, and whether hereditary, self-appointed, or elective,
may justly be pronounced the very definition of tyranny.
—James Madison (*Federalist* No. 47)[1]

If the Boomers had been just another generation, their sociopathy would
be merely lamentable, but demographics and history granted Boomers
the power to reshape the nation in devastating ways. No other American
generation had been as large and enduring, and no other generation had
origins as homogeneous, or ambitions as focused, as the Boomers. Nor has
any other group, or even combination of groups, of comparable size and
cohesion yet risen to oppose the Boomers. America over the past thirty-odd
years has been a Boomer America.

What establishes the Boomers as a *political generation* is that the Boomers' overriding policy ambitions have been defined not in conventional
terms like race or gender, but by age and life cycle. This has been the case
from the very start. The Vietnam draft was, obviously, age based, as were
the domestic responses, like lower thresholds for voting and drinking.
And Boomer (and thus American) politics will continue to be driven by

life cycle, with the Boomers' desire to maintain old-age benefits overriding all other political concerns.* The true power of the Boomers has been partly disguised by the nominal political divisions within the Boomers and also by the culture wars of the 1980s and 1990s, which provided colorful headlines but rarely distracted the Boomers from pursuing the many economic policies on which they agreed, and, given their strength, achieved.

Appreciating the vast scope and influence of Boomer power is essential to understanding that the events of the past few decades have not been an accident, the product of grand consensus across many groups, or the anti-democratic perversions of a plutocratic cabal, but rather the generally democratic expression of a uniquely influential generation and its self-serving priorities. Colorful as Freemasonry, the Trilateral Commission, and Bilderberg may be, we can doff the tinfoil hats in favor of straightforward explanations: the awesome size of Boomer voting power and the generation's demonstrable interest in using that power to promote its own agenda at everyone else's expense. The Boomers would eventually resort to less conventional mechanisms to retain power, as we'll see in Chapter 16, but for almost its entire length, the Boomer revolution was democratic.

The Power of Majority

More than anything, Boomer influence is a story of sheer numbers. As of the early 1980s, when the Boomer revolution really kicked off, the generation represented no less than 42 percent of the voting-eligible population and up to 51 percent, depending on whether one calculates the Boom's start from 1940 or 1946.[2] Under either analysis, the Boomers have been by far the most important political group for several decades—e.g., there were roughly as many white Boomers in 1990 as *all* ethnic minorities, of *all* generations,

*Age thresholds may seem to be generationally agnostic and indeed would be if programs linked to them were maintained in perpetuity. That is not the case—there's no Vietnam War anymore, no draft, and in the next two decades, there will be no Social Security as we presently understand it. Transience makes many age thresholds a mechanism of Boomer empowerment masquerading as general legislation.

combined.[3] The Boomers' numerosity meant that even a modest tilt in any one direction (self-serving sociopathy, as a pointed example) influenced outcomes profoundly. In matters where the Boomers identified themselves by generational interests, as they often did, their power would be overwhelming, allowing Boomers to set policy essentially by themselves, without any of the usual coalition building, compromises, or concessions to other interests. It has been an extraordinary situation in American democratic history.*

Toward a Lower Voting Age

In essential matters, the Boomers have from the start identified their interests on a generational basis, quite literally from the moment they got the vote. Before 1970, the voting age in the United States had generally been twenty-one—"generally," because states were free to adopt lower voting ages for their own elections. Before 1969, only four states did so.[4] It just didn't seem worth the expense to maintain separate registries of eighteen-year-olds for state elections and twenty-one-year-olds for federal contests. More important, most adults did not believe that teenagers possessed the maturity to exercise the franchise. However, during the 1960s, momentum gathered behind the idea that drafting an eighteen-year-old while denying him the vote was unjust. So in 1970, Congress amended, and Nixon signed, the Voting Rights Act to lower the voting age to eighteen, and the states ratified the Twenty-Sixth Amendment the following year, to the same effect. By definition, none of these actors were Boomers, but they all understood the consequences of failing to cater to a group that would gain the vote soon enough. The results of the revised thresholds can be seen in the jump in the next chart.

The only immediate beneficiaries of the Twenty-Sixth Amendment were the Boomers. Right from the beginning, the generation's political identity

---

* The key word here is "democratic." There have been other groups, even individuals, who had greater influence than the Boomers, but none effected change in ways we would now understand to be democratic. For example, the Founding Fathers were a tiny and immensely wealthy oligarchy—George Washington was one of the richest men in the Colonies, thanks in large part to his slave holdings—operating during a time when the franchise extended only to white men.

Boomers: The Essential Electorate

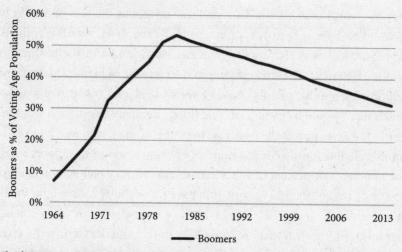

What's going on here? The Boomers have been hugely influential in politics for many decades. While their raw votes peaked in the early 1980s, their true influence kept growing as they aged, gathered offices, made political donations, and most importantly, as their voting participation rates increased.[5]

was based not on conventional characteristics like gender, income, or race, but on age. That was a political landmark in itself. The only comparable equivalent was the enactment of Social Security, which united seniors in 1935 and will serve as the Boomers' final rallying point.

Of equal consequence was how the change was achieved, because the justifications for the lowered voting age were shaky and the mechanisms not without risks to others. That these infirmities made no difference provided an early lesson to the Boomers that the critical factor in obtaining political goods was not logic or prudence, but generational strength.

The conventional and superficially appealing justification for the change in voting age was "old enough to serve, old enough to vote." By that logic, the voting age should have changed not in 1970, but in 1942, when the draft age was lowered from twenty-one to eighteen (or reaching back to World War I, perhaps sixteen). And in the ensuing decades there were, in fact, dozens of proposals to reconcile the ages of voting and draft. All of them failed.

So what changed in 1970? Certainly, not the merits of the arguments.

Senator Ted Kennedy trotted out the old saw that it was unjust for a democracy to draft a man who had no political say about the war he would be required to fight. Kennedy's argument had deep flaws, starting with the obvious, which was that modern nations shouldn't be in the business of drafting teenagers. The obvious place to start was the right place to start, and beginning from that premise would have avoided a lot of tortured logic, of which there would be plenty. For one thing, Kennedy's argument wouldn't justify the extension of the franchise to young women, who weren't draft or combat eligible (only a limited number of women served in support roles). For another, ~70 percent of the Vietnam-era military had volunteered, so obviously the substantial majority *did* have some choice in the fight. While injustice should always be rooted out, there were also vastly fewer teenage conscripts in Vietnam than in World War II. In numerical terms, the argument had gotten weaker, not stronger, and it was further complicated by the fact that so many Boomers avoided the draft by means legal and otherwise. The argument, anyway, would soon be mooted—as everyone understood. One of Nixon's 1968 campaign pledges was to end conscription, and a presidential commission in early 1970 cleared the path to do so. The draft had been declining radically since 1969 and would be formally abolished in 1973. Nevertheless, while the arguments to reconciling the draft and voting ages were slight, flawed, and transient, teenage Boomers were granted the vote. The begrudging service of a tiny minority was used to confer benefits on tens of millions.

Draft or no draft, the extension of the franchise might have made sense if teenagers would be prudent stewards of their new rights. This was exactly what Kennedy argued, saying that eighteen-year-olds "possess[ed] the requisite maturity, judgment and stability for responsible exercise of the franchise."[6] Cognitive research disagrees: Personality and judgment do not fully mature until the early twenties. (Perhaps, in Kennedy's case, the bloom of judgment did not open until even later, given the events of Chappaquiddick shortly before his voting-age crusade.) For proof, one can just review the catalogue of sex, drugs, and draft dodging during the 1960s, or for the more digitally minded, peruse their own histories on the time machine of Facebook. Kennedy also optimistically pointed to the better educations of modern teens, but the necessary classes in civics were cursory at best, both then and now, and while American civic knowledge overall is abysmal—more people can identify Beyoncé than name the three branches of government—it has always been by far the worst among young people.[7]

A more persuasive explanation of the timing of reform is that in an era of close elections, the prospect of capturing a large population of new voters proved irresistible. In 1970, every Boomer under the age of twenty-one stood to benefit, some 60 million new votes available for the taking.[8] The immediate expansion of the electorate was smaller, of course, but still enormous in political terms: some 10–11 million voters, around 8 percent of the voting-eligible population.[9] From World War II to 1970, four presidential elections since World War II had popular margins of less than 10 percent. Kennedy and Nixon (in his '68 campaign) each carried the country by less than 1 percent; Carter would win by 2.06 percent. Even if only half the newly enfranchised youth voted, it might change the electoral balance. To the country's great cost, this speculation would soon be proved out.

Congress duly amended the VRA to permit youth voting, an early concession to Boomer numerosity. Like many Boomer-oriented policies, it put other groups at risk. Granting Boomers the vote through the VRA gave courts a prime opportunity to revisit other portions of the act, including the ability of the federal government to police states that had historically discriminated against racial minorities in the voting booth. Nixon, a lawyer, knew when he signed the VRA amendment that it was likely unconstitutional, and cynics about Nixon could reasonably question whether he was inviting the Court to restrict the VRA's application to blacks under the guise of expanding its protections for Boomers.[*,10] And indeed, something like that happened, albeit decades later, when a Court led by Boomer John Roberts was happy to take advantage of sloppy congressional work to dispatch with parts of the VRA. In any event, the pre-Boomer Court of 1970 allowed Congress to lower the federal voting age but prohibited it from enforcing this result on the states, and went no further.

Nevertheless, with the federal voting age lowered it became politically imperative to pass a constitutional amendment to bring state laws in line,

---

* Nixon had long wanted to limit the VRA to take the "monkey…off the backs of the South," a region that was becoming an important Republican base.

and the speed with which this was achieved confirmed the considerable power of the Boomers.* The Court's ruling subjected all congressmen to the sub-twenty-one vote; any congressman daring to oppose the amendment could expect a backlash. The House duly passed the amendment 401–19.[11] Faced with a fait accompli, states submitted additional ratifications, and Nixon signed the whole package five days after the requisite thirty-eighth state ratified. It was the fastest approval for any amendment, essentially one hundred days from start to finish. By comparison, it took more than two years for the Bill of Rights to achieve the same result; the guarantee of the franchise for blacks through the Fifteenth Amendment took 342 days, to say nothing of the Civil War and the centuries of slavery that preceded it; and, the Nineteenth Amendment's delivery of women's suffrage took 441 days and decades of work.[†,12]

The lesson for the Boomers was that they were uniquely powerful in contemporary politics and perhaps even especially deserving, which reinforced their sociopathic predispositions.[‡,13] In this case, the Boomers were given the privilege; in later years, they would simply take it. As it happened, Nixon expected first-time voters (Boomers) to vote for him, and it appears they did if by a slim majority; then again, so did most Americans in 1972.[14] The Republican advantage in Boomer votes would grow over time, though it would sometimes be overcome when Democrats offered up a particularly charismatic cogenerationalist like B. Clinton. Even then, prominent Boomer Democrats tended to pursue policies any New Dealer/Great Society-ist would have viewed as fairly conservative.

---

* Some have argued that legislators caved to provide students with a formal outlet for their rage, in the hope of diverting campus unrest. The implications of this depend on your view of the degree of violence prevailing on campuses in the 1960s and the philosophical acceptability of morally compromised protests about one issue leading to a response on a tangential issue.

† Intriguingly, the Twenty-Seventh Amendment (resisting modifications to intrasession congressional pay) was proposed in 1789 and ratified only in 1992.

‡ The Twenty-Sixth Amendment may yet serve the Boomers—its expansive language provides that the right to vote "shall not be denied or abridged...on account of age." As Eric Fish noted, that could prevent laws from restricting mentally incompetent seniors from voting, or be used to force states to provide busing, special voting machines, and other accommodations to ensure that graying Boomers can vote.

Capturing new under-twenty-one votes became an urgent matter, and we labor still under the heritage of those efforts, which helped establish the Boomers' permanent political orientations. Democrats, the natural party of the young, failed to capitalize on the opportunity presented by the Twenty-Sixth Amendment. At the time, the Democrats' youth wing was in disarray. In the 1960s, the College Democrats had split from the Democratic National Committee over Vietnam and would not be reabsorbed until 1990. Given student political preferences, the loss was probably not so much in immediate votes as in failure to build an effective Leftist youth machine or establish lasting party affinities.

The Republicans, sensing an opening, quickly occupied it. Hewing to (pre-Trump) stereotype, the GOP had its act together and aggressively courted youth. Just after the Twenty-Sixth Amendment was ratified, the Republican National Committee made College-RNC its official youth arm. C-RNC became a sort of training camp for future Republican organizers, starting with Karl Rove, who sought the C-RNC chairmanship in 1973. Rove was already an operator, having run a Watergate Jr., breaking into the office of a Democratic candidate (per Rove himself, it was a "youthful prank" of a nineteen-year-old; so much for Ted Kennedy's "requisite maturity, judgment and stability").[15] His contest for the C-RNC chairmanship was equally unsavory, involving an electoral kerfuffle and contested results, resolved by the personal intervention of RNC chair George H. W. Bush— foreshadowing, perhaps, *Bush v. Gore* (where all the members of the Court's majority held appointments due to Reagan/Bush I).

The Democrats flubbed a prime chance to make loyal millions of newly minted voters, while the Republicans turned their youth organizations into effective finishing schools. Over time, white Boomers drifted Rightward and stayed there, pulled along by effective youth organizations and the GOP's success in assembling a platform that, overall, might not have mirrored any voter's total preferences but always managed to include the *dispositive* issue for many voters, be it taxes, guns, cultural matters, Social Security, whatever worked in the moment. The sociopathic personality guaranteed that this sort of pander-pick-and-choose politics would succeed, because there was only one issue that really mattered: the free exercise of Self, as defined by that Self, not some theorist committed to coherence. As the Boomers moved

Rightward, their outsized demographic and other powers pushed the system along toward conservatism.[16] For a centrist fixed circa 1972, the Boomer political galaxy experienced a sort of Doppler shift, becoming redder as it moved further and faster away.

Fighting for the Right to Party

The voting age debate had a corollary, of temporary but significant benefit to the Boomers, and that involved alcohol. We've already seen that the Boomers had a certain fixation on substances, and if legal pot was then impossible, teenage boozing was not. Again, this involved a considerable and risky departure from prior practice. From Prohibition's end to 1970, the drinking age in most states had, like the voting age, been twenty-one, and for the same reasons. In the wake of the Twenty-Sixth Amendment, old-enough-to-serve became old-enough-to-be-served, and by the 1970s, thirty states reduced drinking ages to as low as eighteen.[17] Obviously, the old-enough argument was questionable as to voting and plainly specious as to drinking. And just as obviously, like the Twenty-Sixth Amendment, the right-to-drink lobby had exactly one demographic beneficiary: the Boomers, who, thanks to the new voting age, were able to influence this issue—one of their first direct exercises of political power.

Despite almost immediate evidence of rising traffic fatalities—another case of benefits captured by Boomers with costs externalized to others, and one which cast further doubt on Kennedy's perorations on the maturity of modern youth—throughout the 1970s, only one state (Michigan) reverted to the twenty-one-year-old limit. A handful of other states did raise their drinking ages to nineteen (as if that made a difference); most did not. Only in 1984 did Congress pass the National Minimum Drinking Age Act, which didn't expressly require states to raise the drinking age to twenty-one, though it would withhold federal highway funds after 1986–1987 if states did not comply, which amounted to a mandate.[18] By then, the very youngest of the Boomers would be twenty-two or twenty-three, and thus unaffected. The law passed and the states reverted to the old system. And so the Boomers had shaped, by virtue of numbers, a new political landscape, one that permitted them, sozzled and acned, to engage in the solemn duty of selecting the nation's political destiny.

The Colonization Begins

Measured by raw voting power, the moment of greatest Boomer influence arrived in the Reagan years, but various dynamics made the Boomers even more powerful over time. A slowly diminishing share of the vote was offset by the Boomers' growing rates of voter participation, increasing wealth and political donations, and the ascent of cogenerationalists into public office.

The Boomers achieved the height of effective political power from the late 1980s until the early 2010s, a period which, as we will see, has coincided with the systematic transfer of wealth to their generation and a set of sociopathic initiatives putting the price to others. Boomer power derived originally from voting strength and then translated into political offices, whose acquisition had been delayed both by the difficulty in displacing incumbents, conventional preference for "mature" candidates (apparently, no one cared about mature voters), and age restrictions on certain offices.

Nevertheless, the Boomer takeover began quickly enough. The first Boomer in the House was Marvin Mathis (b. 1940), who got the job in 1971; the first Boomer senator was none other than our previous vice president, Joe Biden (b. 1942), who arrived in the Senate in 1973 and more or less proves the case for Boomer political longevity. Just as Boomers took over Congress, they took over the governors' mansions, with David Boren (b. 1941) leading the way in Oklahoma's 1974 gubernatorial race. The concurrence of youth enfranchisement and the near-immediate election of Boomers was not coincidental.

By the 1980s, the Boomers already represented a substantial fraction of Congress, and by 1994 they accounted for more than half of the House, reaching a peak of 79 percent in 2007–2008.*[19] Boomers remain powerful, with over 70 percent of House seats in the 2015–2016 Congress, a greater share than they had even in the early 1990s. At the start of 2016, they controlled 86 percent of governorships. Nor will Boomers relinquish power anytime soon, given the Boomers' expected longevity and a political process

---

* Congresses run two years from January 3 of the calendar year following an election. For simplicity, I omit the last 2.5 days of a Congressional term for ease (it avoids the prospect of multiple Congresses in a single year, which is not really how things operate). For example, the 110th Congress ran from January 3, 2007 to January 3, 2009, but I simply consider it to be the 2007–2008 Congress.

that favors incumbents (about 95 percent of incumbent Congressmen were reelected in 2014). The 2017–2019 House is set to be 69 percent Boomer, so the generation still maintains supermajority control over the national agenda in the legislature, executive branch, and courts.

Even over the coming years, as age finally whittles away generational majorities, Boomer power will remain. Moreover, with most of the socio-pathic agenda in place, the Boomers need only to block new legislation, eas-ily accomplished by minority actions like vetoes, filibusters, shutdowns, and litigation. The Boomers will retain power for a long time.

Another dynamic that will prolong Boomer power is that an America under the influence of graying Boomers now tolerates ever-older candidates. The pathbreaker in this regard was non-Boomer Ronald Reagan, who won his first term at what has become a now-unremarkable sixty-nine—though back in 1980, his age was a concern, and a valid one, given subsequent revela-tions about his Alzheimer's. By 2016, voting may as well have been for presi-dency of the local senior center. Hillary Clinton (b. 1947) was sixty-nine on election day and Trump (b. 1946) was no younger. Both were spring chick-ens compared to the ostensible champion of youth, Bernie Sanders (b. 1941), who shuffled into the 2016 Democratic primary at seventy-four. If the young-est Boomer can do the same—plausible given improvements to longevity, though not competence—we could have a Boomer president as late as 2045. For the apocalyptically minded, if Boomers repeat Strom Thurmond's feat of serving to one hundred, there could be a Senate of Methuselahs into the 2060s (making "senator" uncomfortably literal, derived as it is from *senex*, meaning "old" and also the root of "senile"). These are extreme and unset-tling cases, but even moderate longevity still produces a Boomer-dominated machine for many years to come, especially in the federal judiciary, which operates by lifetime appointment—meaning the Supreme Court could not only become entirely Boomer over the next decade, but remain substan-tially so until around 2050. The lower courts have already been packed with Boomers.

The mere fact that Boomers will retain office for some time does not auto-matically ensure Boomer policies will continue, but obviously people are predisposed toward concerns with which they themselves can identify, cre-ating a receptive audience for Boomer demands, especially in the judiciary.

What senior senator, lubricated by a Metamucil mimosa, could resist a little gray-panther lobbying? And what Boomer Justice, peering over his bifocals at a writ of certiorari, could fail to see the immense application of the Twenty-Sixth Amendment to the senior franchise?

In combination with Boomers' still substantial numbers, the greater tendency of older people to vote, the fragmentation of other interest groups, and the concentration of wealth in Boomer hands—truly unleashed by the *Citizens United* decision in 2010 and other expansions of monetary speech condoned by the Boomer Chief Justice—the Boomers remain a force to reckon with. Boomer lobbying groups are robust and well-funded, and their links to politics close even in the physical sense: of the two major embassies closest to Congress, the first is Canada's and the second, AARP's, located a five-minute Rascal-ride from Capitol Hill. But demographic changes mean that it will soon become possible—for the first time in decades—for a union of younger voters to contest that dominance, and the possibilities of doing so will be considered in the final chapter.

Boomers Invade the House

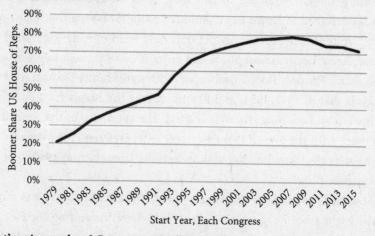

Start Year, Each Congress

What's going on here? Boomers controlled Congress by the first half of the 1990s. Although Congressional votes tended to break on party lines, the parties themselves began converging as their Boomer leaders pushed policies toward a new, Boomerish consensus. This convergence helped produce striking (and unhelpful) instances of Boomer bipartisanship on matters of prison policy, tax, and entitlements. The trend in the House was mirrored in state legislatures, the judiciary, bureaucracy, and other powerful offices.[20]

The Continuing Evolution of Boomer Political Identity

There are various ways to measure Baby Boomer political affinities, by surveys and by outcomes, and while these do not always agree in their particulars, they all surprise in the same general way. With the Leftism of the Sixties hanging like a permanent cloud of political patchouli, it's easy to assume that the Boomers are die-hard Democrats. But exit polls—which measure how respondents say they voted right after leaving the voting booth and are often more reliable than opinion polls leading up to elections—show that while many Boomers have a weak Democratic bias, Boomers are more conservative than the population *overall*, and the generation has been drifting Rightward over time.

Boomer preferences can be assessed in another, perhaps more revealing way. Presidential approval ratings, which are measured more frequently, also show Boomers hold opinions further to the Right of the general population. For this task, it's helpful to strip out minority voters, who generally trend Democratic (e.g., blacks on the order of 85+ percent), and whose very reliability allows Democrats to take their votes for granted while offering policies designed to entice less committed groups. Making this adjustment shows white Boomers generally not only have been moving Rightward but are net Republican, almost all on the order of +1–8 percent depending on birth year.[21] The only Boomer subcohort with significantly Democratic leanings was that of 1947–1954, and like the rest of the Boomers, they drifted Rightward and are now relatively neutral. The sheer size of the generation, combined with the overall Republican tilt in its preference, has dragged the entire white electorate into Republican territory from the mid-1980s onward.

Rightward Ho!

At some level, none of this is surprising: The entire country has moved to the Right since Reagan's election. This is notwithstanding the fact that from Carter to Obama, Republicans and Democrats have evenly split time in the White House. Equal time in the Oval Office doesn't matter so much as the actual policies pursued in that office, because the net drift Rightward in the white Boomer electorate has freed conservative politicians to move further to the Right while politicians on the Left have also moved Rightward to remain viable. Except on certain social matters, Obama was far more conservative than Richard Nixon, for example, and this has been the Democratic story since Boomers started voting en masse. The initial deregulatory impulse began under Carter, not Reagan; it was Clinton, not Bush I, who promised to "end welfare as we know it" and declared that the "era of big government is over"; it was Obama who made most of the Bush tax cuts permanent, and so on. But there have also been some odd spectacles on the Right: the provision of prescription drug benefits to seniors under Bush II (Medicare Part D; apparently the era of big government was not quite over), and substantial increases to Medicare and Social Security taxes under Reagan and that president's decidedly statist salvation of the savings and loan industry. What accounts for these odd paradoxes? Shouldn't Bush II have been the one taking an ax to welfare and Clinton been pushing Medicare Part D?

The answer is that these events, inexplicable in conventional political terms, all had one thing in common: they benefitted the Boomers, who had the political muscle to realize their preferences. This is the most effective way to understand the political influence of the Boomers—not by their expressed sentiments, but by the hard realities of the policies that they enacted. As we have seen, when even reasonably united, the Boomers had more than enough political power to get what they wanted. So the question remains: On which policies could the Boomers agree?

One of the features of the sociopath is that, lacking empathy for others, he favors only himself. It may seem that in a diverse body of sociopaths, no agreement would be possible any more than you could ask anarchists to form a police department. True enough: Only when sociopaths are similarly situated will they vote in similar ways. And the way in which Boomers were similarly situated is that—within the long spans over which policy making has its effects—Boomers are all about the same age. This is particularly true on certain economic matters and explains how otherwise gridlocked legislatures—ones that allow members to stall votes by reading from a phone book (or, in Senator Harry Reid's case, from his own book)—actually managed a comprehensive economic restructuring.

We will presently take up the many consequences of the Boomers' generational unity regarding taxes, debt, inflation, trade policy, and so on, but we can preview one extremely clear example: Social Security. Social Security is a policy defined explicitly by the age at which benefits are paid, and therefore for the purposes of uniting the Boomers, the only thing that matters is that Social Security holds together long enough to pay off the majority of the generation. The median Boomer was born in 1952, and for those alive today, they can expect to live to roughly eighty—i.e., until 2032. The Social Security Trust Fund is expected to be exhausted between 2030 and 2037, with 2034 being the frequently forecasted date of depletion. Again, not a coincidence.

The Roman tribune and jurist Ravilla began his investigations with a simple question: Cui bono? To whose benefit? It is economic interest that frequently unites the Boomers as a generation, it is their sheer size that allows them to determine policy, and it is their shared sociopathy that struck off the restraints that once fettered other generations. It will be the task of the succeeding chapters to trace the flow of money over the past several decades, decades in which the Boomers have been firmly in control, to the Boomers themselves. Cui bono? Boomers.

CHAPTER EIGHT

TAXES

Average federal tax rates in 2013 for households in all but the
top income quintile were significantly below the average rates
over the 1979–2013 period... Over that period, the average
individual income tax rate peaked at 11.9 percent in 1981,
declined [and then varied] in 2008 and 2009 to a low of 7.2
percent, as a result of declines in income and changes in tax law.
—Congressional Budget Office (2016)[1]

In general, the art of government consists in taking as much
money as possible from one class of citizens to give to the other.
—Voltaire (1764)

Etymology always has something to reveal, even about itself: It comes
from the Greek *etumos*, the word for truth. In the case of "economics,"
its origins are also Greek, also illuminating: It derives from οἰκονομικός, a
term that originally referred to the management of the household. Economics was first applied to the administration of national households in the seventeenth century as "political economy."[2] That older term was vastly more
apt than the adjectiveless, modern "economics," because all economics

are *political* economics: the shuffling of money according to the preferences of those in charge. No shuffling is more political and more economic than taxes—and no group more powerful over the past decades than the Boomers.

So it should be no surprise that a prime theme in the Boomers' sociopathic ascendancy has been the consistent manipulation of taxes to serve generational ends. There were two major mechanisms by which Boomer enrichment (and national impoverishment) was achieved. The first was straightforward, a general lowering of tax rates that coincided with both the Boomers' ascent to political power and the beginning of their prime earning years. The second mechanism required constantly adjusting specific tax policies to favor the interests of Boomers as they moved through their financial life cycles, lowering income taxes during periods where Boomers labored for wages, reducing capital gains taxes as Boomers became stockholders, and limiting and even briefly abolishing estate taxes when Boomers expected to inherit. However, taxes did not always move downward. When Boomers perceived tax hikes to be in their interests, some rates (like Social Security and Medicare taxes) were allowed to rise, though only enough to benefit Boomers, many of whom can expect to retrieve more from the system than they put in, before the system falls apart as the Boomers die off.*

Indeed, if you were to construct a wish list of tax policy (aside from no taxes, a situation that even the Tea Party reluctantly acknowledges is unfeasible), the best possible one for Boomer sociopaths would produce tax policies that mirrored Boomers' progressions through their life cycles—a menu that looks like Appendix B and whose most salient parts are covered in this chapter. The sociopathic tax wishlist corresponds rather tightly with how policy actually developed. The consistency in the beneficiaries of these

---

* Because of the diversity of tax regimes in the states, this chapter focuses on federal tax policy for clarity. State taxes vary considerably: Some states have no income tax, while California taxes income at rates up to 13.3 percent and has no special treatment for capital gains; some states have no sales taxes, while others have multiple and often high rates. These effects can be important, but it would take fifty chapters to cover all of them (plus a bonus section for territorial taxes). Local taxes are mentioned when they are especially important to the argument and to the Boomers.

policies, enacted by both political parties regardless of economic climate (in booms, busts, and everything in between) demonstrates both the true power of the Boomers and their sociopathic lack of foresight and empathy.

The sociopathic appeal of generally lower taxes to the consumption-oriented Boomers is self-evident. The sociopathic consequences are made clear by the reallocation of financial burdens to everyone else: other payers of present-day taxes and future payers in the form of debt, piled up after decades of unrestrained spending not accompanied by corresponding tax collections. The system we have is the system the sociopaths wanted.

A Brief History of Income Taxation

Taxes occupy a strange position in the emotional landscape, oscillating between moments of great passion (April 15 and election days) and near-lethal boredom (every other day), and this is what makes fiddling with taxes so enticing: Politicians can always whip the electorate into a lather, winning a mandate for change, but rely on dullness and complexity to obscure the true consequences of tax adjustments. All that matters is making sure that a plurality of voters understand that they will be beneficiaries of favorable treatment (even if not the *primary* beneficiaries), without focusing overmuch on what the consequences will be and what others will bear them. That plurality of voters has, for many decades, been the Boomers.

To the extent it's necessary to prove taxes are boring and difficult, one need only point to the fact that most Americans pay someone else to do theirs.[3] As for passion, there is the evidence of history. Disputes over taxes have erupted into disorder and often violence many times, including the event that notionally led to our nation's founding, the Boston Tea Party, whose name has been appropriated by contemporary antitaxers.

The physical violence has subsided; the anger has not. Instead, tax fury broadened to encompass the idea that all taxes are effectively consumption taxes, and for the sociopath, thievery, rather than a social tithe. So yesterday's handful of moonshiners wielding pitchforks in the Whiskey Rebellion (1791–1794) have been supplanted today by entire Boomer governments grinding to a halt over money disputes (1995 onward) before reaching a sociopathically palatable outcome. All three full peacetime government shutdowns in American history happened during Boomer Congressional control, and each featured taxes and related budgetary matters as main events.

The primary source of dispute today is income tax, and Boomer politicians find there is always plenty to be angry about. Flip open the twenty-plus volumes of federal tax law and pick a line—injustice will be found wherever the fat finger of the Boomer Congressman from Middle Nowhere, animated by the Holy Ghost of the AARP, happens to land. At least as to income taxes, it was not always thus, for the simple reason that for a long time there was nothing like a modern federal income tax. This tax-free Eden remains relevant, because it is to this prelapsarian condition that Grover Norquist and his highly influential Americans for Tax Reform wish to return. Let's be clear: This is not an overstatement. Norquist (b. 1956, prime Boomer) has opined that the America he wants to re-create is the one that existed right "up until Teddy Roosevelt, when the socialists took over....[and imposed] the income tax, the death tax, regulation, all that."[4] "Regulation, all that," of course, means everything we understand to be the modern state; it is, per Norquist, anathema.

Norquist—an executive director of the College Republicans until 1983—emerged as a national figure during the Republican campaigns of the 1980s and has been a force ever since. In 1986, Norquist prepared "The Pledge," a pseudo-contract between candidates/officeholders and the electorate, that required its signers to "oppose any and all" personal and corporate tax increases, whether these hikes were accomplished directly or through the elimination of deductions; candidates signed on in droves.[5] In the 1990s, Boomers Norquist and Gingrich coauthored the Contract with America, another tax-hostile agreement between electorate and GOP representatives (and again, at odds with the notionally elitist concept of representative democracy). In the 2000s, Norquist allied closely with Bush II, who pushed tax cuts further than Reagan. In the present antitax era, Norquist is a sort of anti–St. Jude, a patron saint of winning causes. (Trump has also prepared his own anti-tax "Contract.")

Before 1913—when "the socialists took over"—income taxes were unconstitutional. The federal government had occasionally experimented with them, including during the Civil War, during which other Constitutional niceties like habeas corpus had also been suspended, but the Supreme Court put its foot down in *Pollock v. Farmer's Loan & Trust Co.* (1895). As originally written, the Constitution required that all "direct taxes" be "apportioned among the several States which may be included within this Union, according to their respective numbers."[6] The government couldn't tax based on amounts of *income*, just on amounts of *people*; in other words, per capita taxes, the simplest, most regressive form of tax possible (watchers of Fox News may now be seeing the currency of this digression). Pre-1913, if the federal government needed revenue, the Constitution allowed customs, duties, and excise taxes, which are a mixed blessing, since they operate as consumption taxes (generally good) but restrain free trade (so-so then, bad now).

Ratification of the Sixteenth Amendment in 1913 allowed for modern income taxation. Taxes started low and then rose substantially over the next thirty years. After World War II, the highest maximum rates reached 70–91 percent. Were Hillary Clinton to have proposed anything like this level of taxation—levels that prevailed under ur-Republicans Eisenhower and Nixon (both implicitly branded by Norquist as "socialists")—the DNC would have been the first to rummage up any willing remnants of the Bush dynasty to replace her. The point of this context is not to demand a return to the era of 90 percent taxation, but simply to remind that in the context of present debates, rates of taxation are relatively low in nominal and other terms. Indeed, taxes are *too low* overall, insufficient to keep the government fully functioning or make essential investments for growth, at least not without major revisions to entitlement programs of which Boomers are and will continue to be the chief beneficiaries.*

It is said the Devil can quote scripture to his own purpose; as the core federal tax code is approximately three times longer than the King James Bible, the various Satans of Taxation (pick your ideological Lucifer: Paul Krugman, Thomas Piketty, or the opinionators of the *Wall Street Journal* and its parent, News Corporation, etc.) never lack for material. Between the

---

* I'm arguing contrary to my narrow self-interest here, which does not make me a good person, only one with some appreciation for the requirements of accounting and probity.

5,248 pages of the Internal Revenue Code, the additional 68,606 pages of "related materials," the tens of thousands of interpretive releases, legal precedents, and so on—all prolix and incomprehensible and amended almost continuously—it seems the only thing one can truly know about taxes is that one's own share is too high.[7]

So how to sort through this thicket, to find some reasonable way to understand how taxes have evolved over the past several decades? There are three basic lenses: (1) nominal rates (i.e., official tax rates); (2) average rates (i.e., the percentage of income actually paid, after accounting for deductions, adjustments, giveaways, etc.); and, (3) total tax paid across the entire tax base (i.e., the government's real take). Alone, each tells a different story. Quoting selectively, both the RNC and DNC can easily find ways to testify that taxes are radically high or dangerously low. Only comparing the three different metrics shows the full picture, a landscape perverted by giveaways to Boomer political power. What they reveal, as we will see, is that nominal rates have been in steep decline, effective rates have been mixed among income groups (tending to favor the middle-class and persons now old), and total taxes have not declined very much as a fraction of the economy—and in combination, that means the history of Boomer tax policy is not so much a history of tax reduction as tax *reallocation*.

The First Tax Revolts

No generation has been quite so convinced of I'm-paying-too-much than the Boomers, though of course, their dependence on magical thinking and moody hatred of rational argument, combined with the sheer complexity of the tax code, makes it difficult to engage with them on the subject. Nevertheless, the data are what they are and the sheer unsubtlety of Boomerism makes it easy enough to see what is happening—as Boomers became more powerful, their taxes declined.

As with so many things, the beginning of the Boomer tax revolt had its origins in the Vietnam War. For the Boomers not only did not want to serve in the war (naturally, for moral reasons), they did not wish to pay for it, either (also, naturally, for moral reasons). Expanding on the protest we encountered in Chapter 3, a group of 448 writers and editors, including leading Boomer student organizer Todd Gitlin (b. 1943), took out a full-page ad in 1968, saying the signers would refuse to pay a proposed 10 percent federal war surcharge because it would be used to fund a conflict of which they disapproved; in an act of freelance accounting, about a third refused to pay an additional 23 percent of their income tax, which they also thought would fund the war.[8] (The word used in the solicitation for signatures was "pledge," which must amuse Norquist.[9]) The *New York Times*, the *Washington Post*, the *Chicago Tribune*, the *Boston Globe*, and others refused to take the ad, the *Times* on the grounds that the ad called for illegal activity (it did), but then as now, the *New York Post* held itself to a different standard and ran it.* But as we all know, taxes are complicated, so just to be safe, singer and antiwar protestor Joan Baez withheld 60 percent of her bill.[10] The explicit inspiration for this little tax rebellion was Henry David Thoreau (quoted in the ad itself), the mystic narcissist and icon of Boomer antirationalism who materialized in Chapter 5. Thoreau said he refused to pay taxes as a protest of the Mexican-American War and slavery, but his Walden jailing actually resulted from failure to pay a local poll tax that had little to do with either war or slaves.[11] Not even the president gets a line-item budget veto, but these Walden-inflected groups proposed to give it to themselves. Society cannot work like that.

No Taxation, with Representation

The arrival of real political power rendered informal protests unnecessary, and Boomers quickly began rewriting the tax code, starting with marginal rates. Marginal rates resemble "suggested retail prices" in that they are the official rates that no one actually pays; yet when the public thinks about taxes, it's marginal rates that transfix. Most of these rates, especially on the last and highest dollars of income, have been in steep decline for some time, a process originally motivated by some good intentions and with some economic justification. Over time, tax cuts became unmoored from their

---

* The day I wrote this sentence, on the *Post*'s homepage eight of the fifteen stories in the page's top half were about sex and/or drugs, including a video essay on the art of penis photography. To adopt McCluhan, the medium was the message.

worthy foundations, pushed along by pure sentiment. The net effect was destructive and enduring, because marginal rates are sticky: Once they go down, it is hard to make them go back up.

For context, the highest marginal rates during and after World War II ranged from 91 to 94 percent, and the tax code was incredibly complicated besides, with a profusion of brackets, thirty-three different ones by 1974.[12] In the 1970s, the complexity of the tax code became worse as inflation drove "bracket creep." Because the various brackets were not linked to inflation, increases in nominal wages drove payers into higher brackets that themselves remained fixed, even though workers' *real* wages might not have increased at all. As a result, people could end up paying a greater percentage of their income despite no real change in the amount they made. These were problems that required redress, but like many revolutions, the tax revolt ran far beyond its original justifications.

Led by President Reagan in the White House, Representative Jack Kemp in the House, and William Roth in the Senate (who later gave his name to the Roth IRA), Congress reformed taxes in 1981. Over several years, the law would lower marginal rates (the top rate would go from 70 percent to 50 percent, e.g.) and index brackets to inflation, eliminating creep. The net effect of the Reagan revisions were that all Americans except the poorest 20 percent would pay less in taxes. Tax cutters argued society as a whole would gain as benefits "trickled down," though when it became clear the flow would really be a trickle, not a flood, the justification was quietly dropped even as the policy (and the deficits it spurred) continued. This was sociopathically irrelevant, of course, because the prime objective of lower taxes was achieved.

Although the tax system clearly needed reform, bad changes were tucked in along with the good, with predictable beneficiaries. The 1981 act not only lowered taxes overall, it had specific generational consequences. Some mechanisms were explicit. Inheritances below $175,625 had been previously excluded from taxation; the exclusion would increase to $600,000 in 1987, more than tripling the tax-free inheritance amount.[13] The chief beneficiaries would be, of course, the Boomers—and the reason the estate tax cut could be safely delayed until 1987 (unlike reductions to the income tax, which had to be immediate) was that the Boomers' parents still had a few years left in them. The second mechanism improved tax-free retirement savings, and again, this was of greatest benefit to workers furthest from retirement age, i.e., the Boomers.

Contrary to popular myth, Reagan not only cut taxes, but raised them, and this laid bare the struggle between new Boomer preferences and the older culture of fiscal responsibility, a battle that would eventually and decisively be resolved in favor of the Boomers. The 1981 cuts spawned deficits vastly larger than predicted. So Congress, still populated by more responsible generations, modified the earlier cuts, slowing their adoption and tinkering with some technical details, and the Gipper assented. The largest tax cut in American history was therefore almost immediately followed by one of the largest increases. The net effect of the two programs was still a significant cut; not exactly a triumph of probity, but indicative of a (fading) sense of responsibility. However, Boomers would soon be thrown another bone. In 1984, to help offset deficits, Social Security benefits for higher earners were taxed for the first time.*,[14] Of course, even

Marginal Tax Rates: The Price No One Pays

What's going on here? These are the highest and lowest marginal tax rates—and while politicians fixate on them, these are not the tax rates anyone actually pays, thanks to deductions, credits, lower marginal rates on the first units of income, etc. As a general matter, marginal rates were notably low in the Boomer years.[15]

---

* Obviously, previous nontaxation of Social Security benefits was of great benefit to the pre-Boomer generation, but given that this generation had taxed itself at rates up to 94 percent, one is inclined to give them something of a pass on this.

the oldest Boomers were twenty years away from collecting benefits and that distance, coupled with the possibility of later repeal, limited Boomer objections.

During the 1980s, Congress also raised payroll taxes—the only taxes to experience sustained increases during the Boomer ascendancy—to keep Social Security and Medicare solvent through Boomer retirements. The immediate costs would be borne by the Boomers and their children, but the Boomers could accept this because the Boomers expected to recoup everything they paid and possibly more. That employers usually bore half of payroll taxes also helped; the Boomers were not yet significant owners of capital, and not all of the effect would flow into changed incomes. The revision of payroll taxes could therefore be viewed as something of a generational win.

In 1986, the tax system was overhauled again, inevitably in ways favorable to the Boomers. The number of brackets collapsed from fourteen to two by 1988, with the lowest set at 14 percent and the highest at 28 percent (down from 50 percent). The limits for tax-advantaged 401(k)s were lowered from $30,000 per year (which had benefitted older, wealthier workers at cost to the Boomers) to $7,000, which was more in line with what younger Boomer professionals could actually save. Capital gains lost preferential treatment, and the maximum rate therefore rose to 28 percent (from 20 percent), but the median Boomer was only mid-thirties, had neither a large stock portfolio nor plans to mass-liquidate anytime soon, and therefore (like employer payroll taxes) the burden fell on the old and the rich, whose ranks the Boomers had not yet joined. So Ronald Reagan, the fabled tax crusader, not only increased taxes, but did so several times—just in very targeted ways that happened to coincide with the needs of the Boomers, who were then an enormous fraction of the electorate.

The one area where the 1986 reform appeared bad for Boomers was the elimination of deductibility of personal-interest payments of any kind—a potential constraint on the consumption the sociopathic Boomers cherished. The more than compensatory sweetener was that mortgage interest would remain deductible, now for up to $1 million in indebtedness, and another $100,000 in "unrelated interest"—and thus, the home equity line of credit was born.* A little paperwork, and the Boomers once again had their personal interest deduction, and indeed, "much of the [new, mortgage] debt finance[ed] vacations, cars, boats, and other consumer purchases."[16] Of course, this was the part of the Boomers' life cycle in which they were snapping up real estate at tremendous volume, and while the numerical bulk of the deduction went to the richest (as is the case with most deductions), the most *populous* beneficiary group was the most-indebted (i.e., youngest) homeowners, whose ranks were swelling with Boomer voters. The reforms of the 1980s did not help as much as taxpayers thought they would, but they definitely adjusted the burden downward and in many cases away from the Boomers, or toward programs from which the Boomers (but not their children) could reasonably expect to fully collect.

Overall, the tax reforms of the 1980s had many benefits—nominal taxes were too high, bracket creep was a real problem, the tax base had been too narrow (i.e., too many loopholes and exclusions), and there were too many brackets and other complexities—but these sowed in the fertile field of the Boomer mind a poisonous seed. And the seed was this: The only appropriate direction for taxes was downward, at least for taxes applicable to the Boomers.

The 1990s—Read Their Lips: No New Taxes

The effect of Boomer tax obsession could be seen in the early 1990s, when two very different politicians raised taxes very slightly, and were punished accordingly. Politician One was George Bush the First, who instructed Congress: "Read my lips: No new taxes." Of course, no such effort was necessary because: (1) Bush spoke the words audibly and (2) he raised taxes. Bush's overall increase was small, with the highest earners bearing 40 percent of the rise directly; another 40 percent of the hike came from increased excise taxes.[17] The reform was responsible, modest, and fell most heavily on a core

---

* Inflation and secular interest rate declines have eroded the real value of the mortgage interest deduction since, so that it is much less valuable for young people than it was for the Boomers.

Bush constituency (the rich) who could be counted on to suffer the indignity and reelect their candidate. Instead, Bush was fired, which was a remarkable outcome. Bush I had just presided over the successful Gulf War I, earning some of the highest approval ratings in history. Though the economy had slowed modestly, the 1990–1991 recession was historically mild, brief, and nothing compared to the crises that followed. True, Bush broke his word, but that alone was unremarkable. Presidents violate promises all the time, and few for reasons as good: Bush sincerely believed that changed facts commanded changed tax policy, and the tariffs that fell heavily on his base. Empirical, responsible, self-sacrificing—another electorate might have found Bush's tax policy commendable. The problem was that Bush violated his word on *taxes*, and for Boomers that elevated the sin from venal to mortal.

Thus, a minor increase in taxes helped pave the way for the first Boomer president, William Jefferson Clinton. Clinton accused Bush of being untrustworthy(!) and campaigned for tax relief for "middle-class Americans" and "families with children," two groups with which the Boomers correctly self-identified.[18] (At this point, median Boomers were forty, had children, and like all Americans rich, poor, and otherwise, viewed themselves as "middle-class" and thus potential recipients of Clintonian largesse.) Bill Clinton also promised to "force the rich to pay their fair share."[19] Let us leave aside, as Clinton did, that this was just what Bush had started to do.

Clinton duly won and then proceeded to repeat Bush's mistake. Clinton is lionized by certain Leftish op-ed pages for raising taxes in 1993, and he did, but that was not exactly what he promised, or what many voters expected him, to do. Indeed, of the roughly 25 percent of voters who thought the violation of Bush's "read my lips" pledge was "very important" in their presidential vote, two-thirds voted for Clinton—and one conclusion, in combination with Clinton's rhetoric about middle-class relief, is that these and other voters expected Clinton to cut their taxes.[20] Instead, Clinton raised taxes, mainly but not exclusively on the rich.[21] It squeaked out of the House 218–216 (more than forty Democrats voted against it) and escaped a Democratic Senate only because Al Gore cast a tie-breaking vote—i.e., opposition to Clinton's 1993 increase was partly bipartisan.[22]

Clinton's was not a blockbuster hike, and it certainly helped that it targeted the rich, among whose ranks necessarily few, still-youngish Boomers, or any-one else, dwelled. (It's called the 1 percent for a reason.) Still, the tax pack-age passed only by Gore's single, fortuitous vote; even the Democrats went berserk, and Clinton found himself apologizing to his own base for daring to raise taxes, however modestly.[23] This aftermath helps show that what people thought they were buying in 1992 was a tax cutter, not a tax hiker.

Thus, another modest tax revision allowed the second great Boomer politi-cian to emerge, Newt Gingrich. The commonalities between the two sociopathic Boomer chieftains is striking—age, philandering, murky financial dealings, ethics violations, tax avoidance, dramatic censures (the second impeachment of a president, in Clinton's case; the first official reprimand of a Speaker of the House, in Gingrich's), a premature graying of hair entirely understandable in light of the foregoing—really, they could have been the best of friends. And they even agreed over time, sort of, on the need for tax reduction.

This time, no political mistakes would be made, no new charges to the rich or sensible supplements to payroll taxes, absolutely nothing that could be misconstrued by the tax-obsessed Boomers. Benefits would be made per-fectly clear to the voters who mattered. The Boomers, then middle-aged, had all sorts of middle-aged issues, including school-age children, decrepit par-ents, homes to trade up, stock portfolios to maximize, and retirements to plan. All of these were duly and expressly catered to: a child credit of $400 appeared (rising to $500 in 1999); the estate tax exemption would increase from $600,000 to $1 million by 2006, and all assets would be "stepped up" at the parents' death, meaning that all unrealized capital gains accrued during the parents' lifetime could be tax free at death (i.e., Boomer inheri-tances instantly became much more valuable); gains on sale of homes up to $500,000 were exempted from tax; and the two capital gains tax brackets were lowered, from 28 percent to 20 percent and 15 percent to 10 percent.[24] An added bonus was the creation of Roth IRAs, which were functionally useless to older generations then retiring, but of great use to middle-aged Boomers, as were the various education credits established, the better to subsidize the schooling of the Boomers' children.[25]

Doctrinally, the Clinton cuts were somewhat confusing: economically unorthodox and contrary to commonly understood Democratic policy. In 1997, the economy was growing and it was by no means clear that a tax cut was required; could it not, perhaps, stoke some sort of speculative bubble in the assets favored by the tax bill, like stocks or houses? And had not Democrat Clinton, after all, promised to soak the rich during his first campaign? The answers were obviously all some form of "yes." Then again, Clinton and his counterparts in Congress were Boomers and beholden to their cogenerationalists. Tax cuts emerged from the legislature with strong bipartisan support and Clinton signed.

The 2000s—Lather, Rinse, Repeat

Fast-forward past the Monica Lewinsky scandal, which effectively ended the Clinton presidency, to Bush II. The situation had changed dramatically: the dot-com crash, 9/11, and a major recession. The prescription, however, remained the same: more Boomer-friendly tax cuts. Essentially all tax rates were slashed by about 10 percent, with Boomers doing by far the best. In their peak earning years and with retirement fast approaching, it was essential to lower income taxes and to cut capital gains taxes to fertilize stock portfolios that would soon be harvested. To better appeal to Boomers, tax-advantaged retirement accounts were modified so that people over 50 (at the time, the Boomers were between 37 and 61, with the median Boomer a predictable 49) could make excess tax-free contributions. And needless to say, with the Boomers' parents having one foot in the grave and the other on a banana peel, it had become essential to modify the estate tax. The estate tax exemption quickly rose from $675,000 in 2001 to $2,000,000 in 2006, then to $3,500,000 in 2009 and was finally to be abolished altogether in 2010, a period corresponding with the actuarially forecasted demise of the median Boomers' parents.[26]

There was some sense in cutting taxes during a recession, but *how* the taxes were cut was illuminating—from a Keynesian perspective, the best cuts would be the cuts that led to the fastest spending, not the fastest squirreling away of retirement funds by older Americans. Theory was, of course, meaningless to the nonempirical Boomers. The political bargain was that many cuts would sunset in 2010, but by 2010, the median Boomer would be fifty-eight, aging out of the income-earning years, and nearing eligibility for

Social Security. Tax cuts might sunset, but it would be a sunset the Boomers could ride into.

So what happened to the Bush II cuts? They were followed in 2003 by legislation that accelerated certain portions of the 2001 cuts and further reduced taxes on qualified gains.[27] Even the election, in 2008, of Bush's ideological opposite didn't change the general trajectory. In 2010, under the leadership of a now Democratic Congress and Executive, almost all Bush II's tax cuts were extended; it was "change you could believe in," if you believed the Boomers were still in control, which they were. Inheritance taxes reappeared, but at a lower rate than before the Bush II cuts (40 percent vs. 55 percent) and with a much higher exemption ($5 million versus $675,000 in 2001), which covered essentially all Boomers still in a position to inherit, since few estates exceeded the exemption.[28] Certain payroll taxes also rolled back for a bit, but the reduction was temporary and small, and while not helpful to the long-term solvency of Social Security, would have little impact on the Boomers themselves.[29] It was a giveaway, and it passed.

There was some justification during the recession's nadir to avoid a tax hike, though that logic had little application to items like lowered estate taxes—then again, logic was not in command. Predictably, even after the recession ended(ish), the Bush tax cuts were essentially made permanent by President Obama in 2013, with the exception of a modest reversion in top rates, from 35 percent to 39.6 percent, for the wealthiest taxpayers (e.g., couples making more than $450,000 a year). FICA (payroll) cuts were also reversed.[30] Maximum capital gains rates were restored to 20 percent, but here's the thing—dividend rates, scheduled to return to 39.6 percent, were kept to a maximum 20 percent.*,[31] Because retirees favor dividend stocks (like utilities), which are perceived as safer and provide current income, the capital gains twist was a direct giveaway to the dividend-collecting classes—i.e., the rich and the old. Even more important, the capital gains tax did not increase for the cherished middle class.[32] As for estate taxes, they had become

---

*A surcharge of 3.8 percent on capital gains/dividends was added for the 2013 tax year for the richest taxpayers, though it did not apply to qualified gains on sales of private residences, qualifying inheritances, and the various other goodies doled out to the Boomer masses.

even more urgent. By 2013, the median Boomer was already sixty-one, and those Boomers' parents who were still living would not remain so for much longer. The already generous $5 million exemption was therefore indexed to inflation to preserve its value.[33] The 2000s, therefore, might have been no more than a tactical success for lower taxes overall, but they were a decisive victory for Boomers.

The Rest of the Goodie Bag

There were two other disguised tax giveaways to the Boomers from the 1970s to the 2010s: property taxes and corporate taxes. Both can be covered briefly. Property taxes before the 1970s had been a mess, riddled with loopholes and anachronisms from the age of farms, land grants, and low inflation. During the 1970s, before the Boomers were fully in control, there had been a number of property tax revolts in several states, most prominently in California. Inflation had driven the assessed values of properties up, and since taxes were based on nominal values, taxes went up faster than any corresponding change in real value. So California voters limited taxes to 1 percent of assessed value and capped the rate of assessment increases.[34] Instead of indexing to reality, California set the maximum rate of appreciation at an arbitrary 2 percent per year. General inflation, of course, was much higher then and the appreciation of California property higher than inflation overall for much of the next forty years. The immediate effect was mild, because California had a larger-than-average government that could be productively trimmed and a budget surplus that cushioned the impact on localities collecting property tax. (The state surplus was $5 billion in 1978 dollars when the proposition was passed, or about $18 billion in present dollars versus large annual deficits in the recent past, reaching negative $20 billion in 2011–2012 before achieving rough balance in 2014.[35]) For a time, property tax limits were not a major problem and, had they been as temporary as the inflation that prompted them, even appropriate to the unusual conditions of the late 1970s.

After inflation had been vanquished by 1982, it became clear that the caps had become less shield than subsidy. By this point, Boomers were homeowners and therefore the beneficiaries of the property tax caps whose calculations grew more unrealistic (and thus more valuable) every year. Given that the Boomers were increasingly in control, they would never give up this cherished perk, forcing budget shortfalls disproportionately onto the shoulders of nonhomeowners—i.e., the young and the poor—in the form of regressive higher sales taxes and the like—anything, that is, but taxes on Boomer homes. The effect was a transfer to Boomers, at the cost of younger people whose rates of home ownership were depressed and who enjoyed less benefit from the housing tax shield.

The second major change, to corporate income taxes, also had substantial benefit to the Boomers, albeit indirectly. Effective corporate taxes rose briefly and sharply from 1979 to 1987 and then fell substantially. And even though the United States still has some of the highest official corporate taxes in the developed world and these rates have remained largely unchanged since the mid-1980s, the *effective* rates of corporate taxation fell somewhat, and for some large companies all the way to zero. Although effective rates overall are not wildly different from other advanced economies, there is now an increasing divergence between corporate profits' share of the economy and the share represented by the taxes on those profits.* The figure on the next page illustrates the trend.

The beneficiaries, of course, were people who owned shares in the companies paying lower taxes. In 1979, the Boomers were too young to hold many stocks, so their huge voting power tilted not so much pro or con as indifferent. As the Boomers joined the stock-owning classes in the mid-1980s, when most were in their thirties and forties, effective corporate taxes began to decline. Higher after-tax profits could then be realized in higher stock prices, higher dividend payments, or both. The only thing necessary for Boomers to maximize those gains were decreases to capital gains and dividend taxes, obediently delivered in 1987 and 1997, by Ronald Reagan and Bill Clinton, and preserved by Bush II and Obama—four radically different politicians, though all with the same critical constituency:

---

*Effective federal corporate tax rates are around 25–28 percent versus an official rate of 35 percent (plus an average 4 percent for state/local). As a percentage of GDP, they have fallen to exceedingly low levels even as corporate profits on this measure have risen—the point here is not to imply (as some do) that corporate taxes are 2 percent—they emphatically are not—only that the divergence between profits and taxes provides some room for further contribution.

Corporations: Something to Contribute

What's going on here? Corporate profits have been rising as a share of the total economy for some time, but corporate taxes have been falling then flattening on the same measure. There is therefore at least some room for convergence and additional revenue (accompanied by meaningful reform of the vast loopholes that allow some large corporations to get away with very low tax bills).[36]

Boomers. Most of the gains accrued to the wealthiest, but everyone in the stock-holding classes, including the Boomers, benefited at the expense of the rest.* This was especially the case for middle-income Boomers, who held their stocks in tax-advantaged accounts. The income/contribution limits of such accounts means that it's the Boomer middle class that's avoiding and/or postponing capital gains taxes to a relatively greater extent than the workaday rich (whose additional wealth is sufficient to place it outside tax-advantaged

---

*A sidenote: Another 1980s tax revolution was the rise of "pass-through" corporations like S corps and LLCs, which had all the benefits of a corporation (limited, instead of unlimited, personal liability, for example) and all the benefits of a partnership (no double taxation of dividends, as with corporations). Not only did these effectively lower taxes, they discouraged investment—S corps are not allowed to retain profits. And who owns tax-minimizing, liability-limiting assets, created during the Boomer heyday, a category that notably includes private equity and hedge funds? Small businesses and the exceedingly rich, categories increasingly populated by Boomers. A second aside: Because no member of an LLC can file his taxes before the LLC does, owners of LLCs always pay an estimate on April 15 and then file final returns by October 15. So, if Brillat-Savarin could tell what you are by what you eat, you can easily tell how rich a person is by when he files his taxes; it's a neat party trick for the nosy.

retirement plans but is insufficient to justify the expense of bespoke tax shelters).

Finally, to the extent explicit tax decreases did not satisfy, the defunding of the IRS and concurrent reduction in the likelihood of audits, especially for middle-income payers, authorized less scrupulous taxpayers to adjust their payments to more desirable levels. Just between 2010 and 2015–2016, enforcement personnel at the IRS declined by 23 percent; by the end individual audits hit an eleven-year low, and new IRS appropriations from Congress were directed away from enforcement.[37] Even though the IRS trumpeted the hiring of seven hundred new enforcement workers in 2016, it would end that fiscal year with two thousand fewer staff than at that year's beginning.[38] Hobbling the IRS was like posting a speed limit and then removing all the cops and cameras; for sociopaths, it was a green light for fraud. The annual "tax gap"—the difference between what the IRS believes is owed and what is actually and timely paid—ran over $400 billion dollars annually for the 2008–2010 period, the most recent years analyzed by the Service, and that was before recent cuts to enforcement.[39] It will hardly be surprising if the tax gap widens.

Taxation and Consequences

> Let us remember that the basic purpose of any tax
> cut program in today's environment is to reduce the
> momentum of expenditure growth by restraining
> the amount of revenues available and trust that
> there is a political limit to deficit spending.
> —Alan Greenspan (1979)[40]

> Hogcock, which is a combination of hogwash and poppycock.
> —Jack Donaghy, *30 Rock*

Notwithstanding all these tax cuts, the government has not simply evaporated or been cut in half, although that was the stated intent of the 1980s tax revolution. Returning to Grover Norquist, the purpose of the tax revolt was to starve the government of revenue so that it would shrink back to its size around the turn of the last century, making government small enough "to drown it in a bathtub."[41] (The government is not a person, but metaphorical murder of an institution that embodies society does reek of sociopathy.) The reason Norquist has succeeded in lowering tax rates but not abolishing the government is that people like the benefits each provides and will not part with either.

This presents a certain mystery about mechanisms—if taxes fell, how could government soldier on? Partly, the government borrowed heavily; we'll take that up in Chapter 9. Secondly, while nominal tax rates have gone down, taxes' total share of GDP remained fairly stable, aside from brief gyrations during the first dot-com bubble and during the Great Recession. That overall stability, against a background of constant changes to the code, implies a reshuffling of tax burdens.

The first and most important aspect of reshuffling was the rising share paid by the rich, who paid a large and increasing share of taxes through 2000, had a respite, and saw their rates rise after 2012. Given all the heated rhetoric about the rich, that might come as a surprise, but the electoral math more or less guaranteed that would be the case. For some time, the real story of declining taxation played out in the bottom 80 percent of taxpayers (aka, the mythical "middle class"). Only in 2000 did tax burdens on the rich really decline, but then again, burdens fell for almost everyone else. Here's what the Federal Reserve Bank of St. Louis had to say in 2010: "Before 2000, the tax burden shifted from the lowest 80 percent of earners to the highest 20 percent; since 2000, the burden has shrunk for all groups, but more so for the highest earners."[42] Since 2013, the rich have experienced the sharpest increase in taxes.[43]

There are several ways to think about what happened, each presented in graphs on the following pages. The first is to consider how average federal tax rates have evolved since 1979. There has been a pronounced downward trend in tax burden on the middle class, especially relative to the rich and the poor, with taxes perking up slightly since 2013. The middle class got relative tax cuts throughout this period, a period that heavily overlapped with the Boomers' prime working years.

The second way to think about taxes are "average" rates. *Marginal* rates

The Government's Stable Share

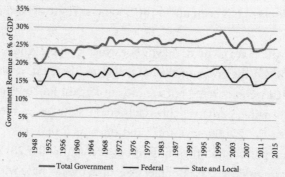

What's going on here? The government's total take, as a fraction of GDP, has remained surprisingly constant over time, with some volatility after the mid-1990s as the economy coped with bubbles, panics, and some large tax cuts. However, the general stability of tax revenue strongly suggests that endless tax adjustments really just shifted burdens around. Because so much of government revenue after the 1980s is accounted for by levies for senior programs and distributed accordingly, and because those programs are not fully funded, the burden has been shifted away from the middle class and old and toward everyone else—i.e., away from the mainstream Boomers.[44]

apply to different chunks of income, starting with low rates on the first dollars of income and progressively rising to 39.6+ percent for dollars of income over $413,200. *Average* rates, by contrast, represent the fraction of total income actually paid, and are always lower than maximum marginal rates because even rich people pay very low marginal taxes on their first dollars of income. These average rates are quite low for most income groups and they can even be negative for the poorest Americans, who can receive more money from Washington than they pay in federal taxes. This leads to another way to think about taxes—the share of government revenue provided relative to a person's share of income. It's not quite "give versus get," since rich people frequently consume more of society's resources than poor people, though it has something of this dynamic. More precisely, most Americans pay less in federal taxes than they earn as a fraction of total income. This shouldn't be surprising, since the point of a progressive system is to subsidize poorer Americans with higher taxes on the rich—what is surprising (or should be to middle-class Tea Partiers) is where the break-even point rests. Only the top 20 percent pays more in federal taxes than it earns as a share of income, showing just how shielded the middle class (and even upper middle class) has been under the Boomers. These dynamics appear in a later figure.

So, wait—did taxes go up or down? For which groups? And with all those tax cuts, how did the government not collapse? There are several answers, some of which we've covered but are included again for convenience, since taxes are confusing, perhaps deliberately so. First, taxes on the rich generally increased until 2000, as a total and often as a percentage of income, subsided for a period, and then moved upward again after 2013. This offset falling taxes on middle-class Boomers. Second, the tax base widened somewhat; i.e., somewhat more people paid taxes. Third, the economy had some one-off spurts, as in the late 1990s (dot-com I) that lifted many payers into higher brackets temporarily.

It's the fourth and fifth answers that are by far the most important,

Tax Cuts for the Middle Class

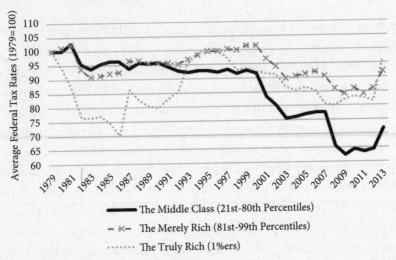

What's going on here? This chart shows how average federal tax rates (what people really pay) have changed relative to the rate scheme in 1979. The story here is that middle class tax rates have been going down while taxes on wealthier Americans have varied. None of this should be surprising, since the stated goal of mainstream politicians is always some form of middle-class tax cut. This chart, by the way, does not say anything about the level of rates—just their relative direction over time.[45]

however, and these heavily involve the Boomers. Answer four is that tax burdens were reallocated substantially, away from the Boomers toward almost everyone else—i.e., the Boomers paid less, and everyone else paid more, and this accounts for both the relative stability of the tax take over time, and many of the fifteen thousand–plus changes to the code, some of which we have covered, like mortgage interest deductions and tax-advantaged retirement programs. The middle-class Boomers faced lower tax burdens during their prime earning years relative to the middle class of the 1940s–1970s and throughout, the middle class didn't pay as much in federal taxes as it earned as a share of national income. The fifth and final answer has the same consequence as the fourth: The nation has not, with (no) due respect to

Who Pays What to Whom?

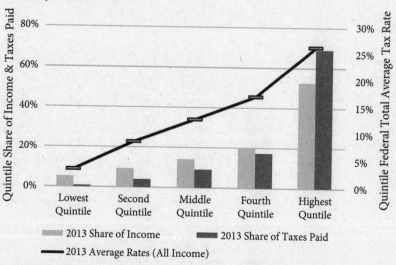

What's going on here? The federal tax system is designed to be "progressive," so that wealthier people pay a larger fraction of their income, which is redistributed to the rest of society—and that is what this chart shows. Only the top quintile pays more than its pro rata share (this is what the bars show). State and local taxes can be more regressive than federal levies and offset some of this dynamic, but what is striking is how dependent the United States is on its richest citizens. The lines, for the record, indicate the average actual tax rate paid by each group—and again, the shape of the line is no surprise (wealthier people pay higher rates), but the *level* may be a surprise, since average taxes are so much lower than the "rack rates" we saw in the marginal rates chart. Moreover, the graph suggests that many Americans may not be contributing as much as they think they do and that tax rates overall are not enormously high.[46]

Greenspan, responded to lower taxes with fiscal restraint. The government continues to spend at a fairly stable (and substantial) rate, and the resulting deficits have been financed with debt, whose burdens will be passed on to younger generations. Finally, the nature of spending changed: There was a shift from investment in items like R&D to consumption transfers like entitlements, the latter as useful to the Boomers as they are unsustainable, at least in their current configuration. It is to these manipulations we now turn, starting with debt.

CHAPTER NINE

DEBT AND DEFICITS

Increasing numbers of baby-boom generation members
are becoming eligible for Social Security retirement
benefits and for Medicare... The aging of the population
and rising health care costs will continue to put upward
pressure on spending and, *absent action to address the
growing imbalance between spending and revenue, the
federal government faces an unsustainable growth in debt.*
—Government Accounting Office (2015)[1]

On January 8, 1835, Senator Thomas Hart Benton stood in Washington
and announced that "the national debt is paid."[2] If it wasn't exactly
true, it was close enough. The Treasury records that in 1835, the national debt
had fallen to just $33,733.05, within spitting distance of zero.[3] The period
between 1835 and 1836 was the exception; debt is the rule. Pre-Boomer, the
national debt usually rose during crises, fell during calm and, between 1950
and 1980, averaged around 50 percent of GDP.*[4] That the United States has

---

* The proper measure for debt is not total dollars, but as a ratio of GDP—a $10 trillion
economy can easily manage a $1 trillion debt, just as a billionaire can easily afford the
payments on a Bentley.

had an essentially perpetual debt without going off the rails shows that the mere existence of some national debt is neither unusual nor, absent other factors, does it pose an existential threat. The keys are size and those "other factors." Over the past four decades—i.e., during the Boomer ascendancy—the nation's debt has risen faster than during any other long period of peace and is expected to grow faster than the economy overall. It now stands at the highest sustained level save World War II, and, per the Congressional Budget Office (CBO), will without correction exceed even that exceptional threshold during the 2030s.[5] The CBO is perhaps being too forgiving—the record will probably be broken noticeably earlier.

So far, the sizable debt has been manageable for two reasons, neither of which is guaranteed to last. One factor is strong demand for US debt, especially from buyers (including many foreign buyers over the past two decades) seeking the relative safety of American bonds and the higher interest rates American bonds offer versus those of other advanced economies. And while American yields are somewhat better than those offered by Germany, Japan, and the like, American rates are abnormally low, which provides the second helpful factor: The United States presently borrows quite cheaply. Again, the debt is quite large and readily manageable only for reasons that may be transient. Our questions, therefore, are straightforward. First, will American debt ever provoke a crisis? Second, who bears responsibility for the debt? And third, is there anything we can or should do about it?

Debt and Danger

A little history of debt is instructive, especially given the necrophilia the supposed debt hawks of the Right have for America's early politicians. America's first leaders emphatically believed that, outside of exceptional cases like war, national debt should be kept small and paid off promptly. Thomas Jefferson argued that passing on a debt to future generations (ahem) was immoral and that setting debt limits was a matter defined in generational terms. "No generation can contract debts greater than may be paid during the course of its own existence," Jefferson wrote, insisting that it was "incumbent on every generation to pay its own debts as it goes."[6] Many of Jefferson's letters focus on the immorality of passing on debt from one generation to another.

Three decades later, the great populist Andrew Jackson, recently deposed from the front of the $20 bill, was so obsessed about debt that he routinely vetoed spending legislation and aggressively sold federal assets to pay off the national mortgage—it was these actions that allowed Senator Benton to proclaim the debt paid.

Though Jefferson and Jackson were derided for their simplistic views on national finance, even more moderate and financially sophisticated Founders believed that debt had limits. Alexander Hamilton famously said the debt could be a "blessing," but *only* "if it is not excessive," noting that "the creation of debt should always be accompanied by the means of extinguishment."[7] So there you have it, straight from the Revolutionary Olympus: Large, intergenerational debts were/are immoral. It's a crosscultural concept, and not for nothing do the German and Dutch words for "guilt" and "debt" overlap (*schuld*). Nietzsche fixated on this, expanding rather darkly on the relationship between debt and punishment.*[,8] One wonders what *übermenschen* would have made of Visa.

Morality aside, large debts with uncertain prospects for repayment can be dangerous. The Founders could not help but know this. In 1780s, three major countries faced debt crises: the United States, Great Britain, and France. The Anglo- and Francophones realized dramatically different outcomes. In the confederated United States, debt had been a mess of state obligations; after the Constitution was ratified in 1788, Hamilton federalized these debts and began repayment, which reassured creditors and eased the flow of funds. As a result, despite its youth and tenuous position, the United States had access to essential finance. France and Great Britain had also incurred enormous debts, in no small part due to the revolutionary wars in the Americas. Like America, Britain's organized system of debt and tax granted it access to credit, and Britain emerged from North American and later European wars as a stable polity, despite giant borrowing.

France went differently: In 1789, just as American credit was restored, France collapsed. The social kindling was in place, with sparks provided by

---

* The German word for "bill"/"check" is *rechnung*, or "reckoning," and menacing clouds of debt judgment lurk in German. Not coincidentally, Germany has both a hefty consumption tax and a cultural aversion to debt, at least at the personal level.

persistent government duplicity about the size of the debt coupled with doubts over the king's ability to tax. It was not that France was poorer than Britain or America; France was larger and richer than both, with an infinitely longer history than the United States and a substantially smaller debt than Britain in the early 1780s.[9] Abstractly, France presented the lower credit risk. In reality, lenders reckoned that France's royalist system could no longer deliver consistent payment, a prophecy that became self-fulfilling. Once the market believed the monarchy couldn't pay, creditors ceased to provide terms, taxpayers refused to remit, and the government, starved of funds, collapsed.[10]

The lesson of this historical detour is that debt becomes a problem when creditors no longer trust a nation's political system to achieve long-term financial stability within its economic context, a situation that can happen at any moderately high level of national debt. That is why Greece, which had a debt-to-GDP ratio of 118 percent in 2008, collapsed into chaos in 2009, spawning a quasi depression that continues still. The Greeks had no credibility when it came to payment, so bankers called in the loans. Meanwhile, Japan experienced no crisis despite having debt-to-GDP ratios significantly higher than pre-crisis Greece; China, too, had very high levels of aggregate debt and no crisis.[11] Not only were these non-Hellenic countries in better economic shape, they also had political systems that seemed, at least in the eyes of lenders, capable of keeping their national finances together. It helps that these Asian nations, unlike Greece, owe much of their debt to their own citizens, rather than unforgiving foreign parties, like German bankers keen on *schuld und rechnung*. (For context, the United States owes foreign parties $6.2 trillion, about a third of its total debt, which doesn't mean that "China owns the US" as some cruder thinkers have it, though it does mark a substantial increase from the roughly $1 trillion owed to overseas creditors as of 2001.[12])

It's worth noting that a major component of Greece's dysfunction was a twinned inability to generate tax revenue and to reform its overgenerous entitlement system—a situation well underway in the United States. Various permutations of the Greek tragedy have emerged at the subfederal level, with cities (Detroit) and counties (Orange County) having gone bust. In 2015 the entire territory of Puerto Rico defaulted on its bonds, which have been downgraded to junk status. The island territory has not gone bankrupt only for the reason that (as of this writing) there is no legal mechanism for territories to do so. And while *territorial* bankruptcy may only require an act of Congress, it may actually be unconstitutional as to *states*, which means states probably cannot engage in the expedience of federal bankruptcy reorganization.[*,13]

Even the federal government has flirted with debt crises, in 1995 and, more dramatically, in 2011, when it came within forty-eight hours of a technical default on its interest payments. In that second crisis, three agencies issued warnings about American credit, with Standard & Poor's actually cutting its rating of US Treasuries for the first time.[14] Yet another debt crisis emerged, on the same lines, in 2013. Although these were major events at the time, people quickly forgot. Still, cracks have appeared, though at present, there are no signs that the United States will have anything like a Greek crisis for the simple reason that people keep buying American debt, partly in eagerness to export money from less politically stable countries to the relative safety of the United States. At some point, however, American debt and dysfunction will rise to the point where that ceases to be the case.

Debt: Its Origins and Amount

There's no mystery to the origins of the national debt: The government spends more money than it takes in, and the result is the deficit, financed by the issuance of government debt. After World War II and until 1974, deficits were regular, but not particularly large. Because the US economy grew rapidly, the ratio of debt to GDP shrank through the 1970s; in other words, the debt got easier to bear, just as a mortgage taken out by a junior associate at a law firm becomes more manageable when that associate makes partner. However, since 1980 the United States has been committed to a combination of stable-to-lower taxes and ever-higher spending, even as growth has decelerated, and this has led to much larger deficits and a growing national debt. It's entirely clear from the next chart which generations are responsible:

---

* To help Puerto Rico, Congress is considering a modification to the bankruptcy law. This would help Puerto Rico, but would not be a good sign, because investors lent money with the legal understanding that Puerto Rico could not go bankrupt. And if the federal government does this for Puerto Rico, it will reinforce what everyone knows but does not believe: that the United States can do this for itself, as many other countries have.

The Boomer Debt Pile

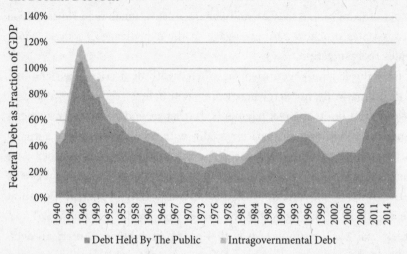

■ Debt Held By The Public   ■ Intragovernmental Debt

What am I looking at? Total government debt has increased to levels not seen since World War II, and given projected deficits of ~3 percent indefinitely, will surpass those historic levels within two decades and perhaps considerably sooner than that. The distinctions between "intragovernmental debt" and "debt owed to the public" will be covered later in this chapter—what's important for now is how quickly and substantially debts have risen.[15]

Some blame lies with the Boomers' parents, but the substantial majority rests squarely on the sociopathic shoulders of the Boomers themselves.

The debt began really growing in the 1980s, substantially the product of tax cuts whose goal was to "starve the beast"—the beast being the government generally and its social welfare system in particular.[16] Not surprisingly, social programs failed to vanish in response to tax cuts. Moreover, Reagan hugely increased defense spending (feeding the beast) while endorsing the implausible Laffer Curve, which said that the tax cuts would pay for themselves (making the beast's food free, presumably). Reagan lowered taxes but ended up starving nothing. In 1985, a White House official concluded that "we didn't starve the beast . . . it's still eating quite well—*by feeding off future generations*."[17] Over the years, the Boomer-dominated political system continued its bizarre debt-dietary policy—all binge, no purge—resisting major cuts to government programs while embracing virtually all tax relief (for Boomers), and deficits and debt grew accordingly.

Nor were there any mechanisms to provide hard restraint. Earlier moves toward a constitutional amendment requiring a balanced budget (not a perfect idea, but indicative of a certain sense of responsibility) had picked up from the 1950s on, so that by 1983—just as the Boomers became a majority of the electorate—thirty-two state legislatures had passed resolutions in favor of the balanced budget amendment. If only two more states had ratified in 1983, starving the beast might have become vaguely plausible. Nevertheless, as Boomers gained power, states rescinded their ratifications and the issue died. The moment has passed, and there probably never will be a balanced budget amendment.

Nevertheless, there was a brief period in the late 1990s when the annual federal budget was in surplus, in part because of a dot-com bubble that boosted tax receipts, in part because of some accounts fiddling, and also because the nation was genuinely growing (though, as it turned out, in some problematic ways). The nation was subjected to Very Serious People wringing their hands about how to conduct monetary policy when the nation paid off its debts. Forecasters predicted a ten-year, $5.6 trillion surplus when Bush II took office, enough to retire essentially the entire public debt at the time.[18] Of course it was a head fake, as the experts should have known. Some on the Left like to trumpet Clinton's budget surpluses, and while they did exist, the share of debt held by the public fell only by a modest $476 billion while total debt, including entitlements debt, actually *increased*. (We'll explore the different types of debt shortly.) Clintonian fiscal improvements were narrow and brief, and while they were real, they were not durable—and not just because of Bush II, but because of Clinton. So instead of a $5.6 trillion surplus between 2002 and 2012, the United States ended up running a $6 trillion deficit, a swing of $11.6 trillion between '90s fantasy and '00s reality.[19] As a result, the United States now has its largest peacetime debt, one that it will grow substantially, gross and as a percentage of GDP, for the foreseeable future.[20]

Just How Much, Exactly?

There are two schools on the debt, the optimists and the pessimists, and each measures debt in different ways, but however you look at it, debt has risen dramatically under Boomer tenure. For the optimists, the federal debt is no larger than 74 percent of GDP as of FY 2015.[21] Optimists look only at debt "held by the public," i.e., the amount the government owes directly to third parties—the people who buy Treasury bonds, like banks, bond funds, and foreign governments. While this is the smallest reasonable measure of debt, the numbers it produces are not reasonably small: $14-ish trillion is a lot.[22] The pessimists take a much broader view and include the amount the government owes to everyone, including itself (via things like the Social Security Trust Fund). On this basis, the debt was slightly larger than GDP, about $18.2 trillion in the third quarter of 2015, $18.9 trillion by the end of 2015 (and rising since then—updates will be posted on this book's website, www.generationofsociopaths .com).[23] Congress measures debt on something like this basis to calculate compliance with the debt ceiling. Of course, the debt ceiling has been raised sixteen times from 1997 to 2015, which makes it something like a diet where the number of permitted calories rises the fatter the dieter gets.[24]

The difference between the two schools turns on intragovernmental debt, so opting between optimism and pessimism means figuring out a reasonable treatment for the entitlements that comprise the vast majority of intragovernmental debt. As a legal matter, the optimists can fairly exclude entitlement obligations, because retirees have no legal entitlement to Social Security, i.e., the government doesn't actually owe anyone any Social Security payments, so if it fails to pay, there would be no legal default, and on that basis, there is no debt per se.

Legal analysis may be fine for the lawyers and accountants, but as a political matter, beneficiaries expect their checks, and the government will make good on its obligations for as long as possible. As a political matter, entitlement obligations for the next two decades are as good as debts, and they should be included in the totals. It may be disturbing to realize that there are no hard assets in the Trust Fund against which entitlement obligations can be netted. That is because, contrary to common conception, Social Security is a pay-as-you-go program: current benefits are paid out of current receipts. The Social Security Administration freely admits that the government collects payroll taxes and spends them immediately; no actual money is deposited.[25] The "Social Security Trust Fund"—some $2.8 trillion allegedly squirreled away to pay for Boomer retirements—is just an accounting entry.[26] Although there is still gold in federal vaults (and there used to be morphine stockpiled there in the glory days, too, which may come in handy at this point), none of it is earmarked for Social Security. The Trust Funds exist only in the sense that the government promises to repay itself (and thus future beneficiaries) at a later date, a promise that takes the form of "special-issue" Treasury securities, available for purchase only by government trust funds.[27]

All this is sufficiently mind-bending to most people—because it is sufficiently complicated and divorced from personal practice (which cynics might argue is the point)—as to require some analogies. If you promise your children to leave them $1 million and you have a net worth of $250,000, and you don't even put any of that quarter million in a bank account bearing the names of your apple-cheeked issue, is it really a "trust fund"?* Or another example—you deposit your paycheck into the local bank, which then uses not the profits on your cash, but *your actual cash* to pay its rent, salaries, and electricity bill—and then deposits its own bonds in your account in lieu of cash. Is this a "deposit"? If a Citibank ATM spits out a corporate bond instead of a wad of twenties, would you be happy?

It is the substitution of your cash for a future promise (made by the same institution collecting your cash) that transforms the Trust Funds into debt in practical terms. Recall that the government has already spent payroll taxes collected to date, so all benefits payable in the future must be funded out of future taxes. A promise to pay from future income that is not offset by hard and sequestered assets is, by all reasonable measures, a debt. (This is not just a Republican conspiracy; Al Gore harped about a Social Security lockbox for the same reason.) Entitlement debts will necessarily be borne by future generations, as the Government Accountability Office (GAO) admits: "intragovernmental debt holdings reflect a claim on taxpayers and the economy *in the future*."[28] Social Security accounts for more than $2.8 trillion, while Medicare accounts for another few hundred billion, though the liabilities of each system are actually much higher, as Chapters 11 and 12 will show.[†,29]

Unfortunately, reasonable measures of total debt go beyond the inclusion of

---

* Government itself has actually undertaken this experiment—during Jackson's presidency, a federal surplus was "deposited" with the States to be recalled in the event the Treasury required it. After a panic in 1837, the money, predictably, did not come back.

† Even if the Medicare portion of the trust fund weren't merely an accounting entry, it is so tiny relative to future obligations as to be meaningless, enough to fund only a few months of benefits at present levels.

intragovernmental liabilities. The government has many other quasi liabilities, and while these obligations, like entitlements, are not legally binding, both the public and the bond markets implicitly view them as such. Given that these groups can compel the government to make good on these obligations (the public via the voting booth) and are necessary to supply the money in the first place (the financiers via the bond market), their opinions are relevant. At least for the purpose of assessing the nation's long-term creditworthiness, it's appropriate to include these sundry, informal obligations in gross debt calculations.

At the federal level, such informal obligations include the government's implicit obligations for entities the government functionally owns or has otherwise backstopped, like mortgage operators Fannie Mae and Freddie Mac, which operate under the telling moniker of "government-sponsored entities" (GSEs).* Netted out against the assets of these entities, the government has probably backstopped several hundred billion to one trillion or more dollars. Some of these liabilities are mixed into things like the Federal Reserve's balance sheet, which reported $1.8 trillion in GSE and agency debt in 2015 (as an asset, by the by). In theory, the Fed adjusts the carrying value of these items to reflect their actual collectability; time will tell how realistic the Fed's accounting is.[30] Others lurk off balance sheet, but as we discovered in 2008 with the big private banks, during economic crises toxins tend to migrate from off balance sheet to on. Even more quasi liabilities of this kind exist, like bank deposit insurance, securities insurance, and pension guarantees. The meager insurance funds on hand for these would be instantly depleted by another crisis, certainly provoking a bailout (funded by more debt). The exact accounting and possible offsets for these potential liabilities can be reasonably debated; what is relevant here is that the mere existence of these items renders the smaller "public debt" calculations somewhat hard to credit.†

---

* The government also essentially owns these companies, collecting all their profits and holding options for the 79.9 percent of their equity (since 80 percent would require the GSE's consolidation on federal balance sheets).

† The government has considerable assets to net against the debt, like land and buildings (French and Russian sovereign land sales are how America ended up with the Louisiana Territory and Alaska). Selling these would be shortsighted—the privatization of certain infrastructure like parking meters and roads in Chicago and elsewhere proved a fiasco—and tempting as it might be to auction off the Jersey Shore to pay down the

Of course, it's not just the federal government that borrows. It's much harder to aggregate the total borrowing of state and local governments, though it's at least $3 trillion.[31] How, you could reasonably ask, can states borrow trillions when every state but Vermont has a balanced budget requirement? How has Puerto Rico, which also has a balanced budget requirement, gone bust? Each state has different rules, but as a general matter, states are allowed to finance capital projects with bonds, and this accounts for the majority of debt buildup. The rest is the product of subjectivity, because while operating budgets must be balanced when passed, bad planning or bad luck can easily tip states into deficits that roll forward. The vast expansion of state debt occurred during Boomer tenure (recall they have been resident in governor's mansions for some time and controlled 86 percent of them in 2016). Whether or not the federal government chooses to bail out Detroit, Puerto Rico, or whichever ill-managed locality goes under next is less important than the fact that should state governments fail, the federal government is highly likely to step in and pay one way or another, either directly through a bailout or indirectly through increased transfer payments like welfare. And the oddity is that while one or two local governments can be safely let go (as has been the case), the more that fail, the more likely a federal bailout to avoid total collapse becomes. In other words, if and when the problem truly emerges, it will be substantial.

The federal government *already* subsidizes state debt, by the way, so federalization of state debts is not exactly unthinkable. The federal government has done so explicitly by extending the benefit of its credit rating to the states (much as Germany does to the European Union) as with Build America Bonds (BABs), issued after the 2008 crisis. For BABs, the Treasury paid 35 percent of the interest on debt issued by local governments. The program ran only briefly, issuing $181 billion in bonds, but the Treasury's own statement makes clear what was going on: "BABs *provide a deeper federal subsidy* to state and local governments."[32] (Which implies what will shortly be discussed: the existence of a permanent federal subsidy in the first place.) The subsidy became necessary because the "financial crisis of 2008 severely impaired credit markets for

---

national debt, gains from the sale of sovereign assets would be more than offset by the signals of desperation sent by those sales.

state and local governments…and many municipal issuers had no access to the capital markets," so the "Treasury pays a 35 percent direct subsidy to the issuer[s]."[33] Local governments used BABs for (mostly) worthy infrastructure projects, but many could not have done so without handouts from the Treasury. Other versions of these quiet subsidies exist, including the exemption of muni-bond interest from federal taxation. That exemption reduces the federal take and, given persistent deficits, emerges on the other end as federal debt. Again, it's important to avoid double counting, so state problems are not included in the federal statistics presented.

Nevertheless, it's important to remember that state and local debts could easily become federalized, one way or another—whether by bailing out their pensions, paying out more federal benefits as local residents slip further into poverty, and so on. However much certain Republicans like the idea of the states as independent "laboratories of democracy," the fact is that they are *united* states, and what binds them is money or, anyway, debt. In the next figure, then, is the total layer cake of American government debt—you can choose how many slices you'd like to consume, but the minimum portion is always sizable.

Unjust Des(s)erts: The Present Debt Layer Cake

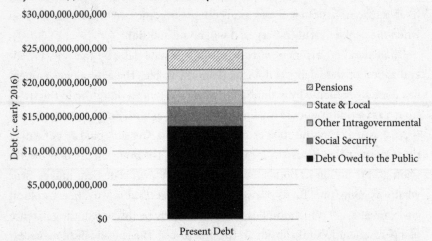

What's going on here? This is the rough total of debt owed by various government entities, plus their likely pension backstop obligations. ("Rough" because no one really knows, not even the government.) Pessimists might add to this the trillions of additional unfunded entitlements obligations, the various and implicit guarantees the government grants quasi-public entities, the deferred costs of infrastructure repair, and so on.[34]

Debt: Maintaining It

Although total debt is substantial, its burden and sustainability are a function of interest rates, because in normal times, interest is the only component of debt the government is functionally called upon to pay. The government rolls over debt constantly. Some $7 trillion in new debt was issued in FY 2016 and $6.7 trillion was repaid, the difference roughly being the deficit, so it was something like refinancing an $18 trillion house with a series of interest-only loans of indefinite duration.[35] So long as the bond market believes in the government's ability to make timely interest payments, there is no problem; if the bond market gets worried, it can inflict a huge price in the form of higher interest rates, or even do unto the United States what it did to Greece in the 2000s, and to France in 1789.

That the bond market holds great power is no secret to either Wall Street or the Treasury Department, and shouldn't be to politicians. After all, it is the bond market—the collection of all buyers, individuals, banks, other nations, etc.—that supplies money in the first place. When disappointed, "bond market vigilantes" have punished the Treasury market. James Carville, Bill Clinton's chief political operative, found himself entirely surprised by the power of the bond market and once expressed a desire to be reincarnated not as the "president or the pope or a .400 baseball hitter...but as the bond market."[36]

Vigilante justice is inflicted through higher interest rates, and this requires a quick refresher on bonds. All bonds are debt obligations that consist of principal and interest. The interest rate is a function of the risk premium the market demands, a collection of judgements about creditworthiness, inflation, liquidity, other market opportunities, and so on, but for government bonds, the two things that really matter are inflation and credibility. The government cannot really force the bond market to buy a single dollar of bonds if the price isn't right, so it auctions off securities in the following way: (1) the Treasury says it wants to borrow $1,000 and will pay 5 percent simple interest ($50 annually), repaying $1,000 in, say, ten years; (2) the bond market can make whatever bids it wants on those bonds—$900, $1000, $1,100—based on its own models. If bonds are bought at the $1,000 face value and held to maturity, the calculation is simple: The government pays $50/year and then $1,000 at the end of year ten. If the market wants to pay only $900 for the bonds, the government must still pay back $1,000 at the end of year ten, but gets only $900 now, and so the implicit interest rate is actually higher; the reverse happens if the market bids over $1,000.

It is this free market dynamic that permits vigilante justice. When the bond market is disappointed, it either bids under face value or sells its existing bonds at progressively lower prices. Both strategies depress bond prices and have an inverse effect on interest rates, as the preceding paragraph showed—the following table presents the mechanics. Faced with a bond-market revolt, the government ends up paying more to borrow until it rebalances its books more to the market's taste.

A Quick Example of the Inverse Relationship Between Bond Price and Interest Rates

	Scenario 1: Everything Happens at Face Value	Scenario 2: Bond Market *Bullish*	Scenario 3: Bond Market *Bearish*
Face Value of 10-Year Bond (amount government must repay—always fixed)	$1,000	$1,000	$1,000
Stated Interest Rate (the "coupon"—also always fixed)	5%	5%	5%
What Bond Market *Actually* Pays for Bond (can vary)	$1,000	$1,100	$900
Effective Annual Interest Rate	5%	<5%	>5%

What am I looking at? Everyone gets confused by bonds, but another way to look at it is this: No matter what, the government is going to pay you $50 per year (the interest) and then $1,000 back after a decade (the principal). Those amounts are fixed. What does vary is what you pay for those cash flows and it may be more intuitive if we make the scenarios implausibly extreme. Let's say you pay $1 for the entire package—you still get $50 per year, $1,000 after a decade, and your return on investment is effectively infinite (every year you get 50 times your money back, plus a bonus 1000x at year 10). Conversely, let's say you pay the government $1 billion for the same bond—you still get $50 per year and $1,000 after a decade, but your effective interest rate is extremely negative.

Again, the bond market considers many things when it trades—indeed, its models often have dozens or even thousands of inputs and outputs, but these can be summarized in two concepts. Input: credibility. Output: effective interest rates. "Credibility" and "credit" have related etymologies and related effects. When credibility declines the price of credit (interest rates) rises.

Credibility is relative, of course. The current price of American credit is unusually cheap for a variety of reasons that have little to do with the inherent credibility of American politics. Partly, the United States is growing somewhat faster than other rich economies and is perceived as somewhat safer/less dysfunctional than almost every other major economy, so money flows into the United States because it is the least bad alternative. This is partly why after 2008, despite a gigantic American financial crisis and ballooning deficits, the dollar rose and interest rates fell; everywhere else looked even worse, and money parked itself in the United States for want of better places to go. Rates have also been low because growth has been anemic and the Federal Reserve has adjusted policy to keep rates down. Experts can reasonably quibble about the details, but in general terms, these have been the recent dynamics.

The result has been extremely cheap financing for the government, and of course, for consumers (think of all those robo-calls and spam e-mails about mortgage refis at "historically low rates"). From 2010 to 2015, the government paid an average of 2.47 percent on new ten-year Treasury debt; subtracting inflation, the real rate of interest traveled to around 1.5 percent or lower.[37] Basically, extraordinary circumstances allow the United States to borrow essentially for free, a situation that will almost certainly change over the very long term.

Hoping for higher interest rates is in some sense an act of optimism, because the past decade of exceptionally low interest rates has been the result of economic distress. Optimism has its own costs, though. During the period of exceptionally low rates, from FY 2010 to FY 2015, gross interest on the debt cost about $360–450 billion annually, and the average was roughly 85–90 percent of the present annual budget deficit (in other words, if we owed no interest, the annual federal budget would essentially balance if we view intragovernmental debt as "debt").[38] Should rates rise, so will interest costs—the question is whether new economic growth produces enough additional tax revenue to cover the increased cost.

The problem with government debt comes from the fact that even though the debt is perpetual, the means of financing it are not. As we've seen, the federal government constantly rolls over trillions of old debt along with a few hundred billion extra (the extra being that year's deficit plus odds and ends).[39] Therefore, every year a substantial chunk of the federal debt can come up for refinancing at new rates—think of it as an adjustable-rate mortgage with a potential balloon payment, and you can guess who will be responsible for the balloon part when the bond market decides it's had enough.

Each additional 1 percent the market demands adds about $180 billion in immediate annual interest payments on the public part of the debt, or about 40 percent of the present annual budget deficit and more over time.* A 2.5 percent gross increase in interest costs would almost double the annual budget deficit, and ceteris paribus, this could spark a vicious cycle where higher interest costs spawn larger deficits, greater concern about fiscal integrity, further rate increases, and so on. Over a few years, other factors—like the flow of money into the United States as a safe haven—can swamp this dynamic. Were tax revenues and economy to expand quickly, that would also make interest payments manageable, though as the rest of the book shows, those outcomes are unlikely on America's present course. Therefore, in the multidecade horizon relevant to people younger than the Boomers, the United States should expect to pay a greater price for its borrowing. For the sociopathic subset of Boomers, this falls into the ever-expanding category of Someone Else's Problem, and that's why the sea of debt has been tolerated.

A return to higher rates could happen relatively suddenly; the bond market is quirky and run by mercurial humans and, increasingly, by inscrutable machines whose processes aren't necessarily transparent to their masters. Were rates to rise to pre-2008 long-term averages, an uptick of about 2.7 percent in absolute terms, the additional costs of servicing our debt by themselves would become as large as the entire present deficit.[40] Slow growth and the lack of inflationary pressures make it unlikely that rates will rise that much very soon, but they will rise—unless the United States remains mired in permanent stagnation, which will make the debt harder to service in other ways.

---

* Over time, because not all of the debt is retired every year, and there's a lag between nominal interest rates and effective rates paid on a portfolio of different maturities.

In ordinary times, the bond market has more power than the government; in extraordinary times, the government can exercise vastly more power than the bond market. After all, the government owns the printing presses (and, the extremists would point out, the army), but it can use extraordinary powers only rarely. Even though implementation was often poor, the government rightly used its emergency powers after 2008, but for reasons we will take up later, it has exhausted much of its conventional arsenal. Therefore, absent a nuclear option like default, compelled purchases, or debasement of the currency, the bond market will exercise greater control in the coming years than it has in the recent past, and the cost of American debt could rise substantially. Still, a nuclear option isn't unthinkable, given that Boomer debt insanity was on full display in 2016 when Trump went so far as to suggest the government issue debt with intent of subsequently renegotiating its terms—i.e., premeditated default.[41] Because that's what many Boomers have done with their personal borrowing, Trump wasn't so much bloviating as reflecting a reality practiced at home.

Private Liabilities

As to that, just as government borrows to maintain its lifestyle, so do citizens. On a personal basis, American debt totaled $14.2 trillion in 2015, of which about $9.5 trillion is mortgage debt, $1.3 trillion educational debt, plus an assorted remainder.[42] Some of these debts, like student loans to pay tuition at elite schools, are really in the nature of debt-financed investments.* Others are offset in whole or part by assets like houses, though as the underwater mortgages in Florida, Arizona, and Nevada show, not as much as one would hope. Nevertheless, there is simply a huge amount of debt outstanding, of every imaginable variety, much of it spent unproductively, and increasingly steadily since 1980 to unsettling levels.

Corporations have also indebted themselves heavily, with gross nonfinancial corporate debt tripling since 1981 on a real basis to a total of $8.1 trillion as of 2015, maybe $6 trillion or so net of cash.[43] (Financial firms,

---

* There's a huge and sprawling debate over what constitutes "investment" in economic terms. Generally, I'm just using the word as noneconomists would.

dark pools, etc. may add even more, though their iffy accounting makes things hard to pin down.) With the creation of junk bonds in the 1980s and the wave of leveraged buyouts, it's tempting to think the Reagan years accounted for the great expansion in corporate debt. Corporate debt did roughly triple from 1981 to 1990, but it was from the 1990s onward, when Boomers were in full control of corner offices that debt really exploded, as a share of GDP and relative to assets.* Debts are heaviest in the financial sector and smaller firms, which is troubling, because small companies struggle during recessions. This development cannot be dismissed as a corporate problem divorced from reality—if companies can't pay their debts, they fail, with very real impacts on stocks, savings, and the real economy.

On every conceivable basis, then—absolute, relative, as a ratio of earnings, per capita—the United States has been on a borrowing binge, public, private, and corporate. The nation has moved into uncharted territory, the kind of place that old maps used to populate with monsters.

Troublesome Trajectories: Bankruptcies

As the economy slows, debt eventually becomes onerous. It can be no surprise that bankruptcies have been mounting; what is surprising is that they have been mounting for quite some time, even during the ostensibly "good years" of the 1980s and 1990s. In the abstract, bankruptcies have enormous social utility, affording bankrupts the chance to reorganize themselves and perhaps create future value, while avoiding the medieval practice of debt bondage, in which debtors became the functional slaves of their creditors. We can acknowledge bankruptcy's use and fairness without giving up the

---

* A portion of this debt has been incurred to pay dividends in the United States, secured by foreign earnings left overseas where they remain untaxed. This little shenanigan will be discussed in detail in Chapter 13. Foreign shelters are also a major reason why newspapers run stories about corporations holding huge amounts of cash (the other reasons relate to wholly normal accounting practices too arcane to bother with here). Much of that cash, taking an extended foreign holiday, secures piles of debt used to pay for things, like dividends, back home. At the personal level, it's like your neighbor borrowing $1 million from the bank, secured against an untouchable trust fund subject to tax penalties. He'd then have $1 million in cash, but $1 million in debt; the ingenuity is more impressive than the wads of hundred-dollar bills.

right to question whether a society in which bankruptcy is frequent is one that is well functioning.

Although the Constitution explicitly authorizes Congress to provide bankruptcy relief, it used to be fairly difficult to obtain. Congress liberalized matters in 1898 and bankruptcies rose, though to the low level of 1.3 per 1,000 adults by 1965.[44] In 1978, when the median Boomer was twenty-six, Congress loosened the law again and has since adjusted the law first to make it easier (when Boomers were primarily debtors and thus beneficiaries of relief). Throughout almost all the Boomers' adult years, bankruptcies remained fairly easy to get and rose quickly, to 7.5 per 1,000 adults in 1998.[45] More recently, debt has become harder to discharge (now that wealthier Boomers have become net creditors).

A casual attitude toward fiscal probity developed under the Boomers, one that would be totally unfamiliar to prior generations, manifesting even in the selection of candidates for highest office. Consider the field of financial improvidence that constituted the 2016 primary contenders. Donald Trump, the only person to make Silvio Berlusconi seem Churchillian, manages to be personally wealthy while presiding over a ramshackle real estate empire whose only products are architectural vulgarity and serial bankruptcies. Marco Rubio presented as a moral crusader (against debt) while tossing away money on speedboats, saving essentially nothing, and appears to have held a long-term credit card balance whose burdens were occasionally relieved by improper use of the GOP house card.[46] Scott Walker, the governor of Wisconsin and a fleeting favorite, had a net worth that ranged from barely positive to outright negative, depending on assumptions.[47] Bernie Sanders had considerable credit card debt, while his family's modest net worth resided entirely and rather questionably in his wife's name; he's said he's paid it off and his spokesman pooh-poohed the whole thing as "normal," but as of 2014, he carried at least four times the national average, though he was also better paid than the average worker.[48] The Clintons, of course, have had their financial ups and downs and long been attached to questionable get-rich-quick schemes like Whitewater and some murkiness around the Clinton Foundation. Ted Cruz received a poorly disguised and highly questionable loan from Goldman Sachs, his wife's former employer.[49] John Kasich, the Ohio governor and, per the *New York Times* editorial board, the only "plausible" Republican candidate (primary voters did not agree), had a previous life as a Lehman Brothers executive from 2001 to 2008, and knew "close to zero" about investment banking when he started, a state of enlightenment apparently paralleled by the bank as a whole given its 2008 collapse.[50] A huge chunk of candidates in recent years have flirted with or had long-term relationships with debt and impropriety. And yet, those now constitute our options, a sea of red ink and imprudence that leaves the American political brow untroubled. The Boomers have habituated the nation to debt and default.

Concerns about bankruptcy abuses prompted Congress to crack down in 2005, decades after it unlocked the bankruptcy door for the Boomers. Like George Orwell's pigs, some bankrupts ended up being more equal than others. One of the 2005 law's most significant changes made discharging student debt exceedingly difficult. The Boomers did not have to worry, as formerly generous subsidies meant they carried relatively little of such debt. Their children, however, carried quite a bit, with interest remitted to companies in which Boomers held shares. That was of no moment for the Boomer legislature. After 2005, student debt would fall into the same legal category as debts like criminal penalties and child support.

A large minority of bankruptcies come from catastrophic health-care costs, and some of these can (and, as an accounting matter, are) just written off as bad luck. Nevertheless, medical bankruptcies have their own sociopathic aspects, given the Boomers' lackadaisical attitudes toward their own physical and financial health, and their failure to enact comprehensive insurance reform. And much of the dollar volume of bankruptcies derives from nonmedical imprudence. The Boomers made mistakes and crafted remedial laws in response; with their errors absolved, bankruptcy reform can trend toward the punitive, except, of course, in the case of medical bankruptcies, where we can expect the Boomers to indulge in more legislative forgiveness.

Repayment

Despite its alarming size, the national debt neither can be nor should be entirely repaid, certainly not within the lifetime of any American now living. Even setting aside 10 percent of the budget—which given the present deficit of around –2.5 percent to –3 percent would represent an impossibly large budgetary swing—would cause a severe recession, if not depression, and still not retire the debt for many decades. It will be a century, if ever, before we need to exhume Senator Benton's corpse for an encore of the debt-is-paid speech. However, at some point in the next decade or so, America must provide the bond market with a more reasonable plan for servicing and eventually retiring much of the debt—that does not mean the United States should stop borrowing, only that it should have a strategy that goes beyond one more crapulent wallow at the trough.

Sadly, we cannot expect any such plan soon. Because interest rates remain low, the debt crisis probably will not emerge until the Boomers are near their ends. Boomers have no personal incentive to address debt and have shown no appetite for doing so. The failure to do anything about the debt (other than add to it) amounts, therefore, to a declaration of generational bankruptcy, financial and moral, with costs transferred to subsequent generations.

The formal debt represents only part of the obligations of the government. The vast system of entitlements represents another. And finally, the true shape of the debt can be assessed only in the context of what has been happening to the nation's net worth. Because not only has the government been incurring huge amounts of debt simply to muddle along, it has systematically dissipated national assets like the military, physical infrastructure, education, and research. It is to these we next turn.

CHAPTER TEN

INDEFINITELY DEFERRED
MAINTENANCE

Impulsivity or failure to plan ahead…
Reckless disregard for safety of self or others…
Lack a realistic concern about their current
problems or their future…
Repeated squandering of money required
for household necessities…
They may minimize the harmful consequences of their
actions… [or] indicate complete indifference…
—DSM-V[1]

If one were to create from scratch a category guaranteed to repel the socio-path, it would be infrastructure—roads, power plants, sewers—or, as the Oxford English Dictionary aptly puts it, the physical "facilities…needed for the operation of a *society*."[2] (Apologies for the high school essay maneuver there, but it was too good to pass up.) Infrastructure demands providence and sharing; sociopaths offer imprudence and shortsighted self-interest, and that translates to neglect. Excluding national defense, gross total infrastructure spending has been falling for some time, to about 2.5 percent of GDP, significantly less than the United States spent in the 1960s (around 4 percent) and less than what many of America's industrialized peers spend today.[3]

The situation in publicly funded infrastructure is especially alarming. Larry Summers, president of Harvard and a former Treasury secretary, argued that *net* government investment was zero, adjusting for depreciation (roads do wear out). Zero was only the slightest exaggeration: it was, under the most generous calculations, 0.5 percent of GDP in 2014 (versus around 3 percent at its midcentury height).*[4] The federal government actually oversaw negative rates of investment in several major categories in 2014, with state and private spending accounting for the modestly positive showing overall. To understand that underinvestment has been serious, you need not pore over eyeball-glazing arcana like BEA's National Income and Product Accounts. You can simply observe the various casualty-producing fireballs that emerged in 2010 and 2014–2015 from California's mismaintained, fifty-year-old pipelines; the poisoned water in Flint, Newark, and elsewhere; sundry train derailments; and (per Joe Biden) "Third World" conditions prevailing in the cesspit that is LaGuardia Airport.[5]

While the Boomers grew up in a country that had the world's greatest infrastructure, they now run a nation where infrastructure ranges from frustratingly backward to downright unsafe. Before the 1980s, no one considered American infrastructure dangerously deficient overall in part because many major systems had only just been completed (though a few systems, like rail, needed work). By 1988, as many systems approached their second or third decades, Congress ordered a review. The grade then was a C, indicating conditions "fair to good…requir[ing] attention."[6]

Unfortunately, matters required more than just "attention," they required a nonsociopathic political class. It did not help that Congress failed to revisit its 1988 report, leaving assessments to industry groups like the American

---

* My assessment is actually *more* charitable and based on slightly more recent data: Summers had the net at 0 percent, Brookings's David Wessel had it at 0.06 percent for 2013.

Society of Civil Engineers (ASCE).* ASCE's independent reports, compiled as the Infrastructure Report Cards, concluded that conditions had deteriorated to a D by 1998.[7] If GenX parents received a similar report card regarding their children, the whole war machine of upper-middle-class Helicopter Fathering and Tiger Mothering would swing into action: money, tutors, apocalyptic lectures, pedagogical investigations, and marches on the PTA. The Boomers, devoted practitioners of latchkey parenting, simply shrug.

Meanwhile, the costs of remediation compound while maintenance is deferred indefinitely even as demand grows, further taxing already worn-down infrastructure.[8] The latest report card, from 2013, marked American infrastructure a D+ overall, meaning that "infrastructure is in *poor to fair condition and mostly below standard*, with many elements approaching the end of their service life. A large portion of the system exhibits significant deterioration. Condition and capacity are of significant concern with *strong risk of failure*."[†,9]

In 2001, ASCE estimated the United States needed to invest $1.3 trillion to bring infrastructure up to snuff over five years; by 2013, rising demand and increasing neglect drove the price up to $3.6 trillion through 2020, significantly higher on an annualized basis.[10] Even the full $3.6 trillion would only drag the mark up to a B ("adequate for now"), a grade whose modesty indicates a certain decline in American ambition. Given the budgets passed since the 2013 Report Card (allocating about 55 percent of the required amount) and emerging news about lead-tainted water in various municipalities, it would be almost impossible to achieve an "adequate" grade by 2020 even if the Boomer machine wanted to, which it does not.

---

* Some small-government types get exercised about ASCE's report card, issued as it is by professional engineers who would obviously benefit from more infrastructure projects. But the government itself abandoned its own Report Card. ASCE has made reasonable attempts to continue that work, and the disaggregated data produced by various governments makes clear that ASCE isn't being unreasonable in its data-based assessment is better than the reductive report cards usually issued by K Street.

† That's the definition for a "D." America gets a D+. The "+" may not be entirely reassuring for those inching over the Tappan Zee Bridge into Manhattan, long past its intended working life and over capacity, witnessing the occasional crane keel over onto Tappan's much-delayed replacement.

For sociopaths, indifference to infrastructure has a certain logic. Bridges and waterworks take years to complete and often decades to return investments. What little interest the Boomers had in infrastructure therefore dwindles with age, especially if such investments risk the entitlements budget. As long as Boomers control government, there will be no smart grid, no public hyperloop, no wholesale move to clean power, not even appropriate maintenance.

The Selfless and Selfish Cases for Public Goods

The argument for infrastructure reduces to two facts: (1) we need it, and (2) it generates a significant and positive return on investment. That we require roads and sewers demands no further comment. That infrastructure generates net positive returns has long been understood by experts (including American governments of the midcentury), though not the present political class. People can and should debate the details, but as a general rule, one dollar in produces more than one dollar out, with gains often shared societywide. Much as some free marketers would have it otherwise, private enterprise usually cannot do it alone: Many projects yield profits that cannot be easily privatized, are simply too large for a given company to undertake, or require the exercise of the government's sovereign power of eminent domain or grant of monopoly to be viable.

If anything, the case for infrastructure has only gotten stronger over the past few years. Use has grown even as the burdens of building have declined. The primary costs of infrastructure, beyond the outright expense, are in the costs of financing and in opportunities forgone (perhaps the money could be more profitably invested elsewhere). Those concerns are not presently germane. Capital is desperate for returns, which is why we can borrow quite a bit at low rates and then profitably invest in roads, bridges, and sewers. Thanks to forces we covered in Chapter 8, America can borrow the whole $3.6 trillion, at forgiving interest rates and without cuts to other services. (One could argue that the bond market might even be encouraged by government spending on something with proven economic benefits.) It is *not* investing in infrastructure that carries greater public and private costs, with congested, ill-maintained roads that cause traffic delays, pollution, poor health, vehicle damage, bigger repair bills, and personal injury claims, collectively far more expensive than filling a pothole in the first place.*

Therefore, unlike Social Security payments, infrastructure is not so much a consumption expense as an investment, and a good one.† The consensus from diverse sources like the IMF, the CBO, private financial institutions, and so on, is that for each new $1.00 invested, infrastructure generates about $1.40 to $1.80 over time.[11] Though the precise variables and conditions are complex, the general conclusion is not. Infrastructure is money well spent, unless a country is already richly endowed, a status the Boomer United States does not enjoy. And while infrastructure provides returns over decades, some benefits can be had almost immediately. Building provides middle-class jobs and favors workers who have recently been underemployed, including certain minorities and the large pool of laborers without higher education. So, by all means, borrow and build. As Larry Summers put it: "*Future generations* will be better off owing lots of money in long-term bonds at low rates in a currency they can print than they would be inheriting a vast deferred maintenance liability."[12]

Getting from A to A, Slowly

A substantial fraction of the (meager) infrastructure budget goes to transportation, and much of that goes to roads, which get heavy use and light funding. In 2015, 260 million American vehicles traveled 3 trillion miles and consumed 173 billion gallons of fuel.[13] It's 3 trillion miles of frustration: congested roads force Americans to waste 5–7 billion annual hours in traffic, at the cost of hundreds of billions of dollars in lost output, wasted fuel, and accidents.[14] Given that America is a car culture and will remain so for decades, it's frustrating that the roads are so inadequate.

As usual, the problem stems from sociopathic improvidence. Transport

---

*Some free marketers hold that public investment in certain infrastructure can "crowd out" private investment, making all projects more expensive and less efficient, but the data for this proposition has never been overly strong; even as a matter of theory, it doesn't hold in the present environment.

†Economic pedants will immediately raise eyebrows, since much of this will be categorized as "spending" in many technical publications, but it quite obviously has more of the characteristics of investment than, say, spending Social Security checks on Twinkies does.

depends heavily on gas taxes, and as with taxes of all kinds under Boomer tenure, these have been falling. The federal gas tax is 18.4 cents plus a (volume-weighted) average 26.59 cents at the state level, for a total of 44.99 cents per gallon as of 2015.[15] Until the 1970s, this arrangement had a certain logic, as prices were stable and road use tightly correlated with gas consumption. However, the oil shocks of the 1970s encouraged citizens to shift to somewhat more efficient cars while spurring inflation that diminished the real value of gas taxes because the federal and most state gas taxes are not indexed to inflation (unlike benefits payments or tax brackets that benefit Boomers).[16] Technology may only exacerbate the disconnect, because if electric cars are ever widely adopted, their use will only expand funding gaps; e-cars are literal free riders.

The federal gas tax rate last rose in 1993, just as Boomers were completing their transition to power, and its value has eroded steadily for almost a quarter century since 1983, even as the number of miles has almost doubled. The net result is that the real value of the federal gas tax has fallen, while use has gone up substantially.[17] Although some *states* have raised their nominal taxes since 1993, hikes have not kept up with inflation. In forty-one states, the total real gas tax (state plus federal) was lower in 2015 than in 1993.[18] Even the liberal bastion of Massachusetts, long inclined to other public works, could not reform its gas tax, with the legislature's attempt to inflation-index the gas tax repealed the following year by direct plebiscite, with Boomer-age groups providing critical repeal support before the vote.[19] Other than a minor experiment in Oregon, replacing automobile gas taxes with sensible alternatives, like fees linked to actual use, has been a dead letter.[20] The federal Highway Trust Fund, in positive balance since its establishment in 1956, went bust in 2008, requiring subsidy from general revenues. In early 2016, the HTF sported a positive (if near-zero) balance, but continues to depend on further bailouts and accounting gimmicks.[21] Notably, in 2008, presidential aspirants John McCain and Hillary Clinton endorsed the idea of a gas tax *holiday* the same year the Trust Fund required bailout.[22] Even the 1993 hike under Bill Clinton was used for several years not for highways, but to pretty up the deficit figures.[23] Clearly, the Boomer establishment does not take this issue seriously.

Starved by Boomers of funding, transportation agencies have been unable to repeat the canal, railroad, and highway revolutions overseen by prior generations. The Interstate Highway System was largely finished by the 1970s and

1980s, and Congress washed its hands, not even bothering to push through the final few miles of the system scheduled for completion in the early 1990s. Given rising demand, it's no surprise that average annual traffic delays per motorist rose from eighteen hours in 1982, the same year Boomers became an electoral majority, to thirty-seven hours by 2000 and then to forty-two hours by 2014.[24] Real congestion costs quadrupled over the same period, to $160 billion annually. (Crucially, *taxes* did not experience the same gains, which was more politically important.) Americans now spend almost as much time in traffic as men do in church, on average.[25] The only reason why Americans don't spend even more time in traffic is a persistently weak economy.

The failure to build new infrastructure makes it all the more important to maintain and modernize existing stock. Each year, poor roads cost over $60 billion in avoidable car repairs alone.[26] Maintenance would save lives and allow for tens of billions in additional (and taxable) economic growth; it also would have required some combination of tax and foresight. That hasn't happened. Instead, as Boomers coast toward a commute-free retirement, neglect has been prettied up as "deferred maintenance." Obviously "deferred maintenance" is not maintenance at all, it is a deferred *liability*.

Inaction has therefore become the rule, a paralysis that transcends liberal or conservative ideology, with terrible conditions existing in cities of all political affiliations. Despite being tiny and rich, San Francisco has appalling roads; its political opposites, Dallas and Phoenix, have horrible traffic. As for Washington, the federal district seems determined to enact in traffic the gridlock many see in Congress. As of 2015, a majority of DC's roads were in "poor" or "mediocre" conditions.[27] It's hard to imagine the world's diplomats cowed by American exceptionalism as they inch along decrepit roads.[28]

Many roads eventually travel over bridges, which have at least been an area of improvement under the Boomers. Notwithstanding the fatal collapse of the I-35 bridge in Minneapolis in 2007 or the floating bridge near Seattle that ceased to be a bridge when it ceased to float, bridges have been getting better. Their grade has improved from a C– to a (by Boomer standards, superlative) C+. That's just an average grade; there are plenty of specific problems. Per the Department of Transportation, in 2015, out of 611,845 bridges, 58,791 are "structurally deficient" and 84,124 "functionally obsolete," with many more being a slightly less threatening "deficient."[29] The positive spin is that these definitions don't imply imminent collapse, though they do mean that bridges are riskier and less capable than they should be. The negative spin is that the bridges ranking as seriously deficient tend to be larger, carry more traffic, and are generally more important.[30]

Many of these problems are a function of age. Bridge stock is fairly old, forty-three years on average, and while some are designed to last for much longer, others are not. The Tappan Zee Bridge, an essential crossing into New York City, was originally designed to last until 2005. Despite being a candidate for replacement since 1980 and carrying more than its designed load for longer than its designed lifetime, Tappan will not be replaced until thirteen years after its sell-by date. The federal government featured the old Tappan Zee on the cover of its 2016 budget as a symbol of (one presumes) what success looks like.* Still, at least Tappan is being replaced, not as a matter of routine prudence but substantially in response to the newsworthy collapse of I-35, leaving 58,790 bridges in need of urgent redress.

Roads are bad enough, and Congress *likes* cars; Congress hates rail, and it shows. Although fast trains are economically viable in populous regions and also ecologically sound, America has no high-speed trains worthy of the name. The best on offer is Acela, which can theoretically muster 150 mph. In fact, it generally averages a bumpy 80 mph between New York and DC, far below the 125 mph that Congress sets as the unspectacular threshold for "high-speed."[31] Only a few segments of track can safely accommodate a full-speed Acela—and given various Amtrak derailments in 2015–2016, perhaps not even that. America can expect no improvement under the Boomers. When Amtrak recently offered a true high-speed option, to debut in 2040, one Amtrak vice president admitted: "There is no mechanism at the federal level to support this today."[32] Amtrak did announce it was buying newer and faster cars to replace an aging fleet, which will do little unless track stock is upgraded.

The American rail system is a bizarre experience for foreign visitors. France has had high-speed trains since 1981, with speeds now averaging over 170 mph on the best lines and despite its imperfections, its system usually has positive margins and offers smooth rides.[33] Japan is set to introduce 300 mph

---

* Let's not even get into the fact that nothing seems to have been specifically allocated out of the 2016 budget for Tappan II.

trains. The fault extends beyond Boomer governments into militant (and often Boomer) backyards, the latter's owners opposed to intrusions into their bucolic suburbs and the former unwilling to exercise their powers of eminent domain to compel sociopathic constituents to submit. That stasis consigns many projects to limbo.

The rest of transportation infrastructure is no better: airports are bad (D), mass transit is bad (D), inland waterways are worse (D–) and each of these experienced significant declines from 1998 to 2013.[34] The subway in DC, the nation's second busiest, has decayed so much that the entire system had to be shut down for a day, and many lines were and will be shuttered for extended periods. The system's own chairman describes it as "*maybe* safe" and "somewhat unreliable."[35]

There is one segment of American transportation infrastructure that is not seriously deficient: the ports. Essential for the import of consumer necessities, these structures have received some attention and earned one of transportation's outstanding grades, a C.

Water and Waste

The various disasters in New Orleans, Flint, the failure of the Lake Delhi Dam, water shortages in the West, and the total absence of any long-term storage site for nuclear waste make clear that the state of water and waste infrastructure is not good. The only improvement seen during Boomer tenure was in the treatment of solid waste. The grade there was up from a C– to a B–, the highest score earned in the entire ASCE Report Card.[36]

There's no need to dwell on the various disasters of the recent past; it's enough to assess the general decline of water and waste management to sense what might happen in the future. The record isn't wholly an indictment of the Boomers, as the treatment of solid waste has improved somewhat and the problems of hazardous waste, especially nuclear waste, emerged long before the Boomers took power. Nevertheless, the Boomer legacy has been one of mismanagement and missed opportunities, as the saga of the Yucca Mountain Nuclear Waste Depository illustrates. As the nuclear industry ramped up in the 1960s and 1970s, it became necessary to find a permanent storage facility for spent fuel. In 1982, Congress commissioned a search for a final resting place. By 1987, Yucca Mountain had been selected, and over the next twenty years, billions were spent on research, planning, and construction. The Department of Energy filed for a license in 2008, but abruptly terminated the process a year later. Per the GAO, Yucca was abandoned for "policy reasons, not technical or safety reasons," the policy reasons being Boomer NIMBYism.[37] Therefore, the United States went from having a decent plan to having no plan, billions of dollars and years were wasted, and the nation is subjected to the tedious theatre of handwringing about nuclear terrorism while leaving piles of radioactive materials scattered across the country in the equivalent of a garden shed.

The neglect visited on Yucca is repeated across the landscape of water and waste, responsibility for which is consigned to a motley group of actors with varying commitments to safety. Although the federal government does a reasonable job overseeing its dams, it operates just 4 percent of the total. Local governments either own or oversee the rest, including the 69 percent in private hands.[38] This would be fine were state officials up to the task, but in the case of Alabama, there are literally *no* state officials: The state has 2,241 dams (with over 600 having substantial "hazard potential") and not one dam inspector.[39] South Carolina has the equivalent of 6.6 full-time inspectors to check its 2,400+ dams.[40] Nationally, there are about 200 dams per state inspector, against about 250 working days per year; if that does not seem like enough, it's because it isn't.[41] While many dams are small and pose little risk, thousands could fail in fatal ways.

As for usable water, needs grow unaddressed. New York City relies on two old water tunnels for its civic supply and now desperately needs a third, both because of growing demand and because the lack of redundancy makes it impossible to close the first two tunnels for inspection, a task last carried out when the tunnels were put into service in 1917 and 1936, respectively.[42] Construction of Water Tunnel No. 3 began in 1970, and thanks to budget cuts and lack of priority, it will not be completed until the 2020s.[43] On the West Coast, California depends on a system whose major components were finished by 1973 and though California's population has roughly doubled, water supply has not. Nationally, pipes, plants, and sewers are all old and in many cases dangerous, and the present level of funding is half of that necessary to keep the system in acceptable order. The whole system is entirely inadequate to supply water or deal with waste. Whether or not cities in deserts or nuclear power plants were originally good ideas, they now exist and need to be serviced. Leaving radioactive debris cooling in pools never intended to be permanent (which is the nation's present strategy) or praying for rain in California instead of expanding the water system is folly.

The Best Defense Is a Funded Defense

Standard accounting does not normally include national defense as an item of infrastructure, though it resembles conventional infrastructure in many ways. Defense comprises a social asset too large for any private corporation to furnish, and of its benefits, all partake. And defense funding doesn't simply vanish when a bullet leaves the muzzle of a gun: Quite a bit supports non-combat operations like R&D, employment (military and civilian), health care, education, physical infrastructure, as well as conventional hardware. These investment and jobs programs have positive social effects that stretch beyond simple "combat readiness."[44] Whatever the accounting treatment—as infrastructure, educational spending, a very weird kind of social engineering—defense has as a practical and political matter long been considered in the same general category as roads and bridges. The Constitution grants the power to provide a "common Defense" in Article I, Section 8, the same provision that allows Congress to provide roads.[45] Older politicians explicitly viewed infrastructure as part of defense, with the converse implicit and natural. (The full name of our highway system is the "Dwight D. Eisenhower National System of Interstate and Defense Highways").[*,46] Defense does differ from other infrastructure in that its economic benefits are much harder to quantify and in having moral dimensions that, say, a storm drain does not. Still, defense is a national asset and one few would be inclined to forgo.

As they have with infrastructure generally, the Boomers squandered their martial inheritance. Unlike other categories of infrastructure, the

---

*The ancient Romans built roads for infantry that also facilitated trade and communication while the Soviets built parts of the Moscow subway especially deep to serve as fallout shelters.

American military still leads, though the growing power of other nations and the gradual hollowing out of American forces has eroded the US's relative position. Though famously large, American military spending has been falling dramatically during Boomer tenure. *Nominal* defense spending is about $600 billion, but measured as a fraction of GDP, defense spending has fallen from an average of 7.9 percent of GDP from 1950 to 1985 to 4.1 percent during the following three decades of Boomer domination. Cuts and sequestration have driven recent spending even lower, to about 3.2 percent of GDP in FY 2016, projected to fall to 2.6 percent by 2026.[47] Even factoring in the various stray programs, one-off appropriations, and the entire budget of the Department of Homeland Security, created in 2001 and responsible for an assortment of security-related noncombat tasks, adds only modestly to the total and does not change the general direction of defense spending.

The Boomers' decision not to invest in the military has, and will continue to have, consequences. The Department of Defense (DoD) cannot openly admit the full degree of its impairment, though it concluded that readiness, already declining, "further suffered due to the implementation of [budget]

The Best Defense Is a Funded Defense

What's going on here? Defense spending has declined considerably under the Boomers. While lower spending made sense immediately following the end of the Cold War, the Boomers have continued America's policy of constant foreign intervention without keeping up levels of spending, and arbitrary sequestration and spending caps will drive defense spending even lower in coming years unless reversed.[48]

sequestration in FY 2013 and the force has not kept pace with the need to modernize."[49] The DoD gamely offers, for it could not do otherwise, that President Obama's partial restoration of funds would allow it to "defeat or deny any aggressor," though at greater risk.[50]

Independent assessments of the military, and by implication government policy, indulge in less optimism. The bipartisan, congressionally chartered National Defense Panel "want[ed] to make two points crystal clear."[51] First, recent budget cuts "precipitated an immediate readiness crisis."[52] Second, (and much more gloomily than the DoD), the Obama administration's proposals for partial funding restoration "are nowhere near enough to remedy the damage which the Department has suffered and enable it to carry out its missions at an acceptable level of risk."[53] The "capabilities and capacities" called for in the nation's master defense document, the *Quadrennial Defense Review*, "clearly exceed budget resources made available to the Department"; in nonbureaucratese, the military simply doesn't have the money to do its job.[54]

Therefore, it can come as no surprise that the Secretary of Defense worried that the Army, Navy, and Marine Corps would not achieve readiness goals until 2020 and the Air Force not until 2023, or that the head of the Marine Corps informed Congress that half of its home-stationed units experienced unacceptable shortfalls that could "result in a delayed response and/or the unnecessary loss of…lives."[55] Various think tanks question the military's capacities, with the (admittedly hawkish) Heritage Foundation rating the military overall as "marginal," and the Army scoring no better than "weak," not an inspiring adjective in any context, especially the martial; other institutions offer chirpier gloss, but generally fret over the military's present size and posture.[56] The Air Force operates the oldest and smallest fleet in recent history, the Navy has shrunk, and overall manpower has been in decline since the Boomers took control of Congress.

It's revealing that the posture of the armed forces has actually weakened since the period 1990–1995, a period of unusual peace. While optimists invoked (part of) Francis Fukuyama's "end of history" to contend that all nations would transition to liberal, Western, and presumably nonhostile democracies, 1991's hopes of global harmony proved no more realistic than Thomas More's *Utopia* of 1516 or any of the many fantasies that followed.* The world remains dangerous and America militant. The United States has been more or less continually involved in military actions of some kind since Independence, and it can no more plausibly forgo conflict than the Romans could close the Gates of Janus with any sincerity.

At a minimum, since the drawdown of the 1990s, threats have grown, with Soviet aggression now recast as Russian adventurism in Crimea, Ukraine, Georgia, and Moldova; the Chinese engaged in island-building menace and cyberespionage; North Korea's deranged kleptocracy now nuclear-equipped and engaged in cyberattacks; the Middle East persistently unstable; and terrorism spreading. At the same time, the scope of territory that America has obliged itself to defend has swollen to include former Eastern Bloc states, some of whom have tiny forces (Estonia has roughly the same number of regular troops as Houston has law enforcement personnel, "about 6,000"), while crucial allies like Germany regularly underspend NATO needs, nowhere near on track to meet the (paltry) 2 percent of GDP goal NATO has set. Europe's inaction implicitly passes the burden to the United States.[57] Despite this, the American military's share of GDP does not even meet the levels of the pacific early '90s.[58]

The military emerged from Vietnam tired and discredited, and over the next two decades—the last gasp of the old guard—it reformed and rebuilt itself into a considerable asset the Boomers have shown no sustained appetite for maintaining. The charitable might wonder how the Vietnam generation managed to embroil themselves in endless conflicts while simultaneously running down the military. The answer resides, of course, in the relentless sociopathy of the Boomer cohort. The seventeen or so military conflicts under Boomer leadership were just the natural products of expediency and sociopathic hostility; military decline the result of improvidence and selfishness. That young soldiers (obviously, none of whom are Boomers) can no longer carry out missions at an "acceptable level of risk," is, for the graying sociopath, not germane. That it will take another five or ten years, perhaps longer, to rebuild a military depleted by

---

*Democracies do go to war against each other; the British burned the White House in 1814 and had plans to agitate against America through the late-nineteenth century—at times, the relationship has been "special" indeed.

Boomer adventurism and neglect simply demonstrates the irrelevance of doing so to a sociopath of dwindling years. All that is required is to avoid wholesale military collapse during Boomers' golden years, while continuing to channel the budget into the retirement and health programs whose gains can be harvested today.

Forecast: Over Budget, Under Expectations, with Rays of Hope

Although infrastructure demands several hundred billion additional dollars each year, the nation can afford it. Leaving aside defense, infrastructure tends to pay for itself. Private and public owners will pick up the tab if the levees break or the bridges collapse, so they may as well maintain them, especially as proper upkeep is usually cheaper than replacement and certainly less problematic than paying off wrongful death suits.

Some on the Right question whether government is competent to be in the infrastructure business; perhaps all the extra money will just disappear into the vast maw of mismanagement. Some on the Left question reliance on for-profit businesses citing, e.g., the privatization of Bolivian waterworks whose mechanics were so suspect that they provided the template for the Bond movie *Quantum of Solace*. These are interesting academic questions and helpful at the margins. They are also of little practical relevance. The government is the only entity that can organize, pay for, and/or inspect a lot of critical infrastructure and by practical necessity, it relies on private enterprise to carry out its plans.

However, it does seem harder and costlier to build things than it used to be. The original San Francisco/Oakland Bay Bridge took about three years to complete and cost about $1.4 billion in today's dollars; the replacement of just its eastern span took eleven years, cost at least $6.5 billion, required immediate repairs, and problems are ongoing.[59] The Empire State Building took 410 days to complete; One World Trade Center took about seven years. Recent expansions to the New York subway are badly over budget, late, and in the case of the recently opened Hudson Yards station, already leaking.[60] The explanations are complex and comparisons difficult. Optimists can point to the growing complexity and capacities of modern building, as well as the generally higher standard of living now, which translates into higher construction wages and costs, as well as OSHA protocols that prevent safety from being lost at the expense of speed. All well and good, and not untrue.

Still, puzzles remain. Wages alone (faltering anyway in the Boomer decades) do not explain vast increases in building costs. Nor does modern complexity explain everything; prices have gone up even for systems that have changed little since the 1950s. An F-35 is different from a Sopwith Camel, but a road is still essentially a path with asphalt. One probable explanation is sloppy and sentimental thinking. It used to be understood that for every mile of tunnel, builders expected a certain number of men to die. Today, there's an expectation that building should be free of direct human costs, with the result that projects are slower, costlier, and have redundant precautions that often do not work. Safety regulations may (or may not, in the case of recent crane collapses in New York) save some lives, but an excessive focus on one type of safety ignores the other, less dramatic fatalities that accrue as drivers rely on deficient infrastructure and waste leaches into water supplies. Environmental impact reviews (EIRs) also slow things down. Genuine and reasonable concern motivated EIRs, to originally good effect, though they need to be considerably rethought as facts change. Reviews can focus too much on avoiding highly specific harms instead of overall benefits, e.g., the impact of a solar plant on local birds instead of maximizing the existential threat of climate change that threatens all birds. They also depend on a judicial system, an item of quasi infrastructure itself, that is sorely understaffed, resulting in protracted litigation.

A particular and relatively new complication is the antidevelopment NIMBYism of homeowners and the craven capitulation of Boomer governments. This movement started in the 1950s and 1960s, with a battle between Robert Moses, who would have bulldozed some of New York City's most charming areas, against Jane Jacobs, who wanted to preserve scenic communities whatever their inefficiencies. While Jacobs then had the better of the argument, a degraded version of her mantle has been assumed by Boomers who refuse to consider change to their personal quality of life as a matter of fixed principle. Boomer bourgeoisie stasis must give way to forward thinking. We do not need to go as far as China, which simply bulldozes the straightest path between points A and B. We simply need to exercise the constitutional means of eminent domain and let a few homeowners stew in favor of the greater good—people with wooden teeth had this figured out 250 years ago; can't we do at least as well? Unfortunately, the Boomer refusal to engage with evidence, to take the long view, or to measure outcomes other than through the tiny aperture of immediate self-interest has made large projects difficult, but not impossible—America is still very skilled at building things, when it wants to.

The Boomers did not inherit a perfect system from their parents, but it was a very good one, certainly better than the rapidly decaying legacy and mounting bills the Boomers propose to leave their children. The sociopaths ran down infrastructure to help pay for tax cuts, and, unless they're stopped, they will run it down further to pay for their retirements. They failed to capitalize on the enormous, positive-return possibilities of proper investment and maintenance. The facts would astonish any thinking citizen. And therefore, the conduct of Boomer policy required the elimination or repackaging of those facts and all the other inconveniencies generated by Boomer policies. This was achieved by the most expedient means of all: lies.

CHAPTER ELEVEN

BOOMER FINANCE: THE VICIOUS CYCLE OF RISK AND DECEIT

They are frequently deceitful and manipulative in
order to gain personal profit or pleasure…
They may repeatedly lie…con others, or malinger…
They may display a glib, superficial charm and can be quite
verbally facile (e.g., using technical terms or jargon that
might impress someone who is unfamiliar with the topic).
—DSM-V[1]

I'm tired of Love: I'm still more tired of Rhyme.
But Money gives me pleasure all the time.
—Hilaire Belloc[2]

Given the Boomers' legacy of mismanagement and misappropriation, how have we gone so long without some sort of counterrevolution? Part of the answer, as we saw in Chapter 7, is that the Boomers still have great raw political power and will for some time—and as to the entitlement budget, they have the support of their elders. Another significant explanation is that, in classic sociopathic fashion, the Boomers have engaged in a campaign of deceit, reaching into their *wunderkammer* of generational duplicity to offer consoling fictions to the population they govern. The mendacious assortment includes disingenuous financial dialogue essential to maintaining the expropriations necessary to fund the Boomers' insatiable consumer appetites and stretches to oppressive political discourse designed to squelch debate (carefully packaged in the form of sensitivity to the various shibboleths of the Right and Left). In the event mere words fail to lull the electorate, the Boomers have resorted to outright oppressions made by the state's monopolies on the money supply and violence, and whether the labels be "crisis management" or "law and order," the oppressive effect is the same. When all other options have been exhausted, the Boomers simply ignore problems whose greatest effects will fall outside their lifetimes and are of correspondingly little concern.

All people lie, and the political class most of all, but the scope of Boomer deceptions goes far beyond the customary embellishment (e.g., the improbable tale peddled by Hillary Clinton, b. 1947, about being named after mountaineer Sir Edmund Hillary, who summited Everest in 1953 and was previously a beekeeper whose first major summit was in 1948, to say nothing of the misstatements emitted by her 2016 presidential opponent).[3] Boomer lies are systemic, sociopathic, and an essential mechanism for both the destruction of wealth and the transfer of what remains from younger generations to the Boomers. The result is a socially dysfunctional but highly effective system of pacification founded on pathological misrepresentation, oppression, and sustained failures to act.

Nowhere are the dynamics of deception more pervasive, in government and the private sector, than in the financial arena. The Boomers' reshaping of commerce combined an astonishing tolerance for risk with widespread dishonesty. Every time the system wobbled, the Boomers' solution was more risk and more dishonesty. It would be convenient, perhaps even comforting, to dismiss financial impropriety under the Boomers as just the product of a few bad actors in a perpetually disreputable industry. The evidence does not fully admit such consolations. For decades after World War II, personal probity and a new regulatory framework produced a calmer and more honest system. With the exception of the Savings and Loan crisis (in which some Boomers participated), bubbles and scandals were comparatively few and small.

As the Boomers took greater control of both the public and private sectors, financial scandals grew to a scale never before seen and we now live in an era of permanent financial emergency. It was not just the work of isolated bankers or sloppy regulators. The transformation required the participation of all parts of Boomer society. Take, for example, the issuance of junk mortgages. These loans required consumers to apply for them, often without any reasonable belief they could be serviced; banks to underwrite them; investors to buy them after syndication; watchdogs to look away; auditors to sign off on incredible accounting; a legislature to gut restraining regulation; and a central bank, trapped in the middle, to engage in the expedient facilitation of all of the above. Subprime mortgages were just one part of a financial fractal where the same story repeated endlessly. In reality, the past few decades have not been so much a financial scandal as a social one, with the Boomers playing a leading role.

The Regulated Market: New Deal to Neoliberalism

Between the Depression and the Boomers' neoliberal revolution, finance enjoyed a certain staid respectability. Scarred by the Depression, earlier generations tolerated less risk and deception than the Boomers would. These cultural traits were codified in, and reinforced by, a new regulatory system that demanded reasonable practices, adequate capital, periodic reporting, mandatory insurance to protect customers, and more. Entities like the Federal Deposit Insurance Corporation (FDIC), Securities and Exchange Commission (SEC), and Commodity Futures Trading Commission (CFTC) enforced fairness and order. Both the public and private sectors were helped by the development of generally accepted accounting principles (GAAP) from 1939 to 1973, which allowed investors and regulators to better understand firms' performance.[4] These innovations favored truth over expedience, and objective fact over subjective projection, helping create a more stable financial system out of the chaos that came before.

Another helpful development, often overlooked, was the collection and publication of statistics. As future Justice Brandeis put it, "Publicity is justly commended as a remedy for social and industrial diseases. Sunlight is said to be the best of disinfectants."[5] The financial Lysol was provided by agencies created in the New Deal and reinforced in the 1970s by entities like the Office of Management and Budget (OMB) and the Bureau of Economic Analysis (BEA). Data helped the market to discipline itself and regulators to make more informed judgments.*

Pre-Boomer governments, markets, and consumers demanded a more orderly system, and they largely succeeded in producing one. The system did not prevent occasional panics and financial failures, but securities frauds were limited in scope, bank failures few, and government intervention to save institutions largely unnecessary. Citizens could reasonably question whether finance, circa 1975, was insufficiently imaginative and somewhat overregulated without tossing overboard, as the Boomers would, essential parts of the system.

The revolutionary Boomer temperament, expressing itself though neoliberal doctrine, disdained incrementalism. Old practices were pushed aside, and as the predictable results manifested, the Boomers swept them under the rug through a wholesale campaign of financial deceit. It is not the mere fact that Boomers engaged in widespread financial deception that makes them sociopaths. In the rough-and-tumble 1870s, the Boomers' practices would have been odious, though not completely deviant. By the 1970s, the case was different. Boomer financial culture operated contrary to prevailing mores while evading, watering down, and sometimes gutting the regulatory framework established by their parents. The result has been a scandalous samsara of fraud, abuse, and bailout.

Deceit and Deregulation

The degradation of words and numbers became an essential front in the war of deception. Linguistically, the revealing opprobrium of old-fashioned terms was dispatched; when old wine tasted rank, it was decanted into new

---

* The only comparably significant source created under the Boomers was the Federal Reserve Economic Data collection (FRED) in the mid-1990s, a compilation of data by the Fed banks and other government sources. The Federal Reserve, which sponsors those activities, was itself created in 1913.

and less judgmental bottles. Yesterday's "borrowing" and "debt" became today's "credit" and "leverage," while "speculation" morphed into "investment" and "junk bonds" transitioned into "high-yield securities." "Second mortgages," a term synonymous with improvidence, were sanitized in the 1980s into "home equity lines of credit" and became a fixture of Boomer finances. In the event any of these bets succeeded, levies on gains could be avoided though "tax efficiency," altogether more palatable than old-fashioned "tax evasion."

The unsettling rise of debt and complexity on Wall Street required not just additions to the financial thesaurus, but entirely new entries in the dictionary of deceit. To pacify regulators after the dot-com crash, Wall Street assigned itself "compliance officers" and "risk managers." Their chief purpose, as the financial collapse just a few years later made clear, was neither compliance nor risk mitigation, but the expansion of portfolios to the maximum extent possible under the least plausible conception of laws. To avoid detection, companies adopted "document retention policies" after the 1980s, whose chief effect was just the opposite: the disposal of inconvenient documents as soon as legally permissible. Arthur Andersen, for example, invoked its compliance with Enron's document retention policy as a defense for elimination, via industrial shredder, of inconvenient evidence.[6]

Even before the books were shredded, they were cooked. An especially important innovation was off balance sheet (OBS) accounting. A conventional balance sheet is supposed to show all of an entity's assets and liabilities, with the difference between them being the owners' equity, a sort of net worth. The large and often disastrous liabilities Boomers accumulated tainted traditional balance sheets.* OBS accounting opened a wormhole into an alternative financial universe into which these problems could be dispatched. The term "off balance sheet" did not really exist before 1968 or so, and didn't take off until the 1980s, before enjoying a truly spectacular heyday during the most recent financial fiascoes. The accounting profession

---

* Originally, selected items were kept off balance sheet because they did not directly relate to the value of the company itself, like assets held in trust for a client by a company, with only the client experiencing gains and losses. The difference between on and off balance sheet can be simplified as a distinction between items that are "my problem" (on balance sheet) and items that are "mostly someone else's problem" (off).

adopted newly accommodating standards during the 1990s and 2000s that made OBS accounting particularly attractive. Obviously, one should always be suspicious of a parallel set of books, traditionally the friends of tax cheats and embezzlers. However, the Boomers' affinity with deceit, irony, and magical thinking not only permitted the creation of this financial multiverse, but deemed it an invention worthy of praise.*

As we saw in Chapter 7, the government itself has enormous OBS liabilities, especially relating to entitlements; here's how it accounts for them. Instead of presenting these items on the main balance sheet, the government deposits them in a footnote. For fiscal 2015, the main balance sheet shows $3.2 trillion in assets (of which almost $1 trillion are student loans) offset against $13.2 trillion in public debt, $6.7 trillion in pensions and benefits for federal employees including veterans, and another $1.6 trillion in "other"—for a total negative "net position" of $18.2 trillion.[7] However, pages 138–165 of the government's financial report consist of two notes to the financial statements, which reveal some $41.5 trillion in unfunded additional liabilities relating to entitlements, which themselves contain various notes and external references of their own, a recursive prolixity that would have stopped David Foster Wallace in his tracks.[8] So, the government has a financial net worth of something between negative $18 and negative $60 trillion. The government doesn't exactly hide the problems so much as reclassify them, for the simple reason that Washington would be in breach of major budgeting rules, like the debt ceiling, if it did not brush them under the rug of OBS and other types of accounting. (This is an example of where the "my problem" versus "not my problem" view of OBS accounting is useful—entitlements are "not my problem" for the Boomers because they won't be paying for them.)

The government also does not have the firmest of grips on its liabilities. Partly, a certain haziness about the figures just comes from the understandable difficulties in accounting for the largest, most complicated entity in the

---

* It did not help that after the 1970s, many auditors collected vastly greater consulting fees from their clients than they did audit fees, creating disincentives to probe too deeply into the books of their clients. The auditors spun off their consulting businesses after Enron made such conflicts of interest too obvious to endure, though many audit firms still collect enormous fees for tax and other work only loosely related to, and sometimes in conflict with, the core audit function.

world, especially over a multidecade time frame. Partly, however, the government has not established adequate procedures for self-comprehension. Like corporate financial statements, government books are subject to audit, and those audits come with an opinion about the fairness, integrity, and reasonableness of the books themselves. The comptroller general's audit opinion of the government's fiscal 2015 books does not encourage, as it notes "certain material weaknesses in internal control over financial reporting," including of the $41 trillion in Social Security and Medicare entitlements in the notes, an "ineffective process" for preparing the entire set of financial statements, and the "federal government's inability to account for and reconcile intragovernmental activities and balances," which presumably includes the critical intragovernmental liability of the entitlements trust funds we saw in Chapter 8.[9] These failings "hinder the federal government from having reliable financial information to operate in an efficient and effective manner."[10] The comptroller says that controls have gotten better since 1996—this has been a long-standing problem—but the considerable weaknesses that remain affect by far the majority of the government's liabilities. Any improvement is small consolation: If you were a General Electric shareholder and the auditors said GE's accounting department was out of its depth but slightly less so than before, GE would not be a stock you'd want to hold.

Government accountants are at least trying to be straightforward about OBS and other accounting. The private sector quickly discovered that for those of less noble mien, OBS was a financial septic tank. Nominally an energy firm, Enron was in reality a financial engineering company whose three most senior and culpable leaders were eventually convicted of fraud (all were Boomers), whose parallel sets of books, OBS accounts, and subsidiaries digested any financial inconveniences. *Fortune* named Enron America's "most innovative company" six times between 1996 and 2001. The magazine was correct, just in the wrong way.

Enron's collapse in 2001 should have served as a warning about these practices. Instead, OBS liabilities grew dramatically, spreading to the center of American finance, now totaling many trillions, though it is impossible to calculate (which is part of the point).[11] Of great utility to the practice was the creation of special derivatives—including collateralized debt obligations, swaps, structured products, and so on—that purported to allow the precise division and reallocation of risk for every taste and budget but which in actuality allowed for huge amounts to be wagered against very little capital, through incredibly complex means, on balance sheet and off.

At moderate size, some of these ideas had merit—it's fine to insure against credit losses through swaps or hedge next year's crop delivery by selling futures. After the 1990s, reasonable uses were eclipsed by derivatives' utility in juicing returns through speculation; one need not understand the mechanics of this to appreciate the consequences. A look at the size of the market alone makes it wholly unlikely that any bona fide insurance or hedging was going on. The "notional" size of credit derivatives is larger than world GDP, and while most of these positions are netted against each other and others are unlikely to produce a total loss, there's clearly a significant mismatch. If you ensure a Camry at the value of a Rolls Royce, are you really buying insurance or are you betting that the car gets stolen before your next payment to GEICO is due? If GEICO wrote you that policy, would it be an insurance company or something closer to a speculator?

The financial establishment now dominated by Boomers had to persuade the accounting profession (also dominated by Boomers) to accept the consignment of these derivatives off balance sheet. Accountants, who had only a generation before set the standard for fairness, prudence, and transparency, rolled over.* The collapses of Lehman Brothers and Bear Stearns were both linked to OBS practices and similar practices would have killed AIG, the giant "insurer," had the government not bailed it out.

The private sector, as its proponents trumpet (and in a different context, I'm a fan of the private sector), is an engine for innovation, though under the Boomers inventiveness slid quickly into fraud, helped in substantial part by a sustained deregulatory push. Again, warnings abounded. The first wave of financial deregulation in the late 1970s helped precipitate the savings and loan crisis in the succeeding years. The S&L crisis was not primarily the

---

* Auditors presently do the same with the trillions of profits American companies have stashed, tax free, overseas. All that's required is for auditors to sign off on their own squishy standard that companies have some reasonable plans for investing the cash abroad. Despite the vast accumulation of uninvested cash that would seem to demonstrate that no such plans are in the offing, the auditors cheerfully waive the financials on their way, and the money goes untaxed.

fault of the Boomers, though some Boomers were involved, like Neil Bush, the red dwarf in the ever-dimming Bush galaxy.* The S&Ls, which had just a few years earlier begged for relief from government oppression, were forced to go back to DC and plead for bailouts. The government obliged, and if Boomers did not learn any lessons about undue risk, they deeply appreciated the government's potential to serve as a backstop to speculation.

Even as the S&L disaster unfolded, Boomers began taking over Wall Street, and in financial engineering they found a vocation in which they could exceed their parents, however dismally. The Boomers pioneered new and riskier ways of doing business, whose consequences would make the S&L crisis seem positively demure. The previously modest market for junk bonds exploded, substantially the creation of Boomer Michael Milken of Drexel Burnham. Junk bonds are debt securities that are not "investment grade," with greater risks of default than conventional debt. They are speculative instruments and have their place, but their use expanded well beyond those limits, and not surprisingly, many worked out poorly. Milken was subsequently convicted of securities violations and Drexel went under; repackaged with the more pleasing label of "high-yield debt," junk bonds soldier on today and in mid-2016 were enjoying a bull run.

Wall Street relied heavily on junk bonds to finance leveraged buyouts (LBOs), a process in which companies would be bought, slimmed down, and flipped back laden with debt to the public markets. The great early practitioner of this was KKR, a firm run by two Boomers, Henry Kravis and George Roberts (the first K, Jerome Kohlberg, who was not a Boomer, had resigned over Kravis and Roberts's decision to pursue larger, riskier, and more hostile takeovers). Although a target of criticism during the 1980s—one of their LBOs was the subject of the book *Barbarians at the Gate*—KKR has generally done well by its investors; its numerous and less apt imitators, decidedly less so.

The restructuring of companies became something of a fashion after 1980, helped along by deregulation and a certain amount of fuzzy thinking. The fashionable doctrine of "synergies," which essentially promised something for nothing, became a great enabler for waves of consolidation

---

* One of the directors of Silverado Savings and Loan, Neil was subsequently found to have engaged in various breaches of fiduciary duty and forced to pay a fine.

and recombination. Synergies were the perfect doctrine for the sociopath, combining deceit, avarice, imprudence, and anti-empiricism. The lumbering conglomerates of old failed to understand the right way to combine (true enough); in the new era, synergy-justified mergers would bring only good. Certainly, they could boost overall profits so long as enough costs were cut and workers fired—legitimate enough—but cost-cutting rarely satisfied market expectations, given all the debt and transaction fees involved. With synergies, Boomer financiers explained, new consolidations would not only be leaner, they would be better, more efficient, and (this could only be whispered) closer to monopolies.

It never quite worked out that way, as spectacular failures like the acquisition of venerable Time Warner by upstart America Online and Hewlett-Packard's acquisition of Compaq showed. Nevertheless, just as Boomer Donald Trump parades his business expertise as a political qualification notwithstanding the financial catastrophes at his casinos, so too did the architect of the Compaq deal, Boomer Carly Fiorina. Briefly a presidential candidate, Fiorina glossed over the price shareholders paid for her bad decisions, perhaps remembering only the handsome payout she received on being fired. That was not Fiorina's only scandal at HP; there were also the iffy sales of equipment to an embargoed Iran during her tenure, though perhaps that counts as a "foreign policy credential."[12]

Irregular Regulation

The S&L crisis had been created, in part, by the loosening of regulatory strictures. Even as the hangover from the S&L crisis lingered until the mid-1990s, the Boomer neoliberal machine and its selective memory were busily forgetting the follies of the past while remembering the lessons that mattered. By the 1990s, Congress was firmly in the hands of the Boomers and could be counted on for two things: (1) watering down regulations, and (2) providing bailouts should anything go wrong. If this sounds like the perverted neoliberalism of Chapter 6, that's exactly what it was.

As Boomer power grew, so did the deregulatory spirit, with support from both sides of the aisle. After a modest pause under Bush (Greatest Generation edition), deregulatory fever returned with Boomers Gingrich and Clinton. In 1994—a year before the S&L crisis was finally resolved—a Boomer Congress enacted the Riegle-Neal Interstate Banking and Branching Efficiency Act (RN), essentially abolishing restrictions on bank acquisitions across state lines. RN passed with broad bipartisan support, including from the White House, paving the way for financial industry consolidation over the next twenty years. Now, a bank could grow so long as it did not control more than 10 percent of the nation's deposits—that would be the threshold for "too big to fail."[13] Maybe.

Abstractly, RN was a fine idea; in practice, RN was fraught with moral hazard. Institutions below the 10 percent threshold had *already* been bailed out, like First Pennsylvania and Continental Illinois. The latter was, until the 2000s, one of the most spectacular and controversial bailouts, and Continental was just a baby bank compared to today's monsters. Continental collapsed in 1984 after acquiring bad oil and gas loans (just the sort of asset now plaguing several Boomer-run banks).[14] Continental's salvation taught banks and depositors that they would not really face the sort of market discipline that was a core assumption of the free market theories supposedly driving deregulation. RN catalyzed the Boomers' privatization of gain and socialization of risk.

To make the most of RN, other laws had to be dismantled, like the Glass-Steagall Act (GS). Passed as part of the New Deal, GS restricted banks from engaging in riskier (if potentially more lucrative) activities that were unrelated to their core business. The Federal Reserve opened some questionable loopholes to GS in the 1980s, but the law remained on the books. By 1998—about four years after the government wound up the last of the S&Ls—Citicorp merged with Travelers Insurance to form Citigroup. The combination would have violated what remained of GS, and unless that law were repealed, Citi would have to divest many assets it had just acquired, making the transaction costly and pointless. However, Citi's CEO was confident the Boomer neoliberal establishment would see the light. It did. By 1999, thanks to intense lobbying of Gingrich, Clinton, et al., the law was officially buried, and the head of Citi sported a trophy lauding himself as the "Shatterer of Glass-Steagall" (hopefully not a conscious invocation of Robert Oppenheimer quoting the Bhagavad Gita during the first A-bomb tests).[15]

Under Boomer control, banks were free to grow and undertake increasingly speculative projects unrelated to their banking businesses, though they were often free to leverage "safe" money when making these wagers. Banks were also liberated, from 2004 onward, to take on increasing leverage thanks to the SEC's modification of the net capital rules. The change was requested by banks made bigger and riskier by previous deregulation (one supplicant was Hank Paulson, then at Goldman Sachs and soon to become Treasury secretary, where he arranged a bailout in the same buildings in which the banks had recently begged to be free of Washington). While the media ignored the changes, some banks did not and expanded risk sharply through direct leverage and/or balance-sheet fiddling.[16]

Meanwhile, in the realm of alternative finance, the hedge fund Long Term Capital Management (LTCM) had collapsed in 1998, the victim of large, levered derivative transactions. LTCM, in short, wagered too much backed up by too little, and the wager went the wrong way. Its three masters were Boomers (one of the Canadian variety) and two had won the Nobel Prize for—of all things—a pricing model for derivatives. LTCM's failure almost destabilized the financial sector. Only the then-unprecedented intervention of the Fed and industry leaders contained the fiasco. Undeterred, another Boomer Congress deregulated derivatives in 2000 and the market for these items, often conveniently kept OBS, vastly expanded.[17]

Just before the 2008 crisis, the largest banks were almost all led by Boomers, like Chuck Prince of Citi, Kerry Killinger and Alan Fishman of Washington Mutual (the biggest US bank failure ever), Ken Lewis of Bank of America, Jamie Dimon at JP Morgan Chase, and Lloyd Blankfein at Goldman Sachs, who became CEO after co-Boomer Hank Paulson left for the Treasury in 2006. All expanded their banks, though to what extent and at what risk remained a mystery, certainly to the SEC. SEC chairman Chris Cox, having relaxed capital rules four years earlier, opined as late as 2008 that he had a "good deal of comfort about the capital cushions at these firms," firms like Bear Stearns, which collapsed days after Cox issued his soothing talk.[18] Was Cox out of his depth, lying, or both? We do know, at a minimum, that Cox was a Boomer.

It wasn't as if some people didn't sense the possibility of things going south—Goldman bet against the housing market while peddling the other side of the transactions to its clients, and Chuck Prince of Citi said in 2007 that the credit-fueled boom might end but that "as long as the music is playing, you've got to get up and dance. We're still dancing."[19] Prince's admission came even as the cracks were opening; he was, effectively, drunk at 2:00 a.m. and ordering another round. Although the situation was clearly fragile, banks' quarterly reports chirped optimism.

While the deregulatory push from the 1980s to 2008 had grounds in free market philosophy, the Boomer establishment that had pushed neoliberalism was happy to ask the government for help when convenient. Both Republican George Bush II and Democrat Barack Obama oversaw a titanic bailout. Congress authorized the Troubled Asset Relief Program (TARP), $700 billion to mop up the various toxic assets produced and consumed by the financial sector. Cox, free market deregulator circa 2004, turned statist in 2008 and temporarily banned short selling of 799 different financial stocks.[20] The SEC's press release opined that short bets against financial stocks contributed to "price declines in the securities of financial institutions unrelated to true price valuation."[21] Of course, the whole logic of free market theory is that the market knows best and gets to set its own price. Anyway, the failures of important firms made clear that price declines were hardly "unrelated" to proper valuations. Taken alone, government intervention might have been fine. In light of the free market parade that had preceded, it was just another example of the heads-I-win-tails-you-lose thinking that has prevailed over the past three decades. The 2008 crisis had another odd outcome: Although the size of AIG, Citi, and their peers made them "too big to fail" (and thus the taxpayers' problems), many surviving banks actually got *bigger* in the immediate aftermath, in part due to mergers that the government helped orchestrate, like BofA's acquisition of Merrill Lynch and JP Morgan's purchase of Washington Mutual (or its remains, anyway).

A major problem during recent crises had been the absence of good data. Even as the need for greater understanding became urgent, the resources assigned to regulation and reporting remained wholly insufficient. The growing volume of financial transactions produced nothing like a corresponding increase in the budgets of the primary regulators, and that should have been no surprise. After all, transparency and data are anathema to sociopathic deception and subjectivity.

The Census, the oldest and most basic system of national reporting, has been perhaps the least visible and most important casualty. In 2012, after

133 years and 136 volumes, the Census privatized the majestic *Statistical Abstract of the United States*, for a grand savings of $2.9 million or 0.0001 percent of the 2012 federal budget. In an era where electronic publication makes the *Abstract* nearly costless to provide, citizens must fork over $179 for a private copy.[22] (It's still worth it.) The Census still happens; its full results are just harder to access. (It doesn't help that older data are available only in iffy pdfs or that some spreadsheets are not compatible with recent versions of Excel—which is why so much of the research for this book occurred on an ancient laptop.)

It's not even clear if budgets had kept pace that many agencies still possessed the requisite will to comprehend their subjects. In the more than eighteen months between April 2007, when the SEC relaxed capital requirements and authorized banks to model their own risks, and the late summer of 2008, when the wheels came off, the special office assigned to monitor the results of deregulation completed *zero* investigations (it also had no director).[23] Even though it is clear that neither government nor firms had adequate insight into systemic risk, the trend has been to less transparency and understanding.

The accounting profession's craven accommodations did not make it any easier to understand what was going on. Sometimes the auditors simply committed fraud, as happened when Bernie Madoff's accountants helped his Ponzi scheme. More usually, it took the form of industry opinions that allowed substantial and unwise discretion on the part of financial officers. Older and more conservative standards, like holding assets at book value, gave way to mark-to-market and mark-to-model accounting. The former allowed firms to price their assets at prevailing market prices (fair enough) and received strong support from financial firms when the market was performing well. The latter—well, the industry terminology for mark-to-model was "mark-to-myth." Whatever CFOs and risk officers needed the model to produce, the subjective adjustment of variables would allow.*

---

* The financial industry has routinely resisted standards of duty long adopted by other professions like medicine and law. The CFA Institute, for example, has members that include many financial professionals; it adopted a truly client-oriented code of professional conduct only in 2006. Given what happened later, one can question its efficacy. The Institute was not, by the way, particularly happy about the Department of Labor's

As matters deteriorated between 2006 and 2008, the accounting profession's governing body continued opening loopholes. These effectively allowed many firms to avoid or reclassify losses during times of market stress. In certain cases, including the highly pertinent case of a crash where no orderly market existed to price assets, firms could assign whatever value they deemed appropriate.[24] Given the rise in private transactions not cleared on conventional exchanges, the possibility of "disorderly markets" was not small and neither was the potential for accounting abuse. Taken together with the complexity of the operations of the biggest, most critical banks, that means the system remains to this day at the mercy of sociopathic subjectivity.

It did not help that the Boomers' psychologically formative years came during a time of great prosperity and that their professional lives were characterized by a long and dubious stock market bubble, allowing critical faculties to wither. Boomer optimism allowed for variables in risk models and accounting statements to be adjusted to their most appealing settings, a parallel to the collective Boomer delusion that the stock and housing markets "only go up." Equally unhelpful was the collision of attractive economic theories with an ugly sociological reality. The considerable beauty of free market theory does not apply well, even on its own terms, to irrationality, improvidence, and criminal deception—i.e., Boomer financial behavior.

Thus the inevitable disasters of the past thirty years, which bore enormous consequences, almost all of which have, and will continue, to pass to the young. Older Americans had more stock and deposits at risk than younger Americans, so they benefited considerably more from the bailouts. Those bailouts required borrowing—years of tax cuts, deficits, and the scar tissue of financial crises left government with no cushion—so the debt finance that saved older stockholders and depositors will be a cost passed to the young. And this also explains why Boomers tolerated bailout culture: bailouts benefit here and now, with costs pushed into the future via debt the

---

modifications (finally released in *2016*) upping ethical standards for brokers, financial planners, and insurance agents. The pre-2016 standard fell well short of "fiduciary duty," generally requiring only that clients be offered "suitable" products rather than those in the client's best interest, or free of conflicts of interest, and so on. In a world of rational actors and/or where government backstops didn't exist, the absence of fiduciary standards would be fine—but again, that world doesn't exist.

young must repay. Returning to automobile analogies, the financial system became a rental car paid for under an assumed name using someone else's credit card. The national Rent-a-Dent was treated accordingly.

Any one bailout, tax cut, or similar would have been fine; indeed, orthodox. But it was not "just one"; the crisis was not so much acute as it is ongoing, beginning with the S&L disaster of the mid-1980s and continuing with the LTCM emergency of 1998, the dot-com crash of 2000, and the housing and financial panics of 2008. And yet, over years of Boomer control the response has always been the same: more deregulation, more spending, lower taxes, and no adequate structural reform during the windows of opportunity between scandals.

Despite the quickening tempo of crisis, nothing about Boomer finance changed. Liberated by the constraints of prudence and the evidence of history, the modest deregulation that began under Democrat Jimmy Carter only accelerated. Despite the cautionary tale of collapse and bailout under Republican Ronald Reagan, the strategy of risk and deregulation expanded under Bill Clinton, continued under his fellow Boomer Bush II, and has gone largely uncorrected under Barack Obama. In an act of macroeconomic heterodoxy, in every major case where laissez-faire consistency might have discomfited Wall Street, Washington provided a decidedly statist backstop. The deregulation, risk seeking, and moral hazard transcended party; it wasn't so much ideology, as outlook. And that outlook was sociopathic.

Monetary Manipulation and Generational Expropriation

Stuck in the middle of this freewheeling disaster is the Federal Reserve, which sets monetary policy for the nation. Since 1977, it has been the unhappy duty of the Fed both to promote growth and ensure price stability (the "dual mandate"), while also serving as an important bank regulator.[25] These goals often conflict, given that the Fed can overstimulate the economy by tolerating high inflation or allowing greater leverage. Reconciling these contradictions takes effort, subtlety, and character. However, as the Boomers took over Washington and the Fed, sociopathic thinking elided any contradictions in the dual (or triple) mandate. Sociopathy required everything to go up and right now, whatever the long-term consequences.

Despite its vast legal powers, the Fed enjoys unusual immunity from critical inquiry and comprehensive criticisms tend to be dismissed as fringe theories. Some attacks really are just Gnomes of Zurich nonsense. But some are quite serious, like the claim that the Fed is unduly secretive. Though the Fed's independence is important, the bank has been unduly opaque and resistant to oversight, and we have no good insight into the workings of the nation's most important financial player. Even the semiotics suggest a closeted world of conspiracy; e.g., the Fed's headquarters resemble a Masonic temple. The one time I visited the Fed to meet with Chairman Ben Bernanke, the vast building appeared totally empty (during the height of the 2008 crisis!), and while we were waiting in the boardroom, the chairman appeared unannounced from behind a hidden door. It was like a visit to Oz.

Indeed, Oz and wizardry are how the establishment tends to view the Fed overall, and this may even be how the Fed views itself, which helps nothing. When the Fed does make mistakes, it rarely admits them and only after a suitably sanitizing interlude, as with Bernanke's public dismay at the bank's response to the Great Depression, seven decades after the fact. While the Fed might be entitled to the benefit of the doubt, it should never get the sort of uncritical deference that prevailed from the 1980s to the 2000s, when it was viewed as some sort of economic magician. (Alan Greenspan, Fed chairman from 1987 to 2006, was called the "Maestro," first as a joke, then as a compliment, then sarcastically, and now not at all.) Moreover, because the Fed has a mandate to protect the economy overall and its tools work best in the short term, it tends to protect the largest classes of interests extant at any given time at the expense of the long view. For the past thirty years, that has meant a bias toward protecting the financial well-being of Boomers.

Some argue that the bank is a perpetual bind, trapped between rapacious private enterprise and a slothful Congress, an apologia that manages to be neither compelling nor wholly factual. The Fed can be endlessly inventive when it wants to be, as its responses to the permanent emergency show: quantitative easing and the unprecedented $3.5 trillion expansion of its balance sheet, its recent consideration of negative interest rates, and so on.[26] Though Boomer candidate Sanders, who crusaded on the subject of bank risk, apparently had no idea how a "moral economy" might be achieved, the process is simple enough.[27] The Fed has long held the tools to restrain the banks, both indirectly, by adjusting interest rates, and directly, through adjustment of reserve requirements, restrictive rule making, and limits on leverage. And indeed, it moves these levers regularly, just not to the benefit of all persons, favoring instead the category of asset holders, comprised heavily of Boomers.

Let's examine what happened when the Fed properly exercised even one of its tools, margin requirements. Margin rules limit how much a speculator can borrow to fund securities purchases, helping tamp bubbles. Margin-driven speculation got frequent blame as a cause of the 1929 crash, so between 1945 and 1974, the Fed adjusted margin every few years, from as low as 40 percent in early 1945 to as high as 100 percent in 1946.[28] Since 1974, margin requirements have been left unadjusted, at 50 percent.[29] During the bubble of the 1990s, the economist Robert Shiller argued the Fed should revive margin tools. A "senior economist and adviser" from the Fed's Boston bank disagreed, stating that "the capacity to borrow against securities has also risen as a result of rising stock prices. It is not clear this exposes the financial system to more risk."[30] Such was a Fed economist's view as of September 2000, as the stock market was collapsing.

A tame economy and stock market gave the Fed no good reason to adjust margin rates between 1974 and 1985; since then, it has had plenty of irrational exuberance to contend with, as even Chairman Greenspan acknowledged. And though the chair has been held by a Boomer only since 2006, Boomers colonized the Fed's other offices much earlier. Under their watch, and despite crashes and bubbles and crashes in 1985–1987, 1998–2000, 2006–2008, and 2012–2016 (more on that in a minute), the Fed has still not adjusted margin rates.

The margin requirement may be a particularly well-tailored tool for stocks, but it is only one of the Fed's many bubble-fighting weapons generally. If the Fed wants to restrain banks, it can adjust reserve requirements, interest rates, etc. If it wants to target froth in certain assets, like the housing bubble that grew from 1998 to 2006, it can limit the value it assigns to syndicated mortgages and other similar assets posted as collateral with the bank. Given the enormous deference the Fed enjoys, it could probably prevent or deflate a bubble in any asset simply by announcing its intention of doing so.

However, it's far from clear that the Boomer Fed wants restraint. It has repeatedly skewed toward a permissiveness whose prime beneficiaries are the Boomers. That is especially the case with the stock market, which has been on a long, if uneven, tear. Had economic growth driven stock appreciation, that would be fine, but much of the growth has been due to an expansion of valuations untethered from growth. (The companies participate in the collective delusion by emphasizing pro forma accounting measurements to exclude "unrepresentative"—i.e., unflattering—results, with the gap between pro forma and GAAP standards being its widest in early 2016 since the ominous dates of 2001–2002 and 2008.[31]) Measured by the cyclically adjusted price-to-earnings (P/E) ratio the stock market seems overpriced, rising from a postwar average of ~15 to 44.2 by the end of 1999 (higher even than in 1929), and remaining elevated, notwithstanding the Great Recession, at 26.6 as of the fall of 2016.[32] Statisticians frequently look for mean reversions, the tendency of extreme conditions to return to long-term averages, and a reversion to postwar averages would imply a very steep drop in prices, all else being equal. But all else is *not* equal and a mean reversion is the last thing policymakers desire: Real rates are at rock bottom and this has provided a tailwind to stock valuations. The institution responsible, of course, is the Fed, which is now a prisoner of its own policies, and perversely, the justification for low rates gets better the longer the process drags out.

Valuation changes have generational consequences. Stocks were relatively cheap in the early 1980s, when median Boomers were thirty-somethings buying stocks (cyclically adjusted P/E ratios ran 9 to 12). Stocks are now expensive, as the median Boomer turns sixty-five and begins liquidating. For each successful seller there must, of course, be a buyer, and domestically, the natural buyers are the young. The generational effect is that the Boomers bought low and sold high thanks to accommodating public and private actors (which they controlled). Should P/E ratios revert to historical norms, the generational transfer will be fully realized. Reversion will make it vastly harder for the young to build retirement savings, as any return to normal valuations will create losses in their existing portfolios, putting young savers even further behind. The young can always invest in something other than stocks, but the long-term trend in interest rates limits their options. Since 2008, rates on bank deposits have been near zero. The same thing applies to bond yields, with the additional difficulty that if interest rates should ever rise, the value of existing bond portfolios will fall.* Generationally, then, both sellers and buyers are forced to participate, with the key difference being that in recent years the transactions have taken place at prices far more beneficial to the former.

A similar dynamic has unfolded in the housing market. While the sources like Case-Shiller, the Census, and the Dallas Fed have their own arcane disputes over the exact level of house prices, they generally agree on the direction and magnitude of house-price changes: up, and by a lot. From the 1980s to the mid-1990s, home prices grew roughly in line with the economy. After 1997, when almost all the Boomers who wanted to purchase housing had already done so (the youngest were by then thirty-three and the oldest, fifty-seven), home prices rose dramatically. It's not that growth in the economy or population accelerated suddenly or permanently. The better explanation was government subsidy.

The Boomer-controlled government expanded housing subsidies during the Boomers' prime home-owning years: property tax caps, mortgage interest deductions, tax exemptions on sales, and so on all favored existing and wealthier homeowners. The government also cultivated the sentimental idea of homeownership as a national virtue. So while renting is often a better financial decision, Clinton, Bush II, and so on extolled this peculiar American dream, and consumers came to view home ownership not just as a necessity or luxury consumable, but as a surefire investment, even a kind of entitlement. People bought bigger and more expensive houses, a consumption problem of its own, while rent control, property tax freezes, zoning restrictions, and other inefficient limits favored existing residents. And the banks willingly facilitated, often reducing down payments from the conventional 20 percent to as low as 3.5 percent or even 0 percent—i.e., allowing leverage to increase from 4:1 to 27.6:1, or in the case of zero down, ∞:1. Many banks competed on the ease of approval, forgoing income verification in favor of borrowers' self-reporting.

When bets turned sour, the Fed intervened, to the great benefit of

---

* The exception is if bonds are held to maturity. If the issuer is solvent, the bonds will be paid off at face value. However, relatively few actors can or want to hold bonds to maturity for reasons not worth discussing here.

Boomers. The bank purchased mortgage assets to hold the market together, and by 2016, housing had almost entirely recovered the losses from the period 2007–2012, for reasons again mostly untethered from economic fundamentals.* The Boomers will soon become liquidators of real estate at these conveniently refreshed prices, harvesting substantial cash from credulous new buyers. Worse, the costs of previous home subsidies will be borne by the young, in the form of national debt passed along due to costs of housing tax subsidies and other goodies handed out by the Boomers to the Boomers.

The other gift to the Boomers—especially the oldest Boomers—has been an interest rate environment helpfully aligned with their life cycle. In the mid-1970s, many *real* interest rates were often quite low.[33] As the Boomers were young and accumulating debt, this was extremely helpful; they were all but paid to borrow. Rates spiked from 1980 to 1982 before a sustained decline during the period of Boomer debt accumulation; rates were higher but moving quickly in the right direction, and that was what mattered.[34] At the same time, the economy was growing, albeit in historically unspectacular fashion, making it easier to maintain that debt. Interest rates have fallen since 2008; the difference this time is that the economy is very weak, meaning new debt is not nearly as easy to service as it was during the period of rate declines from the 1980s to 1994. (Another difference between Boomer-then and Millenial-now: In the transition from net borrower to net saver, older generations benefited from meaningful real interest on their cash deposits—a helpful bonus many Millenials, habituated to banks offering 0.5 percent APYs, have never experienced.)

Ultra-low rates pose challenges for all ages, but they have least effect on those with net savings. Should the United States tip into outright deflation, so long as nominal rates are zero or above, the burden of debt will grow in real terms. At the same time, the value of deposits would automatically rise. In the long term, no one wins, but in the short term terms, savers—i.e., older Americans—do the best. Also, as Keynes noted, in the long run we are all dead, and the Boomers sooner than everyone else.

---

* There was a new, independent phenomenon of speculation by foreign investors, though this was limited to high-end real estate primarily on the coasts and was of limited national effect.

A final note on monetary policy: In many ways, the Fed's arsenal of recession-combating tools, including its credibility as an institution, represents an asset. Since 2008, the Fed has been spending down this asset to prop up the economy, especially stocks and houses owned by Boomers. The Fed exhausted its conventional arsenal (interest rate cuts) fairly quickly, forcing it to experiment from 2008 with quantitative easing, purchasing vast amounts of risk assets like mortgage paper for its own account. The risks of inaction were certainly real, though the benefits, while also meaningful, remain hard to quantify and really evaluate. Regardless, the Fed has now used all of its good tools, leaving less to fight whatever comes next. (At the same time, the bubble-fighting tool kit, as we have seen, went essentially untouched during the Boomer era.) In the event of another crisis in the medium-term, the next step is aggressive and unprecedented: setting nominal interest rates at less than zero. Japan and parts of Europe have begun this experiment, and initial results do not encourage. So, like the Army, the Fed has been depleted by Boomer improvidence, leaving future generations without good means to combat the next and inevitable recession. Obviously, the working young will suffer the most. The Boomers, meanwhile, are embarking on the long cruise of a tax-subsidized retirement.

CHAPTER TWELVE

THE BRIEF TRIUMPH OF LONG RETIREMENT

When the end of the world comes, I want
to be living in retirement.
—Karl Kraus

A long and pleasant retirement is both a historical curiosity and a financial improbability. Until relatively recently, only the rich could retire. Everyone else simply worked until the arrival of disabling infirmity and then waited for the gruesome end; that was it. Life offered too few productive years and economies too little growth to prepare for a lengthy retirement. The only assets vouchsafing infirmity were nonfinancial: children, who could take care of parents in dotage and disability. Unfortunately, that medieval dynamic has become depressingly current. The giant mass of Boomers has just begun to retire and because too many of them are unprepared for the future, their children will bear the consequences.

Retirement planners assume clients need about 75 percent of preretirement income to live comfortably; it's probably more, given the rise in medical costs and that, five to six years after retirement, both average and median households actually spend 83 to more than 86 percent of pre-retirement income.[1] On a cash-savings basis, a fifteen-year retirement after a forty-year career therefore entails annual savings of over 25 percent of income, almost quadruple the Boomer-era savings rate of roughly 6.6 percent.[2] Low personal saving must be compensated for by a combination of government/family subsidy, and strong returns on non-cash investments. That's the kernel of the retirement problem and suggests to the antisocial what levers to manipulate.

From the 1860s to the 1970s, fast growth in economy, population, productivity, and the introduction of public and private programs created the possibility of mass middle-class retirement for the first time. But like everything in life, retirement is contingent. Given how long and expensive old age has become, unless people are willing to save more, work longer, or encourage faster population growth through either bigger families or immigration, mass retirement will be difficult to sustain without some uncomfortable trade-offs. The absence of any of these changes in recent years means that while almost everything about retirement has changed over the past century, one essential thing has not: the dependence of the old on the young. It's just that today, youthful contributions are now heavily intermediated/mandated by state and private plans. Ideally, redistributionist policies as large as America's present old-age benefits (OABs) programs should involve some degree of informed consent on the part of those bearing the costs. This has not happened, because Boomer sociopaths do not want to risk an honest dialogue.

Every year of inaction—and there have now been many—makes the retirement problem more expensive and difficult. That much is beyond dispute. It is also mostly beyond dispute that these programs will continue more or less intact for another quarter century, as substantial majorities of all important groups, young and old, Republicans and Democrats, want to keep the system as is, and it is financially plausible to do so for two more decades (just). So we can dispense with theoretical arguments about whether OAB programs are economically efficient or inefficient, corrupting or humanitarian, in favor of the reality that OAB programs will persist for years.

How many years? Without reform, no one—not even the trustees of the systems themselves—believes that scheduled benefits programs can be maintained much beyond 2034–2037, i.e., just as the median Boomers die off. In the meantime, older Boomers have begun collecting benefits and the entire generation will be on the dole by 2028–2034, at which point it will be infeasible to cut Boomers' benefits. The Boomers' OAB maneuvers are as well-timed as they are deliberate. The result is that every generation born after the Boomers will bear disproportionate costs, while most of the Boomers and their parents harvest disproportionate gains. There is still time to rescue the system and the United States has the means to do it, but we only have about a decade before the choices become very painful.

Private Improvidence

The apocalyptic figure often cited is that half of Americans have no retirement savings; that's roughly correct, though these sorts of headline-grabbing calculations usually exclude important items like pensions, Social Security, and the fact that many households are young and do not yet need to save aggressively.[3] Nevertheless, private savings are crucial, so let's begin there. The situation is dismal. Perhaps 30 percent of middle-aged households will have sufficient private resources to retire without major lifestyle changes (precisely the sort of sacrifice many middle-class Boomers should, but are unwilling, to make). The other 70 percent will not, with Boomer improvidence as a chief explanation. Since the 1970s, the national savings rate has been on a downward trend, falling even as the very large Boomer generation entered its prime working years and should have been pushing the rate up.[4] Despite a modest (and probably transient) rebound after various crises, savings as a percent of disposable income ran just under 5 percent from 1996 to 2016, when Boomers were 44–64, in their prime working years, and should have been aggressive savers.[5] (It's difficult to do cohort analysis of savings, but the signs point the same way.) Contrast this to the period 1950–1985, when America's savings rate approached 10 percent (even when pensions were in better shape), or to Germany and Sweden today, which have both more generous pension schemes and higher savings rates (about 9.5 percent and 15.2 percent respectively).*,[6]

---

* There are some methodological differences discussed in the endnotes, and while they are important, they tend to make the American comparison substantially *less*, not *more*, favorable.

Modern Americans have not been serious about retirement planning. People spend more time planning annual holidays than planning the permanent holiday of retirement.[7] If the argument on the free market side has been that private citizens will take care of themselves, everything in this chapter is strong evidence to the contrary, at least as it pertains to the Boomers.* Franklin Roosevelt, just before Social Security was enacted, expressed "hop[e]" that "repeated promises of private investment and private initiative [might] relieve the Government in the immediate future of much of the burden it has assumed" via his welfare programs.[8] FDR might have feared nothing but fear itself. Then again, he never knew the Boomers.

The government has intervened and will continue to do so. Indeed, even free marketers may concede that the government has an obligation to do so, by implicitly authorizing a lower savings rate in exchange for the promise of Social Security. (The counterargument is that for years, the savings rate was higher despite the existence of old-age programs; the rate fell as Boomers entered the workforce.) In any event, the bottom half simply cannot retire without outside assistance: The poorest 20 percent have a negative household net worth, and the next 20 percent don't have enough personal savings to last a year at the poverty line. Adjusting for age—i.e., looking at the wealth of the cohorts closest to retirement—improves the picture somewhat, but not nearly enough.

The number of poor might be surprising, but the parlous condition of the middle class is what really shocks. On an income basis, we already know that "middle class" is no more than a statistical artifact. The same is true on a wealth basis. Median household net worth was just $79,901 in 2013 (essentially no change from $79,212 in 1992), maybe two to three years of self-funded retirement spending, a shortfall even households distant from

---

* As everyone involved in these debates gets accused of bias, let me just state mine for the record. Although I will shortly argue for heavy government intervention as a practical necessity, as a theoretical matter, I'd prefer to rely on the free market. But this is not 1776 or 1935; we cannot start anew, we can only deal with the facts we have.

retirement cannot really hope to close.* Subtracting housing wealth makes things even bleaker (retirees have to live somewhere), slicing off no less than 30 percent from net worths.[†,9] In other words, despite giant bubbles in stocks and housing, modest economic growth, largely free education, and some historically unique advantages bestowed on the Boomers by their predecessors, sociopathic improvidence leaves many Boomers in an all-too-familiar position. Like the delusional Blanche du Bois, legions of Boomers will depend on the kindness of strangers—indeed, strangers they have economically abused.

Nevertheless, many Boomers did stockpile ill-gotten gains and the wealth of older households is notably higher than that of younger households (and thus higher than the median), though few of them have saved enough to retire without major adjustments to living standards. But that is as much a function of expectations about how the "golden years" should be lived as it is of actual wealth. Older households have been getting wealthier at about the same pace as the top 5 percent of Americans generally, as we will see in Chapter 15. Someone has to pay, and the old and the rich have the most to contribute, even if the price is a less comfortable retirement. The alternative is heavy and indefinite borrowing, the growing possibility of fiscal crisis, and the certain exacerbation of generational inequity.

---

* A quick resolution of a paradox: How do Americans have any meaningful net worth at all? The answer is asset appreciation, in homes, stocks, etc. The value of speculative assets has often, however, evaporated at inconvenient times, for example, in 2008, when the first Boomers began to retire. Thus, I've presented both savings rate and household net worth. The difference between the two shows just how dependent Americans are on the various asset bubbles the Fed is increasingly desperate to maintain.

† The housing wealth of older Americans is a highly uncertain retirement asset for other reasons. Many seniors take out second mortgages, reverse mortgages, and other debt that reduce their home equity; indeed, the government even established a program to help seniors do this. The problem will get worse given that Boomers will be selling their homes roughly simultaneously, to say nothing of the negative effects of higher mortgage rates or property tax reforms, should those ever come to pass. By facilitating reverse mortgages, the government has again used the credit of younger taxpayers to subsidize the elderly.

The False Friend of Pensions

Pensions will help, and these the Boomers have (mostly) earned, though they provide less comfort than many might assume. First, a quick review, because pensions will be personally unfamiliar to most readers under fifty. The proportion of workers participating in pensions had been falling from no later than the 1970s, and from 1980 to 2008 declined from 38 percent to 20 percent overall, and is almost certainly lower today; however, Social Security Administration (SSA) models show about half of *Boomers*, many of whom started working before the shift, holding some form of classic pension benefits.[10] "Classic pensions," to clarify, are defined-benefit pensions, with payouts fixed in advanced and the provider bearing most of the financial risk; i.e., they're real pensions. Many public sector workers like firefighters and teachers still have such pensions. In the private sector, classic pensions have gone the way of the dinosaurs, replaced by defined-contribution systems, where the employee pays in a fixed amount and bears most of the risk (e.g., 401(k)s, Employee Stock Ownership Plans—query whether these are pensions at all). In either case, pensions either mandate or motivate savings, reducing the direct burden on the state (though the state bears an indirect burden through tax subsidy). That's the theory. The reality is that so long as society refuses to tolerate gross poverty among the elderly, should pensions of any type fail, society bears the final risk, paid for by taxes on its wealthier members (of all ages) and on its working members (overwhelmingly younger).

Unfortunately, because most pension plans have not collected adequate contributions from older beneficiaries, they depend on an increasing flow of new workers into the system and very high rates of return on invested assets, assumptions that have been problematic for years. If pensions are not exactly a Ponzi scheme, neither are they well managed. Private pensions are badly underfunded—in 2012, there was a $355 billion shortfall for just the companies in the S&P 500.[11] Public pensions cover vastly more workers and have correspondingly bigger problems. The most optimistic estimates come, not surprisingly, from the association of public pension administrators, who even at the acme of self-service admit about $1 trillion in shortfalls; the most pessimistic academic estimates pegged underfunding at $1–3.74 trillion, with $2.66 trillion as a probable estimate, and that number will likely grow.[12] As it turns out, the academics were the Cassandras of retirement: In fall 2016, it was revealed that California's public pensions maintained two sets of books, one with the official, high-return figures and a second with grimmer calculations based on the same sorts of assumptions underlying the academic analyses.[13]

As pensions fail, the oldest will almost certainly be paid first, leaving little or nothing left over for younger beneficiaries. Given where we are, that represents another generational transfer to the Boomers. The Teamsters' Central States Pension Fund provides an early example of the systemic crisis to come. Central States had been (supposedly, only) $8 billion in the hole in 2013 and discovered just two years later that it was actually $52.3 billion short, thanks to a combination of new accounting and a long-overdue encounter with reality. For Central States to have any chance of surviving long term, benefits had to be slashed—math left no other option—and Central States submitted a plan for reducing benefits. Dozens of congressmen, offering the usual incantations of "middle class" and "seniors," objected. In May 2016, the Treasury refused the Fund's benefits revision plan for reasons both sensible and otherwise, and as the parties dicker over how best to rearrange the deck chairs on the *Titanic*, the crisis grows.[14] Absent an overhaul, Central States will be exhausted around 2026, with Boomer pensioners continuing to collect benefits at patently ridiculous rates until the grisly end.

Surely, you might protest, society must have insured against such catastrophe. It has, sort of. Classic pensions have been insured since 1974 by the Pension Benefit Guaranty Corporation (PBGC). It's just that PBGC itself is more a source of liability than comfort, with no less than $60 billion and possibly more than $230 billion in unfunded future liabilities.[15] Those are PBGC's figures per its 2015 report, and they are almost certainly too optimistic, given the crisis in PBGC's insured funds. (As PBGC puts it, "Barring changes, neither [insurance] program will be able to fully satisfy PBGC's long-term obligations...the risk of multiemployer program insolvency rises rapidly, exceeding 50 percent in 2025 and reaching 90 percent by 2032"— there are those magical years again.[16])

To be fair (and cruelly accurate), it's unlikely that PBGC itself has any idea what the real range of its liabilities might be. Outside auditors concluded the Corporation has "material weaknesses" and "significant deficiencies" in its practices and internal controls, and this has been the case for some time.[17] Neither political party has addressed the problem, and the only major reform of PBGC recently may have made matters worse, allowing for some dubious accounting while sweeping away important protections. Again, it's impossible to know—PBGC's books and management are a mess.

Still, when the inevitable crisis arrives, it will be through the Host of the PBGC that liabilities are transubstantiated into intergenerational welfare. With tens of millions of (older, Boomerish) Americans enrolled in pensions, it's improbable that the government will let pensions wholly collapse, any more than it was willing to let major banks fail in 2008. To the extent PBGC does not effect salvation itself, subsidies will flow automatically through new welfare transfers, as pension failures push seniors below poverty limits. Because the Boomers were the last generation to have significant private pensions, any form of subsidy will tend to operate as a generational transfer, even though it was the Boomers, who in their roles as executives and government officials, oversaw pension mismanagement in the first place. As the crisis deepens, so will the favoritism.

Antisocial Security

All OAB programs struggle for the simple reason that they never received enough funding in the first place. FDR may have hoped Social Security would be self-sustaining and perhaps eventually redundant, but this has not happened, and not enough money has been allocated to cope with that reality.[18] Therefore, the essential task is to convince younger people to continue supporting their elders while presenting a subsidy as the earned return of enforced savings. Accordingly, all OABs have been subject to sustained campaigns of deceit and misinformation, from all political corners—the Right, which claims government programs are bankrupt (not true, yet); the Left, which claims programs are equitable (not in generational terms); and various interest groups espousing all manner of self-interested fixes like privatization. The unifying theme, however, has been to keep the system going at minimal present cost until the Boomers die.

Although precise calculations are complex, any numerate person can understand how these plans work generally, and who the winners and losers are in the shell game. All pension-like plans depend on a few key inputs— the longevity and number of participants, inflation in cost of benefits, interest rates and the rate of return on investments, and the number of payers. The variable the actuaries cannot (and in some cases, are forbidden to) forecast are political changes. In our model, which assumes sociopathy, we simply twirl the political dial to mendacity, a setting that produces outputs coincident with the Boomers' interests and that are supported by the evidence.

Turning to the inputs, the good news is that people are living longer. While a lot of life-expectancy gains have been driven by lower infant mortality, people who make it to sixty-five can expect to live another 19.2 years, up from about 16.8 years in 1982.[19] The problem is not that the actuaries didn't predict these improvements, it's that citizens didn't adjust their savings or retirement expectations. Despite living longer, people now retire slightly earlier. The average retirement age for men has fallen by one year from 1970–71 through 2011, and combined with increased longevity, the period of retirement has extended by a third, from 13.6 to 18 years.*[20] Bluntly, that's too long.

To maintain living standards, the median household would want about $800,000 in private, nonhousing assets on retirement.[21] Median households have something like 10 percent or less of that amount, and even though older households have higher net worths, they too face a large gap that even the rosiest assumptions about pensions, welfare transfers, and stock market returns cannot close. Most studies conclude that about half of households are materially underprepared for retirement, and surveys show that only 17–25 percent of workers are very confident in their retirement planning versus 35 percent who aren't confident (the rest either being "somewhat" confident or not knowing or refusing to answer).[22]

---

* The data on women is less robust due to their lower labor force participation in earlier decades; it has been rising, but they still retire slightly earlier than men (62 versus 64 in 2011) and, being longer lived, their retirements are even more extended.

Moreover, any major illness could exhaust private savings, and even for the reasonably healthy, old age will also be exceedingly expensive, driven by the generally rapid rise in health-care prices. Since the period 1982–1984, health-care costs have more than quadrupled in gross terms and have been rising faster than inflation overall.[23] Medical inflation has slowed over the past few years because of involuntary sequestration and Obamacare's mandated prices, which over the long term will be roughly as effective as ordering the earth to stand still. The Medicare Trustees accordingly believe Obamacare's price fiats "are uncertain," will "probably not be viable indefinitely," with their actuaries being blunter, saying the price limits have a "strong possibility" of "not be[ing] viable in the long range," and the government's overall auditor says the same thing.[24] Why? Because medicine is in large part a service business, and service businesses are hard to make more productive, especially without the R&D the Boomers have assiduously defunded. The best one can reasonably hope for is that inflation in health care falls into line with inflation overall. Until then, health care will take an ever larger fraction of GDP, on an absolute basis and per capita basis, with graying Boomers consuming the most.

Two other price-related variables require discussion, the rate of general inflation and the return on investments. For certain pensions with fixed payouts, the higher the rate of inflation, the lower the "present value" cost of that stream of benefits. Many aging economies, including the United States, have experienced extremely low levels of general inflation since 2008. Even so, many pensions and other benefits programs assume much higher levels of inflation than we have seen or can reasonably expect, and this tends to artificially depress the size of their liabilities.* (Should the United States experience outright deflation, liabilities could increase in real terms.) At the same time, retirement plans forecast strong rates of return on their assets. The assumed returns of many pensions, especially state pensions, are quite high—on the order of 7–8 percent annually, a combination of their higher inflation expectations (which is at least internally consistent, if factually unreasonable) and, more substantially, unadulterated fantasy. In the end, the exact interplay between inflation, returns, and so on doesn't matter. What does is this: Are pensions going to get an 8 percent total return or not?

---

* Especially if there are gaps between discount rates and cost-of-living adjustments.

In prior decades, pensions' estimates were not wildly different from market returns; but this is not the glorious past, it is the diminished present, and the potential for a significant mismatch between assumed and likely returns has been evident since at least 2000. Given a prudent portfolio and the probable overvaluation of stocks in 2016, expecting 7.6–8 percent annual returns is too sanguine; indeed, the Treasury said the failing Central State's 7.5 percent return assumptions were "unduly rosy."[25] Given the mix of cash (present return: depressed) and stocks, pension plans need their equity portfolios to produce something over 8–12 percent annual gains which, as Warren Buffett once pointed out, would imply something truly spectacular about the value of the markets in the future. Compounding at 10 percent would have the S&P 500 around 240,000 fifty years hence.* You may recall that in 1999, just before the crash, a book called *Dow 36,000* predicted a golden age for stocks. It was, of course, utterly wrong—but far less wrong than the pensions' implicit forecast: Dow 2,000,000 by 2066.

Recently, some public pension funds have reduced their expectations somewhat—by about 0.5 percent gross (i.e., to 7.5 percent or so)—which concedes the problem of lower returns without doing anything meaningful.[26] Nor do they want to, as doing so would trigger immediate lawsuits, receiverships, and above all, inconvenient reform that the ostensible fiduciaries of these funds want to avoid. Nor is much political relief, in the form of sanctioned benefit cuts, likely. Just as Central State does, so other pensions will: They will pay Boomers until the money runs out. At that point, no return, however astronomical, will make a difference for younger pension members.

Generational Shifting: Social Security and Medicare

Because so many seniors do not have sufficient private savings to sustain retirement, the task falls to the government. The two chief programs are Social Security and Medicare, both operating under a permanent cloud of misperception and misinformation. Senior entitlements seem dull and

---

* The S&P's annualized returns, assuming all dividends were reinvested, were under 5 percent from 2000 to 2015, and for much of 2000 to 2010, they were actually negative. Only the extraordinary rise after 2009 dragged returns into significantly positive territory, and that depended on huge federal interventions that cannot be repeated—i.e., a bubble.

complicated, but they are too important to ignore and, anyway, it can be unhelpful to focus overmuch on the operational details. If anything, considering the programs in the financial aggregate—which is the way busy legislators must view them—is the best way to understand these programs. You don't have to know much about the reimbursement forms for prescriptions to understand that the prescription drug benefit is exceedingly expensive overall.

Again, there's no legal entitlement to entitlements. Interestingly, "entitlement" was formerly a term of abuse, a comparison to the psychological entitlement conservatives saw in young Boomers. Today, outside of the far Right, "entitlement" has been leached of negative connotations and the public has become confused, developing a sense of proprietorship over these benefits. As the Social Security Administration admits, "There has been a temptation throughout the program's history for some people to suppose that their FICA payroll taxes entitle them to a benefit in a legal, contractual sense."[27] That is collective (perhaps collectivist?) delusion, a fact the Supreme Court made abundantly clear way back in 1960, in *Fleming v. Nestor*, when it denied Social Security benefits to a deported communist.[28] Still, even Congress gets muddled, sometimes saying that people do have a right to these funds, as it seems to have in a 2014 CRS report.[29] The Social Security Act itself makes things perfectly clear, though. It permits Congress to "alter, amend or repeal any provision of this Act."[30] Entitlements can be modified at any time, and have been—and this is important, because they will need to be again.

Paying It Backward

The confusion over entitlement—i.e., between earned asset versus welfare/intergenerational gift—had limited import before the 1970s. Since then, the size, failings, and consequences of OAB programs have grown dramatically. OAB taxes, meanwhile, have become a crucial part of the federal take; they are the only taxes that escaped permanent cuts. It helps that many payers chose to believe that OAB contributions are not really "taxes" so much as a sort of deposit into a personal account to be refunded with interest. The

government has reconciled itself to this misapprehension, as it usefully paci-
fies taxpayers into not asking too many questions about where FICA taxes
are going or who is paying for what. The success of this policy of confusion can be seen in the statistic showing more than 40 percent of Americans
receiving Social Security and/or Medicare benefits in 2008 (i.e., the Boomers
and older) did not believe they had used a "government social program";
presumably they think these OABs are somehow private property.[31] Even
the Right, whose collective antennae are normally sensitive to the workings
of big government, seem confused: Many Tea Partiers believe entitlements
are a kind of earned right, or at least that they are "deserving" of them.[32] As
we'll see, except for the richest, entitlements are welfare, both factually and
legally.

As an accounting matter, entitlements must be welfare for the simple
reason that most older Americans extract more money from the system
than they paid in. The overage is not an entitlement; it is a handout, paid
for mostly by other generations. Per the Urban Institute, a medium-income
two-earner couple born in 1955 taking retirement in 2020 could expect
$1.15 million in benefits offset by just $728,000 in payroll taxes (in real dollar terms), a payout of 1.53:1.*,[33] Obviously, the extra money has to come
from somewhere, and it's easy enough to trace. Any excess return can only
be interest or a gift; as it turns out, it's interest *as* a gift. The reason is that
interest (the .53 of 1.53:1) is paid out of general revenues, and general revenues derive disproportionately from taxes on the rich: The top tier subsidizes the retirement of everyone else, especially medical care. Were it the
case that people understood that dynamic and had knowingly voted for
it, that would be one thing. But clearly, the whole theatre of the doughty
middle-class taxpayer making prudential deposits into Social Security and
Medicare renders that idea absurd.

---

* Experts can reasonably quibble about discount rates and assumptions, disclosed in
the endnotes and cited material, *but the whole political point of entitlements is to serve as
a subsidy to most beneficiaries*, so there should be nothing surprising about payouts of
more than 1:1 for Boomers. The generation preceding the Boomers got off the best, with
those born in 1915 getting a nearly 3:1 payout, e.g., but they are dead or nearly so, and in
terms of remedies, that moots the discussion.

Increasingly, subsidies will flow not just from the rich to the less rich, but from the young to the old. We can see this in shifting payouts for people born after the Boom. In theory, a sixty-five-year-old couple retiring in the 2030s—i.e., the first of the post-Boomer cohorts—will receive Social Security and Medicare (SSM) benefits at a ratio of 1.62:1, basically the same payout as the middle Boomers. However, that's only while the Trust Funds have a positive balance, which of course, the various Trustees admit they will not by the 2030s. When the Funds run out, Social Security benefits will automatically fall 16–27 percent; it's also possible for Medicare to experience a version of this.[34] Automatic reductions would reduce the payout 1.25:1 or so. For average workers born after 1975, the ratio will probably be significantly worse than that. Benefits will be cut and payroll taxes increased, driving realistic payout ratios down toward 1:1 or less. The SSA views these changes as inevitable and models them for years after the Trust Funds run out. While SSA still calculates a positive return for younger workers, its projections are low, enough to question whether returns will be truly positive at all for post-Boomers, if politicians delay action (as they have for thirty-plus years).[35] Either way, the net effect will probably be a greater subsidy from the young to the old.

Even before the Trust Funds expire, the OAB system effects transfers between groups. High-earning single males who retire today have already paid more in taxes than they can expect to collect in benefits. If rich, old men don't seem sympathetic, consider also that men generally, along with African Americans and the plain unlucky, also implicitly subsidize other members of the system. These groups tend to live long enough to pay into the system but die relatively soon into the collection phase, notably sooner than, e.g., white women, so there is already redistribution. As life expectancies between men, women, blacks, and whites converge, subsidies will then flow overwhelmingly to the old, from the rich and from the young.

We do not have to wait until the Trust Funds fail before intergenerational dynamics become important. In 2010, Social Security tipped into "cash flow deficit," as the first wave of Boomers began retiring en masse; the recession didn't help, either. The shortfalls were made up by nonpayroll taxes (in the form of interest payments), not many of which are paid by Social

Security recipients who are, for obvious reasons, basically retired.* So far, the redemptions have been small, but over time they will become exceedingly large. If it continues in present form, Social Security will in the 2030s look like Medicare does today, receiving heavy subsidies from general revenues (instead of from the notional Trust Fund).[36] Income taxes will therefore be increasingly spent, not on roads, schools, and science (all underfunded as it is), but simply to keep OAB benefits flowing to Boomers.

Welfare: Good for the Geezers, Bad for the Gander

Before we take up potential fixes, it's worth looking at conventional welfare, i.e., welfare for the nonelderly poor. Even as the Boomers were preserving welfare for seniors, they were eroding welfare for everyone else. This Boomer stratagem is especially rich, given that welfare was itself largely created by Social Security, which is not just a program for the old. Social Security also delivers substantial assistance to the disabled and to children, if a working parent suffers disability or death. These programs are less fraught than programs for seniors and we can leave them to the specialists. Only one fact need detain us. In 1992, Bill Clinton campaigned to "end welfare as we know it." Doing so required gutting Aid to Families with Dependent Children (AFDC), a creation of the Social Security laws. In 1996, Clinton succeeded in replacing AFDC with something much less generous. (Therefore, when Boomers argue that Social Security is "untouchable" and an inviolable social bond, they forget their own record.) Neoliberal magic promised Clinton's reform would induce the slothful masses to get jobs—though of course many were genuinely unable for reasons of disability, lack of education, and, after 2001 and 2008, poor job markets. Two senior Clinton officials resigned

---

* Because politicians have been less than candid about how Social Security works, here's a recap: (1) the "assets" of the Trust Funds are just an accounting entry, so (2) when the "assets" are redeemed, the government has to come up with the cash somehow, and it does so by (3) collecting current taxes and debiting the Trust Fund by the same amount. Those taxes are payroll and income taxes, which means they are paid mostly by working Americans, a category that largely excludes retired Americans collecting OABs.

in protest. A major gutting of benefits, therefore, happened under the first Boomer president, a Democrat.

The campaign against welfare had been long underway, especially after Ronald Reagan fixated on the case of Linda Taylor, a fur-wearing, Cadillac-driving convicted criminal whose bizarre life certainly included multiple welfare frauds and possibly stretched to murder, kidnapping, and bigamy.[37] Taylor became in the popular imagination a "welfare queen," a slothful sovereign suckling at the welfare teat and eventually, a synecdoche for all (non-senior) welfare recipients. Of course, Social Security has had its own share of senior fraud and abuse: double-dipping schemes, dead spouses collecting checks, etc., but every president after Reagan has expressed an undying affection for senior benefits even as Republicans and Democrats have cut welfare to other groups. The ax was swung at the young and the poor, not Boomers.

Social Security Fixes

This is not America's first entitlements crisis. In 1983, various factors combined to nearly exhaust the Social Security Trust Fund. Benefits were subsequently reined in through adjustments to inflation-indexing and by taxing benefits to higher earners. In 1983, when no Boomer was a senior, it was fine to cut senior benefits. However, it was clear in 1983 that benefits adjustments would have to be accompanied by changes to the retirement age. Because this *did* impact the Boomers, adjustments to retirement age were carefully tailored to engage in generational favoritism. For workers born before 1938, the age of full eligibility would remain at sixty-five. Fair enough; these workers were already getting on. For the core Boomers, it would rise by just one year—much less reasonable, as they had decades to adjust. For only the very youngest Boomers, and all of every subsequent generation, retirement age would rise to sixty-seven. Meanwhile, payroll taxes went up, but only enough to help Boomers and their parents (a buy-off, but something of a moral offset).

When new reforms come, they will not look like those of 1983. Boomers will resist any changes to their benefits. They can, and will, endorse changes to retirement age and FICA taxes—after all, these will fall almost entirely on younger groups and will be of no consequence to the Boomers themselves. So the generational inequities, already significant, will deepen.

As I wrote this chapter, the 2015 book *Get What's Yours: The Secrets to Maxing Out Your Social Security* had been a substantial best-seller. Imagine if the topic were not the sacred heifer of the senior set, but tips for maxing out food stamps or tax shelters. All three are welfare, but any best-seller treating the latter two would have seniors burning down the nearest public housing project before trundling downtown, on Medicare-funded scooters, to blow up Goldman Sachs.[38] Undaunted by hypocrisy or fact, *Get What's Yours* blithely argues that Social Security is for "nearly every one of you who's ever earned a paycheck and wants every Social Security benefit dollar to which you are entitled—entitled because you paid for it. You've earned it."[39] Not at all, but shame has been excised from the Boomer dictionary, which is what allows the authors of *Get What's Yours* to maintain that benefits "can even be yours if you never contributed a penny to the system but have or had a spouse, living or dead, who did."[40] That's true and not entirely unfair, but the book devolves, going from "you've earned it" to "get what you can." The latter category even includes "playing Social Security's marital status game."[41] It's not clear if the book is some kind of metajoke. Whatever it is, the book does acknowledge the long-term funding crisis and blithely consigns these problems to the young. The back cover shrugs its shoulders, saying, "However Social Security's long-term finances are addressed, you deserve to get what you paid for."[42] The "and more" is implied; the "you," obvious.

In a society where *Get What's Yours* is a hit, it seems deeply unlikely that Boomer seniors will accept a repeat of 1983's reforms. The Trust Fund will just deplete, after which benefits will be cut automatically, and for the Boomers, that's fine. By 2034, the median Boomer will be eighty-two and, per the actuaries, dead. Therefore, cuts will fall purely on people born after 1952. However, by 2034, every single Boomer will already be collecting, and it's doubtful that Congress will allow cuts to those already on the rolls. So the likely course is no meaningful change to Boomer benefits, larger cuts for everyone younger, with the additional insult that taxes for the working young will rise, even as their wages remain flat. (At that point, Social Security will be Central States recapitulated at national scale.) Yet young people, despite having low confidence that they will receive OABs, overwhelmingly support these programs, in empathetic counterpoint to their elders, who view benefits with unjustified proprietorship and self-interest.

The Generational Burden

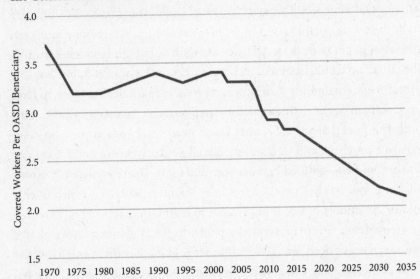

What's going on here? This chart compares the number of workers paying into the entitlements system as a multiple of those people taking money out of it. Figures after 2015 are based on the SSA's "intermediate" estimates. As the Boomers age and lower fertility and other factors reduce growth in the pool of younger workers, the burden the old place on the young will grow—and you can already see the inflection point around 2008–2010, as the Great Recession began and as waves of Boomers started collecting Social Security. Unless the economy and youth incomes grow rapidly, transfers to old people will represent a much larger fraction of taxes paid by the post-Boomers than they ever did for the Boomers.[43]

Leaving aside the political challenge, fixing Social Security requires only modest fiscal adjustments. Let's dispense, however, with the neoliberal fantasy of privatization. It's conceptually attractive, but the citizenry shows no inclination to save enough on its own and—knowing the government will be there in the end—workers will feel free to take undue risks with their private savings. Privatization works only if we are willing to let seniors suffer the consequences of their improvidence; we don't seem to be. Instead, there is merely a theatre of reform. The most newsworthy reform in recent years was forbidding benefits to ex-Nazis in 2014; well and good, but of limited budgetary effect.[44]

What would work now is what worked in 1983: a combination of cuts and taxes. Reducing the generosity of inflation indexing would solve at least half the problem. Tacking on an additional ~3–4 percent gross to the 15.3 percent payroll tax would, by itself, solve the whole problem—if done today. (Raising the tax cap would also help.) An extra 3–4 percent is not, as some on the Left like to present it, all that small—as the Right reminds us, it's a 20+ percent relative increase in payroll taxes. But it's far from catastrophic. The longer we wait, the higher the figures become, not least because the future taxpayer base will shrink. The ratio of workers to retirees has already shrunk from 3.4:1 in 2000 to 2.8:1 in 2014; by 2030, it will be 2.2:1.[*,45]

Medicare Maybes

If Social Security has relatively easy fixes, Medicare does not. Medicare is today where Social Security will be in the 2030s; Medicare's Trust Funds are exceedingly small, leaving the program dependent on general revenues. Most of Medicare's problems are the same as Social Security's, with two additions. The first is that the cost of medical care has generally outstripped the pace of inflation, and so consumes an ever larger fraction of the economy. The second set is that old people, like old cars, get more expensive to maintain even as their productive lives diminish, and seniors remain committed to consuming as much health care as they want.

After the early 1970s, there were few comprehensive changes to Medicare coverage. However, in 2003, the first Right-leaning government since 1955 to concurrently control the Presidency, the House, and the Senate suddenly added prescription drug coverage to Medicare, just in time for the Boomers to benefit. Medicare Part D was the largest new program since Medicare's establishment and came from a deeply unlikely source. This alone should raise suspicions about what was buying off whom. Seniors, a group now including the older Boomers, started collecting drug benefits

---

*You may see different "dependency ratios" in the media, many more alarming than what I present. However, for our analysis, the proper measure is not the total dependent population (which includes dependent children), but the ratio of seniors to workers in the system.

without having paid in for it, so almost the entire cost of Medicare Part D will be borne by younger generations. We still need more time to assess the program—the long crisis post-2008 skews the data—but costs were originally estimated at "$407 billion for fiscal years 2004 to 2013" (it ended up being $474.6 billion), estimated to rise to over $100 billion *annually* by 2017, or roughly doubling the previous run rate, and then another rough doubling from there by 2024.[46] The fact that the government, the most powerful buyer of medications in the world, was forbidden under the legislation from negotiating discounts with drugmakers doesn't help. Already, we've seen price spikes as new drugs are introduced; the sticker price for Gilead's hepatitis C therapy is $94,500.[47]

Hep-C provides an interesting case study. In 2014, 75 percent of those infected in the United States were born between 1945 and 1965 (i.e., Boomers). New York's acting health commissioner urged the Boomers specifically to get tested, entirely understandable in light of the pungent gloss offered by New York Presbyterian's head of liver transplants: "The typical patient is a baby boomer born between 1945 and 1965 who may have experimented with drugs when they were in college years ago."[48]

So, expensive treatment, and mostly for the Boomers. Gilead does offer the government a discount; not all drugmakers do or have to. Discount or not, hep-C treatment is so expensive and pervasive that the Medicare Trustees attributed budget overruns in 2014 to the therapy, one whose primary beneficiaries appear to be Boomers who partied too hard in their youths.[49] Medicare covers any number of expensive medications consumed by Boomers, and, in the case of tax-advantaged plans, can even end up subsidizing Viagra. There is something decidedly off-putting about indebting GenXers to pay for their fathers' erections.

Whether or not public medical costs are driven by private improvidence, any attempt to interpose reason gets ugly. Boomers of all parties melt down over the same basic issue—rationing—whether costumed as "death panels," inequity, whatever. Of course, in a finite world *all* resources are rationed. Perhaps if the Boomers had subsidized medical education, there would be more and cheaper gerontologists; if they had generously funded the National Institutes of Health, better medicines; if their neoliberal doctrine had permitted negotiations with drug companies, cheaper therapies. But they did not. Anyway, *Medicare itself is rationing*, one that discriminates based on age—over sixty-five, the government will help, under sixty-five and nondisabled, your ration is usually zero.[50]

What kind of medical care should the public provide to seniors and others? Already, 5 percent of health-care users consume almost 50 percent of health-care resources, and a plurality of these are poor or elderly—i.e., beneficiaries of public programs.[51] The public is entitled to ask whether (a) it wants to spend this money, or (b) the money can be better spent improving the welfare of a vastly broader and more productive population. But a tedious combination of sentimentalism, anti-empiricism, and self-interest prevents this dialogue. The standard diatribe is that government is killing Grandma. Actually, God and/or nature are killing Grandma, as are some of her life choices. So let's start with that.*

Other major nations more explicitly ration care, as in Britain. America certainly does not want to reproduce the National Health Service wholesale, just adopt some of its better cost-management practices. Thanks to NHS rationing, Britain's medical costs are notably lower than America's. It also helps that Britons, Germans, Australians, etc. are in better shape than their American counterparts (as were prior generations of Americans).[52] And we are, in any event, on the verge of expanding the rationing that already exists. Clinton- and Obama-era policies depressed physician reimbursements, predictably leading to an ever-growing body of doctors who refuse to take Medicare. Having fewer Medicare doctors automatically rations care by making it less available.

There are many worthwhile proposals for reform, but the size of the problem defies incremental solutions. It would be convenient if curbing Medicare fraud and abuse were enough and, given the sociopathic nature of the cohorts now entering Medicare's embrace, it will become a more urgent

---

* Heaven forfend the (unlikely) possibility that cryonics should work—would we then be obligated to freeze the elderly, to defrost and cure them at public expense circa 2200? That's the reductio ad absurdum of the "death panel" crowd, pioneered by Boomer Governor Sarah Palin, who envisioned a world of bureaucrats dispensing life and death on the basis of godless administrative whim.

task. This might save 10 percent of the budget, at most. The larger questions are about waste (which includes a serious conversation about rationing) and funding (which entails higher payroll taxes). There are, of course, some principles to address, such as whether we have a genuine commitment to public health. We may discover we don't. Once upon a time, even the American Medical Association opposed public medical care.[53]

Just how expensive will Medicare become? The average beneficiary's medical costs were $12,432 in 2015 against median income for seniors of $22,887 for individuals and $38,515 for heads of households.[54] Given income and effective tax rates, for the average recipient all of Medicare is a gift on a current basis; everything else, roads, army, EPA, etc., are lagniappes. By 2024, $12,432 will bloat to at least $18,822.[55] As for the total cost, no one really knows, and the government itself is not wholly honest about these issues. The unfunded liabilities of the hospital insurance portion of Medicare alone are at least $3 trillion.[56] If that amount were deposited today—a sum not far from the entire federal tax take in 2014 and one that the Medicare Trustees rather demurely term "sizable"—the program might be in long-term "financial balance."[57]

Nevertheless, existing estimates of a multi-trillion shortfall across all Medicare programs depend in part on an unlikely deceleration in costs; higher taxes, lower benefits, or coverage shortfalls seem inevitable. Both the Trustees and the actuaries assigned to review their reports harbor skepticism that the slowdown in cost growth from 2010 to 2014 can be sustained or that physician reimbursements will be sufficient to attract doctors to provide services. Over time, the gap between what Medicare pays physicians and what private insurance pays may widen from 30 percent to 60+ percent, at which time a majority of Medicare providers would incur huge losses on Medicare patients and will, presumably, stop taking them.[58] Rationing exists, and it will grow.

Here's where some trickery creeps in. While it is "conceivable" that the medical industry can improve enough to keep costs at Medicare's baseline assumptions, doing so would be "unprecedented" and "very challenging and uncertain" (Medicare's own words).[59] In other words, it won't happen. The Medicare overlords assumed in their 2014 baseline scenario that Congress will have to override current cost controls. An alternative projection commissioned by the Trustees agrees that projections under current law are "clearly unrealistic."[60] Under alternative assumptions, if Medicare providers do no better than providers overall, costs will grow 30–50 percent higher over the long term. The more realistic alternative scenario starts showing major divergence around—and this should come as no surprise—2030 and getting worse after that. The Trustees don't believe Congress, the independent panel doesn't entirely believe the Trustees, the comptroller general doesn't believe anyone and throws its hands up in despair, with the only consensus being that the whole system is projected to start falling apart right as the Baby Boomers pass from the scene.

Think tanks regularly produce any number of dire statistics—the dramatic reduction in the number of young workers supporting retirees, OABs' share of the economy (doubling or more over time), the fact that uncorrected entitlements will eventually consume the bulk of the federal budget. Just as these figures contain a kernel of truth, they also contain a certain disingenuousness. Yes, Medicare will probably consume almost a tenth of GDP in fifty years, but GDP will hopefully be larger and the number of old people larger, too—that's the natural progression of things. No losses in quality of life are implied *if* economic growth is rapid enough.

Even if growth continues to be slow, the United States can afford to subsidize basic OAB benefits indefinitely if it chooses, though at major cost to other priorities. The question is whether doing so is fair. Voters have not been presented with clear and honest data about the costs, and the beneficiaries of this obfuscation are those who will be collecting until the crisis can no longer be kept hidden. Those people are the Boomers and their parents. OABs are not enshrined in the Constitution; they can be changed, but we have not had the dialogue appropriate to programs on which a huge portion of the population depends and that consumes an ever-growing fraction of the budget. This is not 1935 or even 1965. The Boomers had every possible advantage, while contributing considerably less than they could have to a retirement they view as their right. Whether we continue to provide Boomers with benefits depends on whether we believe they deserve them, and this is a far more urgent discussion than the usual parade of distractions offered during election seasons.

The Center for Retirement Research at Boston College estimates that about half of working Americans risk material reductions in quality of life during retirement, a figure rising "substantially" from 1992's modest numbers to today's alarming ones, for Americans fifty-one to sixty-one (i.e., for the Boomers).[61] The Center's estimates do not fully account for any of the catastrophes lurking in the pension system, stock and housing markets, or the other crises that have accumulated during Boomer tenure, and the "conventional" (i.e., sunny) scenarios the Center presents can depend, rather darkly, on seniors taking out reverse mortgages to subsidize their retirements. And still, despite the forced smile, the Center still shows huge swaths of America in the hole. The problem has not been economic growth, because though the economy has failed to live up to its potential, it has grown, and the value of housing and stocks has risen even faster. The Boomers had more than enough tailwind and time to prepare for retirement. They chose not to, and they have not been honest with themselves or with the population they govern. While Boomers retain power, they will do their utmost to ensure that the consequences of their improvidence are borne by anyone other than those really responsible. And so the Boomers will leave us with a titanic entitlements crisis. It is not the only existential crisis to unfold under the Boomers.

CHAPTER THIRTEEN

PREPARING FOR THE FUTURE

Decisions are made on the spur of the moment,
without forethought and without consideration
for the consequences to self or others.

A failure to plan ahead....
—DSM-V[1]

For 350 years, from the time colonists arrived on the East Coast until the mid-1970s, America prepared for a grand future. How would New York better the original York, New England exceed an aging Albion, the New World surpass the etiolated Old? Aboard the Puritan ship *Arabella*, John Winthrop exhorted his flock to build a shining "city upon a hill," a reference to the Gospels of Luke and John (and much quoted by politicians). This New Jerusalem, Winthrop preached, would require of his shipmates sacrifice, saving, and mutual assistance (details politicians now omit).[2] If freedom required revolution, prosperity demanded land grant colleges, and liberty necessitated civil war, these would be done. At the American beginning, all projects were long-term projects. If some present profit came of it, well and good. But the real rewards always lay ahead, salvation in the next life and prosperity for future generations.

America largely fulfilled Winthrop's wish, at least until Boomers installed themselves as the Herods of the New Jerusalem. The city on the hill has, under the Boomers, picked up hints of the favela; the end date for salvation set not at eternity, but the 2030s. Any investment that cannot be fully recouped by then must be forgone. Unfortunately, the nation faces a number of challenges, some potentially existential, not amenable to the antisocial mentality and its time line. But posterity is not in charge, the Boomers are, and inaction prevails on the long-term projects of environment, technological progress, and education. America has slipped from visionary leadership to indifference and occasional obstructionism, with costs to be, inevitably, passed along.

It's Not Easy Being Green

It's almost impossible for anyone under thirty-five to imagine a time when the United States was an international leader on environmental matters, much less that it achieved this status under Republican administrations, even when economic and political costs were significant. Nevertheless, that was the case, once upon a time. In the past, environmentalism was sometimes forward thinking, and at other times, a response to imminent catastrophe. Overall, motivations were generally good and so were the results.

It was only during Boomer hegemony that American policy became recklessly indifferent to threats that are simultaneously more dangerous and, paradoxically, that we have vastly greater resources to confront. Those who argue that climate change, the major existential threat of our time, cannot be tackled by a national system prone to partisanship, indifference, and inability to wrangle multilateral solutions ignore a long and successful history of American environmental leadership in equally difficult circumstances.

Environmentalism became a national concern during the Industrial Revolution, when aesthetic and other considerations drove Americans to preserve some of the natural grandeur on which civilization was rapidly encroaching. By 1872, the Grant administration had designated Yellowstone the nation's first national park. It took Canada thirteen years to follow, and Europe about thirty more; the situations have reversed, and the American government is now usually in the rearguard.

Neoliberal fantasy notwithstanding, environmental protection has always been and always will be a mostly government project. Private citizens make necessary contributions, but environment is a public good that only state power can effectively preserve, and the state was formerly vigorous about this. Grant's fellow Republican, Teddy Roosevelt, expanded the National Forest system, eventually protecting some 230 million acres in total (the modern United States covers about 2.3 billion acres).[3] Democrat Woodrow Wilson signed legislation formalizing the National Park system. These were positive, inventive, and international examples and even in a vast and thinly populated country, they represented a sacrifice for a nation obsessed with industrialization and expanding frontiers.

As environmental problems changed—parks were not going to be enough—the modern environmental movement took shape. In 1948, Donora, Pennsylvania, was afflicted by a toxic smog, and citizens demanded action. In the 1950s, Congress passed the Pollution Control Act to begin study of these problems, with regulation delegated to the states. Devolution didn't work (though neoliberals and their allied "federalists" remain committed to that failed experiment) and in 1963, Washington largely federalized the issue by passing the Clean Air Act (CAA), which was substantially expanded and supplemented in 1967, 1970, 1977, and 1990.[4] A companion bill to the 1970 amendment created the Environmental Protection Agency—its original patron was none other than Richard Nixon, and its first and arguably most successful administrator, the establishment Republican William Ruckelshaus (b. 1932). Before 1991, environmental bills were generally passed with bipartisan support and were signed into law by presidents as ideologically diverse as Eisenhower, Johnson, Nixon, Carter, and Bush I. Businesses predictably foamed at the mouth before falling into line, sometimes even lobbying for federal legislation, if only to avoid a welter of competing state laws that led to conflicting regulation and compliance nightmares.

However, as Boomer power grew, bipartisan environmental consensus has become one of the few endangered species that could not be brought back from the brink. As the Boomers became Washington's most lethal invasive species, environmentalism waned. The CAA has not been meaningfully amended in twenty-seven years.[5] That has made it ever more important to expand the effective remit of existing agencies to cover new threats. A unanimous pre-Boomer Supreme Court had done just that, requiring broad deference to the EPA and other agencies in their enforcement and interpretation of existing laws—so-called *Chevron* deference, after the relevant case *Chevron USA v. NRDC*; *Auer v. Robbins* is another famous and related case for the legally inclined.[6] Deference was not, of course, congruent with Boomer anti-elitism, anti-empiricism, or antisocial personality disorder, and Boomer litigants and Justices have been trying to undermine *Chevron* and *Auer*, removing environmental issues from the realm of bureaucratic expertise to that of political expedience.[*,7]

What accounted for earlier achievements? Certainly, the absence of Boomer power helped, but former success did not come simply because it was easy. In the early years of the environmental movement, the United States was more dependent on heavy industry than it is now. And the United States of 1960 was neither as rich nor technologically advanced as it is today, making the costs of environmental regulation proportionately higher. It is true that conventional pollution then was more tangible to voters than invisible and incremental warming is now. The Cuyahoga River in Ohio repeatedly burst into flames due to industrial pollution, for example, which proved hard to ignore. Nevertheless, the CAA regulated both visible and invisible pollution, at considerable cost to living taxpayers (having been passed before the era of unrestrained intergenerational reshuffling via debt). The older generations paid up and cleaned up, even when legislation might never have direct or obvious benefits for those footing the bill. For example, the Endangered Species Act of 1973 (ESA) protected wildlife most Americans had never seen and—even when species are returned to healthier levels (as with the California condor)—remain unlikely to see.

All that changed in the 1970s, as Boomers began arriving on the environmental scene, led by Al Gore, Jr.—not in Gore's later role as enviro-evangelist, but in his original form as pork-barreling scenery wrecker. The stage was

---

* One of the landmark rollbacks of *Chevron* and EPA power was argued for by former liberal lion and Boomer Laurence Tribe on behalf of a coal company. Tribe also defended GE in an environmental case. Tribe, by the way, had been reprimanded by Harvard for plagiarism and also served as counsel to environmental hypocrite Al Gore, whom we shall soon encounter.

the Tellico Dam and the *dramatis pices*, the snail darter, a fish protected by the new ESA. The dam would be good politics, but it required special exemption from the ESA. Maneuvering around a displeased, pre-Boomer Court, Congressman Gore stepped in and saved the dam (plus another questionable dam, and a breeder reactor).*[8] Should one have expected different from a Boomer whose father engaged in a complicated three-way transaction that ultimately left land (acquired from a church) in the hands of Gore Jr., with extraction royalties paid to Gore Jr. at a suspiciously favorable price by oilman Armand Hammer (who had provided slush money to Nixon and campaign funds to Gore)?[9] Or that Boomer Gore derived income from transactions whose origins were linked to Hammer's carbon-spewing coal and gas empire and also received royalties from some environmentally questionable zinc mining?[10] Gore Jr.'s legacy embodies the environmental policy of the Boomers—expedience and hypocrisy—even as he now crusades (via inefficient private jet to and from his massive, energy-sucking mansion, greened up after 2007 with some solar panels and efficient lightbulbs) against climate change, which Gore helpfully reminds us is the great challenge of our time.[11]

Gore is correct that global warming is a serious challenge. It is also a problem compounded by Boomers like Gore. America's failure to confront warming is a product of unrestrained consumerism, the anti-empirical and hysterical rhetoric of the Boomer Right, and the unreconstructed, antitechnological Boomer Left, and endlessly confounded by a bipartisan machine that resists sacrifice—namely, Boomer sociopathy. Whether the young, especially those in developing countries, live somewhat better or dramatically worse lives depends in substantial part on whether America ever takes the lead on global warming.

First, a word on the science, for it is controversial, and much of the controversy derives from the Boomers' curious habits of mind. Let's quickly lay

---

* Besides a certain hypocrisy, Gore ticked off a few other boxes in the standard Boomer sociopathic inventory: marital collapse, a minor financial scandal, certain economies with the truth, etc. Unlike his running mate Clinton, he did not avoid the draft—he served for about six months, near the war's end, mostly out of harm's way. The reasons for his volunteering were dubious: He donned the uniform in large part to assist his father's reelection campaign.

to rest the basics—humans can and do contribute to dangerous warming. Yes, the world's climate has always fluctuated and indeed, some scientists (though not the majority, as some on the Right have implied) actually worried about global cooling in the mid-1970s. Nevertheless, it had been understood since the nineteenth century, thanks to Joseph Fourier, John Tyndall, and Svante Arrhenius, that humanity's reliance on fossil fuels could eventually warm the environment. (They even showed that without existing greenhouse gases, the Sun wouldn't provide enough energy to keep the Earth above freezing.) What they could not agree on were the consequences of further emissions. Arrhenius thought more warmth might be good (as Elizabeth Kolbert pointed out, Arrhenius lived in Sweden, which might account for his enthusiasm for warmth). Others harbored reservations; Alexander Graham Bell worried about an "unchecked greenhouse effect" as early as 1917. Still, even as the West industrialized, humanity's effects remained modest—per capita energy consumption was low and world population about a quarter of what it is today. The rigorous science also lay ahead. Environmentalists cite Arrhenius's remarkably accurate predictions of temperature change, but there was nothing like a scientific consensus in the nineteenth century, and the alternatives to fossil fuels remained highly limited. Less coal-fired industrialization in 1900 meant mass poverty, disease, and a shocking level of backwardness, weighed against the (then) modest and speculative consequences of warming. The basic principles, however, remained, and all that was required was continued emissions before climate became a real and quantifiable issue.

By the 1970s, three switches flipped. First, total energy use greatly increased, per capita and in total (two billion people having been added to the world population). Second, viable alternatives to fossil fuels had emerged. Finally, the problem itself had become clear. The first international body to study warming was not the famous Intergovernmental Panel on Climate Change (IPCC), established in 1988. The first was the 1979 World Climate Program, convened partly at the behest of the Carter administration; Congress had also begun looking into the issue around the same time.[12] It took seven years from the establishment of the clean air research panel in 1955 until the passage of the first major air quality legislation, so one might have hoped for climate action by, say 1986—a date which unfortunately coincided with a surge in Boomer political power. Nothing as significant as CAA was undertaken in 1986, though CAA was occasionally revised until the Boomers completely controlled government. Inaction prevailed even as the scientific consensus became nearly universal and increasingly dire: Humans *do* affect climate, with consequences including warming, famine, flooding, rising and acidifying oceans, and so on.[13] In essence, the consequences are serious, and we will shortly approach the point of no return if real efforts aren't made. Unfortunately, the point of no return is toward the end of Boomer lifetimes and the consequences will start arriving—you can already guess the dates—between the 2030s and the 2050s.*[14] Millennials will not be eager to retire to Florida.[15]

Of the many impediments to climate reform in the United States, two stand out. First, many Boomers do not believe that global warming exists or, even if it does, that it poses a real problem, another example of the generation's anti-empirical bias explored in Chapter 5. In 2014–2015, less than half of Boomers believed that humans were causing the planet to warm—48 percent among younger Boomers, 31 percent among older Boomers and the shrinking set of their elders.[16] By contrast, 60 percent of those eighteen to twenty-nine believed in anthropogenic climate change, a major difference, though still depressingly short of the 82–97+ percent of scientists who hold that view.[17] Consistent with their (self-serving) climate beliefs, Boomers and their elders have more favorable views about fossil fuels than younger Americans.[18] The influence of the Boomer+ cohort means that overall, the United States is roughly split on climate change, and given the bias toward the status quo, little action can be expected in the near term.[19]

---

* Like all scientists, those of the IPCC are careful in their phrasing and analysis, with politics probably driving them to obscure the implications of their work—they're really only comfortable predicting bad things around 2081, when their employers will be safely dead. But irreversibility and consequences will probably much come sooner, as the IPCC labors to imply without too much impolitic specificity; the endnotes provide references to more explicit discussions of climate impacts. Dangerous levels/effects could be reached by the 2030s–40s and catastrophic levels/effects by the 2060s–2070s, within the lives of many reading today. New York would feel like Bahrain and Bahrain would be functionally uninhabitable.

This leads to the second problem: To avoid problems in the future, expenses will have to be borne today. Only 21 percent of people over fifty (largely Boomers) are "very concerned" that climate change will affect them, and in this, they are largely correct.[20] By contrast, there is a 100 percent chance that reforms today will have costs that affect Boomers. For sociopaths, the timing mismatch makes climate reform a nonstarter. Boomer views about the science of climate change may be divorced from reality, but their other views are narrowly rational and consistent. They are just not empathetic or forward thinking.

Unsurprisingly, there has been no major progress on climate change. US emissions rose throughout the Boomer years until the recession of 2008, and after a modest decline, they have begun rising again. While emissions are still, as of this writing, lower than they were in 2008, they are also still unsustainably high. That the only absolute reduction of US emissions came as a result of a major recession hardly constitutes progress.[21]

Bad as the emissions statistics are, they somewhat understate American climate impact. While emissions growth from US tailpipes and smokestacks has decelerated (though not nearly enough), the United States emits in other ways, chiefly by importing goods from nations that emit quite a bit to produce those consumer necessities. Emissions by America's Asian suppliers have grown rapidly, with the net result that America imports cars and smartphones and effectively exports pollution. Adding the "embodied carbon" of imports adds meaningfully to American emissions, on the order of at least 9 percent and possibly substantially higher—it may seem modest, but against plans to cut emissions 26 to 38 percent, it is a relatively large target.[22]

It also does not help that the United States has again become something of a petrostate. Decades ago, the US was the largest producer of oil in the world, then the Saudis temporarily took that title, and now, thanks to fracking and other developments, the US is again the largest producer of oil and equivalents (e.g., natural gas, coal-derived synthetics).[23] Including nonconventional production, as of 2014, America's daily extraction pace exceeded Saudi Arabia by 20.6 percent, and the nation produced more than Iran, Iraq, Kuwait, the United Arab Emirates, and Oman combined.[24] The US has long sent huge amounts of coal abroad, and thanks to recent laws—signed by none other than President Obama—oil producers can export other fossil fuels; the first tankers sailed in 2015.*,25 One should be careful not to double-count embedded carbon and exported fossil fuels, but the precise accounting is less important than the general dynamic, which is that the United States is both a profligate consumer and producer, and that has been a choice.

The sins of the oil industry are easy enough to appreciate, but they have been abetted by the mistakes of the environmentalist movement, led by the oldest Boomers and their immediate seniors. In the 1960s and 1970s, parts of the movement cried wolf about the world's ability to feed itself, the dangers of nuclear power, and resource scarcity generally. None of these arguments had much scientific credibility, and essentially all of them have proved wrong. (Whole Earth Catalog founder Stewart Brand, once a prominent antinuclear activist, has now reversed his stand; too little, too late.) The enviro–Chicken Littleism of the 1960s has been dredged up by warming deniers as evidence that scientists and environmentalists cannot be trusted. That is, of course, untrue. Real scientists can be trusted; Boomer ideologues of the 1970s and 2010s cannot. Such is the price of rampant anti-empiricism.

The Boomer machine has not even bothered to extend fairly painless programs previously enacted. During the 1970s oil crises, Washington quickly imposed car efficiency legislation. The CAFE standards became effective in 1978, requiring 18 mpg for passenger cars; by 1983, just as Boomers took over the electorate, CAFE demanded improvements of 44.4 percent, to 26 mpg, peaking at 27.5 mpg in 1985.[26] Though CAFE had its origins in self-serving immediacy, it continued demanding improvements even as gas prices fell. CAFE worked, and it could have continued. But between 1986 and 2010, the prime years of Boomer hegemony, which included Al Gore's notionally environmentalist tenure as VP, CAFE standards did not improve on 1985. Only in 2011 did standards rise, by a paltry 9.8 percent, to 30.2 mpg (i.e., nothing compared to the giant gains of CAFE's early years, making the Reagan years seem a veritable ecotopia in this regard).[27] Future goals set in Obama's second term are more ambitious, and it certainly helped that young

---

* The bans were imposed when the United States was "running out" of oil in the 1970s.

people care more while older people approaching retirement care less, but new CAFE standards do nothing that would compensate for a quarter century of lost opportunity—had CAFE kept up, America would be demanding 64–120 mpg today, considerably better than a 2016 Prius gets.[28]

It also does not help that consumers blithely purchase "Zero Emission Vehicles," which any thinking person should quickly realize means nothing more than "zero emission *at tailpipe*," since the energy has to come from somewhere. Although power plants, especially gas and nuclear facilities, are greener than gasoline engines, there is no such thing as a truly zero emissions vehicle—they just outsource pollution to a plant, just as the United States outsources factory emissions to China.

So the Boomers leave us a challenge. To avoid a temperature rise of 2°C, above which scientists voice concerns about severe consequences, humans can emit at most ~1,000 gigatons of CO_2 equivalent; this is the "carbon budget."[29] Budgets, as we saw in the chapters on deficit and retirement, are not a Boomer forte. More than half the carbon budget has been spent, and without change, the rest will be exhausted over the next three decades (i.e., roughly coincident with Boomer disappearance). What happens then is up for debate; it will range from somewhat bad to outright terrible. The defense community already ranks climate change and the conflicts it will provoke as an "urgent and growing threat to our national security," a "present security threat, not strictly a long-term risk," to be managed by the Boomer-depleted military.[30] It is not only chaos abroad that concerns; American naval bases are already at significant risk of flooding.

Pessimists argue we can achieve nothing without the help of the developing economies and Boomer politicians have used this as an excuse for inaction. China surpassed the United States as the largest greenhouse gas emitter around 2007.[31] India and the rest of the developed world are also heavy polluters. China's number one rank is based on *total* emissions from its 1.3 billion people; China emits fairly little per capita. The developing world has a long way to go to match American per capita emissions, and that is part of the problem. Rising emissions in the developing world have long been a challenge, but had the United States acted vigorously, emissions might not have been as bad. The United States had the power, after all—it was buying so many of the goods produced by China's smoky industries.

America has exercised trade levers to get what it wants in other areas; could Boomers not have done the same with emissions?

For decades, the United States has made no serious efforts to wrangle a compromise. In 1998, the Clinton administration signed the Kyoto Protocol, which bound parties to curb emissions, but it was an empty, costless gesture (like Gore's environmentalism) because the Senate, which has treaty ratification powers, had voted 95–0 against Kyoto the year before.[32] The ostensible justification: potential harm to the US economy, potential benefits to developing nations. Europe, which did sign, did not plunge into a recession because of Kyoto, so the harm argument was, while not implausible, still shaky; it also wasn't as if the Clinton administration could not have wrangled some multilateral compromise by early 1998. After that, of course, Clinton's infidelities made him a lame duck.

As it happens, the defense community, which has been busily wringing its hands over the security implications of climate change from the mid-2000s, has recently been overseen by Boomer Chuck Hagel, who in his prior Senate life cosponsored the bill scotching Kyoto. Hagel became a keen if ineffective advocate for more defense spending, part of which will doubtless go to dealing with problems deriving from Hagel's own actions in 1997.[33] And what time frame do national security experts use to assess climate change? Why, now until 2030—the end of Boomer history. Until 2030, impacts are estimated to be modest; after, who knows and who cares?[34]

While China, India, and others present problems, the United States has been able to force multilateral solutions when it cares to, even in periods of Boomer influence (though not in periods where Boomers were in complete control). That was the case with ozone-depleting chemicals, restricted by the Montreal Protocol in 1989, the acid-rain regulations in the 1980s (negotiated under Republican administrations), and in some ways, even the CAFE standards, which applied to domestic and imported cars. Each required corralling various nations, interest groups, and businesses; each happened reasonably quickly after the problems were identified as serious; each has been a substantial success. What accounts for the difference? Smog, scenic despoliation, and skin cancer—the consequences of inaction on acid rain, ozone, etc.—would be borne immediately by the Boomers. And significantly, until 1992, non-Boomers still had the White House and some influence in

Congress. Bush I, an exemplar of self-sacrificing decency (a concept now as dead as the dodo), corralled the Senate into ratifying his signature of the Rio accord, a predecessor to Kyoto—it was not much of an agreement, but the best the United States managed for a quarter century afterward.[35] Could not the vastly popular Clinton have done the same, at a time when the economy was doing better and the threat more obvious? Could he not have drummed up a single vote? By 1998, of course, the old guard had long since been swept away, and Boomers did nothing.

Paths Forward

Although the time to avoid some kind of man-made climate change—and the potentially enormous financial and human consequences of it—has probably passed (as will the costs, to future generations, naturally), the worst can be mitigated. We already have the models, including cap-and-trade pioneered under the Montreal Protocol, and outright restrictions, practiced in the United States on some airborne pollution and in Europe for many chemicals. Certainly, China and India must be included, and have some willingness to participate, as the 2015 talks at Copenhagen showed, though as an agreement without much legal force, Copenhagen is no better than the Rio accords. Late in his final year, Obama reached an accord with China on the Paris protocols, but its demands are too modest and mostly unenforceable, and they can be undone by a future president because Obama did not send the agreement to the Senate for ratification, opting instead for reversible executive action and creating the possibility for protracted litigation. At least the Paris talks opened the door, and the United States has the means to truly force itself and other nations through it, though it should have done so years ago.* Given the recent election, this is unlikely.

In the meantime, the United States should resume its work on alternative

---

* In the second half of 2016, the Obama administration took a meaningful step to reduce hydrofluorocarbons (HFCs), a major climate hazard, but was only able to do so because HFCs fell into the language of the Montreal Protocol agreed to before Boomers controlled Congress—a Congress that would not, in present Boomer form, have consented to a new treaty on HFCs. The burden of the HFC switch will, naturally, fall onto future generations; the Boomers already have their HFC-equipped air-conditioners.

sources of energy, including the nuclear effort so badly stymied by 1970s Boomer hysteria over the perceived dangers of nuclear power. There is no denying that there was an accident at Three Mile Island (TMI) in 1979. It was bad, but not that bad—less costly in lives and treasure than the *Valdez* and *Deepwater Horizon* accidents. The United States has never seen anything like TMI in the almost forty years since, despite operating dozens of nuclear plants.[36] And while people debate whether TMI caused any excess cancer deaths, what cannot be debated is that the numbers were so small that they remain hard to detect. Compare that to thousands of people who collectively die in mining and drilling accidents, and from black lung and the by-products of conventional power, numbers both considerable and undeniable. Unfortunately, TMI coincided with the release of the disaster flick *The China Syndrome*, and the televisual Boomers conflated movie with reality, with the result that we have a China Syndrome of an entirely different type: Asian factories belching pollution to produce wares for Sam's Club.

After TMI, sentimentalism largely halted new nuclear undertakings. The potential of nuclear is evident in the fact that, construction halts notwithstanding, American nuclear facilities produce about a fifth of the nation's electricity, at functionally zero ongoing carbon cost.* We could do much more. France derives 76.3 percent of its electricity from nuclear stations at virtually zero carbon cost, for example, and while it has plans to reduce its dependence on nuclear, it will still generate vast amounts of near-emissionless power.[37] And nuclear technology and management have gotten much better since TMI and can get better still. Should we achieve breakthrough reactor designs, they can be aggressively licensed to China and India—these will not meaningfully assist those countries' extant

---

* Another paradox quickly resolved: Even though total energy use has grown, nuclear plants can supply 20 percent of needs because existing facilities have been expanded and become significantly more efficient. However, many plants are necessarily quite old and need to be replaced. New reactors have an initial carbon cost, as all major construction projects do, but produce very little carbon afterward. As most plants are expensive and require significant initial borrowing, the present era of very low interest rates significantly mitigates their once considerable expenses, which were often disastrous during the years of high interest rates, but should not be so now.

nuclear weapons programs, and any competitive benefits will be more than offset by dollars America does not have to spend combating climate change.

Sentiment cannot trump physics, whatever the Boomers want to believe. The biodiesel Mercedes that formerly trundled around Boomer Berkeley were a farce, and so were many equivalents peddled by a dim or cynical establishment (e.g., fuel cells—remember those? switchgrass? ethanol?) Many of these are either giveaways to rackets like the corn lobby or merely perverse, energy-intensive means of converting solid fuel to liquid and public dollars into agricultural subsidy.

As for the most popular alternatives, many are good, but can never be sufficient on their own. Solar and wind have inherent limitations. There just aren't enough consistently sunny or persistently windy places, which means using storage technologies like batteries that bear their own poisonous compromises. Batteries themselves have not improved nearly as fast as other technologies and represent a limiting factor. Most batteries also use highly toxic materials, some of which are rare, expensive, and presently produced in regions whose attitudes to the United States and overall stability range from ambiguous (China) to simply bad (Bolivia, West Africa). Absent genetically modified breakthrough sources, biofuels are also inefficient, as the crops frequently consume more energy to grow than they ultimately provide. Government intervention is fine—polluters can and should be charged for the externalities they produce, and Montreal's cap-and-trade proves that there are market-based remedies that suit both public and private needs. But subsidies to inherently unworthy energy projects waste money; we need genuine alternatives, not fake ones.

Weird Science

America could have had a much larger technological arsenal to confront its problems, and not just in matters of energy and climate. Unfortunately, Boomer sentimentality has stymied progress by failing to allocate appropriate funds while raising bizarre and unhelpful barriers. Whether presenting in its religious form on the Right or as the sentimental technopessimism of the unreconstructed Left—two fruitless branches stemming from the same anti-empirical root—the result has been less innovation.

For many on the Boomer Right, there is nothing to like about the phrase "government-funded science" and research suffers accordingly. This is especially the case for research that might call into question any preexisting beliefs, violate Norquist's tax pledge, or disturb the evangelical or business sensibilities of core constituencies, which is to say, most research. The Higgs boson may be the "god particle," but it is not God, and definitely costly, so: super-colliders canceled. Alternative energy being "alternative" to conventional energy: out. And so on. The Boomer Right ruled out areas of research as a matter of prejudice and convenience, which is no way to create a future.

However, the dogmatic Right does occasionally participate in a sort of scientific process, if only by accident, as in the case of stem cells. Researchers discovered the therapeutic potential of these entities but were forced, early on, to rely on fetal tissue as a prime source of material. The Right sensed a chance to score points with the dogmatists, whatever the lost opportunities for wellness. It spun up the whole apparatus of the pro-life movement, and the Bush II administration limited federal funding for embryonic stem cell research. These bars were ultimately lifted in part by the Obama administration, which helps (though a new, if limply supported, witch hunt by Boomer Congresswoman Marsha Blackburn does not), as did the development of nonembryonic sources.[38] While stem cell research is now proceeding well, years were lost—though not by everyone. Even as some states were banning stem cell research, others (e.g., California and New York) saw beyond the nonsense and promoted stem cell research at their own expense, and this is what gives the Right its walk-on role in science history. Over the coming years, we will see the results of a certain rough experiment, comparing New York's and California's achievements in biology to whatever is going on in the various places that restrict such research.* It may seem odd to mention the arcane world of stem cells in a chapter about existential issues, but stem cells *are* existential, at least for individuals. If the therapies work, people live longer; if they don't exist, people die. And stem cells are but one example of potential and serious losses due to underfunded science.

---

* To be fair, several other countries, including normally forward-thinking peers in Europe, have taken restrictive positions as well. They have their own, often different, reasons for the strategy and we will see how they do, too.

The Boomer Left has a much healthier attitude toward R&D, though it has made its own dogmatic mistakes and in its early years was much too skeptical about the net benefits of research. For example, many young Boomers leapt at the neo-Malthusian nonsense peddled in the 1960s and 1970s by a slightly older generation of writers, which prompted a baseless conversation about scarcity and the self-defeating nature of technological improvements. A parade of books, like Paul Ehrlich's *Population Bomb* (1968) and the Paddock brothers' *Famine 1975!* (1967), predicted a world of too many people and not enough resources, and advocating involuntary culling (Ehrlich) or even the abandonment of starving states (the Paddocks re: India). There were speeches about man's hubris and technological futility, and these left an imprint on certain minds.

In the event, there was no famine and no culling. Science and technology came to the rescue, just as science and technology made nonsense of the prediction that we would run out of certain essential resources in short order. The Stone Age, as has been famously noted, did not end because humanity ran out of stones; it ended because we discovered bronze, iron, and steel. With the possible and temporary exception of rare earth minerals, technology assures us of plenty of industrial resources; the first private efforts to mine asteroids have just begun. There can be, as Futurama put it, a "world of plenty" if we choose to invest in one.

Ehrlich et al. would have been a Sixties sideshow but for two reasons. First, certain strains of pessimism still infect the Left, and the results can be seen in anything involving genetic engineering. Second, neo-Malthusian arguments were recycled by a cynical Right as proof that Leftish predictions of apocalypse were always off base, a process now repeating with climate change. It did not help that even after Ehrlich was discredited, some on the Left kept presenting technology not as a vehicle for net improvement, but as an addiction—in David Foster Wallace's terms, a problem that presents itself as its own solution, and is therefore unworthy of investment. This is only true in the weakest of ways: Global warming certainly is the product of industrialization and will probably kill many people, and we will need new technologies to cope, but technology and industry also allowed for the birth of billions of people and the prevention of billions of early deaths. Measured in lives and their quality, the danger is almost certainly not from too much technology but not enough. We have plenty of problems that only technology can solve.

None of the dogma of the stranger versions of the Right or Left provided a helpful context for R&D, though in the end, they were probably just set dressing for an argument that was really about money. In the zero-sum world of Boomerism, there were only two options: energetic investment (for everyone's eventual enrichment) or maximal consumption (for immediate personal enrichment). We know which option Boomers chose.

Winthrop never would have foreseen his city on a hill buzzing with drones, slopes planted with GMO tomatoes, peopled by seniors playing tennis aided by replacement parts grown in a vat. He would have seen many specifics as downright ungodly, but he would have recognized the general motivations that could produce such weird greatness; they were, after all, his own.

Thinking Machines and Unthinkable Consequences

The only technology, besides nuclear weapons, that could potentially kill the majority of humanity is not the emission of greenhouse gases (that will endanger only a billion or so), but the creation of artificial intelligence.* This is an area where philosophy, politics, economics, and science heavily overlap, each able to make valuable contributions. Regrettably, the Boomers do not take AI seriously, in part because many of them do not understand technology well enough to understand the threat it poses. And because the first truly human-equivalent AIs are still a few decades away, the Boomers feel they can safely ignore the issue.

Nevertheless, the day will arrive, probably within the lifetime of this book's younger readers, when AIs begin to replace humans in many or even most tasks. They will become our helpers, then possibly our competitors, and we have no real plan. In the 1990s, the threat did not seem credible, and inaction then might have been excusable. But AI, which had been a joke for years,

---

* It's doubtful that a malevolent Skynet will be the author of catastrophe; more likely, AIs responsible for essential systems like power plants, autonomous weapons, dams, and so on will make mistakes that could unleash catastrophe. Then again, the possibility of a rogue supercomputer is not zero, though it remains distant.

constantly failing to live up to its promises, has begun to exceed even more optimistic forecasts. In 2016, DeepMind's AlphaGo program beat a human master at Go 4–1, an achievement many thought unlikely to occur before 2025. Because of the flexible way AlphaGo learns, and the enormous difficulty of the game it was playing (Go is to chess what chess is to checkers), an AI that can win at Go is something we need to take seriously. The government has essentially shrugged its shoulders, and by default, AI has been consigned to private hands, to private ends, and private gains.* It is no coincidence that AI, which is comparatively cheap to develop and has received sustained attention from private institutions, is a bright spot in the R&D landscape. Again, private, unregulated masters can shape AIs to their own purposes, as they can with genetic engineering and space colonization (all are underway). That's fine for me and my Silicon Valley set—as for the other 320-odd million Americans, the Boomer government doesn't seem to care.

AI is not, by the way, an aside to the central issues of this book. AI will directly impact problems like the slowdown in growth, stagnating living standards, and rising inequality—though whether it exacerbates or alleviates some of these problems is as much a matter of policy as technology. The point where AI starts to have a substantial impact is near: Baumol may have been correct that it takes the same four players to perform a string quartet as it did in 1800, but technology has already provided us with recorded music and will soon furnish robotic players. What does society do with its cellists? (Ehrlich and the Paddocks would say: Cull them. The AIs may agree.)

Yo-Yo Ma is safe for now, but low-end labor is not. Machines already stock warehouses (Amazon has a fleet of robots that have replaced manual labor), and robotization is underway with longshoremen and other traditionally well-paying blue-collar jobs.[39] Some waiters have already been replaced by

---

* Full disclosure: I invested in DeepMind personally in its earlier years; the company was then acquired by Google, in which I now hold stock. Wall Street has long dismissed Google's side projects like self-driving cars and AI as money sinks, but Google has a thoughtful plan and one you may not be fully comfortable with. Google (in the verb sense; may as well start there) "self-driving car," "AlphaGo," and "Android Marketshare" and you'll get a sense for the future Google might have in mind. You can add in Boston Dynamics +Atlas +Google, and you might get a sense of Google's terminal ambitions, even if it ultimately ditches Boston Dynamics in favor of other robotics companies.

iPad menus; computers render pilots increasingly superfluous and will soon do the same for drivers. It is a future where humans are increasingly liberated from less skilled labor and, by implication, no longer needed for a broad range of jobs. National planning that does not consider the challenges and opportunities of AI will be necessarily incomplete and ineffective. AIs can free humans to do what machines cannot, and if they make cashiers redundant, perhaps they can also free cashiers to be artists or philosophers. Or perhaps not—really robust AIs may render almost all workers redundant, and we ought to think about what that sort of society might look like, including how gains might be transferred to displaced laborers and how those laborers may fit into a world that does not need them as workers.

And this brings us to the other great matter of the future: education. What sort of schools, producing what sort of graduates, will we require in a future that no longer has much place for semiskilled labor? It is not a question the Boomers care to ask, much less answer.

CHAPTER FOURTEEN

DETENTION, AFTER-SCHOOL
AND OTHERWISE

He who opens a school door, closes a prison.
—Victor Hugo[1]

Had Victor Hugo witnessed Boomer educational and penal policy, he might have reconsidered the truth of the foregoing, thrown up his hands and inverted the whole sentiment, added a stream of qualifiers, or just parroted Émile Zola in a hearty *J'accuse*. Under Boomer control schools and jails have intertwined, the degrading former providing sustenance for the swollen latter. Boomer schools and jails are no longer systems of uplift and remediation; they have become mechanisms of mass containment and deferred liability.

Educational erosion began when the Boomers were themselves in school, wasting the opportunities their parents granted, a casual disregard of school that continued in more virulent form when Boomers took power. Despite ritual genuflections before the altar of excellence, Boomers revealed their fundamental unseriousness in education policies that ranged from negligent to ludicrous. After decades of promises made and broken, the United States continues to underperform against its peers. What improvements have been achieved are often misleading, the product of lowered bars, statistical manipulations, and in some cases, outright fraud.

As economy and education faltered under the Boomers, a parallel system rose to contain the factory seconds, kept company by whatever portions of society Boomers found it expedient to impound. That parallel system is history's largest penal regime, and it extends well beyond the needs of deterrence and containment. Erected at enormous cost to the fisc (as usual, mostly debt financed), the corrections system has become a state within a state; indeed, in 2014, it was America's thirty-sixth most populous state, larger than New Mexico, and if those in probationary regimes are included, its fourteenth largest, just ahead of Massachusetts.[2] Many of its charges could have been saved by the schools the Boomers failed, by social programs the Boomers let decay, or by the exercise of empathetic clemency instead of automatic punishments that appealed to the Boomers' crudest Old Testament instincts. Instead, Boomer policy created a conveyor belt that leads from school detention to its lifetime equivalent.

Boomers as Students

The educational crisis began in the early 1960s, the Boomers' own school years, when American scholastic performance began a downward slide. At least for the white, middle-class majority, it was as much the students failing the system as vice versa. By the time America realized Boomer test scores constituted a national embarrassment, the Boomers themselves were taking over the instruments of school policy. It was therefore society's great misfortune that demographics and timing consigned responsibility for any educational renaissance to the hands of the generation whose underperformance had prompted calls for reform in the first place.

Aside from crude measures like literacy, the longest continuous data on American educational achievement are SAT scores, and what they show is a decline that overlapped almost perfectly with the period Boomers took those tests. After a period of stability from 1952 to 1963, scores fell nearly continuously for two decades, a slide that began just after the first Boomers sat for the SAT (using my date of 1940 for the start of the Boom, or, using the conventional definition of 1946, *exactly* when Boomers started taking the test) and ended in 1982–1983, precisely when the last Boomers left high school.[3] If one wanted to define the Boom by other than mere fertility statistics, the downward curve of SAT scores would identify essentially the same population.

While the slide was alarming, observers correctly detected a partial triumph hidden within the embarrassment of overall scores. Thanks to integration and greater gender equality, the pool of SAT takers had become more inclusive from the 1950s onward. Because these new kinds of takers traditionally scored lower (women on math, minorities on math and verbal, a discrepancy due in part to historical discrimination), their scores temporarily depressed results overall.* But that was only part of the story. Per the College Board, which administers the SAT, "compositional changes" of these kinds explained between 66 and 75 percent percent of the decline from 1963 to 1970 and "only about a quarter" of the even steeper decline after 1970 (in which year the median Boomer would have been seventeen or eighteen and of prime test-taking age).[4] Declines after 1970 affected "virtually all categories of SAT takers," top students, mediocre students, blacks, whites, almost any way you sliced it.[5] The SAT slide was paralleled in ACT scores.[6] GRE scores, in line with Boomer progression through the education system, began declining somewhat later, with "almost half the drop concentrated in 1969–1970," as older Boomers would have begun sitting for those tests.[7] College Board analysts tried correction for any variables they could, even subjecting students to both the 1963 and 1973 tests as a control, and if anything *that made matters worse*—the 1973 test appeared to give a lift of eight to twelve points versus the 1963 test (it was, effectively, more generous with points).[8] In the end, much of the decline was attributed to "pervasive" factors that the Educational Testing Service danced around, but can really only be read as: Boomers.[9]

---

* My subject is generational; I stake little territory in the largely unhelpful and mostly pseudoscientific debate (on both sides) regarding the inherent capacities of a given group for a given subject. The purpose of general education is to produce citizens competent at managing their own lives and capable of participating in representative government. Either all ethnicities and genders are capable of at least that much or we are going to have to call a Constitutional Convention.

Scholastic Inaptitude

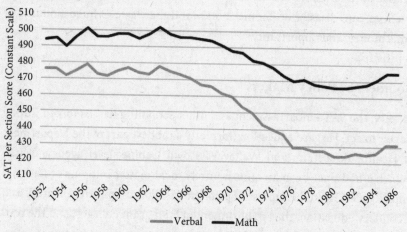

What's going on here? The first Boomers starting taking the SATs around 1957–1959 and the last around 1981–1983. The declines in SAT scores defined Boomers in their own way; once the Boomers were no longer of traditional test-taking age, scores improved (modestly). The SAT subsequently tinkered with its scoring formulas, but during the period presented, the methodology was consistent—i.e., the changes were driven not by the test, but by the test takers.[10]

The Boomers' poor SAT scores were somewhat surprising, given the context. America was affluent and schools reasonably provisioned. Getting into college, for which SATs served as a gateway, had become widely important: College provided an exemption to the draft (if one were so inclined—and as we know from Chapter 3, millions were) and the growing wage premium for college degrees offered the easiest path to higher incomes in the era of stagflation. Was it perhaps something about the test takers themselves, televisual, self-interested, permissively raised, bottle-fed, and politically distracted? The correspondence between Boomer test-taking and falling scores is suggestive, as it is what happened next.

As soon as the Boomers left high school, SAT scores rose—i.e., matters improved *before* the tentative reforms of the late 1970s could work any real magic. And while scores continued improving over the next decades, the gains should not be seen as some unqualified success for Boomer educational policy. Absolute scores remain unimpressive overall and flatter only relative to the Boomer-era fiasco. The failure to achieve real excellence represents a core disaster of Boomer policy and the waste of huge amounts of time, money, and opportunity.

Boomers as Policy Makers

In 1979, the SAT embarrassment and other schooling fiascos forced Jimmy Carter to act. He gave education (formerly a modest part of the Department of Health, Education, and Welfare) its own Cabinet-level agency, elevating what had once been an almost purely local matter into one of national importance. Given the success of prior efforts like compulsory primary and secondary education, the establishment of land grant colleges, and the progression of American research universities from second-rate status to international leadership, national optimism in 1979 was wholly understandable. What America had done before, could it not do again? Critics worried that Reagan would derail the project, as Reagan's first campaign had a plank calling for abolition of Carter's new department. Reagan never did—in fact, he chartered a bipartisan National Commission on Excellence in Education in his first year as president.[11]

In 1983, the Commission produced *A Nation at Risk*, a remarkable document that offered a candid assessment of American secondary education and provided wholly sensible ideas for reform. Quite a bit of *ANAR* remains depressingly current—if you strip out the dates, parts could have been written yesterday. That is the core of *ANAR*'s present relevance: more than three decades later, most of it a period of almost complete Boomer power, the problems remain the same while many of *ANAR*'s recommendations languish ignored and untried. It was not that Boomers did not know what to do, it was that they did not do it.

The report found that much of the American high school curriculum was mediocre and that nonacademic classes like "bachelor living" could, if a student wished, account for a substantial portion of graduation credits.[12] The previous generation should have kept these nonclasses off the menu, but nevertheless, it was the Boomers who chose to take them. *A Nation at Risk* also bemoaned the imposition of "minimum competency" standards, which fell "short of what is needed, as the 'minimum' tends to become the 'maximum,' thus lowering educational standards for all."[13] The report also worried about America's short school year (almost 40 percent fewer hours than some international peers), the paucity of homework, persistent grade inflation, and the automatic shuffling along of children to the next grade (as the College Board noted, rather aptly, automatic advancement was perceived as an "entitlement, rather than something to be earned—or denied," and we know how Boomers feel about entitlements).[14] Some of these problems were not the fault of Boomer policymakers, but once *ANAR* made the problems clear, they became the Boomers' responsibility. Could the United States return to its former position of eminence in international league tables? Well, that depended on who was in charge, and from the 1980s, it was increasingly the Boomers.

The Boomers—beginning to rear children of their own—clamored for reform, or at least its Kabuki equivalent. Of course, as we have seen, they were unwilling to tax themselves to furnish necessary funds, for schools or anything else. Nor would Boomers of any political stripe engage with the substance of education itself, as that would require money, effort, compromise, and other irksome undertakings. For Democrats, *ANAR*'s demand for longer school days and teacher accountability would require confronting the teachers' unions, a prospect from which Democrats recoiled. For Republicans, more teaching days would inevitably require higher pay, and that would mean higher taxes, anathema to the Republicans and, over time, resisted too by Boomer Democrats. The sociopathic solution would be theatre without sacrifice (or results) and the constant shuffling of responsibility between federal and local governments, to ensure minimum accountability.

Much as Boomer economic neoliberalism provided a nothing-for-nothing "third way," so educational neoliberalism would provide its own third way, to similar effect. The charge was led by Bill Bennett, the nation's third secretary of education, appointed two years after *ANAR* came out. Rather than pursue *ANAR*'s recommendations, Bennett (a Boomer, naturally) and his successors held that the *market* would improve education, in the form of vouchers, school choice, charter schools, the federalist laboratory of the states in edifying competition with each other, and all the other neoliberal nostrums manufactured from the 1980s on and embraced by both parties. It was a risky bet, but then again, Bill Bennett, erstwhile educator and moral crusader, was nothing if not a risk taker, as his $8 million in gambling losses would subsequently reveal.[15]

However convenient it would be to dismiss Bennett as a Reaganite anomaly, the neoliberal experiment accelerated as Boomers gained power, under Democrats and Republicans, in states, blue, red, purple, and all the other dismal colors of the Boomer political rainbow, starting with charter school initiatives, passed in many cases by direct referendum—and thus not attributable to politicians alone. Minnesota and California granted the first state charters in 1991–1992; as of 2016, forty-three states and the District of Columbia have them, a period that coincided with near-total Boomer control of state politics. Charter schools have records that are, at best, mixed. Some are effective institutions, others achieve a facsimile of success by siphoning off the naturally talented and jettisoning the less apt, and many are simply terrible. Overall, their performance is not radically different from that of public schools.[16] Various other initiatives with merit pay and tenure reform produced equally mixed results.[17] Some of these projects were worth trying, but after decades without satisfying results, it's difficult to applaud policy makers for repeating the same experiments and expecting better outcomes.

The experiments Boomers did not want, or bother, to run were the substantive reforms outlined in *ANAR*. Levels of homework, length and number of school days, teacher compensation, and curricula are not substantially better than they were decades ago—the school year remains the same, teacher compensation remains moderate relative to better-performing nations (in part because American teachers work less—Leftists tend to overlook this point), and hours of homework have not budged.[18] As for curricula, a 2016 survey by the Education Trust found that "students are meandering toward graduation," with high schools "prioritizing credit accrual" instead of "access to a cohesive curriculum that aligns high school coursework and students' future goals."[19] The survey concluded that 47 percent of students had no "cohesive curriculum" and at most, 39 percent had a college-ready curriculum.[20] If this sounds familiar, it's because *ANAR* said the same thing decades ago.

Some problems identified in the 1980s actually got worse, particularly grade inflation. In Boomer culture, all children are "special," bound for college and greatness. Therefore no child could receive any grade to the contrary. UC Berkeley, for instance, is a good school but hardly the most selective in the country, yet its 2015 freshmen had gross average high school GPAs of 3.91 and 4.41 on a "weighted" basis—in other words, the nation's twentieth-best university had freshmen whose transcripts were essentially perfect, and on some metrics, *beyond* perfect.[21] This is why focusing on test scores rather than transcripts has become so important: Not only are curricula poor, grades reflect no objective reality.

As for the schools themselves, budget limits consigned them to physical decay, which could not have helped the learning process. Returning to the Infrastructure Report Card, the physical plant of schools has traveled from a D in 1988 to an F in 1998, and then hovered around D since, though ASCE doesn't quite know, because not enough data are available.[22] It was a tad ungrateful of the Boomers—for whom about half of existing school capacity was built—to let their former schoolhouses languish in squalor.[*,23]

Against international peers, the United States has not fulfilled any education secretary's goal of excellence. Not only have SAT scores failed to surpass their 1950s peaks (no surprise given the lingering curricular issues), but on international scales, the United States remains middling at best. The latest international comparisons are the Programme for International Student Assessment (PISA) tests, and from 2000 to 2012, the years for which PISA data are available, they showed that the United States achieved "no significant change in [US] performances over time" despite endless state and federal initiatives, with reading scores average and math performance "below average" (PISA is being polite: The United States was twenty-seventh out of thirty-four developed nations).[24]

It could come as no surprise that in 2010, Education Secretary Arne Duncan found himself in the position of repeating the same vows as all of his predecessors. Duncan promised that the United States would (somehow, one day) "lead the world in educational attainment," as "nothing, nothing,

---

* Nevertheless, the United States spends more per student than every other advanced country except for the exceedingly wealthy and smaller countries of Austria, Luxembourg, Norway, and Sweden, according to the OECD. It's fairly easy to guess where this money goes.

is more important in the long-run to American prosperity than boosting the skills and attainment of the nation's students."[25] True, but measured by action, "nothing, nothing" is more important to Boomers than low taxes, entitlement spending, and debt-fueled consumption.*,[26]

There have been only three, highly dubious, areas of improvement: class size, certain nominal test scores, and gross graduation rates. Class size has become something of a fetish, and the overall pupil/teacher ratio has declined at a slow rate since the 1970s. It's now—with enormous variation between grades, schools, and geographies—about 20:1.[27] However, it's not clear how important this metric is. A Nation At Risk didn't trouble itself over class size—it focused on teacher quality; anyway, during America's scholastic heyday, class sizes were much larger in both public and private schools, 26:1 and 31:1 in 1960.[28] The problem in 1983 is still the problem now; teachers are notionally competent in methods of pedagogy, but not necessarily the substance of the class they teach—and therefore it doesn't matter whether there are twenty students in the room or forty.

As for test scores, thirty-odd years of reform produced a far from enviable record. Among younger students, reading and math scores have drifted upward, but by age seventeen—the age that really matters as it roughly mirrors the conclusion of K–12 education—progress has been slight to nonexistent.[29] The one major improvement has been a narrowing of the white-minority achievement gap, though it's convergence of the wrong type, with white groups treading water and most minority groups converging on majoritarian mediocrity.[30]

At least the race gap has converged in its own unsatisfactory way; gaps between rich and the not-rich have widened. As economic inequality has vastly increased under the Boomers, and as younger couples increasingly tend to pair with mates of comparable educational and economic attainments (both strong predictors of a child's success), we can only expect these gaps to grow. Encouraging statistics do pop up from time to time, though

---

* Duncan (b. 1964) resigned in 2016, as scandals over manufactured test scores started percolating and after revelations that charter schools, of which Duncan was an enthusiastic supporter but an indifferent administrator, were wasting federal dollars.

few withstand investigation. For example, graduation rates have improved. As high school seniors do not possess the full benefit of a proper education, those results provide only limited consolation. All in all, the picture is disheartening: some improvement in math, no improvement in reading, a narrowing minority performance gap (albeit to the wrong levels), a widening socioeconomic gap poised to grow wider still, and graduation rates leached of meaning—after thirty-odd years of "reform."

As failures mounted, promises grew. In January 1989, Bush I assumed office as the "education president" and encouraged governors to endorse goals where, by the year 2000, American children would lead the world in math and science achievement, all children would be prepared for "challenging subject matter," high school graduation rates would reach 90 percent, and so on.[31] How this would be achieved was left badly unaddressed and, of course, Bush I's goals went unfulfilled (math, thirty-fifth; science, twenty-seventh; graduation rates 81 percent and of dubious meaning anyway; children prepared for challenging material, far from all, as we will see).[32] The goal of prepping "all" children to high levels, by the way, did not reveal seriousness of purpose, but its absence. The goals were unachievable and would grow only more absurd as Boomers colonized education departments. That's not to say that real improvement could not be achieved, only that the targets set were wrong and the results achieved failed to impress.

Thus, while 2000 brought no computerized reckoning (being a matter of profits, Y2K was taken seriously), that year did reveal Bush I's promises as unfulfilled. The problems were therefore consigned to the hands of...Bush II. In 2001, the new Bush ginned up the No Child Left Behind Act, offering equally outlandish promises: that "all" students would be "proficient" by graduation, instructed by "highly qualified" teachers (or "distinguished" ones, query what distinguished them).[33] It passed with overwhelming, bipartisan support. The federal government would set the standards, the states would figure out how to achieve them, and Washington would apply various carrots and sticks along the way. It was the perfect combination of Boomer foibles—anti-empirical fantasy and/or cynicism (no society can make "all" of a group "proficient"), neoliberal federalist magic (incentives! states' rights!), and, of course, de minimis diversion of tax receipts away from the entitlements programs that were becoming matters of urgency for undersaved Boomers. Echoing the fantasy-by-fiat of Soviet planning, No Child demanded triumph by 2014.

The success of the No Child act may be inferred from its uncontested repeal and replacement in 2015. It was reincarnated as the Every Child Succeeds Act, another title of utterly fraudulent Boomer promise, passed (again) with bipartisan support and signed by President Obama. The new act retained testing but removed certain penalties for poorly performing schools, forbade federal imposition of curricula, and devolved many powers to the states (again, tried before, failed before).[34] The states remain mired in the process of figuring out what to do, because Every Child Succeeds does not provide adequate funds, guidance, or accountability. The one thing that is certain is that "every" child will not "succeed."

In any event, the definition of educational "success" in Boomer education policy is roughly the same as Bush II's "mission accomplished" was in Iraq—some transient bare minimum, defined as whatever the conditions on the ground already were or could be made out to be, after which matters can be left to devolve on their own. Because Washington (like Moscow) would impose some penalties for failure, the Boomer educational machine relied on the same strategies as the Boomer financial machine: Take what numbers you have, cast them as victory if remotely plausible, and adjust them to the desired level if not, i.e., fraud. A parade of scandals ensued, with teachers focusing overwhelmingly on how to *take* tests instead of the substance tested, a parallel to teachers' own training in methods of teaching, rather than achieving mastery of the subject to be taught. If that cynical ploy failed, higher scores could be realized through blatant cheating, like leaving answer sheets out for students to copy or simply fabricating scores (in Atlanta, the results were numerous indictments, pleas, sentencing, etc.).[35] Even with cheating—some schools inflating their scores in utterly implausible ways in just a few quarters, tactics that might have shamed Enron—schools did not meet Bush I or II's promises, and they will not meet Obama's, either.

The murky, misguided, sentimental, and fraudulent nature of Boomer educational goals more or less guarantee bizarre outcomes. Now, not only must no child be left behind (didn't happen) and every child succeed (not happening now), every child must go to college (will never happen). Universal college education has become the last uncontroversial virtue under the Boomers, even though it is not achievable for reasons of logistics, attitude, aptitude, and personal and national economics. Other nations know this and divide students early on into vocational and other tracks suited to children's abilities and needs, as Germany does with its *Realschulen*, *Hauptschulen*, *Gymnasien*, and vocational training in the *Duale Ausbildung*. These systems are more efficient and effective, though their realism offends Boomer sentimentality. Boomer-run schools cannot be complicit in confirming displeasing realities, like the fact that not all children can, want, or should go to college. Anyway, the marketplace can be relied upon to supply its own brutal curriculum soon enough.

The college fetish is an anomaly, as only over the past few decades has the ostensible purpose of K–12 education become the production of a nation of college graduates—or more precisely, those touched by college, however slightly. In 2009, President Obama called upon every American not to *graduate* from a good college, but simply to *go* "one year or more" beyond high school.[36] While the president offered career training as an option, an American culture extolling every child's specialness must have understood the president to mean a year at college.

Obama justified his objective on the grounds that "this country needs and values the talents of every American," a statement that can be described as naïvely aspirational at best and totally disingenuous at worst.[37] Leaving aside normative issues, compensation data show that while America values the talents of college graduates generally, it does not particularly value the services of those who have not finished college. Since 1980, wages have fallen for groups without a college degree, and that includes declines for those with only "some college."[38] In virtually every case, Obama's one year of college will produce debt, probably add little to knowledge that could and should have been acquired during high school, and is unlikely to produce wage gains: Therefore, it is sentimentality with a price.

Even assuming students do complete college, what college, what major, and how financed matter as much as or more than simply collecting a credential from a random institution. On a pure income basis, not all colleges or majors justify their expense, in terms of direct and opportunity costs. An English degree from a second-tier liberal arts college is generally a *consumption* good, which is fine by itself, but cannot be justified on policy grounds, and possibly not even social ones.

The worst offenders are not the English departments at Bennington and Bard; the cardinal sinners are for-profit colleges. Because the United States has not adequately invested in conventional nonprofit institutions like community colleges, for-profit colleges have been absorbing the excess supply of the college bound. Between 1998 and 2008, postsecondary enrollment increased 32 percent generally, but 270 percent at for-profit colleges.[39] By 2010, almost a tenth of college students enrolled in for-profit institutions.[40] These neoliberal confections transform vast amounts of public dollars into private gain, little of which is realized by the students much less the public. Part of the reason is that these institutions provide very little education at considerable cost. Per a Senate committee, "evidence suggests that for-profit schools charge higher tuition than comparable public schools, spend a large share of revenues on expenses unrelated to teaching, experience high dropout rates, and, in some cases, employ abusive recruiting and debt-management practices."[41] Half of student borrowers who entered repayment in 2007 and had defaulted by 2009 had attended for-profit institutions (despite being just under 10 percent of the student population) and for-profit colleges, and by the latter year, for-profit institutions were consuming almost a quarter of federal loans and grants.*[42]

Many for-profit colleges are either nonaccredited, or functionally so, and worse than useless. When one of the largest providers, Corinthian Colleges, went bust it left its students indebted and taxpayers holding a very large bag. (Along the way, this showed that these institutions, which are not "colleges," are also often not, except for their executives, "for profit"). Nor could students pick up where Corinthian left off, as that institution's loose academic standards made its coursework difficult to transfer and functionally valueless.[43] Although for-profit colleges have existed for some time, their arrival as a significant part

---

* Intriguingly, Bill Clinton was the honorary—and well-compensated—chancellor of a for-profit institution, though not one accused of the sorts of extravagant frauds practiced elsewhere. But question what he did to earn his eight-figure compensation and what that bought for students. Meanwhile, the presidents of Stanford and Harvard, who do real work, each made about a third as much.

of the educational landscape is pure Boomer.[44] If the government investigations, private lawsuits, and other actions have any merit at all, the Boomers' for-profit innovations range from the incompetent to the fraudulent.

The flip side of the terrible for-profit colleges are the indignities visited on traditional public institutions and their students. In the 1960s, when Boomers were on campus, public colleges charged nominal, and often zero, annual tuition; today, in-state tuition runs around $13,500. The existence of tuition itself is not necessarily bad, though it is hard to reconcile with the rhetoric about a universal college experience. It is also no substitute for public investment, especially when it comes to adding entirely new schools, which take billions of dollars to create (for tuition alone to support that expense, students would need to pay several hundred thousand dollars annually). In the two most significant public university systems, those of California and Texas, low funding has permitted the creation of only one genuinely new campus during Boomer reign, the highly dispiriting UC Merced.* (Compare this to the list of University of California campuses opened between 1900 and 1965: UCLA, UCSB, UC Riverside, UC Davis, UCSD, UC Irvine, and UCSC.) Deposited in a dusty hellhole, opened almost two decades after authorized, accredited six years after inauguration, and with a decidedly unselective 2015 admissions rate of 64.6 percent, vs. about 17 percent for UC Berkeley and UCLA, Merced is essentially doomed to failure.[45] Even as the populations of California and Texas dramatically increased—the latter roughly doubled from 1980 to 2015—systems have not kept up.

While conventional public colleges may be overcrowded and underfunded, they do vastly better than their for-profit equivalents. Unfortunately, here again, the doctrine of college-for-all reveals a seedy Boomerism. Much of that one year of postsecondary work Obama called for will be remedial, for the simple reason that K–12 education has not been doing its job, nor has it done so for some time. At least 20 percent of students at colleges arrive unprepared, wasting space and money.[46] The job of topping up high school education often falls to (usually underpaid) adjuncts and part-timers, an old practice that reached new and astonishing scale under

---

* Texas's "new" campus was mostly an agglomeration of older sites.

Boomer administrators. Adjuncts have been hired in droves, now representing something like 40–50 percent of instructional faculty, depending on the survey and the institutions.[47]

Because the vast majority of new appointments are no longer for conventional, tenure-track positions, the proportion of adjuncts—precisely the type of instructor usually assigned to teach Obama's magical first year of college—will continue rising. The presence of adjunct faculty does not bode well for students, as freshmen taught by adjuncts have a lesser propensity to continue to a sophomore year, though this is not necessarily the fault of the adjuncts. However, there has been one major expansion in permanent staff growth, in noninstructional personnel, comprised of various administrative positions created, and subsequently occupied, by Boomers to oversee the growing fraction of campus life that does not involve actual teaching.

Presiding over the adjunct bazaars are, of course, the Boomers in capacities administrative and otherwise. To create the adjunct market, there must be demand and supply. Demand is provided by things like Obama's sentimental injunction to get that "one year" of college and by for-profit universities that need cheap labor. It is further stoked by traditional universities, which consign many introductory undergraduate classes (beneath the dignity of Boomer professors) to low-paid adjuncts. The Boomer professorate, meanwhile, focuses on producing the supply of graduate students required to serve as adjuncts, few of whom are likely to get tenure themselves, since Boomer professors seem determined to die in their endowed chairs.[48] That many older professors are expensive, unproductive and, in fields like mathematics, decades past their prime disturbs not one whit a bloated administrative apparatus.

Student Debt

What is the net result? Too many badly equipped students and an explosion of debt. We saw the bill in Chapter 7; now we know the reason. The $1.3+ trillion in educational debt in the first quarter of 2016, which has overtaken credit card debt over the past decade, burdens both students and society—though Boomers+ least of all.[49]

Defaults have already begun, because the education funded by those loans has been so dubious and the Boomer economy so inadequate to the task of providing good jobs. Potential losses run into the hundreds of billions, and while these liabilities will be amortized over time, the burden will hit younger taxpayers the most. Meanwhile, the gains have been transferred to the Boomer-dominated educational bureaucracy and leadership of for-profit institutions.

A foreign observer may think American policy had been run by people who had no experience in education or simply hated it. That observer would be wrong. The White House has been occupied by an endless parade of former educators. Since 1952, educators-in-chief included: Dwight Eisenhower (president of Columbia University); Lyndon Johnson (high school teacher); George H. W. Bush (briefly a business school lecturer); Bill Clinton (law school professor); Barack Obama (same). So, for about half of the time since Eisenhower's inauguration, the White House has been occupied by a former teacher of some kind or other. Bush II was not an educator, but was married to one, so if you include Laura, you could argue educators have resided in the White House for about two-thirds of the period between 1952 and 2016. And that's leaving aside the degraded future, the contest of

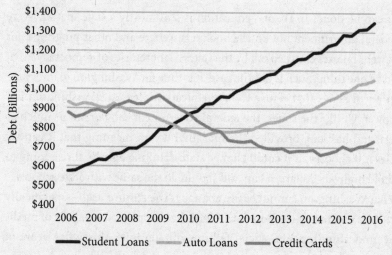

The Changing Shape of Consumer Credit

Student Loans ——— Auto Loans ——— Credit Cards

What's going on here? Sadly, this chart needs little explanation: student debt, formerly so minor the government barely kept statistics at all, has become thanks to Boomer policies a giant feature of the debt landscape.[50]

2016 having been between various ersatz educators, Hillary Clinton (who, notwithstanding her failure of the DC bar exam, taught law in Arkansas, whose less demanding test she did pass) and Donald Trump (of the distinctly Boomerish Trump "University"), who fended off challenges from yet *more* ex-teachers like Ted Cruz (adjunct law professor), and Bernie Sanders (briefly a college lecturer).

Not all presidents or candidates were great educators; then again, statistics show that many full-time educators aren't great educators, either. The only modern presidents to really succeed in education (in limited ways) were Eisenhower and Johnson; the former, because he had very specific needs and curricular goals in mind (the disciplines necessary to win the Space Race and Cold War) and the latter because he helped alleviate the discrimination and poverty that had made it impossible for many students to learn at all—and both, because they spent real money to achieve meaningful and specific outcomes. All the other educator-leaders either had Boomer students to contend with (eventually, an insurmountable task) or were Boomers themselves, who pursued rhetoric over results.

A Return to A *Nation at Risk*

What can be done? In theory, education is still mostly a state matter. Were the federal government not on the hook, via welfare and other programs, for the various failures churned out by the states' "laboratories of democracy," that would be one thing. Such is not the case. It is time for Washington to intervene or set adrift states that refuse to take education seriously. Washington has the power. Unlike the states, the federal government can borrow as much as it likes, and has long provided the marginal dollar, meaning that it can set policies if it chooses. If it could change state drinking ages by threatening to withhold highway dollars, it can and should do the same with state schools.

What Washington cannot easily change is the culture itself—specifically the culture created by the Boomers. Until that happens, the parade of mediocrity, underfunding, and social failure will continue, thirty-five years of wasted opportunities whose moral and financial debts will be handed off to the young.

Serving No One by Serving Time

Instead of providing education and opportunity, Boomers focused their energies on the creation of an unforgiving penal state, furnished with intolerant laws and panoptic enforcers to supply the inmates. For many, school is just the waiting room before formal incarceration. Perhaps mass detention would be acceptable if prison served as an effective deterrent or society lacked alternatives; neither is or was true. While society had better options, the Boomers favored ever-stricter laws and processed ever more people into the prison system, the spectacle of law and order always being more satisfying to Boomer psychology than any reality of justice or efficacy. While Reagan often gets the blame for the rise of imprisonment, it was Boomers who (frequently in bipartisan accord) passed the most odious laws and Boomer administrations that presided over the most spectacular and fruitless phases of mass incarceration.

In the 1960s and 1970s, the argument for expanding incarceration had a certain reasonable dimension, because the United States had problems with crime—young people have a higher propensity to commit crime, as do antisocial people, and the United States was well supplied with both: Boomers. Crime rose until 1991, after which Boomers had begun to age out of the brackets most liable to commit crimes. (Notably, the large Millennial generation does not seem as disposed to crime as its forbears.) And had Boomers maintained fast economic growth, crime might have fallen without the need for a penal state, as economic growth tends to depress crime, all else being demographically equal.[51]

Even with these failures, the prison population should have leveled off in the 1990s, instead of growing. The traditional justification for mass imprisonment is deterrence, but on that basis the prison population had reached some efficient peak no later than the early 1990s—subsequent prison growth was costly and ineffective. A survey by the Brennan Center found that prison growth in the 1990s had "relatively little to do with the crime decline," concluding "that the dramatic increases in incarceration have had a limited, diminishing effect on crime."[52] (An aging population did, however, seem to help from 1990 to 1999; there was no evidence of aging's effects after 2000, notably.[53])

The anti-empirical Boomers, of course, had no patience for analysis: Going forward, it would be "three strikes, you're out." It was a perfect system

The 51st State

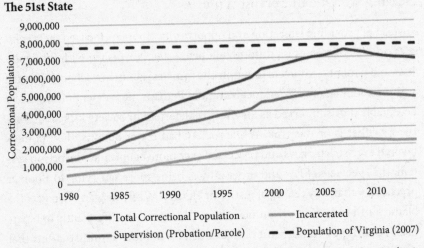

What's going on here? This chart shows the total number of Americans either in physical custody or under correctional supervision (probation, parole). The rise in corrections began before the Boomers took power, but there was, at the time, a serious problem with crime (often perpetrated by then-youthful Boomers). By the early 1990s, crime had already plateaued, but thanks to punitive, bipartisan laws, the correctional population just kept growing, at undeniable financial and human cost and without any strong evidence of a deterrent aspect. Only recently has the fraction declined modestly, and quite a bit of that has been driven by a few states like California releasing masses of prisoners, in some instances because prisons were so overcrowded that they violated Constitutional requirements for decent treatment, which counts as a fairly meager improvement. Even correcting for overall population growth, the prison explosion remains—the total correctional population rose from 0.81 percent of the population in 1980 to 2.46 percent in 2007.[54]

for the nation's chief judicial officer, Boomer John Roberts, who during his Supreme Court confirmation hearings compared the role of a judge to that of an umpire counting balls and strikes. Given the Boomers' test scores, it's helpful strikes were limited to three. America was at least spared the vista of Boomer judges discalcing themselves to add past ten or, God forbid, disrobing entirely to get past twenty.

It was the arrival of laws like three-strikes that drove so much imprisonment during the 1990s and 2000s. Even if the need for deterrence had waned, the desire for Levitical justice waxed. The Boomers were fed up with crime, which their own generation had helped drive to high levels, and rather than engage in self-reflection or a detailed study of humane alternatives, opted as usual for the most expedient response—crude and often indiscriminate punishment. Historical discretion for clemency would be progressively removed from the mid-1980s by mandatory sentencing guidelines, the better to ensure that pre-Boomer judges (another detestable elite) would not allow legal knowledge, intimacy with the facts, or human compassion to interfere with the punitive task at hand. Discretion and mercy were further circumscribed when Washington State held a referendum that approved the first modern three-strikes law in 1993, followed over the next two years by twenty-three other states as diverse as California, Louisiana, and Vermont, a situation that proves that even red and blue states could find some toxic common ground under Boomer leadership. There has been some relaxation of these laws since, but not nearly enough.

The relentless prosecution of nonviolent drug and property crimes also padded numbers. Nixon appointed the first drug czar, but the war on substances entered a new phase with the Boomers. One of the first Boomer drug warriors was, appropriately enough, Bill Bennett (Reagan's second secretary of education), who transitioned along with his students from the school to the justice system, the instantiation in a single person of the Boomers' school-to-prison pipeline. Didn't-inhale Bill Clinton also participated, appointing drug czars with a remit to do everything from hunting down doctors advising on medical marijuana to funding aerial dispersals of herbicides to kill coca plants in Colombia, a strategy that recalled the whole scandal over Agent Orange in Vietnam and proved about as effective.[55] (Clinton also supported, for some time, a ban on funding needle exchanges as part of the law-and-order spectacle.) The list goes on, including the zero-tolerance policies and "Broken Windows" policing endorsed by New York City's (Boomer) mayor Rudy Giuliani and practiced by his cogenerational lieutenant at the NYPD, Bill Bratton.

Even as Boomer police forces grew and were given ever stricter mandates to pursue even the most minor crimes (like turnstile jumping, an original object of the NYPD's zero-tolerance policy), the offices of public defenders were slowly starved of funds. The public defense system, never well funded, needed to at least keep up with the human inventory stockpiled by newly vigorous police departments. Because compensating defense funds were not forthcoming, when prison populations reached a peak in 2007 the nation had the full-time equivalent of just 15,000 conventional public defenders against a caseload of 5.6 million.*,[56] How this math allowed the justice system to fulfill its constitutional duty to provide defendants with adequate counsel went unpondered by the Boomers.[57]

After the 2008 crash, prison populations declined somewhat, the product of a minor transition to leniency, a certain lack of funding after the 2008 crash, and in some cases, court-ordered release of prisoners held in institutions so overcrowded as to violate the Eighth Amendment's ban on cruel and unusual punishment. It is too soon to tell if the pattern will persist. Certainly, the aging of the Boomer blue-collar criminal class helps, as does the absence of mass detention for white-collar crimes associated with recent stock market crashes.†,[58]

Regardless of the recent and minor dip in prisoners, the United States still has the largest prison population in the world on an absolute basis (despite being a distant third in population; China and India are each four times larger). A quarter of the world's prisoners reside in US prisons, although less than 5 percent of the world's population is American.[59] Of all major countries, save perhaps Russia, the United States has by far the largest prison population per capita—around 0.7 percent of Americans are in detention (1 in 143) and 2.1 percent in the correctional system in total (including supervised parolees, or 1 in 47).[60] These numbers are down from their peak in 2007, almost entirely due to the decrease in probationers, rather than prisoners, and even Obama's worthy grants of clemency in his final year are a rounding error.[61] Many prisoners deserve to be where they are, but many others could have ended up somewhere else had the Boomer system not

---

* Not all these cases are active or complicated, but these figures do not even permit a cursory review of anything except the most extraordinary cases. It doesn't help that the United States spends virtually nothing on public defense—0.0002 percent of GDP versus 0.2 percent for the UK, or one-thousandth on a relative basis—nor that a public defender's salary can be less than an annual bonus for a midtier associate at a big firm.

† Boomer white-collar offenders are, of course, almost never prosecuted and will be free to misbehave for another two decades without adding to the prison statistics. Four years after the 2008 crisis, the Justice Department had no statistics about financial executive prosecutions (data that had been collected in the S&L crisis), a decision one law professor called "smart" for the depressing reason that the data would be "really embarrassing."

failed them. Instead, they reside in prisons full to bursting, which is less hyperbole than numerical fact. In 2014 federal facilities were at 128 percent of rated capacity, with states ranging from a low of 50 percent (New Mexico) to a high of 150 percent (Illinois), and combined population averages almost 112 percent of maximum ratings—in other words, the prisons are stuffed.[62]

Beyond normative issues, this massive prison population is an economic liability. Prisoners produce almost no economic value and are expensive to house (though private prisons have partly offset costs by monetizing inmate labor, a situation uncomfortably close to slavery). A survey of forty states showed each additional prisoner had an official real cost of $31,286.[63] In California, the government estimates it cost $47,102 annually to incarcerate a person as of 2009, a price that rose by $19,500 in less than a decade; this trend will continue.[64] California is an expensive state for anything, but the federal government, even with the dubious benefit of economies of scale and facilities in cheaper states, has an average inmate cost of $30,620 per year.[65] We can debate what an "average" taxpayer is, but given effective tax rates and ranges it would take the entire tax revenue of at least four and up to a dozen middling taxpayers to support a single prisoner—or, to use state analogies again, it would be like taxing Virginia to imprison Nebraska.* Depending on assumptions and tastes, different states could be chosen, but the point is simply that there's something off about a society that spends so much to achieve so little.

Naturally, the neoliberal machine has offered its services (private prisons) to siphon off public funds to be transferred to their shareholders and Boomer executives. The largest of these private prisons are Corrections Corporation of America and GEO—the first founded by Boomers and the second by a Boomer-age immigrant raised in America and well immersed in Boomer culture. These completed the neoliberal custodial trinity: charter schools, for-profit universities, and now their barbed-wire equivalents, privatized prisons. There are indications that this experiment may be

---

* Of course, given the skew in income, it's really the rich paying the taxes to incarcerate the poor. That doesn't necessarily mean the rich decided to imprison the poor (though some may think so—the voting math, however, means it's the Boomer middle-class that taxes the rich to imprison the poor). In any case, it's not a healthy dynamic.

faltering, but with public prisons full, there will be private prisons for some time.

The total costs of the prison state are necessarily large: about $86 billion across federal, state, and local prisons.[66] (For context, California's corrections budget considerably exceeds that state's grants to the entire UC system.[67]) Only part of the costs are paid out of current receipts, given the federal deficit, and states' reliance on long-term debt to pay for prison construction; therefore, many of these costs will be passed down. The biggest cost, perhaps, will arrive when prisoners fulfill their sentences and return to the general population, a process only just beginning. These future parolees include huge subpopulations of the old, the mentally ill, and the badly educated, whose infirmities and convictions preclude them from many jobs. They will therefore be transferred from one form of state-subsidized living to another: welfare, Medicaid, etc.[68]

The American justice system has always had its biases, against minorities and the poor, and these are not the Boomers' creations. What Boomers are responsible for is the explosion in the prison population, vastly increasing the numbers of those exposed to institutional injustice while providing no real path for these prisoners to become self-sufficient on release. As ex-convicts bleed into the probation system and then the general public, the costs will be disproportionately borne by current and future taxpayers, not the Boomers who presided over mass incarceration in the first place.

One notable perversity of Boomer justice is the creation of a police state by Leftists of the very same generation so heavily associated with protesting the "pigs" during the Vietnam War, the 1968 Democratic Convention, and so on, their supposedly libertarian cogenerationalists, and even small-state Rightists. Ideological consistency proved no restraint, and the Boomers sanctioned the police to be the sword and arm of newly discovered middle-class moralism. What changed? Now, it was not peace symbols being spray-painted on public buildings, but crimes against Boomer properties. The junkies were no longer the (whitish) denizens of 1967's Love Fest, but people of discomfiting hues despoiling dog parks and other conveniences required by the Boomers. Blacks for whom the Boomers had supposedly rallied in the 1960s were swept into prison at rates vastly greater than the whites, with black men 3.8 to 10.5 times more likely to be serving a year or more than comparable whites, depending on age.[69]

The Brennan Center noted that an "aging population" contributed somewhat to the decline in crime. Young people historically have a greater propensity to commit crime, but the arrival of the very large Millennial generation prompted no crime wave, nor was there anything comparable before the 1960s. The Boomers may be more entangled than anyone realized. After all, *something* changed from 1967 to 1991, and we will pay the price for decades to come. Alas, the Boomer decades have left the country ill equipped to pay for anything, including a spectacularly ill-advised prison state.

CHAPTER FIFTEEN

THE WAGES OF SIN

From 1989 until 2007, median wealth increased for families
headed by someone over age 50, rose somewhat for families
headed by someone between 35–49, and stayed much the
same for younger families...Marketable wealth—the measure
used in this analysis—significantly understates the resources
of a family that expects much of its retirement income to
come from Social Security or defined benefit pension plans.
—Congressional Budget Office (2016)[1]

One of the more curious artifacts of the Boomer decades is luxury
voyeurism, a phenomenon that began in 1984 with the *Lifestyles of
the Rich and Famous* and continued through the various *Real Housewives*
series and *Downton Abbey*. The last is at least nakedly fictional, though no
less bizarre for it: an antimodern melodrama of entitled toffs, stately homes,
and dubious-though-usually-deferent staff, and generally celebrates the very
system of antidemocratic immobility against which America had originally rebelled. *Downton* manages to affront both the nation's liberal origins
and, given its theme and state sponsorship (PBS), also runs counter to the
muddled anti-elite, anti-government populism of the Republican prole-
tariat. It succeeded nonetheless. There is something decidedly odd about a

nation ostensibly tied in knots over income inequality drooling over, as the critic Robert Hughes remarked in another context, "the spectacle of privilege enjoying its own toilette."[2] Maybe America is okay with inequality after all. Or maybe the Boomers are. Or maybe TV has simply narcotized the population into accepting a fait accompli.

TV, America's defining leisure/cultural activity and thus of immense sociological importance, no longer offers the relatively realist middle-class of *Leave It to Beaver* (c. 1960), the blue-collar grit of *All in the Family* (c. 1970s), or the aspirational movin'-on-up-ism of *The Jeffersons* (c. 1975), to say nothing of the edifying splendor showcased in Kenneth Clark's *Civilization* (c. 1969), one of the last shows to assume viewers' ability for, and predisposition to, being uplifted. The great pacifier in an age of inequality, TV since the 1980s has helped inoculate against resentment so long as participants have the right accent—British, for class; suburban trash, for accessibility or derision, as the audience requires.* In the 1950s, rich Americans knew better than to flaunt wealth. Now, as long as display is leavened with degrading, preferably televisual, exhibitionism, it can be tolerated, enjoyed, or under the Boomers, even used as the basis for candidacy, e.g., Fred Thompson, Jesse Ventura, Al Franken, Sonny Bono, Donald Trump, and so on. And TV's window into the 1 percent has become increasingly important, as a moderately priced flatscreen has become the only aperture through which most Americans can reasonably expect to inhabit the moneyed world. When George Jefferson, after amassing a dry-cleaning fortune in the outer boroughs, moved to his "deluxe apartment in the sky" in 1975, just before middle-class wages started their long stagnation, he was not in the vanguard of mobility, but a final straggler. *Jeffersons* watchers witnessed a funeral, not a future.

The reason for that, of course, is that the Boomers' sociopathic strain of

---

* *Roseanne* was the last big hit to deal squarely with the problems of the working class, and to the extent it was realistic, it was not exactly optimistic until its final season. *Roseanne*'s resolution itself was sufficiently fantastical that the entire French critical establishment would have keeled over with excitement if it could have gotten beyond the plastic flowers and girth: not only do the Conners *win the lottery*, but *the show itself* is revealed to have been an unlikely therapeutic tool for its millionaire Boomer auteur, Madame Roseanne Barr-Pentland-Thomas-Arnold. We'll see the Boomer lottery/*pecunia ex machina* make its reappearance in the epilogue.

governance has not lived up to its promises, as the mediocre economy has made abundantly clear. Once upon a time, slow growth might have been chalked up to an "output gap," the difference between the economy's actual performance and true potential. Because systematic underinvestment and bad policy have reduced potential, there's not so much a gap as convergence toward a new and depressing normal, a "secular stagnation." After 2007–2008, the Fed regularly revised its estimates of potential downward, from 2.8 percent to 2.5 percent, 2.4 percent, 2.2 percent, and then 2.0 percent in 2016, at which point one Fed governor gamely tried to put a floor under things, saying that it would be "hard" to make the case for 1.0–1.5 percent growth.[3] Hard, perhaps, but not impossible; Fed governors more or less said the same thing about 2.0 percent growth back when they were predicting 2.8 percent. In the first quarter of 2016, annualized real growth dropped to 0.8 percent before rebounding somewhat the following quarter to 1.4 percent, so it was not only *not* "hard" to make the case for sub-1.5 growth, it is what actually happened.[4] At some point, one must bow to years of lackluster numbers and admit that there is little gap, "output" or otherwise, between what is happening and what could be happening.

While Americans regularly rank the economy as a top concern, many have little idea what secular stagnation entails, a situation politicians have been careful to encourage. Judged by the Clintons' exhalations, the 1990s were an era of uninterrupted prosperity rudely curtailed by Incurious George. (Skip over, as you are meant to, the fact that many of the problems George made worse were originally created by Bill.) Meanwhile, per the Obama administration's rhetoric, the economic repair job had been mostly completed as Obama left office—one more coat of paint, and the economic house would be as good as new. None of these stories are true: What we have now is a very fragile new normal of very low growth, hollow employment, mounting inequality and, on the present course, far too little to look forward to.

Income, Growth, and Intergenerational Transfers

GDP growth has been decelerating under the Boomers, as the next chart shows. For the period 2000–2015, the economy managed real annual average growth of 1.9 percent versus over 2.9 percent in years between 1970 and 1980 (which were viewed at the time as something of an economic horror show). The economy of the 1980s and 1990s performed somewhat better than the 1970s, though not by as much as commonly believed—and the '90s, presently felt to be an era of prosperity, underperformed most of the postwar/pre-Boomer period. The relative mediocrity of the 1990s was a loss made worse by the desperate and shortsighted manner in which it was achieved. As we've seen, quite a lot of Boomer-era growth was debt financed and consumption driven rather than a product of strong fundamentals. Much of the near stagnation after 2000 was the result of choices made in the late 1980s and 1990s, and the worst of the bills will come due in the next decades. The capital gains cuts, bubbles, deregulation, disinvestment, and so on of the Bill Clinton years cannot be detached from the inequality, crashes, bank consolidations, and slow growth that immediately followed, however much Hillary Clinton would have had it otherwise.

The Era of Slowly Diminishing Expectations

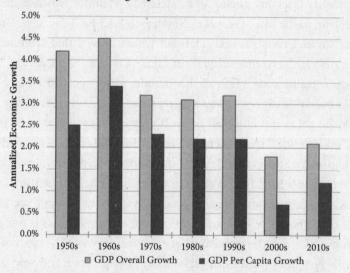

What's going on here? Economic growth overall and per person grew faster in the pre-Boomer years. Even the 1990s, a "success story," appears to be nothing spectacular in context. By the 2000s, growth slowed considerably as the full weight of Boomer policies manifested. Decades are arbitrary divisions, but the distinctions between growth, before Boomer power and during, are not arbitrary and not small.[5]

As the unusual anger of the past few elections demonstrates, America's concerns were not limited to slower growth overall, but also the distribution of wealth within a faltering economy. Median income has been essentially flat for many years, aside from an outlying (and perhaps anomalous) blip in 2015 which did not change the general shape of things. Gains in *average* income have been almost entirely driven by gains at the top of the distribution. Without belaboring the specifics of a problem well treated elsewhere, economic inequality has vastly expanded since the 1980s, with money flowing to the top segment and almost nowhere else. It is, in substantial part, a Boomer phenomenon, because while inequality has risen in other countries, in no other advanced economy has the shift been quite as pronounced as in the United States, with the limited exceptions of our cultural cousins in Canada and Britain. The tax and monetary policies that led to this were already covered in Chapters 7 and 11.

While helpful in calling attention to the issues of inequality, some of the post-2008 jeremiads about the 1 percent were too facile, ignoring as they did that even fairly large degrees of inequality have a certain inevitability. Inequality is a consequence of a capitalist system for which there is no replacement, as the utter failures of North Korea, Cuba, Venezuela, Bolivia, and the Soviet Union showed (many of which proved that "communist" regimes also had extreme inequality). Deng Xiaoping, himself the leader of a then socialist state, realized this decades years ago and loosened the communitarian leash on Chinese entrepreneurship. Whether Deng actually said "to get rich is glorious" or openly acknowledged that some people would "get rich first," that's been the People's Republic's modus vivendi ever since, and successful (so far).[6] That's the nature of capitalism everywhere, even "socialism with Chinese characteristics."[7] Capitalism is, if not a perfect machine for generating general prosperity, then the best one yet devised and the only one conceivable in America. One of its outcomes is some very rich people—indeed, the enticement of extraordinary wealth is part of what makes the system work. The critical issues are *who* gets rich and *how*; society has never been agnostic about these matters.

If Boomer-era inequality had simply been the product of fast growth and innovation, with rising tides lifting all boats and a few yachts besides, that would have been fine. That was not the case. Inequality has been driven by debt, speculation, lower taxes, lower social investment, redounding in the short term to the benefit of the rich—but those rich people are not merely rich, they are overwhelmingly old (which is why they tolerate the short-term aspect). Wealthier households tilt Boomerish, with the balance sheet inflated not so much by real growth and investment—the sluggish GDP figures imply as much—but by the transfer of wealth from other generations to themselves. The only households to experience gains in median family wealth from 1989 to 2013 were those headed by people age sixty-five or older, so the oldest households in 2013 were wealthier than their peers of 1989. The younger Boomers also got richer from 1989 to 2007, and while the crash produced some losses, they were much less affected than non-Boomers. Although older households are usually wealthier than younger ones for obvious reasons, the *gaps* between younger and older, Boomers and non-Boomers, grew. In 1989, fifty- to sixty-four-year-olds (non-Boomers) were ~1.7 times wealthier than thirty-five- to forty-nine-year-olds (Boomers). By 2013, Boomers *were* the fifty- to sixty-five-year-olds, and they were ~2.5 times wealthier than the new set of thirty-five- to forty-nine-year-olds (almost all of whom were non-Boomers). And that calculation of wealth does not include Social Security or pensions, which probably drag the entire Boomer cohort into positive territory; everyone else did and probably will do worse.[8]

The Boomers' extraction of wealth from other generations helps explain why the Organisation for Economic Cooperation and Development (OECD) ranked the United States dead last among peers in a 2013 survey of "intergenerational equity."[9] The United States, an "outlier" among developed nations, had an "exceedingly high" rate of child poverty (21 percent), compared to Northern Europe (4–7 percent). Achieving lower rates of senior poverty at the expense of the young, present and future, has been a choice. Per the OECD, US spending on the old outpaces spending on the young by almost 5:1. The ratio will only get worse as more Boomers retire and absorb benefits, a process that will continue as Boomers join entitlements rolls and remain there until the last Boomers die out after 2050. On intergenerational terms, America is not doing well. Only Japan, Austria, and a few other countries with much older populations (many of which are, for reasons related and not, perpetual basket cases like Italy and Greece) have a worse skew when it comes to spending on the elderly versus the nonelderly.

International comparisons are illustrative, not definitive, because each country has its own quirks and accounting. Regardless, the OECD has almost certainly been too lenient with the United States on three critical inputs—debt, senior spending, and ecology. As we've seen in prior chapters, one cannot take the various numbers that serve as OECD's inputs at face value, starting with the debt. And despite OECD's forgiving calculation, the United States is still last. It's also notable that America's closest cultural parallel, Canada (whose citizens will doubtless detest the comparison), also languishes near the bottom. It has been subject to its own, if less odious, generation of Boomers, like Stephen Harper (b. 1959), Canada's answer to Bush II and its first real Boomer prime minister.*

The poverty young people currently experience will reappear in old age. The heavy tilt toward senior spending has reduced (for now) poverty among current seniors. Senior poverty rates are now lower than poverty rates for the general population and less than half youth poverty rates.[10] That's fine for the Boomers, but when the Social Security Trust Fund is exhausted, benefits will automatically be cut absent drastic political action. Therefore, more future seniors (GenX and younger) will revert to the conditions Boomers have already imposed on the young: a lot of poverty. The rates of senior poverty, driven down to 10 percent by 2014, will after 2034–2037 resemble or exceed today's youth poverty rates of 21 percent.[11] The young will not remain youthful, but many will remain poor.

The enrichment of the old at the expense of the young shows the fundamental absurdity about crude fixations on the 1 percent. The 1 percent cannot control a democracy on their own. A giant population of aging Boomers can and has. It is no surprise that the rich are old, or that the patterns of wealth accumulation of the two groups over the Boomer decades look so similar.

---

*Technically, the title of first Boomer PM was held by Kim Campbell, but she lasted less than 5 months. Harper lasted nine years.

Rich vs. Poor or Old vs. Young?

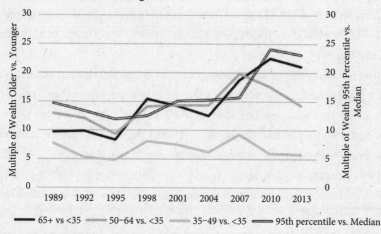

What's going on here? The conventional narrative is that the richest Americans have been getting very rich, very quickly, and that is mostly true, with the top half of one percent doing by far the best and the very rich top 5 to 10 percent doing quite well. The double line shows the multiple of worth of a family richer than 94.99 percent of other Americans vs. the median family as a proxy of the very, but not billionaire level, rich. The other lines show the same dynamic, except with households grouped by age vs. households headed by people under thirty-five. The gaps between rich and middle-class and the gap between the old and young have been growing in the same way. People exercised about trends in wealth inequality should also be worried about age inequality. The exception to the trend is for the late-middle-aged, whose housing wealth was hard hit by the Great Recession. Once post-2013 data is in, even this group should be in better shape, as unprecedented intervention has rescued many Boomer homeowners. Part of this is natural: Households should be wealthier as they get older, but the striking thing is how the dynamics of old vs. young mirror the much more politically prominent dynamic of rich vs. middle class.[12]

The Many Flavors of Unemployment

The recovery since 2008 has been one of the weakest and slowest recorded, so fragile and with so much risk of reversal that it hardly seems a recovery at all, notwithstanding the perky jobs reports the Obama administration routinely issued. We have already seen that the official unemployment rate, which hovered around 5 percent in Obama's last year, has been driven in part by declining labor force participation. The official unemployment rate is called "U-3," and measures total unemployed, but counts only those without jobs who are still looking for work—*not* the permanently discouraged or the underemployed, two categories of increasing importance in the recent and iffy recovery.*,13

Broader measures of unemployment offer a less heartening picture, one that squares more easily with the rage of certain populists (the Trumpenproletariat and unreconstructed Bernie fanatics, e.g.). If unemployment were really just 5 percent, the Republican and Democratic primaries would have been without their stranger fauna—creatures that were, like many exotic consumables, imported. Trump is a billionaire, probably; a cipher, certainly; and a Republican, absolutely not. Sanders is not a Democrat, though registered as such for the primary, and as of early 2016, his Senate homepage made clear what he was and really is: the "longest serving *independent* member of Congress."14 Sanders *is* a permanent creature of government, albeit of an odd socialist hue, but not an "outsider" (per Chapter 5), a Democrat, or even a cogent thinker on his key issue of financial reform (for that, one must turn to Elizabeth Warren, one the comparatively rare examples of thoughtful Boomer legislators despite her recent inflammatory tack). Market-based democracies with true 5 percent unemployment just do not produce these sorts of oddities, or produce as their onetime front-runner the wildly unpopular and protean mystery that is Mrs. Clinton, ex–Goldwater Girl and present Democrat, alternately for and against free trade depending on the moment, and so on, her compass pointing not to an ideological pole but its political homonym, much less ditch her for the even stranger Trump.

More realistic metrics than conventional unemployment figures explain these oddities. The Bureau of Labor Statistics' broadest measure is U-6, which dipped below 10 percent only six years after the Great Recession officially "ended."15 U-6 includes the conventionally unemployed, plus the underemployed, and others "marginally attached" to the labor force. Combined with those who have totally given up, U-6 offers a less heartening picture; 10 percent is not great, and it's reasonably possible to calculate bleaker numbers

---

* For most purposes, people in prisons don't count toward the unemployment rate, though they are basically unemployed, and were US incarceration rates at developed world norms, unemployment would be about half a point higher.

Unemployment: Larger, Longer, and Worse

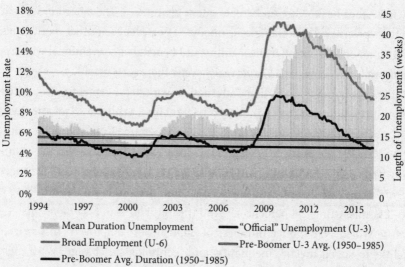

Legend:
- Mean Duration Unemployment
- "Official" Unemployment (U-3)
- Broad Employment (U-6)
- Pre-Boomer U-3 Avg. (1950–1985)
- Pre-Boomer Avg. Duration (1950–1985)

What's going on here? The simplest way to look at this chart is whether the squiggly lines are above or below the horizontal lines—above means the economy is doing worse for the unemployed than in the pre-Boomer years. During the course of Boomer power, things have tended to drift distinctly above the lines. Six years after the Great Recession, official unemployment finally dropped below its pre-Boomer average (the double horizontal line). However, looking at other measures, unemployment remains a problem: broader measures of unemployment remain elevated and the duration of unemployment (the bar field) remains very long, especially relative to the pre-Boomer averages (the solid black horizontal line). People out of work for long periods tend to be less successful at ever getting good replacement jobs, so this is in some sense a predictor of future troubles.[16]

(but nothing quite as high as what some politicians have offered—e.g., it's not 25 percent). In economic terms, Obama spent both of his terms getting the country from panic to a place that is at best disappointing, though this is not primarily his fault. These facts explain some of the popular rage.

That the Obama administration has emphasized the narrower U-3 falls well short of sociopathic deceit, given the long history of U-3. Nevertheless, focusing on U-3 does not acknowledge fundamental shifts in the economy; it's akin to fixating on America's lead in the production of Necco wafers—i.e., simultaneously true and somewhat beside the point. Jobs have been created, but not all jobs are created equal, and quite a few do not provide the opportunity to work as many hours as people would like or need. A declining fraction of jobs offer full benefits and a degree of security; many others offer (at most) flexibility instead of health care and employment guarantees. The latter kind of job features prominently in the "gig" economy.* Whatever their other merits, gigs and temp jobs do not offer the stability and benefits of conventional employment, and only some participants really prefer these sorts of jobs.

The gig economy and other "alternative work arrangements" accounted for quite a lot of recent job growth, probably at least a third of all jobs created, and per preliminary findings by Harvard's Lawrence Katz and Princeton's Alan Krueger, perhaps *all of the net employment growth in the U.S. economy from 2005–2015 appears to have occurred in alternative work arrangements*" (emphasis original; in a recent update, the authors revised "all" to a no-less-unsettling "94 percent").[17] And this returns us to *Downton Abbey*—before World War I, huge numbers of English were employed "in service," thanks to social inertia, inequality, and technological change. With gigs, this is happening again, only now the chauffeur comes in the livery of Lyft's pink moustache, not *Downton*'s white tails. And this time, there will be no intermarriage between passenger and driver à la Lady Sybil and Tom, especially in the coming decades when the driver becomes a robot. The Dowager Countess of Grantham has become Lady Brenda of the Colonies, residing in Sun City, Arizona, couriered from aquarobics to gerontologist by rideshare and nursed by a contractor workforce, often composed of the immigrants her ex-governor Jan Brewer so detested.[18] At least, however, there's still staff; indeed, Lady Brenda can expect more, albeit younger, browner, poorer, and occasionally inanimate.

The question of jobs and who fills them opens messy questions of trade and immigration, two fixtures of American policy that have recently returned to the forefront of debate. In theory, trade and immigration bring net benefits, but for whom? Over the very long term, everybody wins, but no voter or politician operates on geologic timescales. In the short run, free trade and immigration tend to benefit consumers in higher-income countries and workers in, or emigrating from, lower-income countries. Over the medium term, beneficiaries tend to be those insulated from displacement

* Another disclosure: I have invested in several gig companies, like TaskRabbit and Lyft, because a few years ago I began to suspect that gigs were the future of work.

either by seniority, skill, or money (whether previously earned or currently doled out courtesy of the government or monopoly power), categories inhabited by older persons.

Over a single (sociopathic) individual's lifespan, an optimum strategy might be to oppose immigration and trade while young and vulnerable to displacement, flip to support in middle age once union rules, tenure, and capital provided some buffer, at that point relying on the government to ensure against the diminishing period of risk between tariff-free binges at Costco and the collection of Social Security. For someone born circa 1950, the 1980s might have therefore been premature for unrestrained free trade; perhaps better to "Buy American!" and support a Republican waging a trade campaign against Japan (as Reagan did). The arrival of the 1990s and middle-aged security might have been a chance to reverse those positions in favor of maximum consumption without any worry of personal replacement (and indeed, this was when NAFTA passed with bipartisan support and when a major wave of illegal immigration occurred). By 2016, with Social Security kicking in and a transfer of spending from foreign goods to domestic services (provided for by millions of illegal immigrants already emplaced), one might have been free to indulge in whatever view aligned with the prejudices of the moment. And this was, of course, basically what happened: heavy-handed statism under Reagan, liberalization starting with Clinton and perhaps ending after Obama, and a certain renewed tolerance among those older, on the dole, or in possession of large portfolios, of nativism and monopoly power (more on the last in a moment).

The details and emotions around trade and immigration are complicated and variable, but one thing has always been clear: Trade would produce dislocations (the polite term for layoffs) and worked best if there were mechanisms for adjustment, be it welfare, job training, R&D to support new industries, or all of that and more. Obviously, nothing quite so thoughtful or extensive took place. Instead, there were purely geographic relocations. Some existing and many potential jobs from the Rust Belt were shuffled off to Mexican maquiladoras or sent to the nearest thing America had to Third World labor and environmental conditions and biddable politicians, i.e., the Southeast. Detroit aggressively expanded south of the border post-NAFTA, while BMW opened a plant in South Carolina, a state refreshingly light of union laws and pollution constraints and always open to tax and regulatory concessions.[19] While trade did cause reshuffling of incomes, some losses were partly offset by increased purchasing power. Prices for consumables from Asia and Mexico fell, and that was fine for middle-aged consumers. Eventually, of course, trade and immigration meant that the prices of services (wages) would follow the price of goods; again, fine, with Social Security on the way. The courses of trade and immigration have not been irrational or unintended. They have been sociopathically perfect as a strategy.

One other item about trade and the Boomers: Of the many reasons to explain America's booming post–WW II economy and its subsequent faltering, perhaps the most labored and Boomerish excuse is that with the rest of the world flat on its back from 1940 to 1970, America had it easy. The facts show that underperformance cannot be excused on that basis. Though physically undamaged, America had its own, if less onerous, war debts and a huge, displaced labor force of soldiers and civilian suppliers. Nothing about 1946 was easy, at home or abroad, though the young Boomers didn't realize this. Still, America managed to pay down debts and retrain workers, achievements that could have been models for handling the much smaller dislocations created by free trade. If millions of soldiers could be transitioned via the GI Bill, could not something similar have happened post-NAFTA?

Moreover, America prospered even as Europe and Japan recovered and became more competitive. America even pursued a policy to its short-term disadvantage, heavily subsidizing many former enemies and allies alike in the form of defense, foreign aid, and open markets; America made itself *less* competitive after the war than it could have been. The midcentury was not an economic cakewalk. It was the product of prudential policies at home and abroad. It was not in the 1950s, when Europe and Japan were in ruins, that America stalled, but much later, even as competitors' wages, regulations, and currencies converged to American levels. That counters the convenient narrative of America skinned alive by the cunning manufacturers of Nagoya and Munich, protected by currency manipulators in Tokyo and Bonn. (Nor have Europe and Japan's demographically driven slowdowns resulted in any sudden uptick in American growth, showing again that America does best when everyone does well.) Finally, there is something not merely untrue, but wholly depressing, even un-American, about the idea that the nation can only compete when the rest of the world is in ruins.

The Fifth Wall

America did enjoy one immediate benefit of European chaos: the mass immigration of highly talented Europeans to the safety of the States. Immigration continued rising in gross terms for decades, though much of it was illegal, and happened under the Boomers. Whether immigration has been good, bad, or indifferent overall is largely beyond the scope of this book, though of course to the extent untrained migrants are an initial drain, the remediation of good schooling might help. Of course, that has not been provided even to Americans of unquestionably native parentage.

What is germane is the utter strangeness of present immigration policy. You may expect that well-educated, motivated immigrants would be precisely the sort of people preferred by the system. Their improvement, after all, was paid for by some other country's tax dollars and represents an outright transfer of value to the United States. These realities motivated Operation Paperclip, which held the national nose and vacuumed up German scientists after the war. And yet, visas like the H-1B for skilled immigrants (now unburdened by Nazi pasts) are notoriously difficult to get, capped at 85,000 (65,000 standard, 20,000 related to master's degrees), though various administrative quirks manage to accommodate about 130,000 such persons annually.[*,20] These individuals—as well as those on student visas—receive training at the partial expense of American corporations and universities. In a move of stunning perversity, many are then shuffled back, laden with American intellectual property and skills, to their places of origin.

While the talented must pass through the eye of the H-1B needle, wide doors remain for others courtesy of the talent-agnostic mechanisms of kinship and plain illegality, slipways not carefully targeted to America's long-term economic advantage. The former might be an area where the

---

* One of which apparently went to the most recent Madame Trump, a skilled...model. A special class of H-1B visas exists for just these exceptional people.

Boomers have displayed a redemptive empathy, or at least, nonsociopathic inertia. The latter has just been a policy failure and one abetted by Boomer employers, who contented themselves to look away or profit—a category that (twice) came very close to including the nation's top law enforcement officer. Hence the spectacle of Bill Clinton's first two nominees for attorney general being scuttled over their employment of undocumented nannies. Clinton blithely proceeded with the first nominee even after she disclosed her knowing impropriety; both Clinton and Joe Biden, then on the Judiciary Committee, seemed to be of the view that "everybody does it," until scandal forced them to proclaim that everybody does *not* do it.[21] Both nominees were (inevitably) Boomers.* Their nominations failed as nativists expressed outrage. Of course, many of those making pilgrimages to Capitol Hill to vent their spleens returned to McMansions tended by their own staff of illegal gardeners, contractors, and nannies. Whatever partisans said, Boomer America wanted these immigrants and the cheap labor they provided, just as they wanted cheap foreign goods. As drug cartels know, where there is demand, there is supply, so immigrants are here, legally and otherwise. It's incumbent on us to find a decent solution to this Boomer mess, perhaps a modified Bracero project (a migrant worker program that ran from the 1940s to the 1960s) or modest enforcement of tax ID laws. Although Obama made some decent efforts, he was stymied by the Boomer political consensus, whose most energetic propositions boil down to the infeasible and indefensible: walls and look-the-other-way.

Monopoly Money

There is, finally, the issue of rising monopoly power, a sociopathic product of neoliberalism coupled with a distaste for the hard work of long-term investment. Monopolies can provide short-term profits at low cost, with nothing more than a quick change to the law, benefits redounding to the (Boomer) capital class. Monopolies are inextricably linked to jobs, inequality, and

---

* Judge (sic) Kimba Wood's nanny appears to have been properly hired under prior applicable laws; her sin was failing to respond forthrightly to the White House's specific questions about nannies.

productivity, because abusive monopolies can maintain profitability while firing staff, outsourcing customer service, and underinvesting in their businesses. They are protected by their market power, whether sanctioned by patent law (acceptable) or regulators being forced by Congress to look the other way (less so). Monopolies relate to trade because many justify their existence on the basis that America needs large national champions to compete in the brutal world of free trade. Perhaps so, but this logic more or less guaranteed that the one place monopoly profits would not flow was to employees. After all, part of the justification for size was to compete against cunning foreigners. As the wages of overseas labor are alleged to be unduly low, thanks to backwardness and currency manipulation (though of course, it's not as if General Motors and Ford sputtered because Mercedes or Honda pay slave wages), the one thing monopolists can't and don't want to do is raise wages. That would contradict the whole competitive argument in the first place. If any benefits were realized, they would flow to the menagerie of Boomer shareholders and executives.

Monopolies and oligopolies grew under the Boomers, a product of the corresponding decline in antitrust regulation. The initial deregulatory push began in the twilight of the 1970s and gathered steam under Reagan, though if the original impulse can be set at the feet of a different generation, deregulation's long continuation and growing consequences are essentially Boomer. Both law and economics recognize that monopolies are not always bad. "Natural" monopolies can produce net social good; multiple competitors in some situations might be inefficient. The state analogy is the public good/natural monopoly. It's helpful that there's only one fire department, and probably just as well that it's run by the government. On the private side, Facebook, at least in America, is an economically acceptable natural monopoly—it's a product that gets better as more people use it (a "network effect"), it's difficult for competitors to re-create and doubtful consumers want a substitute, and there have been no real charges that Mark Zuckerberg has abused his position to dispatch competitors.

Still, not all monopolies are natural, and there has been an alarming rise in the market power of megafirms. That is not to say that size automatically guarantees abuse, only that it creates its potential and, given the occupancy of corner offices by Boomers, should alarm. While we have not returned to the days of Standard Oil by any stretch, many companies do possess significant market power and seem to extract monopoly profits, returned to their owners and executives, not workers, consumers, or R&D departments.[22] Corporate giants do not remit overmuch of these rents to the Treasury, given the decline in corporate taxation and the creation of megafirms to avoid taxes through inversions. The rise of firms with monopoly power and their ability to generate profits without the usual sorts of investments may also explain why the S&P 500 has experienced better profit growth than revenue growth over long periods (notably, after 2008). It's not that these firms are growing so much as they are making easy profits, cutting costs, and buying back stock with the proceeds (which boosts earnings per share without increasing the intrinsic value of the business).[23] Market power permits these easier options instead of the harder work of innovation.

Some of the more abusive participants, as anyone who has interacted with their local (and probably only) cable provider knows, are telecom companies, though high degrees of questionable power now exist in agriculture, pharmaceuticals, retail, beer, and elsewhere. In the land of endless choice, you may select from many different brews, but not many different brewers. You can journey to the oligopolist Wal-Mart, within fifteen minutes' reach of 90 percent of Americans, to select from many different beers, almost 80 percent of which are likely to have been produced by only two companies, Anheuser-Busch InBev and MillerCoors (regulators approved the sale, subject to some divestments, of the latter's parent company to the former while I was editing this book, creating the world's largest beer company).[24] For the temperance minded, online giant Amazon can ship you a soda produced by duopolists Coke or Pepsi, made with high-fructose syrups derived from corn seeds provided by oligopolists like Monsanto (the subject, in 2016, of an acquisition offer by fellow agricultural oligopolist Bayer), along with snacks from Frito-Lay (a Pepsi subsidiary), delivered by Amazon's oligopolist partners UPS and FedEx, the better to enjoy streamed shows traveling over your local telecom monopolist's fiber, whose bills will be paid via cards issued by oligopolists Visa, MasterCard and Amex, or by debiting an account held at one of the giant banks. Whether any of this is good or bad is hard for individuals to resolve; it's the province of the regulators. What is clear is that the rise of megafirms has taken place substantially under Boomer watch.

Antitrust regulators report, of course, to their sociopathic political masters, so we can expect concentrated market power for some time, *and this may actually be the best possible outcome* until the era of sociopathic governance concludes. Addressing potential monopoly problems requires a sense of justice and a mastery of data that has been notably absent in these past sociopathic decades. The prospect of Bernie Sanders breaking up the banks was truly alarming given the near-total ignorance he revealed in a New York *Daily News* interview—it would have been a Boomer bull in the china shop.*[25]

Of course, Sanders will never get that chance, but the interventions that have occurred do not hearten. Sanders was correct that the most urgent sector for reform in the past two decades has been finance. The government's solution was more consolidation, not less, while providing backstops to banks of all shapes and sizes. The same has been true in agriculture, an industry necessary for life itself and always a subject for showboating, if not effective action. (Must Iowa have its primary first?) As for those cherished farms, input costs have risen faster than crop prices, which means the few remaining independent farmers exist as expedient middlemen who funnel subsidies upward to the four firms that by 2009 controlled 50+ percent of the markets for seeds, pesticides, equipment, and so on (up from ~20–30 percent in 1994).[26] With our food supply concentrated in so few hands, the spectacle of feckless sociopaths breaking up seed suppliers for the sake of political theatre is truly alarming. For better and worse, nothing will happen.

———

The Boomer economy has been disappointing, but to repeat, the United States is not poor, nor has it stopped growing. What has happened is that growth has slowed and will slow further still, and the nation's balance sheet

———

* The *News* kept asking Sanders "how" he would break up the banks and if the government had the powers to do it, and the answers were vague, including "well, I think the Fed has [that authority]"; then another question about Fed authority to do various things "by fiat," to which the response was "Yeah. Well I believe you do," and all sorts of similar vagueness on a supposedly signature issue, all *from a member of the Joint Economic Committee.* It's hard to provide a cogent summary of Sanders's rambling, contradictory, and woolly plans, but you can follow the link in the endnotes and subject yourself to the full thing if you're inclined.

has eroded. Wealth has been redistributed from the young to the old, paralleled by the concentration of power in ever fewer corporations, who in the absence of competition provide less innovation and fewer jobs. The result has been far from a resounding success.

Certainly, given America's commanding lead right through the 1970s in almost all critical areas, the job market's successful absorption of returning soldiers in the 1940s and the vast legions of Boomers in the 1970s, and the peace dividend after the Cold War, the story of American economics could have been one of widespread prosperity instead of the mixed picture we do have. Coupled with the astounding burdens visited upon the young, including mediocre schools and a giant prison-industrial complex, and the sheer insanity of the Boomer political class that reached its acme in the 2016 contest, is there anything to which the Boomers can point in their defense?

CHAPTER SIXTEEN

THE MYTH OF BOOMER GOODNESS

> We were taught in the sixties to award ourselves merit
> for membership in a superior group—irrespective of
> our or the group's accomplishments. We continue to do
> so, irrespective of accomplishments, having told each
> other we were special. We learned that all one need do is
> refrain from trusting anyone over thirty...we were the
> culmination of history, superior to all those misguided
> who had come before, which is to say all humanity.
> —David Mamet (b. 1947, in 2011).[1]

It would be gratifying if the Boomers admitted their mistakes wholesale and ceded power to other groups. A little contrition might recommend sympathy to a generation sorely in need of some, while new management might finally begin to address the accumulated problems of the Boomer years. But contrition requires a guilt the Boomers don't feel, and new management may demand reparations the Boomers don't want to pay. Anyway, what the disgruntled multitude fails to grasp is that the Boomers are *Good People*, and Good People do not need to apologize for or explain, much less repay, anything. Boomers have always taken this view, believing that they are more moral, just, freedom loving, and generally deserving than other generations—"special," to use Mamet's term, and worthy of special treatment. Reality has forced a few Boomers to express retrospective doubts about their generation's actual virtue (notably Mamet and Erica Jong, from different angles). These turncoats are exceptional cases, and most Boomers retain an unshakable faith in their moral credentials, credentials that cancel any obligation to atone. Rising debt, melting ice sheets, crumbling freeways, and faltering schools are just small-minded entries in a spreadsheet with no cell large enough to contain Boomer goodness.

If anything, the sociopaths believe it is *we* who should be thanking *them*, our betters, without the ungrateful backtalk. In 2016, when young Black Lives Matter protestors dared to question Bill Clinton about his 1994 crime bill, legislation whose carnage was covered in Chapter 14, Clinton lashed out. Not only were the protestors wrong, Clinton argued, they were "defending the people who killed the lives you say matter."[2] In Clinton's view, he was the savior, and the protestors just confused apologists for the sort of scum Hillary Clinton referred to in 1996 as "super-predators." Clinton seemed surprised that anyone might question his wife's use of "super-predators"; how else would protestors describe "gang-leaders who got 13-year-olds hopped up on crack, and sent them out in the streets to murder other African-American children"?[3] Per Bill Clinton, "maybe you"—you, the thankless multitude—"thought they were good citizens, [Hillary] didn't."[4] Well, no one did or does. The debate wasn't over the imprisonment of a relatively small number of violent gang leaders, it was over the legions of petty drug criminals locked away for years by indiscriminate sentencing laws. In Clinton's Boomerish mind, though, if you were against the crime bill (or more pertinently, against Clinton) then you were clearly for the criminals.

This same Manicheanism stretched beyond the admittedly strange Clintonverse. When libertarians raised questions about the excesses of the Patriot Act, the Bush II administration knew what to do. It was "with us or with the terrorists," and any questions invariably landed you on the wrong side; don't ask what intelligence fiascoes abetted 9/11, because questions merely establish you as an ungrateful partisan on the wrong side. Bush II, of course, derived enormous support from the evangelical Right, itself a

Boomer creation (Chapter 5) and convinced enough of its moral bona fides that it implicitly sanctioned the murder of abortion providers and embraced, until 2000, a ban on interracial dating at its flagship, Bob Jones University. The administrators of real universities, not to be outdone in repressive goodness, nurtured a culture of political correctness so sanctimonious and restrictive as to negate the principles of inquiry and open debate their institutions had fought for centuries to achieve. Naturally, all this was painted as protection of helpless innocents who would one day grow up and thank the Boomers for their kindnesses, and if the golems of goodness occasionally went berserk, that was their fault, not their creators'. The whole faux-moral lexicon of Boomerspeak, whatever its sources, is the language of tyranny, not virtue.*

If the idea of Boomer sociopathy is valid, the whole idea of Boomers as Good People is absurd, and it may seem like an unnecessary frustration to explore Boomer morality. Nevertheless, the notion of Boomer goodness warrants a thorough factual debunking. First, the Boomer propaganda department has so assiduously promoted Good People branding that many people accept it (once, even I believed it).† Crediting the myth of Boomer goodness may deter voters from the important task of asking the Boomers to pay their fair share. For example, the peace-and-love narrative about Vietnam collapses in the face of the facts described in Chapter 3, just as the whole I-feel-your-pain motif of Bill Clinton's presidency was belied by the various crime, welfare, and other policies then pursued, to say nothing of the "compassionate conservatism" practiced by the GOP in the 2000s (being neither, it failed even on its own terms). Second, questioning the record not

---

* Shoddy self-righteousness is, to some extent, just part of politics and has been practiced before, as in the toxic witch hunts prosecuted by Joe McCarthy in the 1950s. But many of Senator McCarthy's colleagues condemned him at the time, and while Eisenhower refused to publicly condemn the senator on the grounds that it would be beneath the dignity of the White House, the president did steadily undermine a senator he found "reprehensible" and whose methods he "despised." Arguably, Eisenhower should have gone public, but in the end, his moves behind the scene helped achieve the right result.

† In general, this chapter conflates "goodness" with the mildly progressive social agenda accepted by a plurality of the electorate or that flows out of the Constitution and settled law. In a democratic society, this seems like a reasonable way to limn a discussion that otherwise tends toward unhelpful sprawl.

only reveals the absence of Boomer goodness, it shows something of the opposite, especially in the antidemocratic methods the Boomers implemented to preserve control at a time when demographic power alone can no longer sustain the sociopathic agenda.

To be clear, this chapter does not argue that the Boomer decades have been without moral advances; it argues that the Boomers don't deserve nearly as much credit for those advances as commonly supposed. Gains came, but not as quickly as before, and were unevenly distributed, sometimes highly so. They often arrived courtesy of mixed motives, as with the expansion of disability rights, or, over the opposition of Boomers, as in the case of gay marriage. And they were offset by some new and very large injustices, especially in economic matters, which affect far more people than the old categories of discrimination ever did. As bills from the sociopathic decades come due, Americans may decide to forgive the Boomer generation some of its misdeeds, but they should do so only as a matter of their own goodness, not as thanks for moral services the Boomers never rendered. Much of that forgiveness will come in the form of money—the flow of senior benefits—making the Boomers' record on economic fairness a natural place to begin.

Money Matters

Economic justice is where the narrative of Boomer morality breaks down completely. The startling rise of income and wealth inequality has been detailed in this book (e.g., Chapter 15) and elsewhere. The general consensus is that high levels of inequality create problems, although there are some debates about whether inequality is immoral or amoral and whether the present levels of inequality are really quite as bad as they've been made out.* What has not been debated as thoroughly is intergenerational inequality,

---

* Some have attempted to sidestep the issue by characterizing inequality as a natural byproduct of technological change and the winner-take-all dynamics of modern economies, an idea which has great currency in certain circles. Even if correct as a description—and I think it often is, as other chapters have suggested—it is not *by itself* a

and the relative silence on that issue is partly because the issues were settled long ago. For individuals, debts die with the debtor; it has been a long time since the West forced children to make good on obligations they had no say in accumulating. For Boomer society, the reverse is true. The mechanisms of perpetual national debt and the deferred obligations of pensions, environment, infrastructure, and so on *do* allow debts to be passed along.

The Boomers inherited some of the lightest intergenerational burdens in American history and will leave some of the greatest. In doing so, the Boomers have authored one of the greatest injustices of a modern nation (mostly) at peace. It's an injustice that is not as overt or violent as the cruelties based on categories of race, gender, or sexuality. And unlike conventional categories of oppression—which were based on minority status (with the exception of women, a minority that is in population terms, a majority)—intergenerational injustice affects not only most Americans now living, but all those yet to be born. The various explanations, excuses, motivations, and contexts for this catastrophe have already been raised and disposed of in earlier chapters; all that matters here is that the intergenerational injustice created by the Boomers, in full service of themselves, by itself moots any idea of Boomer goodness.

The more abstract type of academic philosopher may dismiss economic issues as crass and collateral—how can a national debt, however swollen, compare to a lynching? For a given family, at a given moment, no comparison can be made; doing so would be grotesque. But over time, and on a social scale, economic injustice becomes a wrong of tremendous proportion, and is the more insidious for being less graphic. In a market society, economic justice and economic opportunity are the ingredients necessary to make all other forms of justice truly meaningful and should not be ignored. It is very hard for one generation to engage in the "pursuit of happiness" if it is busy paying the bill for another generation's sociopathic pursuit of the same. Worse, it can be hard to even participate in democracy at all. If a younger citizen, saddled with educational debt, paying taxes to service obligations taken

---

serious contribution to the moral discussion, since it conflates inevitability with moral neutrality and ignores the possibility of redistribution.

out by prior generations, working a crummy and inflexible job, cannot take time off to vote, then his vote has been rendered nugatory. Economic injustice is a more roundabout way of disenfranchising people than the Jim Crow laws of old, though it has its own considerable power. It is also not the only way the Boomers have failed to uphold the central principle of democracy.

One Person, How Many Votes?

Aside from odd liminal cases, the incontestable virtue in America is the right to vote. None of the debates that muddy the waters around abortion or the death penalty are pertinent to the franchise. History's judgment of Americans who seek to disenfranchise other Americans is invariably harsh. The principle has been settled: Citizens have a right to vote and to do so freely, without prejudice, and with minimal inconvenience.

The struggle to arrive at that principle—a struggle that has provided history with so many opportunities to judge prior generations, to whose ranks the Boomers will eventually be added—has been long. It started in 1776 and continued until 1965, and the length, general direction, and the bloody fights it engendered show how central the free vote is to the moral arc of the United States. At the Founding, not many people could vote. There were a lot of qualifying adjectives: You had to be a citizen who was also white, adult, propertied, and male. After the 1790s, the limiting adjectives were white, adult, and male; after the Civil War, adult and male; by 1919, just adult (and even the definition of adult was broadened in the 1970s to include semi-adult teenagers). There was resistance every step of the way—the old guard liked as many adjectives in its democracy as it did in its prose—and if "white" and "male" could no longer be employed as overt qualifiers, "stakeholder" and "literacy" would do, enforced by poll taxes, residency requirements, and reading tests. Those who did not have the means to pay the tariff to vote, had not lived long enough in one place, or could not meet the standards of literacy, could not vote. Such people were usually poor blacks (and not a few poor whites), which was the point.

By the early 1960s—i.e., before Boomers could participate in the dialogue—Congress had had enough. No more adjectives, no more qualifiers, no more tests. The Constitution, as then understood and amended, required no less. To guarantee against backsliding, Congress passed the Voting Rights Act of 1965 (the VRA). The VRA paid special attention to places that had been historically abusive about the franchise. The act was an essential part of ensuring that citizens who cared to vote would have those votes counted, without the old impediments.

Under the Boomers, Right and Left, adjectives and qualifiers have started to return, and the moral arc has begun to reverse. Felons had long faced voting restrictions, but these restrictions were of limited numerical impact until the Boomer justice system started mass-producing millions of felons, starting with Bill Clinton. If poll and literacy taxes were out, proxies like voter ID laws could be employed, and have now become something of a vogue with Boomer legislators. You still have to be able to read and to cough up money to get, say, a driver's license, though since these filters are applied at the DMV instead of at the voting booth, they don't count as poll taxes or literacy tests. To take another example, many states have no explicit provisions that require employers to provide paid leave to vote, so a stagnating economy also serves as a filter, one that can favor older people, who are either retired or are senior enough to have flexible jobs.

As exclusionary techniques mutated faster than Boomer morality evolved, laws like the VRA remained important protectors of the franchise, helping root out new and subtle discriminations. In the Boomer years, however, the VRA has been eviscerated by the Supreme Court, with the implicit consent of Congress. On the Court's part, Chief Justice John Roberts (a Boomer, appointed by a Boomer, and confirmed by Boomers) effectively gutted the VRA in *Shelby County v. Holder* (2013), a decision Roberts wrote himself.[5] He was well prepared for the task: Even as a junior attorney in the Reagan White House, Roberts had been plotting VRA's demise.[6] Once on the Court, Roberts limited the VRA, partly relying on legal theories and assumptions implicit in *Dred Scott v. Sandford* (1857).[7] This might seem like so much dusty legal arcana, but it's stunningly perverse. *Dred Scott* is one of the Supreme Court's most infamous decisions, a long-discredited slave case. To resurrect its latent reasoning as a doctrinal weapon against a law designed to protect the black franchise took gall, and it also took Boomers.

If you removed all the Boomers from the *Shelby* Court, the VRA would have emerged intact.* Since the Court is only nine (or sometimes, if the Boomers on the Senate Judiciary Committee are being particularly moody or ineffective, eight) people, this a slightly trivial thought experiment. What is not trivial is that *Shelby* devolved power to the states, allowing them to impose new voting restrictions without worrying about intervention by federal bureaucrats—those meddlesome elites, again. Boomer state legislatures had a field day, imposing ID laws, restricting online registration, redrawing voting maps, and limiting same-day registration and the preregistration of citizens about to turn eighteen, all strategies that tend to make voting harder for minorities and the young.

Equally important is that Roberts could not have sunk the VRA if Congress hadn't opened the door. The VRA depends on data to determine which places, based on historical practices, are prone to voting abuses and need federal preclearance before they adjust their voting laws. Unless that data were updated to account for new information, the VRA would become an arbitrary burden—which was one of Roberts's points, and a valid one. For a time, Congress had paid attention to the VRA, adjusting and expanding the act. In 1982, Congress even overturned a court case that had made it somewhat harder to implement certain parts of the VRA.[8] And then Congress mostly lost interest. Certainly, by 1984, it was time to think about updating the VRA's formulas; the Census of 1980 had published its results in May 1983.[9] The VRA was not especially endangered then, but as the years passed, fresh data came in, new voting abuses came to light, and the Supreme Court started to raise technical questions about the VRA, so legislators should have realized the VRA was growing brittle.[10] In 1992, just before Boomers seized control of the executive branch and the legislature, Congress made its final truly substantive revisions to the act.

After 1992, in the following years of untrammeled Boomer power and under both parties, the act was simply renewed in a cursory fashion, without meaningful revision or update.[11] The most charitable interpretation might be that no congressperson wanted to revisit the math and discover that work

---

* The Boomer vote was 3–2 to limit the VRA. Removing all Boomers would have left the vote 2–2, and the lower court rulings upholding the VRA would therefore have stood.

remained to be done in a home district in, say, Alabama, which if not intentionally malicious was certainly a dereliction of duty. The more realistic interpretation was that the Left couldn't be bothered to do the math or spend the political capital needed elsewhere (like expanding entitlements) while the Right perhaps understood that inaction would undermine the VRA itself. If the *Shelby* Court was just nine people, the inactive Boomer Congress was a literal cast of thousands operating (or not) over several decades.

Erosion in voting-protection laws also keeps the federal government from doing much about scandals like the paucity of voting booths, as in Phoenix, where voters in the 2016 primary had just one polling place per 108,000 residents.[12] In a democracy, that is an outrage, though perhaps retired Boomers can afford to wait in line. Older people are also less itinerant than younger people and have no problem furnishing a permanent address to obtain more convenient absentee ballots, or producing a local identity card to comply with the ID law du jour.

Meanwhile, the once minor category of people disenfranchised by felony records has become a major one, swollen by the huge rise in Boomer felony prosecutions. These ex-felons tend to be substantially younger and less white than the Boomers, and even if the intent of three-strikes laws was not to adjust the voting balance, that was its effect. Recently, Boomer Democrats have started to let small numbers of felons vote, a ceremony of minor consequence except when it isn't—as with the suspicious concurrence of such reforms during close elections, with Virginia's governor in 2016 performing a recent act of decency-cum-self-service by allowing up to 200,000 felons to vote.[13] (Virginia can be a swing state, and its governor had ties to the Clintons and probably some reasonable beliefs about how his new voters might cast their ballots.)

If Virginia in 2016 provides a compromised precedent about felony-voting reforms, history has better and grander examples. Before the advent of Boomer power, felony disenfranchisement had been dropping, a trend that continued even under law-and-order Nixon. According to the Sentencing Project, the number of disenfranchised felons was about 1.76 million in 1960, dropping to 1.18 million in 1976—and then it started rising again, faster as Boomer power grew, ballooning to 5.85 million by 2010.[14] Some of those ex-felons even legally have the right to vote in their states, though a lack of funding, outreach, and policy reversals as new governors undo prior revisions functionally deprive many ex-felons of rights they actually have. The point is not to argue the merits of whether ex-felons should vote; it is to point out areas where the Boomers have shrunk the franchise or have failed to protect the existing rights of qualified voters, often with intergenerational consequences.

There have been other antidemocratic frustrations, like the antique rules surrounding the party system, baroque arcana fit for the Holy Roman Empire. These rules also have intergenerational consequences, as many independent and younger voters discovered in 2016. The Democratic nomination was not rigged, as some Sanders supporters had it, because the Party can set its own rules and it complied with them. It's just very hard for the young, lacking the money and personal influence that accrete with age, to change the rules or become super-delegates (who, based on average age, are Boomers). With Boomer votes waning, these legal techniques are of increasing importance to perpetuating generational power. Many operate at the expense of what we, at least emotionally, understand democracy to be. However slippery notions of "goodness" might be, in a democracy, interfering with the voting rights of others is, as *1984* would put it, doubleplus ungood.

Questions of goodness aside, chipping away at the power of other groups is a strategy with limitations. New voters arrive faster than they can be plausibly disenfranchised, and no new Boomers are being born to replace those that age is stealing away. Fortunately, coping with the depletions of age is a Boomer specialty. Like broken hips, fallen compatriots can be replaced by something altogether stronger and more durable: all it takes is money and a willingness to tolerate the introduction of something artificial into the body politic.

Companies Are People, Too

Even as the Boomers eroded the franchise of many human persons, they vigorously expanded the power of money and corporations, reversing a series of reforms enacted between 1905 and 1975. As a result, money and companies have more direct and potent influence in American politics than they have in decades. Whether this is good, bad, or indifferent in theory depends on your political philosophy. In practice, history suggests that too much money, especially from nonhumans, warps the proper functioning of democracy by subverting the principle of "one person, one vote." Without regulation, companies, PACs, and the rich can dominate the media. Sometimes this influence is effective, sometimes it isn't, but it always takes money, and the people with money, as we've discovered, also tend to be old, i.e., Boomers.

The pernicious effect of money politics is not merely theoretical, as the nineteenth century showed. Industrialists and union bosses regularly purchased influence, directly and through the organizations they controlled, gaining the power to control executive appointments and direct convenient legislation. By the beginning of the twentieth century, this had become intolerably noxious, and Teddy Roosevelt asked Congress to look into campaign finance reforms. Over the following decades, various limits were emplaced, including a law requiring campaign contribution disclosures signed (doubtless with some irony) by Richard Nixon in 1972.[15] After the Watergate scandal, which had been tied to slush money, Congress redoubled its efforts, setting up the Federal Election Commission (FEC), whose duties are to "disclose campaign finance information" and ensure compliance with campaign contribution rules.[16] There had been abuses, but a pre-Boomer Congress tried to do something, however tardily, to address them.

The triumph of campaign-finance reform was brief and in many ways prefigured the collapse of the VRA.* In both cases, Congressional blunders and subsequent inaction created the possibility of legal challenges; in both instances, the legal challenges materialized; and in both instances Congress failed to respond effectively. In the case of finance reform, the legal challenges arrived as *Buckley v. Valeo* (1976), which upheld some Seventies

---

* The fact that money politics and voting rights abuses were widespread in prior eras provides the Boomers with no moral cover, any more than the existence of gladiators in the Roman Empire would justify blood sport today. Gilded Age practices grant no protection from the charge of sociopathy. Sociopathy involves departures from prevailing social norms, and in the 1970s, when the Boomers were starting to accumulate power, norms had moved against money politics.

reforms, like financial disclosures, while striking down others, notably the restrictions on spending by candidates and interested groups.[17] For the Court, it was all a question of balance of the government's interest in fair elections against citizens' interests in free speech (which in a commercial society involved spending money), and the Court found that the right balance had not been struck. As long as *Buckley* stood, it would be a win for rich candidates. One of the *Buckley* dissenters worried about self-funded campaigns for the rich; prescient indeed, given Perot, Trump, and to a much lesser extent, Romney. That many self-funders failed to secure office does not mean self-funding had no effect, since many self-funders did capture their party's nomination, and therefore adjusted the choices available to the electorate.

Buckley was a victory not only for rich humans, but the nonhuman rich, i.e, corporations. The whole idea that corporations were people (and thus entitled to speak and influence as humans did) was worrisome. In a later case, even William Rehnquist, a Nixon appointee, expressed doubts on that subject.[18] Nothing about *Buckley* prevented Congress from another try at combating money politics. *Buckley* was a young case, without a legacy and supported by a fragile majority, and spending was initially light, so Congress might have found a different path.

So, just as *Shelby* opened the door for Boomer state legislatures to refigure voting rights, *Buckley* made it possible for big money to return to politics. At first, the intrusions were modest, but once Boomers had colonized boardrooms and the legislatures, the various strategies of unlimited evasion took off: dark money and superPACs, thinly disguised "think tanks," cryptolobbying, and so forth. By 2002, matters had gotten unseemly enough to provoke new regulations in the form of the Bipartisan Campaign Reform Act, sponsored by John McCain and Russ Feingold.* That law was sloppily

---

* The oddity of anticorruption legislation being sponsored by one of the infamous Keating Five, a group accused of taking kickbacks from the failing S&L industry years before, was not helpful. Then again, with Boomers, you take reforms where you can get them, as with Dodd-Frank, whose sponsors were previously enmeshed in ethics violations, prostitutes, abuse of power investigations, receipt of major funds from Fannie Mae prior to its 2008 bailout, and so on.

drafted and far too late. The time to act had been sometime in the 1980s or 1990s, before there were billions of facts/dollars on the ground, all eager to undo McCain-Feingold. By the 2000s, it became trivial to dispose of irritants like McCain-Feingold, and courts dispatched them in a series of cases culminating in *Citizens United v. FEC* (2010).* Anyway, political theatre aside, the Boomers were largely content with the idea of corporate personhood and speech, and the culture of political money. Hillary Clinton said she despises the idea of PACs, but she's enjoyed several, most quite large.

Lest this seem merely academic, the corrosive money politics of the Boomer era have become so entrenched and pervasive that the Supreme Court now seems unable to even *define* corruption. During an appeal by Virginia's ex-governor (Boomer Bob McDonnell) in a trinkets-for-favors case, the defense boiled down to this: behavior of McDonnell's sort had become so widespread—that Boomer favorite, "everybody does it"—that the Court should no longer find these sorts of transactions corrupting. So what if McDonnell (who had campaigned on a promise to convene an ethics panel and then wisely dropped the issue) had received vacations, the loan of a Ferrari, or had a $15,000 catering bill picked up by a donor open to the occasional kindness (wholly nonreciprocal, of course)?[19] After all, McDonnell had not issued any legislation with a receipt for "services rendered" in lieu of a signing statement. Rather surprisingly, Justices of various stripes seemed to agree with McDonnell during oral argument and eventually, and unanimously, vacated the conviction. It's hard to see how a generation can maintain its moral credentials when it has created a political culture so distorted that *no member* of the nation's highest court can distinguish between bribery and business as usual. Who is bribing whom and why are questions that, by this point, have obvious answers.

---

* For the record, I'm sympathetic to the Court's rulings as a conceptual matter, if the proper disclosures are made. If a citizen can't understand what a corporate ad looks like with various mandated disclosures, or appreciate corporate intention, the idea of the competent citizen-voter vanishes. But this presupposes a world where civics and critical thinking are taught in properly funded schools, which hasn't existed for some time.

You Have the Right to Remain Silent, You Do Not Have the Right to an Attorney

Because most federal judges hold lifetime appointments, and because so many of them are Boomers and were appointed by Boomers, the judiciary will be an important redoubt of Boomer ideology for many years. (Let's not even get into the farces that are elected state judges.) As the sociopathic agenda is now the status quo, judges can simply strike down laws inconvenient to the Boomers. Given that many important cases are close, with almost equally compelling legal arguments, and future disputes over things like entitlements are without much precedent, outcomes may turn on a judge's ability to identify and sympathize with the arguments of a particular group. Boomers will certainly prefer to argue before judges who share their same views and problems. That dynamic may not be an affirmative evil, but neither is it wholly neutral.

Nor should we rely on courts, as the nation did midcentury, to serve as a font of personal rights. With the notable exception of gay marriage, courts are getting out of that business and in doing so, are giving Boomer legislatures a freer hand to whittle away at rights Americans take for granted. Even when victories are achieved, they frequently depend on the whims of a single Justice, Anthony Kennedy, making them more fragile and less credible. The entire appellate bar now finds itself in the position of the wine industry during the glory years of the peerlessly influential critic Robert Parker: catering to the idiosyncratic and often odd tastes of a single man, with some strange and labored outcomes that may not prove reliable over time.

This was not always so. When the Court handed down *Brown v. Board of Education* (1954), the decision was unanimous—an act of real moral imagination considering that all the *Brown* justices were old, white men born before the Model T and the airplane. Prior courts also created the modern concept of defendant's rights, notably in *Gideon v. Wainright* (1963) and *Miranda v. Arizona* (1966), a permanent feature of *Law & Order* ("you have the right to remain silent, you have the right to an attorney," etc.). Given that the show's suspects are usually guilty, this senior staple conditions its viewers to understand *Miranda* as a noxious impediment. The Boomer justice system seems to agree, displaying impatience with *Miranda*, the Eighth

Amendment, and the rest; the Boomer modus operandi is Jack Bauer's of *24*, knee-capping swarthy suspects without so much as a constitutional curtsey. Anyway, what "right to an attorney" can there be, given the defunding of public defenders we saw in Chapter 14? Once, courts might have acted to reverse these sorts of policy abuses. Now, Boomer legislatures and voters can be reasonably confident their intrusions will be tolerated by judges—in part because they selected those judges in the first place.*

Abortion is another example of the *Shelby* dynamic—as courts become less committed to rights, they create avenues for rights to be taken away. Legal contraception and abortion started appearing in individual states through the 1950s and 1960s and were established nationally in the line of cases culminating in *Roe v. Wade* (1973). The social controversy over abortion never went away, but the *law* seemed settled until 1992, when the Court took up *Planned Parenthood v. Casey*. A mostly non-Boomer Court revised *Roe*'s trimester system in favor of the squishier "undue burdens" test for abortion access.[20] Fair enough; *Roe*'s trimester system was pseudoscience anyway. However, Boomer legislators knew what to do—they started erecting all sorts of barriers, undue and otherwise. With even the youngest Boomers now past menopause, that generation can indulge in God-fearing regulations that will have no impact on them or, if liberal, can save political capital for more Boomer-specific challenges.† (*Roe/Casey* were on the ballot in 2016; a vote for Trump was tantamount to a vote against *Roe*. Boomer women seemed not to care.) Thus, the accelerating closure of abortion clinics, the renewed drama over anything relating to fetal tissue, sex ed, evolution, and other matters that were and/or should have been settled long ago.[21]

---

* For those holding out hope (or fear) that conservative Justices drift leftward over time and render transient cases like *Shelby*, *Citizens*, etc., it's probably time to let go of that idea. Pre-Boomers Souter, Blackmun, Stevens, and occasionally Kennedy did drift left. Boomers Alito, Thomas, and Roberts have performed as advertised.

† The erosion of the church-state boundary has been another Boomer-era loss. A humanist republic must now endure the humiliation of watching various Boomer supplicants like John Boehner and Bernie Sanders pay obeisance to a medieval theocrat as their counterparts busily misquote the Bible. Jefferson would have thought the whole thing ridiculous, while JFK would be astounded, since his own election suffered from the perception that JFK would be obedient to Papist idolatry at the expense of the Protestant-civic tradition. Such are the odd switchbacks of the Boomer years.

Gender, Generations, and Greens

Most conceptions of "goodness" involve fairness, and fairness has not been a Boomer priority. Economic inequality expanded greatly during Boomer tenure—helped along by bipartisan cuts to capital gains and estate taxes, and the strangulation of quality public schooling. Gaps, however, were not limited to those between rich and poor.

Although women have been a significant part of the workforce for decades, they still do not receive equal pay for equal work. The Equal Rights Amendment would have provided a foundation for redress. ERA even had Republican champions in the White House through the 1970s, and nearly achieved ratification. The amendment's momentum evaporated just as the Boomers were rising to power. While the ERA is dead, the imbalances it sought to eliminate live on. Women still only earn about $0.76–$0.78 to a man's $1.00, and improvement almost entirely stopped after 2001 (when Boomer control of management neared its apex).[22] Women remain under-represented in government: 19.4 percent of the 2015–2016 Congress was female, and women make up a minority of the Supreme Court. In America, 2016 was the first year a woman had a strong chance at her nation's highest office. By contrast, Tory Britain had a female prime minister by 1979, Canada (briefly) had a female prime minister in 1993, Germany elected its first female leader in 2005, Brazil in 2011, and so on. American gender equality has not been achieved, and that has been a choice perpetuated by the Boomers. Boomers have long been free to vote for women and pay women equally. Boomer-led companies that trumpet their ability to predict what flavor of Doritos a consumer wants on a given day can certainly figure out how to pay Ms. X the same wage as Mr. Y.

Finally, on the international stage, the consumer-driven, neoliberal Boomer culture has unleashed vast environmental and social problems, and just because some of these manifest offshore does not mean they vanish from the moral equation. The sociopathic society of consumption depends heavily on goods turned out by dismal sweatshops (e.g., Boomer Kathie Lee's/Wal-Mart's Dickensian workshops, Boomers Steve Jobs'/Tim Cook's subcontracted factories, so depressing that they feature suicide nets to prevent employees from leaping to their deaths).[23] Asking other countries to improve their labor conditions would not only be ethical, it would improve America's competitive position. The only thing Boomers really ask for now, however, is that their purchases be cheap and the moral quandaries offshored. As for pollution, geographic felicity will make America one of the last countries physically affected by global warming. Countries like Vietnam, for which liberal Boomers had affected so much sympathy in the Sixties, will be inundated by the consequences of Boomer energy policy. (Henry Kissinger was right: Consumer capitalism could defeat Hanoi.) By then, of course, the Boomers will be in their expensive, environmentally unsound caskets, manufactured by funeral oligopolist Hillenbrand. At least Hillenbrand is an American company featuring "predictabl[ly] strong cash flows"; it's even, as Wall Street would put it, "acylical."[24] The next time someone tells you that America makes nothing, has no growth industries, a one-word riposte: caskets.

Mixed Victories, Mixed Motives: Gays and the Disabled

Civil rights have posted two major victories during the Boomer decades, for the LGBT community and the disabled, but no one should grant the Boomers too much credit. On the first, the Boomers contributed, though not nearly enough, and many stand Canute-like (without Canute's irony), trying to roll back the transgender waves emanating from the toilets of the nation's decaying public schools. LGBT rights have been anything but a Boomer victory. *Obergefell v. Hodges* (2015), granting gays the right to marry, would have come out the other way were it not for the coalition of non-Boomer liberals and Anthony Kennedy.*,[25] To ask whether Obama's tardy support

---

* Interracial marriage, which in some ways presaged gay marriage, was also a non-Boomer phenomenon that picked up steam many decades ago in various states and was sanctioned nationally by *Loving v. Virginia* (1967). Fifty years later, white Boomers+ remain least enthusiastic about interracial marriage and are the only group to display really significant differences of opinion on white/black versus white/other miscegenation (if you have to marry across lines, make it an Asian, it seems); they are also, consistently, the least likely to have family married across racial lines.

of gay unions gave Kennedy cover or lower courts gave cover to Obama is to miss the point. *Obergefell* reflected the mores of younger people, not the Boomers. The Boomers remain more ambivalent about gay rights than succeeding generations, as shown in opinion polls and their sporadic efforts to amend state constitutions in gay-unfriendly ways.[26]

Let us not forget, also, that the Clintons, the epitomes of Boomerism who now labor to present themselves as eternal champions of liberty, were deeply on the wrong side of history when Bill was in power. As president, Clinton had the opportunity to integrate openly gay members into the armed forces. It would have been a step far smaller and less controversial than Truman's order to integrate black troops half a century earlier—about 60 percent post–WW II were *against* black integration, and while opposition to gay integration in the early 1990s was substantial, it was considerably weaker than opposition to racial integration had been decades before.[27] Could Boomer Clinton take a step requiring half Truman's courage?

No. Clinton acquiesced to Congress's "Don't Ask, Don't Tell" policy. That law found "the presence in the armed forces of persons who demonstrate a propensity or intent to engage in homosexual acts would create an unacceptable risk to the high standards of morale, good order and discipline, and unit cohesion that are the essence of military capability."[28] Of course, a special study commissioned by Clinton and his defense secretary had found nothing of the sort would happen. The most cogent voice urging integration came not from gays' putative ally, the youthful Clinton, but the grizzled and distinctly un-Boomerish Republican Barry Goldwater.*,[29]

While Clinton personally opposed Don't Ask Don't Tell, expedience proved irresistible, and having digested the unjust appetizer, Clinton could hardly wave away the inevitable entrée. Thus, the gratuitous sequel, the Defense of Marriage Act, passed overwhelmingly by Congress, which Clinton did not even bother to veto. DOMA was an act of pure animus to the gay rights cause, affording only heterosexual marriages the protections of

---

* Of course, when it came to defunding the military resulting in higher levels of risk to troops, but lower levels of risk to entitlement spending, we know how the Boomers chose. The gay menace, being of no consequence to the fisc, could be taken at whatever level of seriousness polls required.

federal law and permitting states to reject gay marriages legally performed outside their borders, with all the predictable consequences.

Notwithstanding Clinton (and Obama in his first term, who was distinctly wobbly on the issue), some Boomers did support gay marriage. But the main impulse came from the young. The long legal struggle that brought about *Obergefell* was entrained by San Francisco mayor Gavin Newsom (b. 1967), who in 2004 ordered his clerks to issue marriage licenses to gay couples.* A majority of Americans have since accepted the idea of gay rights, but Boomers were tepid to hostile in 2004. Just before *Obergefell* was argued, Boomer support was 18–28 percent lower than that of the young, and the only group with net opposition to gay marriage was the sixty-five-plus set.[30] Obviously, the struggle for gay rights did not begin and end with Newsom. It stretched back to Stonewall and its many Boomer participants. Then again, it also stretched back considerably further than that, to the Mattachine Society (c. 1950) and its predecessors. All one can say is that the Boomers played a partial and ambiguous part in gay rights, and many have not reconciled themselves to new realities. Americans are obviously free to take whatever position they like on gay rights, with one exception: believing that the Boomers were unalloyed champions of the cause.

The Boomers did achieve some major advances in equality, for disabled persons. The watershed was the Americans with Disabilities Act of 1990 (ADA), passed by an increasingly Boomer Congress and signed by the non-Boomer Bush. As a utilitarian matter, ADA was expensive, unwieldy, and sometimes muddled; the moral impulse was commendable, though.

The ADA would subsequently be tainted by Boomer self-interest when Bush II signed an expansion in 2008. The key fact: The 2008 amendments substantially broadened the ADA's definition of "disability." Now, in addition to the limbless and the lame, disability would include dysfunctions in "caring for oneself, performing manual tasks, seeing, hearing, eating, sleeping, walking, standing, lifting, bending, speaking, breathing,

---

* The Massachusetts case authorizing gay marriage in the Bay State in 2004 was authored by a jurist of South African extraction with votes from Boomer and non-Boomer Justices, but all the dissents were by native Boomers.

learning, reading, concentrating, thinking, communicating, and working" and impairments of "major bodily functions."[31]

Why might a reactionary Boomer Republican sign such a law, one that required overturning a 1999 Supreme Court case on the same subject? For the same reason he signed Medicare Part D. The ADA's newly expansive definition swept in a sea of seniors now swelling with Boomers. A win, but a self-serving one, and quite well timed: In 1990, no Boomer was really elderly; in 2008, the oldest was sixty-eight and the mean age was fifty-six, quickly approaching the point where "caring for oneself" was becoming a concern. Predictably, the late-night landscape became cluttered with commercials for Medicare-reimbursable scooters, stair movers, and other government-subsidized aids.[32]

As went the ADA, so went health care generally, a landscape of mixed outcomes and motivations. Medicare Part D, as previously seen, was a huge subsidy, to the old and to the drug companies. Because there is no long-term plan to finance Part D, it is a temporary gift to the Boomers and a permanent liability to everyone else. It is a liability made larger by the Boomers' lack of antitrust enforcement, which permitted huge consolidation in drug, insurance, and hospital companies. As for Obamacare, which barely squeaked through, it is too soon to tell. Certainly, Obamacare's implementation has been rocky, and it appears that the law could be significantly less effective than anticipated, though it does seem to be improving matters meaningfully. Despite its compromises, Obamacare may be the one truly significant social accomplishment of the Boomers, and perhaps their only substantial gift to young people, as it allows those under twenty-six to remain on parental policies. At least for now, Obamacare should not be discounted in the moral calculus, whatever its practical results and likely gutting post-2016.

Privacy: We Can Hear You Thinking

Privacy once held great value for Americans; in California, it's enshrined in the very first paragraph of that state's Constitution.[33] No similarly explicit right to privacy appears in the federal Constitution; it was "discovered" by pre-Boomer Justices. Nevertheless, it's clear that the Founders considered privacy important, adding the Fourth Amendment to protect the sanctity of the home from unwarranted intrusions. A century later, privacy remained an essential civic virtue. In 1890, before he joined the Supreme Court, Louis Brandeis wrote that the "right to be let alone" was necessary to protect the person and to avoid "what is whispered in the closet" from being "proclaimed from the roof-tops."[34] When the telephone caught on, Brandeis worried about the abuses of wiretapping.[35] Without privacy, as Brandeis and the Founders knew, the institutions of democracy wither. The indiscriminate collection of vast amounts of data transforms free expression into the ability to self-incriminate, while rendering transparent an otherwise private ballot to the good people of Langley and elsewhere. The intrusions have been mild so far, but the precedent is set, and it is hardly encouraging that we know that the government spies on American citizens, abetted by a secret court system that routinely accepts 99+ percent of all government surveillance applications. What this means for privacy is unclear, because the secret courts' opinions are not released and only the government is allowed to present evidence—which does not sound very court-like.

Under the Boomers, justice and privacy are increasingly treated as optional goods, to be sacrificed on the altar of panic as political needs demand. Not many remember, but it was Bill Clinton who pushed the snowball downhill with the Antiterrorism and Effective Death Penalty Act of 1996 (ATEDPA), which among other things, substantially modified laws about habeas corpus in the United States, making it harder for prisoners to contest their detention—the law even barred recourse to the Supreme Court. ATEDPA was passed after the Oklahoma City and first World Trade Center attacks, and its efficacy as a response to those incidents has been made clear.

When 9/11 happened, the Boomer machine once again rolled into unthinking action, producing the Patriot Act, legislation of breathtaking hysteria and invasiveness, with warrantless searches, intrusive requests (which, until tardily disbarred, required no probable cause, carried no judicial oversight, and forbade the recipient from even disclosing that a request had been made, and thus were about as *un*-American as possible, by the standards of the Founders), and of course mass data collection. Patriot embodied the whole apparatus of *1984*, with technology considerably more advanced than Orwell's telescreen. Perhaps no generation might have summoned the courage to resist such lawmaking in the immediate aftermath of crisis. Even Roosevelt, a man with a good temperament and an even keel, ordered the internment of American citizens of Japanese heritage during World War II. The internment camps were closed a year after the war ended, eventually replaced by America's great healing artifact, a shopping mall called Tanforan. Later, both Reagan and Bush I issued apologies for the wrong, letters were sent to the survivors, as well as the truest act of governmental contrition, checks. These were late, but seemingly heartfelt.

So far, the Boomers and their hysterical policies are drifting on a different course; if they had followed the internment camp time line, we would have been done with all of this by 2003 at the latest. But ten years after the events that inspired it, Patriot was renewed. In 2015, critical provisions were extended for another four years, as the USA Freedom Act of 2015.* Even after Edward Snowden et al. revealed the flaws of the security state, in part by the simple fact that an only modestly talented and low-level contractor was able to scamper off with secrets (many of them potentially yours, since the government was recording vast amounts of e-mail, though it was trying to "minimize" the impacts on Americans), even after Ground Zero went back to being just "downtown" (complete with another shopping mall), even after all that, Patriot/Freedom continues.[36] It is surely time to reconsider—thoroughly—laws conceived in haste and mourning, that have always lived in considerable tension with the freedoms they notionally sought to protect, and whose efficacy has never been entirely clear. It would seem that Boomers Right and Left, who have long agreed about the degrading effect of an intrusive state on the cherished good of liberty, would have done so by now. They have not.

---

* It's difficult to get over the sheer mendacity of Boomer legislative names, which essentially effect the reverse of a given title: Every Child Succeeds, USA Freedom, Pay-As-You-Go Act, etc. The parallel is on K Street, where lobbying firms employ equally obnoxious conventions, the formula generally being appending a noun describing what one is trying to destroy to the Trump-classy "Institute"—e.g., the Kochs' Institute for Justice.

Bellum Americana

Despite, or anyway, probably not because of the Patriot Act, the world has, in general, become a more peaceful place, measured by casualties overall and per capita. Peace being a universal virtue, and the subject of so many Sixties homilies, you might think that the Boomers were the prime movers. Once again, the details show otherwise. Not only has the phenomenon been international, Boomer America runs somewhat against the trend, both in military adventures and its love affair with guns, which remain surprisingly easy to buy. Anyway, it was never true that the Boomers were wholly pacific; as Chapter 3 showed, the young were the most ardent supporters of the war. But "hostility" is a trait of the sociopath, and however many peace symbols might still be dangling in the Haight, the Boomers have always been willing to reach for the pistol.

For the record, there have been at least seventeen military interventions under Boomer presidents, some lasting many years. For context, America has been more or less continually involved in a conflict since the Revolution, but after Vietnam, these tended to be fast and small—e.g., Reagan's swift (if theatrical) rescue of students in Grenada and Bush I's quick deposition of Panamanian dictator Manuel Noriega—and when larger, genuinely multilateral and confined to specific objectives, as with Bush I's liberation of Kuwait.*

That has changed again, and the generation that pledged "not another Vietnam" has found itself with several. Chief among the Boomer military fiascos are the quagmires in Iraq and Afghanistan, but there were others, active and otherwise, usually with murky motivations. Compare Bill Clinton's tardy response to the human rights crisis in the Balkans to the swiftness of his missile attacks on Sudan, conveniently coincident with the Lewinsky investigation.[37] Consider the debacle in Libya under Secretary of State Hillary Clinton, partially disowned even by her own boss, however elliptically, in an interview with *The Atlantic* and more candidly by Vice President Biden elsewhere.[38] Peruse the entirety of the foreign policy under Boomer

---

* The CIA, including under Bush I in a previous role, had worked with Noriega. At least Bush I's generation was of the type to clean up many of its own messes.

neocons (Dick Cheney, Paul Wolfowitz, and Condoleezza Rice chief among them), which established overt regime change as part of the national mission, against which the covert expeditions of the CIA in the midcentury in Central America and Iran seem downright limited and gentlemanly.

If Boomer foreign policy had questionable motivations and enormous costs, it did achieve one thing at the cost of another—vastly fewer American lives have been lost than were in Vietnam, at the cost of relying on drones and the toleration of failed states, which themselves represent liabilities deferred. Some may argue that it's hard to compare reconstruction in Libya, Iraq, and Afghanistan with state building in West Germany, Japan, South Korea, and Israel during the 1940s to 1960s. Certainly it is, in large part because the Boomers didn't make a real go of reconstruction: Much money was spent (some on dubious military contractors and local cronies), but thoughtful planning and follow-through were notably absent. Partly thanks to forward thinking like the Marshall Plan, when Germans and Japanese arrive in the United States today, they do not carry resentments about occupation, firebombing, and nuked cities; they arrive as some of our friendliest allies and most civil tourists. From the countries the Boomers have invaded, mired as they still are in chaos and corruption, we may receive less amiable visitors. All one can say about Boomer military policy is that its motivations have been no better than they were in prior years, the gains more elusive, and follow-up—perhaps the most morally revealing aspect—has been a failure when it has been pursued at all. Indifference, incompetence, whatever it is, it is not goodness.

What progress was achieved during the Boomer decades compares unfavorably with the revolutionary accomplishments of prior generations, and this was not the product of rogue and regressive politicians, but elected representatives who reflected the will of their Boomer constituents, as revealed by voting patterns and opinion polls. At best, Boomers failed to maintain the pace of gains prevailing before 1970. At worst, Boomers have begun to actively thwart progress. For those who believe these moral failures come purely courtesy of the Republican Party, and not the Boomers generally, there are two counterpoints: (1) Boomers overall, especially younger

Boomers, are net Republican (Chapter 7); and (2) many rights lapses have been enthusiastically bipartisan, like the prison legislation of the 1990s.

The Boomers did not inherit a perfect America. But the nation was making quick moral progress. At the end of the twenty-first century, the same cannot be said, and several hundred million Americans will live with the consequences of these missed opportunities and moral lapses. We have seen how the Boomers have failed on almost every important issue they had the power to control, and how in many cases, they did so out of pure self-interest, to enrich themselves and preserve their own power—in some ways, the very persistence of Boomer power is testament to the generational injustice practiced by the Boomers. Very little of this was consistent with, or motivated by, the notions of equity, fairness, privacy, democracy, or peace that we customarily associate with "goodness." Many of the illusions of Boomer goodness were dispelled by the specifics covered in prior chapters, but now that the remains have been dealt with, there are no excuses left. It's time to call for the check.

CHAPTER SEVENTEEN

PRICE TAGS AND
PRESCRIPTIONS

Behold, I was shapen in iniquity; and in
sin did my mother conceive me.
—Psalm 51:5[1]

W hen the original Bad Parents, Adam and Eve, took the serpent's
advice over God's, they lost the family home (Eden) and gained an
enduring legacy (original sin). The Old Testament does not explicitly record
how the first children, Cain and Abel, reconciled themselves to this dismal
inheritance, though we can infer from the subsequent fratricide that the family's reduced circumstances produced some tensions. To our post-Freudian
eyes, Cain's murder of Abel seems like classic displacement; surely, there were
more obvious targets. But Adam and Eve endured (the former for 930 years),
snakes multiplied, and the celestial grandfather hung around until Nietzsche
killed finally him off circa 1882. Laboring under the burden of their pro-
genitors' sin, succeeding generations had a rougher go. The rest of the Old
Testament reads like the files from a psychiatric hospital, filled with murder,
revenge, theft, and war, to say nothing about the *really* unsettling bits like the
tales of Lot and his daughters. Despite engendering this whole mess, Adam

and Eve eventually trended heavenward, an ideal vantage point from which to view their offspring's descent to less hospitable climes.

Coping with the legacies left by bad parents is an eternal challenge, in which grace and fairness rarely feature. The millions of Americans who will shortly partake of this ancient drama, individually and as a society, should do so with care. The temptation will be to frustration, and the danger, that frustration will be misdirected: toward siblings, spouses, nurses, estate lawyers, Medicare bureaucrats, and everyone else tasked with taking care of people who didn't take care of themselves—i.e., at society, instead of at the sociopaths. Misdirected squabbling would suit the Boomers, since it would distract the young from pursuing the real culprits. The Boomers should not be granted that satisfaction.

Instead, we should remember who caused the problems in the first place and do as a society what decent people do individually with their own cranky, aging, and culpable parents. The first step is to appreciate when the elderly are no longer competent and to remove from them the ability to harm self or others, or run up any more debts. That accomplished, you can tabulate the mistakes: the second mortgages, inadequate insurance, accumulating doctors' bills, leaky roofs, the lot of it. You then, the estate planners tell us, liquidate what parental assets there are to meet those obligations and the additional costs of long-term care. Any shortfalls will be your obligation, one way or another.

Many of those who have already been through this saga know that no real gratitude will be forthcoming. At best, these good deeds will be viewed as nothing less than your duty, and at worst, the elderly will let fly accusations of churlishness and ingratitude. This will be infuriating, especially considering that any money you spend will come from a paycheck depleted by various deductions for senior programs you may never fully enjoy, even as those deductions supply Social Security checks that parents brandish as proof of their self-sufficiency. The mechanisms of a national, sociopathic agenda subverts Tolstoy: Each family can now be unhappy in the same way, and multiplying the above frustrations by 75 million, the remaining Boomer population, equals a lot of unhappiness and more than a little rage. Whether these feelings can be channeled into a productive coalition instead of fratricidal conflict over collateral issues, is this book's final subject.

If the Boomers can be removed from power, then the tallying and division of liabilities can begin. Alas, America cannot rely on a refreshing fiscal baptism to remit sin, even though this is essentially what Candidate Trump proposed, through his unprecedented suggestion of national default. Nor can America force Boomers into the confessional in the hopes that the bridges, schools, and the prison-state repair themselves after a sufficient number of Hail Marys, or their political equivalent, the hollow apologies of the politician caught out. There will be no moment of grace, no great catharsis, only a succession of checks written and budgets reallocated. It is a process not without a quiet nobility. It also has its cold satisfactions, including the collection of funds from the Boomers themselves.

Remediating the sociopathic Superfund site of Boomer America will be expensive. In money alone, the project will require $8.65 trillion soon and over $1 trillion in additional annual investment. Given the past chapters, the size of the bill will not come as complete shock. What may be surprising is that the United States can afford all of it.

Though dormant for many decades, the argument for investment remains as powerful and straightforward as ever: Proper investment enriches society over the long run. Good as this is, there is no getting around one frustrating reality, which is that the size of the tab and the age of its originators are considerable, so that those doing most of the paying will be the least culpable. It's plausible that the youngest Americans will eventually receive a decent return on their investment. If they are forward thinking, it shouldn't be difficult to convince them to support the necessary reforms. The harder task is to persuade middle-aged Americans, who will succeed the Boomers in power, to pursue costly change. By virtue of their age, Americans in midlife have substantial incomes, making them prime targets for new taxation, while also being sufficiently old to make full recoupment unlikely. These Americans (mostly GenX but also including the youngest Boomers of the nonsociopathic variety) will need to be motivated by patriotism and the interests of their own children. They will be called upon to do much, and they deserve an honest treatment of what needs to be fixed and how much

that will really cost. There can be no more Laffer Curves, free-lunch privatization schemes, or any of the other delusional neoliberal theology that offers
salvation without good works.

As to those good works, they are legion and expensive. While the totals
are necessarily imprecise and debatable, the bill's general enormity is undeniable. Whether the sum is $6, $8.65, or $10+ trillion, it's always trillions
and always many of them. Collecting all the strands covered before, the next
table shows the rough tab, excluding the $18+ trillion in national debt about
which we can and should do nothing immediate.

The Bill

	Near-Term Costs	Ongoing Additional Costs
Infrastructure	$3.6 trillion	$100 billion
Pensions	$1 trillion	$200 billion
Military	$800 billion	$100 billion
Entitlements/Health Care	$750 billion	$200 billion
Climate	$1 trillion	$150 billion
Education/R&D	$1.5 trillion	$250 billion
Extra interest	—	$170 billion (minimum)
Total	$8.65 trillion	$1.17 trillion

Note: "Near-term" means the next few years, a window that reflects both the cheapest
time to remediate and also the period in which part of the sum can be collected from the
Boomers; it is for those reasons more front-loaded than it could otherwise be. "Ongoing" simply means the additional, unbudgeted expense over the next thirty or so years,
at which point certain items like education, pensions, and climate should be in good
enough shape that they can be maintained fairly cheaply and we can finally begin repaying part of the national debt.

These are the rough prices to keep the system going the way it is, and we
may decide that these are unacceptably high prices to pay for certain items.
But we have to *choose*, not just let the system drift along, spawning deficits
to uncertain purpose. Significant reductions to entitlement programs, limiting foreign intervention, reducing spending in thinly populated areas—all
items to consider—would greatly reduce the total. Keep in mind that TARP
alone, designed to clean up the financial mess of 2008, was authorized to

expend/invest up to $700 billion just on the financial sector and could have been a complete loss (in the end, it was not). A slightly larger sum for ongoing investment, instead of crisis management, does not seem undue in that context. Certainly, it would help if the government passed along a digestable summary of its financial position to taxpayers—it supplies projected benefits information, which is about as complicated and political a figure as one can imagine, to Social Security contributors. Could goverment not also provide, with a receipt for every annual tax filing, a one-page statement of the government's financial position and the use of monies? This might assist taxpayers in deciding what they really want to fund, allowing for a degree of informed consent.

Even slimmed-down, some parts of this agenda cannot be easily avoided—major spending on infastructure, R&D, and some welfare seems like a precondition to a growing, functional society and these alone will cost trillions. Investments at this scale demand sacrifice, not a favorite Boomer word. These are sums associated with major wars, and they demand commensurate effort, meaning higher taxes, more investment, and less profligacy. Collecting the money requires exquisite care, since sloppy tax hikes can punish growth, and the whole point is to return America to a trajectory of quick upward growth.* That rules out the cruder mechanisms of austerity in the Teutonic mold (practiced recently, and to devastating effect, by Berlin on Athens) and the self-limiting let-the-rich-pay-it-all populism of the extreme Left and Right.

What could work is an investment program, much of it administered by the state, initially funded by debt and ultimately paid for by moderate tax increases on most Americans. After years of neoliberal conditioning, such a program may seem irretrievably Leftist, fundamentally un-American, or antithetical to growth; none of these descriptions are warranted. All of these strategies have been pursued before, often quite successfully, and by both parties. Using tax revenues to support even the most expensive and state-centered programs, e.g., infrastructure and defense, would not strike

---

* "Quick" doesn't mean the fantastical 4–6 percent increases proposed by some Republicans, but something like 3 percent real growth, which would double national income over twenty-five years. It's a hard goal, but not implausible.

a 1950s Republican like Dwight Eisenhower as creeping socialism, for the simple reason that he did so himself. Doubtless, some of this book's proposals are to the notional Left of Obama and Clinton; then again, those politicians offered policies that frequently lay to the Right of Nixon, except in certain matters of civil rights. It's all a matter of perspective, and that perspective should be supplied by data and social consensus, not the idiosyncratic worldview of the shrinking Boomer electorate.

The Boomer mess is the largest challenge the nation has faced in some time, though once the Boomer establishment has been replaced, it will be helpful to view reform as a process of manageable fiscal adjustments, instead of an opportunity to avenge a cosmic injustice. The Boomers might deserve to bear almost all of the burden, but as a practical matter, they cannot. Everyone will have to participate, though to the extent Boomers can be targeted without ruining them, they should be.

The Easy(ish) Part: Borrowing and Investing

After so many chapters skewering the Boomers for their addiction to debt, it may seem odd to call for more borrowing, though more borrowing is the appropriate course. No level of taxation can provide enough immediate funds, and borrowing is unusually cheap in the post-2008 world. The difference between the borrowing of the Boomer years and the borrowing of the future rests in how funds are used. The old practice of subsidizing transient consumption with perpetual debt needs to go. The way forward must be tax and invest, not tax and spend, and new debt should be viewed as an instrument to deal with a temporary difficulty, to be reduced when the challenge abates.

Distinguishing between investment and consumption is a subject treated at length in policy literature and worthy of considerable pondering by bureaucrats, but no voter has time or opportunity to do the same. When bond issuances arrive on the ballot, the options are "yes" and "no." To resolve that binary in the three minutes allotted in the voting booth, a rule of thumb helps: if a project does not provide benefits for at least as long as the term of the associated debt, that project should be viewed with (nondispositive) suspicion. Projects with fleeting and unquantifiable benefits are likely to be disguised consumption. It should also (though it hasn't, for thirty-odd years) go without saying that total ascertainable benefits should exceed total costs.* These are not rules to be applied with unthinking narrowness. Some worthy projects are inherently speculative and may seem to fall outside the rubric, like California's 2004 proposal to fund stem cell research. At the time, it was not clear when or if the state's $3 billion investment would be recouped. In the end, California voted "yes" and that was the right choice, both ex ante and post hoc. Moreover, while any specific R&D project might be speculative, in the aggregate, R&D has a long history of positive and enduring returns. A little perspective is all that's required to make these rules functional guides to the profusion of bond requests made of voters. Olympic stadium: out. Decent schools: in.

When good projects do arrive, even debt-obsessed voters should not (for now) be deterred by the scope of obligations incurred. American interest rates are near zero in real terms and the arrival of subzero returns on Japanese and European sovereign debt will limit the upward pressure on rates that huge new debts usually entail. The world has vast amounts of cash looking for a positive yield and very few good places to find it: Swiss banks in 2015–2016 actually charged major depositors for the privilege of holding ready funds. In such a world, America can offer rates that are both absolutely low and extremely competitive, perhaps 1–2 percent, eminently affordable even to a highly indebted nation. This happy climate is not guaranteed to last, any more than rotting bridges are guaranteed to stand absent repair.

This brings us to infrastructure, sorely in need of investment, in everything from filling potholes to upgrading systems like Amtrak's increasingly rickety Northeast Corridor, which also happens to be by far the most profitable and rational part of the Amtrak system, though it has the misfortune of serving urban corridors that rural congressmen despise.[2] Bridges to nowhere and vanity projects have given infrastructure a bad reputation. But making sensible, data-driven investments provides safety, profit, and new

---

* Many laws require bureaucrats to engage in cost-benefit analysis (CBA), but voters have never been required to do the same. To say that sociopathic politicians have tried to pervert CBA by appealing directly to the basest instinct of voters and by manipulating CBA variables would be something of an understatement.

jobs. If doing so benefits the coasts (and it will), so be it; they pay the taxes anyway.* Given systemic underemployment, infrastructure investment will provide jobs without much upward pressure on wages. One could easily envision spending $3–4 trillion in the next few years, reaping a net benefit and little inflationary damage. It's a substantial investment—an order of magnitude more than anything proposed during the 2016 election—but anything meaningfully less will do equally little good.

Given the unusually good environment for issuing government bonds, it is also a good time to relieve student debt. Government borrows much more cheaply than students and may as well use its advantage by assuming many student debts directly—including the $150 billion owed to private parties as of 2012 (the date of the latest comprehensive data).[3] Many loans are already "impaired," and the government is already in the forgiveness business through front-end mechanisms like means-tested repayments, deferrals, and outright forbearances (i.e., write-offs). On the back end, the government is on the hook through guarantees and automatic programs like welfare and other safety net entitlements. So it is really just a question of timing, costs, and allocation, the sorts of arbitrage and fiddling Wall Street loves in other contexts; we just have to be honest about the mechanics.

The gains of forgiveness would be substantial, emotionally (student borrowers are "distressed" in various senses) and fiscally. Federal student loans carried an interest rate in 2015–2016 of between 4.3 and 6.8 percent, with private loans carrying higher rates, to say nothing of the even higher

---

* It's time to get away from saccharine notions about the "Heartland" promoted by the Boomer Cult of Feelings. This is a capitalist republic, and that means the Heartland is where the money and people are: New York, Los Angeles, the San Francisco Bay Area, etc. Reason commends that this is where many infrastructure dollars should be sent, though not enough are. The reason the Heartland plays a substantial role in the political dialogue, vetoing progressive legislation and able to demand net transfers from Washington (despite being the redoubt of conservative "virtue"), is because of antidemocratic compromises made by the early Republic, a system two hundred years out of date. If Brooklyn had as many senators per resident as Wyoming, the borough would have a delegation of nine, out of New York City's total of about thirty. The vetoes and pork-barreling of middle-state senators are blackmail and should be treated as such.

costs of credit extended to cover student living expenses.[4] By contrast, the ten-year Treasury yield was, in mid-2016, about 1.8 percent. If only half of student debt were retired, this interest rate arbitrage would save $20–30 billion annually. Any savings are, of course, from the student (and, long-term, social) perspective; the various and often predatory corporations who issue or hold these loans would be deprived of an equal sum (and the Treasury of some revenues, though by relieving students of some debt, the government might help students live more productive lives and eventually generate more tax revenue). Rationalizing student loans could also shore up the financial system, since many private loan holders have shaky finances—this was a problem in the 2000s for Sallie Mae, the sort-of-private-sort-of-public loan provider—and dealing with systemic problems early is invariably cheaper than cleaning them up during a crisis. No one should be deluded that this is anything other than a bailout, and one with very distasteful aspects, subsidizing some very bad decisions by students and helping out some dubious participants in the loan business. That is the dirty nature of all responses to financial crises. Better the government address these problems now, before crushing debt derails younger lives prematurely and the costs arrive, compounded, via the back doors of welfare and other programs. Student debt is just one example of the flexibility permitted by the currently low costs of government borrowing.

In a less sociopathic political environment, even America's largest programs can be fixed fairly easily with minor adjustments, entirely affordable relative to the giant consequences of inaction. Returning Social Security to long-term balance requires moderate increases to FICA taxes and minor increases of the retirement age to reflect increased longevity (Chapter 12). Climate policy needs appropriate investments in energy infrastructure and R&D and reforms like cap-and-trade, which are not terribly expensive in the short-term and bring long-term benefits to public and private parties. The cap-and-trade programs implemented to deal with acid rain in the 1990s provoked no recessions and California, which has had its own carbon cap-and-trade program in effect since 2012–2013, is prosperous. Any temporary dislocations would be small compared to both the total economy and the damage averted. Even the military can be brought back to full readiness in just a few years at fairly modest cost by undoing the arbitrary damage of sequestration and culling the self-serving fauna of congressional pork and white-elephant systems.

Because debt is presently so cheap and many of the largest challenges like Social Security and climate have costs that can be spread over many years, some of the largest problems are actually the easiest to address, conceptually, if not politically. The real challenge is equitably allocating the various costs and avoiding the waste that attends any large reshuffling of funds.

The Harder Adjustments: Healthy Debt, Tax Increases, Benefit Cuts, and Avoiding Waste

Except in severe recessions, any additions to the debt should be accompanied by budgets that pay current interest out of current revenues and come with reasonable plans for their eventual extinguishment.* Investing $8.65 trillion immediately would add considerably to nominal interest payments, though because real interest rates are near zero, even borrowing at this scale carries modest costs. Still, even nominal obligations must be paid and interest plus ongoing investments would add about $1.2 trillion in spending, and that means new taxes.

Total tax receipts in the United States are close to $7 trillion across federal, state, and local, taxes, so meeting new expenses implies a relative tax increase of 21–25 percent, substantial but not unbearable. To allay any heart attacks, that means the highest nominal federal rates might rise to around 50 percent (from 39.6 percent, though the effective rates would be much lower). For average taxpayers, their effective 15 percent rate would creep up to 18 percent or slightly higher. These figures assume the current tax and benefits systems otherwise stay the same, which, just to calm down the Rightist reader, they palpably should not. We can and should rejigger the brackets, FICA allocations, benefits, deductions, and so forth. Pulling a few of the tax codes' many levers might leave new tax rates much closer to current rack rates, raising revenue while eliminating the distorting subsidies

---

* To emphasize again: It's neither practical nor desirable (for technical reasons that aren't pertinent here) to extinguish the entire national debt. However, over the next fifty years, we can certainly reduce debt as a proportion of GDP by being disciplined about borrowing and by accelerating economic growth.

embedded in the code. It's possible to be fiscally prudent without dismantling the government or flirting with confiscatory taxation, though no one
should be deluded that the total tax take must go up, starting with taxes on
the Boomers. (It seems impossible that this will happen in 2017, but the elections of 2018 and 2020 offer new opportunities.)

Seniors—i.e., Boomers—will view higher taxes as an unfairness not to
be borne and the prospect of reduced benefits as an outrage; anyway, they
will argue, they don't have the money. Like much of Boomer dialogue, such
assertions are mostly self-serving and false. The Boomers did not pay their
fair share of taxes, as the national debt and general decay attest, and Boomers should make good on their debts. As for pensions, benefits, and other
senior citizen bonuses, the Boomers might argue that they are at the end
of their working lives and so any cuts would be an unprecedented cruelty.* Well, it might be an inconvenience, but it would not be a cruelty, morally or fiscally, and certainly not unprecedented. The moral facts have been
established. So have the fiscal facts: Older people *do* have a lot to tax. The
richer ones own a disproportionate amount of wealth, much of which
generates income whether the Boomers are working or not. Even less rich
seniors receive all manner of benefits, pensions, and other overly generous/
unsustainable payments that can be reduced either directly or through the
tax, whether or not they have considerable money assets (and many do not).
Some age-targeted taxes may be unconstitutional and others, however legal,
may be effectively quashed by stalling litigation that allows the Boomers to
make it to the grave untouched. However, the very Boomer policies designed
to protect their generational interests also create many unambiguously legal
and fair targets, correlated with age and ripe for harvest.

Social Security is the obvious place to start, and the retirement age
should be raised for anyone reasonably able to work, including the younger
Boomers, by at least three years. ("Early" retirement would then happen at
sixty-five, and "full" retirement at seventy or later.) Similar revisions were

---

* Society has a long history of forgiving old people; criminals, for example, can apply for
clemency based on age. Society also has a long history of specially penalizing those who
have done a major wrong to the nation or who fail to show remorse. The principles of
clemency are at best a wash for the Boomers.

made in 1983, in a way that protected the Boomers (Chapter 12). It's time to do it again, without generational indulgence. Wealthier Boomers can also have their benefits taxed more aggressively, another strategy backed by precedent. Clawing back old-age benefits has the advantage of being generationally targeted and also sends a message to younger workers that the state cannot (and indeed, never intended to nor did) cover all of retirement. Northern Europeans have vastly more generous welfare states *and* higher personal savings rates; they understand that even in generous systems, individual responsibility remains paramount.

There are other areas where taxes can be reasonably, generationally targeted. The Boomers are the cohort presently reaping the greatest gains from inheritances, and these can be taxed at something above the functionally zero rate that generally applies. Indeed, doing so would be downright republican (lowercase), given that low inheritance taxes are oddities in a nation founded, however glancingly, in opposition to inherited privilege. The exemption, now at $5.45 million, can be lowered dramatically, allowing sentimental items to be passed along without abetting dynastic wealth while shoring up the fisc. Other exemptions can be reduced or abolished, including the "step-up" basis at death, a loophole that directs the IRS to exclude any qualifying gains that accrued during a giver's lifetime, which can be most of them.* When Britain decided its parasitic and antidemocratic gentry needed to go, the mechanism was "death duties." That was a century ago; certainly twenty-first-century America can be at least as progressive as Edwardian Britain. Why, precisely, do the senior viewers of PBS care so much about how Downton Abbey will survive the predations of Lloyd George and his death duties? Because Boomers have their own McDowntons to worry about.

Even before they change hands, American McDowntons are already protected by some generationally discriminatory exemptions that themselves

---

* Estate rules are mind-numbing, so here's a simplified example. If a parent buys an asset for $10,000 and it's worth $1 million at death, there would normally be a taxable gain of $990,000. Step-up ignores this gain. You, the inheriting child, would be taxed only on the postmortem gain—e.g., if you later sold the asset for $1.5 million, you would be taxed only on $500,000, not $1.49 million.

deserve revision, especially the property tax caps enacted since the 1970s. The Boomers have long profited from these anomalies at the expense of schools, infrastructure, and the residential aspirations of younger Americans. The longer one stays put, the more valuable the cap becomes—caps assume that the taxable value of property increases at an arbitrarily low rate, say 2 percent, even if in many markets appreciation is much higher. So a long-term resident in Malibu might be taxed as if his home were worth $1 million, even if an identical property next door just sold for $25 million and is taxed accordingly. Revising these caps would be progressive, both in standard terms and generational ones. It would also be efficient, as caps distort all sorts of economic decision making, reducing labor market flexibility by encouraging people to stay put, which makes no sense in an era where lifetime employment has vanished and jobs migrate. (The same is true of rent control, another strategy that favors seniors while constraining supply and forcing the price of unrestricted rentals upward.) The usual counterargument is that such revisions will displace seniors who cannot afford to live in the homes of their choice, to which the answer is: tough. The law confers rights of citizenship in the United States, not a right to reside in a particular place. Abolishing caps and rent control may create short-term price declines, though this would serve as something of a generational equalizer, putting more homes in reach of younger cohorts, among whom rates of homeownership are notably depressed.

Vast as the generational subsidies of property tax protections are, they pale in comparison to medical spending, consumed by seniors in disproportionate amount and substantially at public expense—a fact the simple existence of Medicare's age-qualification underlines. The most reasonable reforms entail more cost-benefit analyses of the sort routinely imposed on other government programs; rationing, to use the charged term. Evangelical Republicans may not care for "death panels," but who are they to defy their God, who sayeth that the "days of our years are threescore years and ten" or, at most, by "reason of strength" (or Medicare) might extend to "fourscore"?[5] Let us grant the evangelical wish that Washington cease interfering with God's design, at least on this matter. Anyway, social programs are supposed to do the greatest social good, not cater to false sentiments about kindly geriatrics. Costly interventions to drag a life out a few unproductive months, at the price of a lost generation of children, do not balance in the Benthamite books. If they were true to their principles, instead of bowing to Boomer hypocrisy, both the Left and the Right would each find something to like about rationing.

The prospect of rationing may also encourage the Boomers to embrace more sensible medical policies. It would expose neoliberal welfare as the unviable chimera it is, a policy that simultaneously requires the government be the single largest buyer of health care while forbidding the state from using its market power to negotiate discounts from the medical oligopolies the Boomers helped create. More thoughtful policies can save a lot, while sacrificing little. Sweden spends 9.6 percent of GDP on health versus America's 16.9 percent (in 2012), and Stockholm isn't exactly littered with the corpses of neglected seniors.[6]

Rich as many Boomers are, many are not, and this means generational taxation alone can never suffice. Taxes will need to rise generally, even on the sacred cow of the middle class, whose teats have been supposedly abused but have actually experienced only the most tender caresses. Nowhere, in the great debates over the progressivity of the American tax system that have raged for years, has there ever been real discussion of asking anything of the middle class. All major candidates in 2016 promised relief for "middle-class" taxpayers, a now-customary ritual. Why the middle class should get a break has never been clearly articulated, for the same reason that the definition of "middle class" is never articulated. The vast majority of the electorate (up to 87 percent) views themselves as some sort of "middle class" and therefore interprets any proposed breaks to be in their immediate self-interest.[7] This is one promise Boomer politicians usually keep, and it has shielded the vast middle from paying its fair share.

Before we get to the middle, let's start with the sins of the bottom and top, the respective fixations of the Right and Left. The bottom quintile or so already receives net subsidies from the government, and these transfers seem like something of a precondition to a functioning society in practice, regardless of their theoretical merits. Presently they seem set to a level that is, roughly, minimally functional, so there is little to trim—the subsidies are small enough that meaningful reductions would create mass unrest without much fiscal gain. Not even the Kochs want to risk repeating Louis XVI's flight to Varennes (or Zurich, at any rate) and there's little we can do here. The lower-middle class, however, does have something to contribute—it is taxed at exceedingly low rates, so that many of its members pay less than they receive in benefits. Nor is the lower-middle some citadel of unalloyed virtue. While the evasions of the upper brackets feature more zeroes, the less wealthy commit their own evasions. Cash-based compensation, like tips and so on, frequently go unreported. Swan in to an upscale hair salon, past the doors proudly announcing the acceptance of Visa and Amex, and you see an ATM, there to dispense untraceable cash for tips, testaments to the culture of low-stakes evasion. The IRS gives this sort of cheating a free pass, because it lacks resources to take action. Aside from examining suspicious returns reporting zero income, the IRS basically does not scrutinize the "middle class" at all: It examines 0.5 percent of filers reporting incomes between $25,000 and $200,000, while it examines 6 percent, 10 percent, and 16 percent of returns reporting incomes over $1, $5, and $10 million, respectively.[8] All parts of the middle class can contribute somewhat more, and the IRS can ensure that they do.

As for soaking the rich, there aren't that many of them, and they can be dunked only so many times. Even dramatic tax hikes on this small population would produce at most an extra $300 to $400 billion, which does not completely close current deficits, to say nothing of the additional investments called for.* Nor would abolishing favorable rates on capital gains and dividends be sufficient, supplying perhaps $200 billion annually, and only if the market holds together.[9] (The amount is notably low because so many

---

* Many on the Right make the theoretically plausible if totally unrealistic argument that very high tax rates would cause productive people to flee the country. An exodus of the rich did not occur in the 1940s and 1950s, when the highest marginal tax rates were 90+ percent, though the midcentury did not have a generation of tax-dodging sociopaths. Tax exile also does not really happen in high-tax places that are extremely pleasant to live in, a wholly predictable outcome of...free market theory. People will pay to live in attractive places, like California or Sweden, instead of eastern Nevada or the Congo. Finally, the United States imposes exit levies that make exile totally impracticable except for the exceedingly rich, most of whom will grumble at higher taxes without actually doing much, since a few extra percent will have no real impact on their quality of life.

capital gains are shielded by middle-class retirement plans.) The wealthy should pay their share, but they already pay quite a lot: the top quintile of earners (households earning an average of about $270,000 annually) paid 69.0 percent of federal income taxes; the top 1 percent alone pay 25.4 percent of taxes.[10] Respectively, these groups account for 52.6 and 15.0 percent of income; they pay more relative to their share of income and other groups pay less, which is precisely the point of the progressive system and the existence of a skew itself is not a critique of the social policies of a progressive system. Whatever your position about the fairness of how the rich generate their income, there's no getting around the heavy dependence of the government on receipts from a very small number of people, and the implications of this have not been much discussed outside of some (self-serving and overheated) Rightist think tanks.

While progressivity is important, the point many have missed is that excessive focus on collections from just the richest risks further social distortions, from the perspectives of the Left, Right, and what remains of the center. Populists should keep in mind that a system that is already disproportionately funded by the rich will become ever more captive to them as taxes increase. The rich will become even more interested in tax policy, while the government will become ever more dependent on the well-being of a tiny class of individuals and cater to them accordingly; if you have only one goose laying golden eggs, the goose had better be happy. Overtaxing the rich also encourages other unhealthy dynamics. Those who pay tend to feel they own; those who do not cannot feel quite the same. After a certain point, extreme progressivity defeats the social purpose it seeks to achieve, reducing society to oligarchy versus mob, with the oligarchy feeling entitled to govern at whim and emotionally justified in evading a burden others do not really share.*[11] The mob, lacking a sense of proprietorship, can hardly be expected to take a proper interest in maintaining society—how much can a

---

* A word on the billionaires who keep saying they pay lower taxes than their secretaries: This is not only factually unlikely absent heavy exploitation of tax avoidance, but easily remedied. Pay.gov allows people to contribute to the retirement of the national debt—and so these disgruntled billionaires are free to adjust their tax rate up to whatever level they like by this mechanism. In FY 2015, the Treasury collected a grand total of $3.9 million, so clearly this has not been a popular option.

person who pays no net taxes really complain about what the government is doing with his "tax dollars"? The tax system should be progressive and perhaps highly so, not utterly lopsided.

Taxes on almost the entire base should rise and levies should be more efficiently collected. The IRS can receive proper funding to collect what people fail to pay. The Service estimates that at least $450 billion goes uncollected every year, and even after audits, more than $400 billion that is owed will never be collected.[12] Proper funding of the Service could retrieve a significant fraction of the deficit by itself, about as much as a major hike on the rich would, without changing a single rate. It is not enough by itself, but it would help, and it would be equitable.

Similar reforms of corporate taxation would provide additional revenue, while keeping things fair and improving American competitiveness. Official (rather than effective) American corporate tax rates are high by global standards, which encourages evasion, of more and less legal means. Large, sophisticated and aggressive corporations, like Apple and GE, have often paid nothing.[13] (It used to be joked that GE was, by attorneys employed, the largest tax law firm in the world; that's not the highest and best use of GE's resources.) Lower and more uniform taxation would be more fair to smaller corporations and encourage larger companies to remain in America, instead of being "domiciled" in micronations that have nothing to do with a company's core business.

Higher taxes would impact consumption, though this is not necessarily bad, especially if consumption taxes helped reflect the real cost of purchases, many of which are subsidized by society (meaning: younger generations). Though consumption taxes have long enjoyed support in policy circles, they are frequently derided as political nonstarters, which is bizarre as many such taxes already exist: sales taxes, regulatory fees like car registration taxes, gas taxes, use taxes, tolls, and even property taxes, capped as they are. Even if consumption taxes of the kind seen in Europe are impracticable, raising existing consumption taxes would not only generate revenue and encourage savings, it would help internalize externalities, i.e., the true social costs of the goods consumed. The anomalously low price of energy in America fails to capture the total costs fossil fuels create, and a simple way to reduce emissions is to raise the price of fuel. As fuel has been relatively cheap for a few years, it is a convenient time to raise taxes on fuel. Some may protest that consumption taxes, or even carbon taxes, are unfairly regressive, but they are small components of a generally progressive tax system and also the most direct means of making consumers bear the real cost of their purchases.

Along the same lines—of making people assume directly costs that would otherwise be socialized—are insurance fees. The premiums that regulators charge the financial sector, for example, have been inadequate, which was why Congress had to cough up a few hundred billion to rescue the banks in 2008. Social insurance premiums for entitlements, as we've seen, are also too low. So are premiums for the semiprivate world of pensions, as the hopeless state of the PBGC shows. Unlike the financial sector, pensions and the PBGC are in sufficiently bad shape that prospective insurance will never be enough to meet existing liabilities. Subsidies will be required from general revenues, as will steep benefits cuts—which the Boomers deeply oppose and must be forced to bear. Again, Social Security and pensions are not promises made by the US Constitution, and anyone who relies exclusively on these programs does so at his peril.[*,14] Pensioners should have known better, and a contrary conclusion implies a paternalistic state of breathtaking scale.

The point of trudging up and down the tax tables is to show that there is no one tax revision that can solve the problem by itself. Only taxation on almost the whole tax base, with special emphasis on the Boomers and the properties they control, can supply revenue on the order required (and do so with any fairness). When politicians say that the wealthy are not paying enough taxes, they are right if only because *no one* is presently paying enough taxes. When politicians say the middle class (whatever that is) pays too much, they ignore both the history and the math. The effective income

---

* However, as a foretaste of things to come, some pensioners have been attempting, with success, to recast pensions as *legal* entitlements; this may be true under some *state* constitutions, but does not apply to the largest federal benefits. And it proves that, despite social necessity—for pensions will absolutely break some states, like Illinois—the Boomers are hell-bent on getting theirs.

tax rate for most Americans runs around 15 percent, as we saw in Chapter 8. The bottom fifth receives outright subsidies, and something like 40 to 60 percent of Americans consume, via tax credits, entitlements, and other public services, more economic value than they pay in taxes.[15] What politicians are really talking about for the bottom half of the middle class is not tax relief, but deepening the tax subsidy from the wealthy to the lower-middle class. Society can do this, but it should be honest about what is going on, and that will entail dispatching all the nostrums of lower-middle-class virtue from political dialogue. The trade of self-regard for a 3 percent gross tax savings doesn't seem like the sort of exchange a healthy republic should make.

Every interest group in the world has plans to reform taxes, and no one person can understand the millions of words of federal, state, local, and agency taxes and fees, or the various glosses on them provided by the lobbying industry. No one person—no one voter or reader—has to. All that has to be appreciated is that the scale of the problem defies any cheap fix and that essentially all taxes must rise for some time. My personal hope would be for the state to recede from its role as manager of perpetual financial crisis, concentrating instead on effective regulation and limiting itself to the various things it does best, like building roads, and schools, and funding basic research, with taxes scaled down to lowest reasonable need. After we repair damage to the system, we should consider a return to lower taxes. That point is many years away.

This book started with an analogy of a trial and now that a verdict has been reached (or anyway, the prosecution is resting), the time has come to ask for penalties. In doing so, it's helpful to revisit the legal framework. In legal terms, what the Boomers did to the country was knowing and voluntary, sometimes reckless but often intentional, and they profited from their actions. This is what the law requires before ordering restitution. While not all of the Boomers directly participated, almost all benefited; they are, as the law would have it, jointly and severally liable. Traditionally, it's up to group defendants to sort out who should pay what, but in this case the analysis simply collapses to a question of who can pay at all. And given the size of the claim, essentially every Boomer who can pay should. Then again, given the sum involved, so must we all. That is the nature of society, sociopaths be damned.

Avoiding a Repeat: Future Generations

All of these reforms and investments would be of limited utility if another generation of sociopaths emerged. It is not enough to undo the damage; we must avoid a repeat. This is one of the few areas where America can enjoy relatively easy optimism. For better or worse, many of the unique conditions that twisted the Boomers into generational sociopathy will not recur. The comfortable world described in the first two chapters, with its assumptions about effortless future prosperity, has vanished.[16] The historical anomaly of bottle-feeding largely disappeared by the mid-1970s (except among the poor). Permissive parenting soldiers on, though plenty of alternative models have arisen to hopefully better effect. Even television, still omnipresent and corrosive, now competes with other diversions that seem less warping. While there are some indications that newer technologies like social networking foster narcissism among the young, and perpetuate the sort of media group-think that prevailed after the abolition of the Fairness Doctrine, nothing quite as bad as television seems to have arrived, though it will be years before we can reach a definitive conclusion. For now, newer technologies do not seem to promote sociopathy in the same way as TV; there has been no Facebook crime wave, or Twitter rampage. (Sometimes hermetic recirculators of misinformation, these platforms allow for crowing and disingenuousness but do not seem to create sociopathic or criminal mind-sets in the first place, with the possible exception of extreme bullying.) As for controversial foreign entanglements, there have been plenty, but the rise of a volunteer army, albeit one distastefully supplemented by mercenaries and black sites, has avoided some of the problems with the draft, problems that anyway seem to have been as much a means to express sociopathic tendencies as a creator of them.

The most important task, if we want to avoid creating another generation of sociopaths, is providing an education in the value society produces and the thoughtful management of personal choices. It is a shame that civics disappeared from the curriculum and that courses on financial literacy never really existed. It is also a tragedy that many view life as a zero-sum game, where wealth can never be created, only reallocated. However disappointing growth has been under the Boomers, the economy has still expanded. These are not the neo–Dark Ages, where the only way to get ahead is for hedge fund managers to practice rapine and plunder on neighboring Westchester villages, though the Boomers seem to believe as much. Naïve as it may sound, inoculating society against the antisocial requires, at bottom, persuading people of what is palpably true: that society has value and everyone should contribute.

AFTERWORD

A revolution does not last more than fifteen years, a period
which coincides with the flourishing of a generation.
—José Ortega y Gasset[1]

Insightful as the Spanish philosopher José Ortega y Gasset was about mass power and historical transformations, he did not live long enough to see Boomers, which might have provoked him to revise his revolutionary time line. It has been forty years since the Boomers began accumulating real power and about twenty-five since they gained command of the nation's highest office and many of its legislatures, and they are still upending the social order in fairly radical ways. Many years remain before Boomers will voluntarily relinquish their holds on the White House, legislatures, courts, governors' mansions, executive offices, and the other important perches from which they continue to practice sociopathic revolution. Even age hasn't slowed the Boomers down, as the reductions time inflicts on Boomer numbers and general energy are offset by the influence of money and specific enthusiasm over the issue of senior entitlements. Like all sociopathic revolutions, the Boomer revolution wishes to be permanent and if it cannot manage that, then 2030 or 2040 will do. Boomers are well on their way to accomplishing their goal.

The Boomers' continuing efficacy is reflected in politicians' ritual obeisance to Social Security and Medicare, now invariably discussed in religious terms like "untouchable," "inviolable," and "sacrosanct," rendering them sacred institutions for which tithing is strictly nonoptional. In 1983, these programs could be rationally discussed. Now, even though these programs—like the rest of the sociopathic program—are known to be unsustainable as-is by all reasonable policy makers, they drift on. Because the problems Boomers created, from entitlements on, grow not so much in linear as exponential terms, the crisis that feels distant today will, when it comes, seem to have arrived overnight. Tempting as it is to wait for age to do its work, unless action is taken soon, America of the 2030s will understand Hemingway's dictum about bankruptcy arriving slowly, then suddenly. By then, the Boomers will be gone, and the moment for justice will have passed. Only the problems, more vast and less tractable, will remain.

David Hume, an altogether more realistic philosopher than his Spanish successor, marveled at how easy it was for a minority to control a society. Hume would not be surprised to see the sociopaths hanging on even though they are now substantially outnumbered by other generations who, if they acted together, could unseat the Boomers. But younger generations have found nothing to inspire the same sort of devotional interest that makes the Boomers so effective. So far, younger voters tend toward single-issue politics, and however worthy any given issue may be, most single-issue politics are self-limiting. A carbon tax does not fix the banks, fixing the banks does not ensure civic equality, transgender bathroom access does not revivify R&D, and none of these reforms really address the huge imbalances that have been accumulating under the Boomers. Comprehensive reform requires younger generations to align closely, to demolish the entire sociopathic edifice, instead of picking at it one brick at a time.

Unfortunately, there is one major exception to the rule about single-issue politics, and it benefits the Boomers—as long as they can win on entitlements, they can keep everything. Entitlements are so large that they essentially determine the budget and the national future, and they are an easy issue to rally around. The nonsociopathic electorate needs to find for itself something as compelling and far-reaching as entitlements are for the Boomers, and paradoxically, entitlement reform is unlikely to serve as the rallying point. Entitlements enjoy immense abstract popularity across all age groups (thanks in part to Boomer deceit about them) and technical adjustments to retirement ages and payout ratios haven't aroused mass passion and don't seem likely to. Given that the actuarial catastrophe has been well under-stood for decades and that the only response has been an *expansion* of senior benefits, it seems unity requires a different catalyst.

What might work is an Other, the common enemy the philosopher Carl Schmitt believed societies needed to push them into decisive action.[2] Schmitt, being a German of a certain era, reached some ugly conclusions about Otherhood, but he was not without a point, and his thinking has recently become something of a vogue even for people who (correctly) find Schmitt himself repellent. A Schmittian menace does motivate society, sometimes to good ends, if the Us is genuinely commendable and the Other, not so much. Over the centuries, the Scots had the English; the English, the nuisances of the Continent; the Continent, Ottomans at the gates of Vienna; everything north of Wittenberg, everything south to Rome; and the Thir-teen Colonies, the bewigged tyrant lodged at Windsor. All these Others triggered political revolutions (and may still), some of which were very good and others definitely not, though many were serious and popular attempts to deal with real problems. But in modern America, in pressing need of reform, there has been a conspicuous lack of motivation; the enemies dis-appeared. George III is long dead, as are the "Evil Empire" and Osama bin Laden. Cuba, the dagger once pointed at the heart of America, is open for tourism, and if the Islamic Republic still officially fixates on America as the Great Satan, Tehran and Washington are at least talking again. Immigrants, the latest target, make for an angry talking point, though a nation content to employ so many of them—not just in factories, but in homes, as gardeners, cooks, and nurses—and so addicted to the cheap labor immigrants provide, won't really kick the habit. What foreign menace, then, could ever prompt a truly positive and comprehensive social restructuring? None, perhaps. But there is a large body of Others, close at hand: the Boomers.

Part of my goal throughout has obviously been to establish Boomers as a highly culpable Other, one whose deposition might lead to some real good. Boomers really are different, as they often and proudly remind. They do not share other generations' values and do not behave in ways that accord with America's better conceptions of itself. They are Other, even, in their own ways, enemies of state and society. Think of Grover Norquist's dream of drowning the government in a bathtub (or, in less virulent form, Bill

Clinton's declaration that the "era of big government is over"), or the despoliation of the environment, indiscriminate imprisonment, and intergenerational expropriation. Are these not proof of Boomer Otherhood?

Rather than repeating the arguments of the past seventeen chapters and their hundreds of endnotes, perhaps it's easier to just let the Others indict themselves. In May 2016, as I was working on this book, *The Atlantic* ran a cover story that demonstrates in the form of one person the story this book has been trying to tell about an entire generation. The article in question was written by Neal Gabler, a Boomer, purporting to expose "the secret shame of middle-class Americans."[3] It was presented as the lament of a man denied the opportunity to thrive, but close reading, under the light provided by the preceding chapters, shows the article for what it really is: a very public disgrace brought on by the Boomers' Otherly habits of mind.

Gabler's premise is that he is one of almost half of Americans who could not conjure up $400 to pay for an emergency. By locating himself in the security of 150 million companions, Gabler has prepared his escape; you know it will be anyone's fault except Gabler's. But Gabler *purports* to fix the blame on himself, providing him the chance to charge you, the *Atlantic* subscriber, for an exercise in confessional therapy.

Gabler's narrative of how he arrived at his particular Station of the Cross is a story of folly unleavened by self-awareness. Gabler, like all Boomers, arrived in a rich and functional America. Yet, despite having teaching jobs, book contracts, a TV gig, a spouse who worked as a "film executive," parents who paid for his daughters' college educations, and "typically ma[king] a solid middle- or even, at times upper-middle-class income," Gabler and his wife find themselves borderline insolvent—although his financial illiteracy doesn't make clear if he's actually broke or just hard up for cash. He does reside in the Hamptons, after all, which are not exactly Nairobi. Let this pass; Gabler says he's in a bind, and we can take him at his word on the biographical details, if not his conclusion.

What follows are a parade of self-admitted bad choices, of astonishing scope, that encompass the whole rotting cornucopia of Boomerism. Per the article, it is Gabler who chose to become a writer (not famously remunerative in any era). It is Gabler who chose to buy a Brooklyn co-op which he asserts he "could afford," though obviously he could not: His Brooklyn address exposed his children to the indignity of public school, requiring Gabler to dispatch the kids to expensive private institutions. The condo eventually had to be sold at a crippling loss. (Another collision of the Boomers' mentality of effortless wealth against hard reality: The housing market does not only go up.) Moving along, it was Gabler who relocated to East Hampton (not as nice as one imagines, mind you—"we live there full-time like poor people [sic]," Gabler notes). Gabler's children were smart enough to gain entrance to Stanford, Harvard Medical School, Emory, and the University of Texas (the latter presumably, given his New York addresses, not at in-state tuition rates; then again, does New York even have public universities? Sixty-four campuses in the SUNY system alone, as it happens). It was not, however, Gabler who primarily paid the bills, it was his parents.

Well, how could Gabler pay? He had blown past a book deadline and was sued by his publisher to have the advance returned (an outrage, since "book deadlines are commonly missed and routinely extended," the same sort of everyone-does-it thinking of Nannygate/McDonnellgate). At some point, Gabler also failed to pay his taxes and now owes penalties; he implicitly rages against a progressive tax system that cast him into a higher bracket due to the offensive delivery of a lump-sum book advance (for which most authors would be grateful, but not Gabler). Alas, Gabler didn't come clean to his wife about their financial position, and she prematurely retired from her executive career, apparently deluded by the prospect of a manly provider tilling the fields of literature. So far, so bad, and on it goes: a daughter's wedding arrives, which Gabler pays for—sounds good, except that he cashed out his 401(k) to pay for the party and at some point had to borrow money from an adult child, practicing at home what Social Security effects at national scale. Now in the financial hole, Gabler teaches MFA students, becoming a cynical accomplice in the production of indebted cannon fodder to be mown down by an industry that, as Gabler has been laboring to explain, does not provide a real living.

So whose fault is it? Gabler says it's his, though the whole hair shirt he weaves for himself is more or less unraveled by a pull quote pleading that "perhaps none of this would have happened if my income had steadily grown the way incomes used to grow in America. It didn't and they don't." That's true by itself, though incomes are still somewhat higher than they were when Gabler came of age, and people once saved a fair amount of those earnings. The problem is that Gabler ignores the Boomer-engineered policies that this book has been laboring to drag out from under their slimy rock, perhaps because he has been too busy living their personal equivalent.

The article, like the Boomers themselves, continues even though it's already done more than enough damage. As it happens, even a degraded America offered Gabler opportunities—think of those prestige writing/teaching/fellowship gigs, and his job as a critic on TV. It's just that Gabler couldn't hold on to the money or the highly paid TV work, the latter because he wasn't "frivolous enough for the medium." Gabler, now eligible for customary senior benefits, is almost certainly on the dole, so this whole tale of woe is subsidized not only by the good people of *The Atlantic*, but by you, the taxpayer, though to be fair it's possible that 15 percent of his Social Security benefits are being garnished to repay his tax debts.[4]

The reason Gabler is put in the stocks is because he embodies in one person the whole Boomer problem and the difficulty in achieving repair. Gabler chose to publish the story, not as an apology, but as an excuse and a justification. He is not contrite; he takes no real responsibility. He is the Other, utterly unfixable and totally oblivious, one example out of millions. Gabler had every opportunity, starting with his studies at the then-cheap University of Michigan and right up through the decidedly untaxing demands of his televised movie reviews. Those opportunities Gabler blew, just as the Boomers generally inherited a healthy nation and leave behind one steeped in difficulty. Gabler wraps up by citing the statistic that 21 percent of Americans view a lottery win as the most practical way to accumulate wealth. Of course, Gabler and the Boomers *did* win the lottery: They were born in the richest and most dynamic economy the world had ever seen, midcentury America. They just did what so many do with lottery lucre: waste it.

This is a deeply negative portrayal, but a certain negativity may be what's required. If dense-print tables of marginal tax rates and federal deficits don't provoke the necessary emotions, maybe Gabler's vivid example will. Would it be more pleasing to frame the coming struggle in terms either more positive or more abstract, a "Struggle for Society" or a "War on Sociopathy"? For many, yes. But palatability is no guarantee of practicability. Positive campaigns take decades to succeed, which America does not have. The record of purely positive campaigns is decidedly mixed in any event: Jimmy Carter tried the sermonizing approach in his Malaise Speech, and we saw how *that* worked out. Even when positive campaigns do work, they tend to have negative aspects. Civil rights were as much a campaign *against* bigotry, slavery, and a literal war on the South, as they were *for* justice and freedom. As for abstraction, a "War on Sociopathy" would probably go the same way as other wars on abstractions like poverty and drugs—pure concept is rarely electrifying, and anyway there's always something tangible behind the scrim of theory. We can probably no more have a War on Sociopathy without proceeding against the sociopaths than we can wage a War on Terror without targeting some terrorists. The difficulty is that if the Boomers are a viable Other they are, in important ways, also an Us.

Eight centuries ago, the Catholic abbot Arnaud Amalric confronted a similar problem, a group of Cathar heretics holed up inside Béziers. Attempts to persuade (heterodox-but-still-Christian) Cathars to embrace orthodoxy failed, so the Cathars had to go. Regrettably, the heretics had sealed themselves in the town along with some orthodox Catholics, mixing up Us and Other. The medieval Church, however, specialized in logic that had brutal internal clarity. The abbot duly instructed his troops *"Caedite eos. Novit enim Dominus qui sunt eius,"* which works out, more or less, as: "Kill them all. God will know His own." The town was put to the sword, the homes burned, and a notice dispatched to the Pope. Doubtless some will see this book as the printed equivalent of the greasy abbot-inquisitor, rubbing its inky paws together as it torches the stockades of Boomerism. Bad as many Boomers have been, *caedite eos* isn't this book's motto. Not all Boomers are sociopaths, and not all of them deserve to be condemned. But many Boomers do behave sociopathically, and as a generation, their management has been disastrous and needs to be terminated.

There is no surefire treatment for sociopathy at the individual level, and therapists generally wait around for a spontaneous remission. America doesn't have the luxury of patient optimism and nothing about Boomer behavior or pathologies recommends anything less than coercion by the state, democratically authorized. Boomers have been getting their way for decades and expect to continue doing so. They are not about to swing open the doors of Congress to let in the forces of social orthodoxy, rainbows streaming down from heaven, doves rising up to meet them, and a chorus of hosannas all around. The Boomers are too old, and benefit too much from their policies, for any of that. Nevertheless, this is not thirteenth-century Béziers, it is twenty-first-century America, and the goal is not to extirpate heresy but replenish society. We cannot destroy the village in order to save it; we can at most do a gut remodel.

Just as Boomer policies began as personal before emerging as political, so reform will have to begin as cultural before it becomes civic, essentially reversing the sociopathic process, starting with a reintroduction to dialogues of reason and difficulty. The Boomer cult of Feeling has gotten out of control. In policy matters, "I feel that" does not have the same validity as "the data show" and "prudence suggests." It's perverse that feelings gained precedence during the same period when technology made thoughtful civic participation truly viable. The defunding of the government's statistical projects has been lamentable, but there is still a huge body of data available, most of it free (for now), and citizens have the means to figure out what works without resorting to the unreliable compass of pure emotion. Americans do not have to "feel" anything about the effectiveness of abstinence education; they can look at the data, download policy abstracts, or even watch twenty-two minutes of John Oliver.

With these resources at their disposal and a few moments of critical thought, almost no major issues are beyond the ken of even the most time-pressed voters. Decades of debt and deficits make clear that taxes will eventually have to go up, or some spending go down, or both. Figuring out whether to vote for an infrastructure bill is as easy as driving over the local streets or reading a few headlines—when a bridge collapses, it does not take a civil engineering degree to conclude that something has gone seriously wrong.

Where self-study cannot suffice, competent experts abound. We regularly and profitably rely on experts for the necessities of daily life, so why not do the same in public policy? No one needs to know the details of nuclear fission or the thermodynamics of methane combustion to turn on the lights; a switch is flicked and the engineers take care of the rest, no personal feelings or special expertise required. Entitlements reform should be no different—substantial revisions including higher taxes and benefits cuts are obviously required. Voters can authorize politicians to pursue these changes, while consigning details like life expectancy and inflation indexing to the specialists. Doing so requires jettisoning the whole disastrous culture of anti-elitism, without abandoning the citizen's obligation to judiciously select which elite experts deserve credence, an obligation easily met. A study on smoking funded by cigarette companies and conducted by a no-name college may not be wrong, but it demands more scrutiny than a Stanford study conducted under the auspices of the National Institutes of Health and submitted to the rigors of peer review. Studies on financial soundness sponsored by banking groups are pertinent, but hardly dispositive. Science, reason, and the intermediation of competent elites provide ample prophylaxis to the sociopathic cult of feeling.

It will also be necessary to reacquaint public discourse with nuance and ambiguity, instead of demanding reductive sound bites like "no new taxes" or "zero-tolerance policing." To take one example, no one knows the exact rate of unemployment. Experts have only a range of estimates, with varying degrees of confidence. That does not mean that there isn't some core consensus or that every opinion (or feeling), however extreme, is equally valid, or that reasonable certainty can't be achieved. In the case of the figure that started this book—the projection of what median incomes could have been absent the nation's long deceleration—it was one estimate within a plausible range. For narrative simplicity, the details and assumptions were consigned to the endnotes, but there they are, available for review and up for debate. That debate is valuable and may lead to other discoveries or more precise estimates. However, the trends have been going on for so long and are so pronounced that no reasonable adjustment will change the general conclusion about a distressing deceleration in American growth. The same is true for many of the policy issues discussed in this book and elsewhere. Given the scale of the problems facing the United States, general conclusions suffice. It really doesn't matter if there are twenty thousand, forty thousand, or sixty thousand dangerous dams, or if the national debt is $14 or $18 trillion and growing at 3 percent or 3.5 percent annually—the numbers and directions are severe enough to demand change regardless.

Returning to a thoughtful, empirical culture will also make it easier to persuade the population of another general conclusion: that society has considerable positive value. After many chapters slogging through the sociopathic wreckage of the past decades, readers may despair of convincing enough voters of that fact, yet there are reasons to hope. Younger groups already have the most prosocial outlooks, even though they have been deprived—courtesy of the Boomers—of direct experience with a really flourishing society. These views can be encouraged through reasoned debate and rerunning an old political experiment: investing for the general welfare and promoting the interests of society. It has, after all, worked before. There is no guarantee that it will work again, but the toxic results of the present experiment commend *some* other course, and we may as well choose one that enjoys both a history of success and normative justification. All that's required to begin is a return to reason, probity, and investment, and reorienting policy in opposition to the sociopaths. And yes, there will have to be some additional taxes. If God will not know his own in this new struggle, we can rely on a properly equipped IRS to stand in His stead.

The goals of this cultural reorientation are straightforward. The first is to provide a foundation for unity against the Boomer agenda, and to do it quickly. If that unity requires a degree of anger about what has happened to the country and at those responsible, so be it. The Boomers deserve America's displeasure and they ought to repay what they can. The second is to remember that the anti-anti-social agenda is, at heart, a *prosocial* agenda, one that strengthens the ideals of a commonwealth. The Boomer Other is only a framing device, hopefully useful, but not an end in itself. Remembering the prosocial goal helpfully limits how far we proceed against the Boomers, because for all their considerable faults, they are part of society, too.

APPENDICES

APPENDIX A

Boomer Sociopathy—Ticking the Boxes

The evidence presented in the book will either persuade or not persuade readers that the Boomers behaved in antisocial (i.e., sociopathic) ways. Readers can intuit what antisocial personality disorders look like, and we could leave it at that. However, clinical guides are useful for framing the analysis.

The Diagnostic and Statistical Manual of Mental Disorders, Fifth Edition ("DSM-V") is the psychiatric profession's standard reference work for identifying disorders.[1] The DSM-V contains two major diagnostic models—its standard model and its "emerging model."[2] These modes heavily overlap and are generally consistent. This book contends that under either model, the Boomers meet the clinical standards for "sociopathy"—i.e., "antisocial personality disorder." The key difference between the two models is that the original model invokes a requirement of "conduct disorder" before age fifteen, and time has made that data hard to get, although the sustained attention to "juvenile delinquency" during the 1950s and 1960s (when the Boomers were under fifteen) is highly suggestive. In any event, the second model dispenses with this restriction.

Generally, each sociopathic individual must meet certain minimum criteria and this book presents population-wide data, with the exception of certain political figures whose personalities are well reported. In some cases, diagnostic criteria autocorrelate. Boomers who did drugs while on combat duty flouted the law, acted improvidently, displayed certain empathetic deficits, etc.: you can basically construct the checklist for one discrete individual. In other cases, conduct may or may not have overlapped, and some may wish to argue that, perhaps, all the Boomers who displayed improvidence (as manifested in the savings rate) did not manifest, say, lack of empathy. But that proposition of random bad behaviors not leading to a composite antisocial whole is very hard to believe, given the vast populations involved and the necessary implications of some actions—e.g., in the case of savings, that the lack of savings and improvidently low tax rates necessarily mean that other generations will have to bear the consequences of Boomer consumption (demonstrating lack of empathy). We can go on like this all the way through.

The DSM-V is, like all works of its kind, filled with various qualifiers, restrictions on use, and so on. It's designed to diagnose individuals, not broad demographic groups, but as this book is not medicating anyone or consigning them to an asylum, the DSM-V provides an important guide to thinking about Boomer behaviors.

DSM-V (3 or more required)	Boomer Behavior	DSM-V Alternate (two or more of behaviors marked A, six or more of behaviors marked B)	Boomer Behavior
Failure to conform to social norms/lawful behavior	Draft-avoidance, divorce, illegal drug use, financial fraud	A.1 Egocentrism	Same, plus narcissism
Deceit	Financial fraud, perjury by prominent politicians, persistent misrepresentations about entitlement program solvency, etc.	A.2 Self-direction (absence of prosocial standards, failure to conform to laws, social norms)	Same, plus same as above
Impulsivity/Failure to plan ahead	Low savings rate, low social investment rate (R&D, infrastructure, and defense deficits)	A.3 Lack of empathy	Environmental disregard, mass imprisonment, entitlements crisis, bizarre immigration policies, etc.
Irritability/Aggressiveness	Violence, repeated military conflicts, institutionalized violence (mass imprisonment), etc.	A.4 Intimacy deficits (incapacity for relationships, deceit, use of domination/intimidation to control others)	Unusually high rates of divorce, mass incarceration, etc., plus some instances of deceit noted above
Irresponsibility (including failure to honor financial obligations)	Low savings, accumulation of personal and public debts, rising bankruptcy, failure to invest (e.g., in infrastructure, schools), environmental despoliation	B.1 Manipulativeness	Persistent fraud/deceit, especially in financial matters; draft avoidance
Lack of remorse	Repeated failure to correct behaviors, post-Vietnam conduct, acceleration of behavior despite obvious effects on others (e.g., entitlements crisis, environment), refusal to give up unsustainable pension benefits	B.2 Callousness (lack of concern for others, aggression, lack of remorse)	Sustained military conflicts, environmental and infrastructure neglect, absence of sustained/successful rebuilding efforts after conflicts, differential outcomes of draft dodging on rich/poor populations, mass imprisonment without readjustment programs, intergenerational debts, etc.

Evidence of conduct disorder before 15		Data hard to gather, but rising rates of juvenile delinquency corresponding with Boomer 0–15 years; drug use, promiscuity, teenage pregnancy against social norms serve as proxy data
	B.3 Deceitfulness	Entirety of Boomer financial culture of bubbles, crashes, etc.; accounting manipulations in private and public reporting
	B.4 Hostility (includes heightened sensitivity to slights, vengeful behavior, etc.)	Continuous military interventions, mass incarceration, government shutdowns based on personal animosity, etc.
	B.5 Risk-taking	Irresponsible savings behavior, drug use, rates of STD infection at generationally unusual levels (e.g., Hep-C and senior STD infections)
	B.6 Impulsivity (acting without plan/ consideration of outcomes)	Boomer retirement crisis, environment, infrastructure, educational deficits
	B.7 Irresponsibility (incl. failure to honor financial obligations)	Bankruptcies, swelling national debt, entitlements crisis, etc.

APPENDIX B

Ask And Ye Shall Receive—The Sociopathic Tax Wishlist

Period	Median Boomer Age	Life Event	Boomer desire	Actually Got	Boomer Win?	Boomers in Power?	Burden Shifted To
1973–1987	21–35	Stock accumulation	Indifferent to capital gains tax; acquiring, not selling	Capital gains increases	Mostly	During later stages	Near-retirement stock sellers (older; Boomers' parents)
1973–1987	21–35	Trading up homes	Elimination, then re-imposition of property tax caps	No change to property tax caps, but various other housing goodies handed out instead	Mostly yes	During later stages	Younger, non-homeowners
1973–2014	21–62	Earning	Lower income taxes	Lower income taxes; some adjustments to technical provisions like AMT	Mostly yes	Cuts begin in earnest and accelerate after Boomers hit max power	Richer, older, and through debt, to younger generations
1980–2032	28–expected death	Earning/ Retirement	Targeted funding of Social Security/ Medicare	Targeted funding of Social Security/Medicare	Yes	Yes	Younger; Boomers pay more, but only enough to keep system solvent until their expected deaths
1982–2017	30–65	Home ownership	Beneficial treatment of homeowner taxation	Property tax caps, mortgage interest deduction, exclusions from home capital gains	Yes	Yes	Non-homeowners (younger, poorer)
1992–2017	40–65	Retirement saving	Retirement savings incentives	Retirement savings incentives	Mostly yes	Yes	Mixed
1992–2032+	40–expected death	Portfolio reallocation, sale of appreciated stock	Lower capital gains taxes	General and substantial decrease in capital gains	Yes	Yes	Non-stockholders (younger, poorer); does benefit Boomers' parents but Boomer loss offset in form of larger inheritances at lower taxes later
1995–2020	43–68	Awaiting inheritance	Reduction in estate tax	General and significant reduction in estate tax	Yes	Yes	Not yet clear, almost certainly those too young to inherit before rates revert

These tax changes, so favorable to the Boomers, emerged from both Republicans and Democrats, often against party orthodoxy and frequently through bipartisan action.

ACKNOWLEDGMENTS

I am grateful for the support of the many people who helped make this book a reality.

First, thanks to my friend Alexandra Wolfe for introducing me to my agency, Janklow & Nesbit. My agent at J&N, Paul Lucas, has been a terrific advocate and a great reader. I always felt Paul Lucas and I were in it together—and not all writers can say the same about their agents. Brenna English-Loeb of J&N also deserves my thanks.

My research assistants April Reino, Griffin Price, and Wendy Lim were tireless in tracking down all manner of data and dealt gracefully with all my requests, no matter how obscure. April in particular was a model of Midwestern fortitude and forbearance; Griffin's excellent work in quantitative analysis was essential. The team was joined toward the end by Rebecca Thomson, and I'm delighted that she and April will join me on future projects. Thanks also to my friend Eric Silverberg, who helped me find my research assistants in the first place.

The entire team at Hachette Books was a pleasure to work with: Michelle Aielli, Betsy Hulsebosch, Lauren Hummel, and the publisher of Hachette Books, Mauro DiPreta. My editor, Paul Whitlatch, was everything I could hope for: rigorous, thoughtful, fair, and with impeccable instincts. The "Pauls," agent and editor, Lucas and Whitlatch, made the book better than it would have been.

Thanks also to Lynn Goldberg and her team at Goldberg McDuffie, including Angela Baggetta and Emily Lavelle, who along with Hachette's team were essential to getting the book noticed.

ACKNOWLEDGMENTS

Much of the data in this book derives from government sources. Americans are lucky to live in a country still committed to the collection and provision of data: the Census, BEA, the Fed, the CBO, the GAO, the National Institutes and various academies, and others. These institutions have suffered endless budgetary indignities but still manage to produce the most comprehensive set of data any society has ever collected about itself. Even after decades of Boomer neglect and hostility, no bureaucracy is as committed to making a nation as transparent to itself as the American bureaucracy. These institutions deserve far greater credit than they get. My thanks to them. My feelings about their political masters, I think, are clearly and abundantly different.

On the personal side, my parents—and yes, one of them is a Boomer—have always been there for me and they have my gratitude and love. They deserve lavish praise, but they're not the sort of people who like to read about themselves. I'll just leave it as: Thank you, Parents. My partner, David, has been a wise first reader, an extraordinary source of support and counsel, and a font of endless patience. (Bruce: "I think the next book could be a little provocative, plus I need your notes on this chapter by tomorrow, and also there are packages downstairs with reference books and would you mind stacking them by the other books on the sofa and just shove aside the two boxes of books that have blue Post-its on them?" David: "Uh-huh. Also, you need an additional citation on your marginal tax stats.") And of course, there's Fuzbo, Cherry, Cola, and the Animal Family. But they're another story.

Various others, from less obvious quarters, deserve thanks. I managed to come down with a surprising number of ailments while writing this book—including pneumonia but (disappointingly) not something more, you know, *writerly*, like consumption. Dr. Clifford Sewell managed to get me through these afflictions. I started and finished this book in a house more or less built by my friend Luis, and if my editor thinks I'm a helpless fiddler, he should meet Luis, who has been a great friend over the twelve years (and counting) that my "remodel" has taken.

Finally, a quick hello to Ruxing and Yena Fitzgerald, Benjamin Levchin, and Francesca Dizon—I'll get to that childrens' book one day, but probably not before you have kids of your own.

A NOTE ON THE NUMBERS AND CONVENTIONS

The goals in presenting data in this book are to be reliable, fair, and clear. Clarity is not always a goal harmonious with the other objectives, and so certain complexities have been placed in the footnotes and endnotes to improve readability. The rest of these notes are not essential for understanding anything in the text—I present them for completeness and because many of the topics discussed are complex, controversial, and the subject of surprisingly...vigorous...academic discussion. (Many think that Picketty and Saez are the last word on income inequality, and while they have done good work, that work is highly controversial—not just in its conclusions, but in its methodologies and data selected.)

Figures presented in this book may also vary from figures cited in the daily news; the latter are often not annualized, not inflation adjusted, and not final—this is no criticism of newspapers, which operate on a different time scale. The following explains why some of these differences appear and why this book's versions should be more reliable and fair.

For historical comparisons, dollar figures have usually been inflation adjusted with nominal figures shown where relevant. Doing so allows sensible comparisons when long periods are discussed. Readers will not need to understand the adjustment mechanism beyond knowing that $1 in 1980 bought more than $1 does today and that this dynamic has been accounted for. Most dollar figures, except when noted as "nominal," are presented in 2015 dollars. There has been very little inflation between 2015 and press date, and 2016 figures were not finalized as of the original press date; however, inflation has been subdued for a long time and most 2015 dollar figures will be close in value to current dollars. In cases where data are presented for after October 2016, they are based on projections (usually the government's) using a source's estimates and "business as usual" scenarios unless otherwise noted. "Now" and "current" in this book refer to the book's original press date, though figures remain substantively current.

Historical data are also generally presented end-of-period, not intrayear, except where absolute highs and lows are relevant. Where there are multiple sources, consensus values from the most dependable sources (usually, the government) are presented; consistency has been sought in methods of inflation adjustment where possible, though the government itself uses various metrics for inflation adjustment, like constant and chained dollars. In cases of conflicting sources, priority is generally given to reliable, conservative sources (where "conservative" means the numbers least supportive of the book's argument). There have also been places where the government has only collected continuous, comparable data over particular periods—for example, for certain items of income, between 1979 and the present. Starting dates and end dates have an effect on *magnitudes* of change, but for the topics covered do not affect the general directions or conclusions.

Because government frequently revises recent data, there may be some minor deviations between the most recent data presented in the book and the final data released after the book's original press date. Readers should also be aware that the government's fiscal year does not match the calendar year and that laws passed in a given year may not be effective until later years; these distinctions are noted when relevant. The government also takes some time to analyze data, and there is usually a multiyear lag for important data, like tax receipts. There can also be quirks in annual accounting—for example, budget deficits can actually vary on the order of $50 billion by virtue of whether the government's fiscal year ends on a workday or a weekend. Again, most of the data presented are long-term, greatly reducing the importance of these quirks. Different parts of the government produce different analyses of statistics that go under the same term (like "income") but which embody different concepts. The BEA and the Census, for example, differ substantially on the definition of income and they present figures that are often notably different. I have tried to use consistent sources for the same concepts wherever possible. The trends and conclusions remain the same, because the differences in methodologies tend to produce roughly the same gaps over reasonable periods, and the directions are generally parallel. Finally, international comparisons are especially challenging because each country adheres to different accounting standards. Again, the general conclusions are unaffected and I've tried to keep things reconciled where possible—it's not so much apples-to-oranges as tangerines-to-clementines in most cases.

In cases where quotes have been modified for readability, changes have been made only to nonsubstantive punctuation and capitalization (e.g., "Government is in Washington" appears as "government is in Washington" instead of "[g]overnment is in Washington"); otherwise, changes are noted. All emphases in quotations are mine unless otherwise noted.

NOTES

Foreword

1. Robins, Lee N., and Darrel A. Regier. *Psychiatric Disorders in America.* The Free Press, 1991, ch. 11. The ECA study was based on surveys and work conducted by UCLA and Yale, Johns Hopkins, Washington, and Duke universities, with a large population in five mainly urban sites, and coordinated with the National Institutes of Mental Health in the first half of the 1980s; the findings were generalized to national populations using 1980s Census data. It used definitions from the third version of the DSM, which had the same general concept of antisocial personality disorder as the fifth and current version, though with slightly different criteria. Not only did ECA find that the prevalence of antisocial personality disorder was higher in Boomer-age cohorts, it also speculated that lifetime prevalence might have been understated relative to older groups, as Boomers had not had as much time to accumulate symptoms.

Introduction

1. Reagan, Ronald. "Ronald Reagan's Announcement for Presidential Candidacy." National Archives, 13 Nov. 1979, www.reaganlibrary.archives.gov/archives/reference/11.13.79.html. Reagan attributed this sentiment to "someone," probably a speechwriter, but wholeheartedly endorsed it.
2. Taylor, Paul, et al. "Once Again, the Future Ain't What It Used to Be." Pew Research Center, 2 May 2006, www.pewresearch.org/files/old-assets/social/pdf/BetterOff.pdf (citing data from 2002, 2006); Stokes, Bruce. "Global Publics: Economic Conditions Are Bad: But Positive Sentiment Rebounding in Europe, Japan, U.S." Pew Research Center, 23 July 2015, www.pewglobal.org/files/2015/07/Pew-Research-Center-Economy-Report-FINAL-July-23-20151.pdf (citing data from 2015).
3. United States Constitution. Preamble.
4. Buettner, Russ, and Charles V. Bagli. "How Donald Trump Bankrupted His Atlantic City Casinos, but Still Earned Billions." *New York Times*, 11 June 2016, www.nytimes.com/2016/06/12/nyregion/donald-trump-atlantic-city.html?_r=0; Carroll, Lauren, and Clayton Youngman. "Fact-Checking Claims About Donald Trump's Four Bankruptcies." *Politifact*, 21 Sept. 2015, www.politifact.com/truth-o-meter/statements/2015/sep/21/carly-fiorina/trumps-four-bankruptcies/; Isidore, Chris. "Everything You

Want to Know about Donald Trump's Bankruptcies." CNN, 31 Aug. 2015, money.cnn
.com/2015/08/31/news/companies/donald-trump-bankruptcy/; Harwell, Drew, and
Jacob Bogage. "What Trump Didn't Say About His Four Big Business Bankruptcies."
Washington Post, 7 Aug. 2015, www.washingtonpost.com/business/economy/what
-trump-didnt-say-about-his-four-big-business-bankruptcies/2015/08/07/bc054e64-3
d12-11e5-9c2d-ed991d848c48_story.html. Trump admitted his casinos filed for bankruptcy in several places, including the Republican primary debates and in an interview
with ABC.

5. White House, Council of Economic Advisers. "The 2015 Economic Report
   of the President." *Economic Report of the President*, Feb. 2015, ch. 1, p. 39, www
   .whitehouse.gov/sites/default/files/docs/cea_2015_erp_complete.pdf. The Report is
   technically presented by the president to Congress, but it's fairly clear that the CEA
   does most of the heavy lifting.

6. Federal Reserve Bank of St. Louis. "Real Median Family Income in the United States"
   (MEFAINUSA672N), www.research.stlouisfed.org (using data from the US Census).
   The St. Louis Fed both produces its own data and aggregates data from other sources,
   primarily government sources. Because the St. Louis Fed's online database is used
   frequently and is a convenient source for readers, I will frequently refer to this source
   (hereinafter "FRED"), noting the applicable series identifier and, if FRED's data are
   based on sources other than the Federal Reserve Bank, the institution providing that
   data in a series's first mention. In the case of family income, the statistics presented
   are for 2015, in CPI-U-RS inflation-but-not-seasonally-adjusted terms (essentially,
   2015 dollars). It's important to note that recent economic data are constantly revised,
   and exhibit some minor fluctuations as final data are collected. Usually, after a few
   quarters, the economists achieve consensus at a final number. These fluctuations
   may account for certain minor differences between figures quoted in this book, in
   the press, and even by a given government agency within a few-week period, but do
   not change any general conclusions or raise any questions about the long-term data
   herein or the reliability of government data generally (though the government's *conclusions* are often suspect, the more political and less technical the data are). See "A
   Note on the Numbers and Conventions" for further discussion.

7. Ibid.; US Department of Commerce, Bureau of Economic Analysis (hereinafter
   "BEA"), Consumer Price Index; author's calculations. For this chapter, I've used
   Census's "family incomes" because they have a longer and more consistent history
   than "median household incomes." The latter is a more common metric now, but
   it has a more complicated history than family income. Both statistics drive toward
   the same conclusion: Analyzing any reasonable metric reveals a significant gap
   between projected and actual income, whether that metric is family income, household income or GDP per capita, and so on. (The projected/actual gaps for GPD per
   capita are smaller, because they would be an average, and blend in the concentration of wealth at the top—though incomes would still be higher even under that
   analysis). Because counterfactuals over such long periods draw in so many different
   variables, this endnote is a long one. First, the composition of American families
   has changed over time but that in itself is partly an economic choice and the general conclusion remains the same even adjusting for changes to family composition. Second, the "mid" scenario encompasses 1981–82, years of recession, while
   the "actual" series includes 2015, well into the recovery, so if anything, the case is

being somewhat understated. Third, it's important to acknowledge that the ways Americans earn income have changed over the years (and how the Census has changed its calculations of income, most recently in the 2013–2014 period which resulted in a 2 to 3 percent jump due to methodology alone). These factors can push the numbers around, but again, they don't change the general direction or rough magnitude of the gap. For example, many Americans work longer hours and more people in American multi-person families work now than they did in the 1950s (so if anything, one could argue that incomes should be even higher). At the same time, people start working later in life and for several decades have been compensated partly in non-cash income which is nevertheless quite valuable and important (like certain health and retirement benefits)—factoring these items in would narrow the gap between actual and potential but not come close to erasing it. (This is especially the case considering the formerly greater availability of defined benefit contributions before the 1980s. The picture darkens when you consider that older people who received employer contributions to retirement plans/Social Security have a much better chance of collecting from those plans at promised value than younger people today will.) All in all, principled cases could be made that projected incomes could be higher or lower than I estimated, but even heavy tweaking still leaves a gap and that gap really grows as the Boomers accumulate power. You'd expect major departures by the late 1980s or early 1990s (a hysteresis) and this is essentially what happens. It's worth noting that the Economic Report of the President completed a similar counterfactual in its 2015 Report and found that household incomes would be 98 percent higher had certain positive trends continued, which is a stronger claim than I advance here. See supra en 5 at pp. 29–34.

8. "64–65 NY World's Fair FUTURAMA Ride Video," www.youtube.com/watch?v=2-5aK0H05jk#action=share.

9. The estimated population at the time I turned in the final draft of this book was 324 million; it was about 321 when I first started working on the book. US Department of Commerce, US Census Bureau (hereinafter "US Census"). Population Estimates, Intercensal Estimates (various periods).

10. Diagnostic and Statistical Manual of Mental Disorders: DSM-5. Washington, DC: 2013 (hereinafter "DSM-V"), 764 (alternative model); cf. ibid. at 659 (default model). A discussion of the specific application of the DSM-V's various criteria and caveats about their application appear in Appendix A to this book.

11. Office of the Independent Counsel. The Starr Report. Submitted by Kenneth W. Starr, endnote 1091, 9 Sept. 1998, www.washingtonpost.com/wp-srv/politics/special/clinton/icreport/srprintable.htm.

Chapter 1: The View from 1946

1. Quoted in Hayden, Deborah. Pox: Genius, Madness and the Mysteries of Syphilis. Basic Books, 2003, p. 133.

2. Ibid., pp. 137–138.

3. US Census, Current Population Surveys (various years and intercesal estimates); Centers for Disease Control and Prevention's ("CDC") Population Estimates (same); author's calculations.

4. Ibid.; US Census, "Current Estimates Data" Population Estimates, 2015, www.census.gov/popest/data/index.html.; CDC. "Live Births, Birth Rates, and Fertility

Rates, by Race: 1909–2003." Vital Statistics of the United States, Table 1–1, www.cdc
.gov/nchs/data/statab/natfinal2003.annvol1_01.pdf; US Census. "Death Rates by
Age, Sex, and Race: 1950 to 2008." Statistical Abstract of the United States, Tables
110, 2012 (various years), available for 2011 at census.gov/library/publications/2011/
compendia/statab/131ed/tables/12s0110.pdf; author's calculations.

5. "October 28, 1980 Debate Transcript: the Carter-Reagan Presidential Debate."
Commission on Presidential Debates, 28 Oct. 1980, www.debates.org/index.php?
page=october-28-1980-debate-transcript.

6. Department of Veterans Affairs, Office of Public Affairs. "America's Wars." www
.va.gov/opa/publications/factsheets/fs_americas_wars.pdf; US Public Health Services, National Office of Vital Statistics. "Vital Statistics of the United States 1945,
part I." Prepared under the supervision of Halbert L. Dunn, Centers for Disease
Control and Prevention, www.cdc.gov/nchs/data/vsus/vsus_1945_1.pdf.

7. Haskew, Michael E., ed., *The World War II Desk Reference*, Castle Books, 2008 at
433–35; author's calculations. "War deaths" includes civilian and combat deaths.
Figures for American civilian casualities are not available, but are usually assumed
to range from negligible to up to 120,000, which is a tiny fraction of the 16 million
estimated civilian deaths in the Soviet Union, the 6 million in Poland, and the 13
million in China. There is considerable debate about the exact numbers each nation
lost, but the general conclusion is that German, Chinese, and Soviet losses were
immense—tens of millions.

8. Davidson, Justin. "The Kitchen Debate's Actual Kitchen." *New York*, 8 May 2011,
nymag.com/realestate/features/commack-moscow-2011-5/.

9. Ibid.; US Census, Current Population Reports, Current Income (1961) at table B (for
1959 incomes).

10. Zillow.com; FRED, MEFAINUSA672N. Long Island is a different place now and
358 Towline Road has had some upgrades over the years, which explains some of
the relative price increase. Nevertheless, housing consumes a larger share of income
for many Americans than it once did, with significant geographic variability; it is,
to be reductive, costlier.

11. National Bureau of Economic Research. Clotfelter, Charles T. "Patterns of Enrollment and Completion." Jan. 1991, pp. 30–31.

12. FRED, UNRATE (BEA). A full discussion of unemployment trends is in Chapter 15
of this book.

13. "American Machine & Foundry Company." Harvard Business School, Lehman
Brothers Collection—Contemporary Business Archives, www.library.hbs.edu/hc/
lehman/company.html?company=american_machine_foundry_company.

14. Public Law 89-10 (1965), Title II, §201 et seq. and subsequent reauthorizations at 20
USC §§6301 et seq.

15. *Brown v. Board of Education*, 347 US 483 (1954).

16. Social Security Administration. Life Expectancy for Social Security; CDC. Life
tables 1900–2100.

17. Tax Foundation. "Federal Individual Income Tax Rates History: Nominal Dollars:
Income Years 1913–2013." taxfoundation.org/sites/taxfoundation.org/files/docs/
fed_individual_rate_history_nominal.pdf.

18. Ibid. (maximum marginal taxes fell through the early 1960s, reaching 70 percent in
1965).

19. FRED, GFDEGQ188S, FYFSGDA188S (US Office of Management and Budget, hereinafter "OMB"). Full discussion of debt and deficits appears in Chapter 9, as do additional and primary sources.

Chapter 2: Bringing Up Boomer

1. Locke, John. *Some Thoughts Concerning Education*, part I, § 1, open-source edition, undated (originally published 1693), https://the federalistpapers.integratedmarket .netdna-cdn.com.wp-content/uploads/2012/12/John-Locke-Thoughts-Concerning -Education.pdf.
2. Ibid., Dedication.
3. DSM-V, p. 661.
4. Brody, Jane E. "Final Advice from Dr. Spock: Eat Only All Your Vegetables." *New York Times*, 20 June 1998, www.nytimes.com/1998/06/20/us/final-advice-from-dr -spock-eat-only-all-your-vegetables.html.
5. Maier, Thomas. *Dr. Spock: An American Life*. Basic Books, 2nd ed., 2003, pp. 199, 202.
6. Ibid., p.130 (quoting Spock, Benjamin. *The Common Sense Book of Baby and Child Care*. 1st ed., Duell, Sloan and Pearce, 14 July 1946). Multiple editions of the *Common Sense Book* have been issued, and Maier has been cross-checked against the *Common Sense Book*.
7. Quoted in Maier, pp. 138–139.
8. Quoted in Maier, p. 321; see also Pace, Eric. "Benjamin Spock, World's Pediatrician, Dies at 94." *New York Times*, 17 Mar. 1998 (quoting Peale slightly differently, but to the same effect).
9. US Department of Health and Human Services, US Public Health Service, Office of the Surgeon General. "The Surgeon General's Call to Action to Support Breast-feeding." 2011, pp. 1–5; Horta, Bernardo L., and Cesar G. Victoria. "Long-Term Effects of Breastfeeding: A Systematic Review." World Health Organization, 2013, (a metastudy, noting a certain heterogeneity of data but many statistically significant outcomes, even adjusting for important variables like socioeconomic status and maternal IQ).
10. "Childhood Lead Poisoning." World Health Organization, 2010, p. 20 et seq.; Godwin, Hilary A. "Lead Exposure and Poisoning in Children." UCLA Institute of the Environment and Sustainability. Southern California Environmental Report Card, 2009, www.environment.ucla.edu/reportcard/index.html; see also Reyes, Jessica Wolpaw. "Environmental Policy as Social Policy? The Impact of Childhood Lead Exposure on Crime." National Bureau of Economic Research, May 2007, www .nber.org/papers/w13097 (for the effects of lead, but coming to different conclusions about generational criminality).
11. US Department of Commerce, National Telecommunications and Information Administration. "Household Broadband Adoption Climbs to 72.4 Percent." 6 June 2013, www.ntia.doc.gov/blog/2013/household-broadband-adoption-climbs-724-percent.
12. US Department of Labor, Bureau of Labor Statistics. "American Time Use Survey Summary." 24 June 2016, tables 1 and 11, www.bls.gov/news.release/atus.nr0.htm. "Teenagers" are defined as fifteen-to-nineteen-year-olds by BLS.
13. Maier, p. 401.
14. Powers, John. "Documentary Revisits the 'Dazzling' Polemics of the Buckley-Vidal Debates." NPR, 18 Aug. 2015, www.npr.org/2015/08/18/432721150/documentary

-revisits-the-dazzling-polemics-of-the-buckley-vidal-debates; Holt, Jim. "Will Intellectual Combat Ever Top William Buckley vs. Gore Vidal? A New Documentary Suggests Not." *New York*, 26 July 2015, nymag.com/daily/intelligencer/2015/07/best-of-enemies-buckley-vidal.html. Clips of the debates are available on YouTube, such as this one, with the relevant portion starting around 10:30, https://www.youtube.com/watch?v=ZY_nq4tfi24.

15. 13 FCC 1246 (1949) and codified in multiple releases afterward.

16. 48 FCC 2d 1 (FCC 1974).

17. Davis, Horance G. "TV: Just an Appliance…Toaster with Pictures." *Hendersonville Times-News* (a *NYT* regional newspaper), 29 Aug. 1987, p. 4; Syracuse Peach Council, 2 FCC Rcd 5043 (1987).

18. "What Americans Know: 1989–2007: Public Knowledge of Current Affairs Little Changed by News and Information Revolutions." Pew Research Center for the People & the Press, 15 Apr. 2007, p. 13, www.people-press.org/files/legacy-pdf/319.pdf.

19. *The Impact of Television: A Natural Experiment in Three Communities.* Edited by Tannis MacBeth Williams, Academic Press, 1986, pp. 2–4, and 14, and tables 1.3–.4.

20. Ibid., pp. 51–52, 61, see also 66 and compare pp.105–106, 120–121.

21. Ibid., p. 67.

22. Ibid., pp. 334, 412.

23. Ibid., ch. 9.

24. Winn, Marie. *The Plug In Drug.* Penguin Books, 3rd ed., 2002, p.109 (quoting NIMH, and referring to studies cited therein); see also, Hancox, Robert, et al. "Association of Television Viewing during Childhood with Poor Educational Achievement." *Journal of the American Medical Association*, vol. 159, July 2005, p. 615 et seq. (noting that the "associations between child and adolescent television viewing and education outcomes [which were negative] persisted after adjusting for IQ, socioeconomic status, and childhood behavioral problems," in a 1972 NZ cohort); Ridley-Johnson, Robyn, et al., "The Relation of Children's Television Viewing to School Achievement and I.Q." *Journal of Educational Research*, vol. 76, no. 5, May–June 1983, p. 294. JSTOR, www.jstor.org/stable/27539990; Borzekowski, Dina L.G., et al., "The Remote, the Mouse, and the No. 2 Pencil: The Household Media Environment and Academic Achievement Among Third Grade Students." *Archives of Pediatric Adolescent Medicine*, vol. 159, no. 7, 1 July 2005, pp. 607–613 (significantly negative effects for children with a TV in the bedroom, controlling for other variables); but compare Gentzkow, Matthew, and Jesse M. Shapiro. "Preschool Television Viewing and Adolescent Test Scores: Historical Evidence from the Coleman Study." *Quarterly Journal of Economics*, vol. 123, no. 1, Feb. 2008. Oxford Journals, qje.oxfordjournals.org/content/123/1/279.short (finding essentially no effects). See also Wright, John C., et al. "The Relations of Early Television Viewing to School Readiness and Vocabulary of Children from Low-Income Families: The Early Window Project," *Child Development*, vol. 72, no. 5, Sept.–Oct. 2001, pp. 1347–1366 (finding educational content may have small positive effects, but general content has negative effects in studied group).

25. Winn, p. 109.

26. Associated Press. "Coast Survey of Students Links Rise in TV Use to Poorer Grades." *New York Times*, 9 Nov. 1980.

27. Morin, Rich, and Paul Taylor. "Luxury or Necessity? The Public Makes A U-Turn." Pew Research Center, Social & Demographic Trends, 23 Apr. 2009, p. 9, www.pewsocialtrends.org/files/2010/10/luxury-or-necessity-2009.pdf.

28. Marsiglia, Cheryl S., et al. "Impact of Parenting Styles and Locus of Control on Emerging Adults' Psychosocial Success." *Journal of Education and Human Development*, vol. 1, no. 1, 2007. "Authoritative" parenting, which is somewhere between permissive and authoritarian, produces the best outcomes.

Chapter 3: Vietnam and the Emerging Boomer Identity

1. Johnson, Samuel. "The Idler." *The Works of Samuel Johnson, Vol. 7*, Essay No. 30, at 120. A. Strahan, 1801.

2. Rucker, Philip. "Trump Slams McCain for Being 'Captured' in Vietnam; Other Republicans Quickly Condemn Him." *Washington Post*, 18 Jul. 2015, www.washingtonpost.com/news/post-politics/wp/2015/07/18/trump-slams-mccain-for-being-captured-in-vietnam/; Felsenthal, Carol. "Bernie Sanders Found Socialism at the University of Chicago." *Chicago Magazine*, 4 Feb. 2015. There are some lingering questions about whether Sanders could have, in good conscience, applied for CO status, since it required at the time a religious objection to all wars, which it's not clear he had. But Hillary Clinton's primary win mooted the matter.

3. US Census Bureau. *Statistical Abstract of the United States: 2014*. Tables 3, 7; author's calculations.

4. Loewe, James W. *Lies My Teacher Told Me: Everything Your American History Textbook Got Wrong*. 2nd ed., New Press, 2007, pp. 244–245 and 255–256.

5. Daggett, Stephen. "Costs of Major U.S. Wars." Library of Congress, Congressional Research Service, 29 Jun 2010, p. 2 et seq. Figures cited are for the wars themselves; the defense budget was higher in the 1940s–1960s overall than it would be during the later conflicts in the Middle East. It is reasonable to debate which basis— all defense, or just combat operations—is the right metric, though it's important to remember that the secular trend in mid-century America was for large defense budgets overall as a fraction of national income.

6. Free, Lloyd A., and Hadley Cantril. *The Political Beliefs of Americans: A Study of Public Opinion*. Rutgers University Press, 1967, pp. 59–60 (citing May 1964 Gallup polling; about a quarter of Americans were unaware "about the fighting in Vietnam").

7. DSM-V, p. 659.

8. Pub. Law 51-144 §1.c-d (1951). The twists, turns, and complexities of the draft are mind-numbing now, but were studied intently during the war. We can gloss over many of the system's quirks without losing the general point, although the quirks themselves provide interesting test beds whose implications are discussed later.

9. US Census, *Statistical Abstract of the United States: 1966*. Table 366; *Statistical Abstract of the United States: 1976*. Table 541; author's calculations.

10. 81 Stat. 102 §6.a.1, .h.1 (1967); see also Selective Service System. *Annual Report of the Director of Selective Service*, 1967, p.14 et seq.

11. Reports of the Director of the Selective Service (various years); see also note 9.

12. Lunch, William L., and Peter Sperlich. "American Public Opinion and the War in Vietnam." *Western Political Quarterly*, vol. 32, no. 1, Mar. 1979, p. 24. JSTOR, www.jstor.org/stable/447561.

13. Ibid., pp. 32–33.

14. Appleton, Sheldon. "The Public, the Polls, and the War." *Vietnam Perspectives*, vol. 1, no. 4, May 1966, pp. 3–13.

15. Ibid., pp. 24, 33; see also Erksine, Hazel. "The Polls, Pacifism and the Generation Gap." *Public Opinion Quarterly*, vol. 36, no. 4, 1972–73, pp. 616–627; Erksine, Hazel. "The Polls: Is War a Mistake." *Public Opinion Quarterly*, vol. 34, no. 1, 1970, pp. 134–159.

16. Carroll, Joseph. "The Iraq–Vietnam Comparison." Gallup Inc., 15 June 2004, www.gallup.com/poll/11998/iraqvietnam-comparison.aspx.

17. Erskine, "The Polls: Is War a Mistake," pp. 134–135.

18. "Every Person of the Year Cover Ever." *Time*, time.com/3614128/person-of-the-year-covers/.

19. Baskir, Lawrence M., and William A. Strauss; see also this chapter's note 9, *Chance and Circumstance: The Draft, the War and the Vietnam Generation*. Alfred A. Knopf., 1st ed., 1978, pp. 4–6, Fig 1.

20. Foley, Michael S. *Confronting the War Machine: Draft Resistance During the Vietnam War*. University of North Carolina Press, 2003, p. 37.

21. Selective Service System. *Annual Report of the Director of Selective Service*, 1967, p. 16.

22. Baskir, Strauss, Fig. 1. See also this chapter's note 9.

23. Foley, pp. 39–40.

24. Kuziemko, Ilyana. "'Dodging Up' to College or 'Dodging Down' to Jail: Behavioral Responses to the Vietnam Draft by Race and Class." Princeton University and National Board of Economic Research, 2010; and Kuziemko, Ilyana. "Did the Vietnam Draft Increase Human Capital Dispersion? Draft-Avoidance Behavior by Race and Class." Princeton University and National Board of Economic Research, Jan. 2010.

25. Miller, Glenn T. *Piety and Profession: American Protestant Theological Education, 1870–1970*. Wm. B. Eerdmans, 2007, p. 699, and footnotes 55, 728. John C. Stocker conducted similar research and reached concurrent conclusions in work for the Lilly Foundation.

26. Kuziemko, "'Dodging Up' to College or 'Dodging Down' to Jail"; Card, David, and Thomas Lemieux. "Going to College to Avoid the Draft: The Unintended Legacy of the Vietnam War." *American Economic Review*, vol. 91, no. 2, May 2001, pp. 97–102. JSTOR, www.jstor.org/stable/2677740; Associated Press. "College Enrollment Linked to Vietnam War." *New York Times*, 2 Sept. 1984, www.nytimes.com/1984/09/02/us/college-enrollment-linked-to-vietnam-war.html (citing research by the Census Bureau); *Opportunity*, no. 113, Nov. 2011, pp. 2–3 (noting anomalous spike in male enrollment not paralleled in women during draft period).

27. Graham, Fred P. "Spock and Coffin Indicted for Activity against Draft." *The New York Times*, 6 Jan. 1968, www.nytimes.com/books/98/05/17/specials/spock-indicted.html.

28. Maraniss, David. *First in His Class: The Biography of Bill Clinton*, Touchstone, 1996, pp. 188–194; see also Ifill, Gwen. "The 1992 Campaign: New Hampshire: Clinton Thanked Colonel in '69 for 'Saving Me from the Draft.'" *New York Times*, 13 Feb. 1992 (reprinting Clinton's rather confusing letter to his ROTC director); Ifill, Gwen. "The 1992 Campaign: Democrats; Vietnam War Draft Status Becomes Issue for Clinton." *New York Times*, 7 Feb. 1992; Brokaw, Tom, et al. "Bill Clinton Tries to Defend Himself on Draft Issue." *NBC Nightly News*, 15 Sept. 1992, archives.nbclearn.com/portal/site/k-12/flatview?cuecard=33559.

29. Seelye, Katharine Q. "The 2004 Campaign: Military Service; Cheney's Five Draft Deferments during the Vietnam Era Emerge as a Campaign Issue." *New York*

Times, 1 May 2004, nytimes.com/2004/05/01/us/2004-campaign-military-service
-cheney-s-five-draft-deferments-during-vietnam-era.html.

30. Foley, p. 51.
31. Appy, Christian G. *Working-Class War: American Combat Soldiers & Vietnam*. University of North Carolina Press, 1993, p. 27; see also Baskir, Strauss, pp. 6–9 and ch. 2 generally.
32. Timberg, Robert. *John McCain: An American Odyssey*. 1st paperback ed., Free Press, 2007, p. 122.
33. Foley, p.12.
34. Baskir and Strauss, pp. 40–41 (172,000 CO classifications); and US Census Bureau. *Statistical Abstract of the United States: 1977*, table 598 (179,000 CO classifications between 1965 and 1975); see also Selective Service System. *Semi-Annual Report of Director of Selective Service, 1973*, Appendix 12 (noting about 300,000 classifications); Fox, Richard P. "Conscientious Objection to War: The Background and a Current Appraisal." *Cleveland State Law Review*, 1982, p. 90; Levi, Margaret. *Consent, Dissent, and Patriotism*. Cambridge University Press, 1997, pp. 164–173. Because of the way CO objections were processed, compilers occasionally double-counted; the consensus is that about 175,000 CO classifications were made and even the largest figures noted were just a tiny fraction of other deferment types.
35. Kuziemko,"'Dodging Up' to College or 'Dodging Down' to Jail"; Kuziemko, "Did the Vietnam Draft Increase Human Capital Dispersion?" p. 2 and secs. 5–6.
36. Ibid.
37. Kuziemko,"'Dodging Up' to College or 'Dodging Down' to Jail," p. 22.
38. Baskir and Strauss, pp. 126–129.
39. Anderson, Terry H. *The Sixties*, Pearson, 2012, pp. 79–80; Baskir and Strauss, pp. 8–9.
40. DSM-V, pp. 660–61.
41. Heinl, Robert D. "The Collapse of the Armed Forces." *Armed Forces Journal*. North American Newspaper Alliance, 7 June 1971, reprinted in Gettleman, Marvin, et al. *Vietnam and America: A Documented History*. Grove Press. 1995, pp. 326–336.
42. Ibid., p. 329.
43. Brush, Peter. "The Hard Truth about Fragging." *Vietnam Magazine,* Oct. 2010, pp. 40–43.
44. Anderson, p. 167.
45. Baskir and Strauss, pp. 134–136.
46. Bell, Bruce D. "Characteristics of Army Deserters in the DoD Special Discharge Review Program." *Research Report 1229*. US Army Research Institute for the Behavioral and Social Sciences, Oct. 1979, p. 2 and n. 4.
47. Heinl, in Gettleman, p. 334.
48. Karnow, Stanley. *Vietnam: A History*. 2nd ed., Penguin Books Group, 1997, p. 20.
49. Plato. *Crito* (generally).
50. Stern, Lewis M. "Response to Vietnamese Refugees: Surveys of Public Opinion." *Social Work: A Journal of the National Association of Social Workers*, vol. 26, no. 4, 1981, pp. 306 et seq.
51. Elliott, Debbie. "A Lesson in History: Resettling Refugees of Vietnam." *All Things Considered*, 14 Jan. 2007; State Department Archives. "Foreign Relations of the United States, 1969–1976, vol. X, Vietnam, January 1973–July 1975." Document

263, 1976, history.state.gov/historicaldocuments/frus1969-76v10/d263; see also for a partisan opinion, Pham, Quang X. "Ford's Finest Legacy." *Washington Post*, 30 Dec. 2006, www.washingtonpost.com/wp-dyn/content/article/2006/12/29/AR2006122901070.html. Chapman, Bruce. "As Governor, Jerry Brown Was Vociferous Foe of Vietnamese Immigration." *Discovery News*, 2 Oct. 2010.

52. Hunter, Marjorie. "Ford Offers Amnesty Program Requiring 2 Years Public Work; Defends His Pardon of Nixon." *New York Times*, 17 Sept. 1974, p. 1. Estimates varied as to numbers eligible for clemency; the government cited figures that were probably too low and were in any event rendered moot by Carter's subsequent pardon. Moreover, under Ford's clemency, the two-year term could be reduced for "mitigating" circumstances like family hardship, so it's not clear that much penance really would have been required.

Chapter 4: Empire of Self

1. DSM-V, p. 662.
2. Ibid., pp. 660–61.
3. Swatz, James A. *Substance Abuse in America: A Documentary and Reference Guide.* Greenwood, 2012, p. 158; *West of Center: Art and the Counter Culture Experiment in America, 1965–1977.* Edited by Elissa Auther and Adam Lerner. University of Minnesota Press, 2 Nov. 2011, p. 57.
4. "Protest: The Banners of Dissent." *Time.* 27 Oct. 1967, content.time.com/time/magazine/article/0,9171,841090,00.html.
5. Gitlin, Todd. *The Sixties: Years of Hope, Days of Rage.* Revised ed., Bantam, 1 July 1993, p. 214.
6. Cottrell, Robert C. *Sex, Drugs and Rock 'n' Roll: The Rise of America's 1960s Counterculture.* Rowman & Littlefield, 19 Mar. 2015, p. 88.
7. *The New York Times: The Times of the Sixties: The Culture, Politics and Personalities That Shaped the Decades.* Edited by John Rockwell. Black Dog & Leventhal, 2014, p. 152.
8. "Gallup Finds Rise in Marijuana Use," *New York Times*, 6. Feb. 1972, p. 36 (polling college students and finding under 5 percent had tried marijuana in 1967, rising to 42 percent by 1970 and then a majority by the end of 1971; of that majority, four out of five had used it in the past year and three out of five in the past month). See also Golub, Andrew, Bruce D. Johnson, "The Rise of Marijuana as the Drug of Choice Among Youthful Adult Arrestees," June 2001, US Department of Justice, at 6 (citing data for general population derived from the National Household Survey on Drug Abuse et al). See also Robison, Jennifer. "Decades of Drug Use: Data from the '60s and '70s." Gallup, 2 July 2002, http://www.gallup.com/poll/6331/decades-drug-use-data-from-60s-70s.aspx (marijuana use among all *adults* under 5 percent in the late 1960s).
9. See notes 8 and 10.
10. Harrison, Lana D., et al. "Cannabis Use in the United States: Implications for Policy." University of Delaware, Center for Drug and Alcohol Studies, 12 Jun. 1995, pp. 181–183. CEDRO, www.cedro-uva.org/lib/harrison.cannabis.pdf; National Commission on Marijuana and Drug Abuse. "Marihuana: A Signal of Misunderstanding." Commissioned by President Richard M. Nixon, Mar. 1972; see also Johnston, Lloyd D., et al. "Monitoring the Future: National Survey Results on Drug Use 1975–2014," vol. 2, 2014, p. 27, tables 9.15 et seq. (sponsored by NIDA and NIH).

11. Johnston, "Monitoring the Future," tables 9.10, 9.12, 9.15.

12. National Institute on Drug Abuse. "DrugFacts, Nationwide Trends." (rev. 2015, most recent data from 2013 surveys), p. 2, www.drugabuse.gov/sites/default/files/drugfacts_nationtrends_6_15.pdf.

13. Twenge, Jean M., et al. "Changes in American Adults' Sexual Behavior and Attitudes 1972–2012." *Archives of Sexual Behavior*, 2014–2015, psy2.fau.edu/~shermanr/Twenge%20Sherman%20&%20Wells%20In%20Press.pdf at 2273 in journal form.

14. Ibid., Finer, Lawrence B., and Jesse M Philbin. "Trends in Ages at Key Reproductive Transitions in the United States, 1951–2010." *Women's Health Issues*. May–June 2014, pp. 5–6 (electronic version).

15. Ibid.; see also Twenge, Jean M., et al. "Changes in American Adults' Sexual Behavior and Attitudes 1972–2012." The Millennials do appear to have very promiscuous subcohorts.

16. Ibid. at 2280. The number of partners peaked in the cohort born during the 1960s generally, and so includes some GenXers. The data cited are not sufficiently granular to make a precise break at 1964.

17. Ibid.

18. Twenge, "Changes in American Adults' Sexual Behavior and Attitudes 1972–2012," at 2279.

19. DSM-V at 660.

20. *Griswold v. Connecticut*, 381 US 479 (1965); *Eisenstadt v. Baird*, 405 US 438 (1972).

21. Kost, Kathryn, and Stanley Henshaw. "U.S. Teenage Pregnancies, Births and Abortions 2010: National and State Trends by Age, Race and Ethnicity." Guttmacher Institute, May 2014, table 2.1.

22. Cowan, Sarah K. "Cohort Abortion Measures for the United States." *Population and Development Review*, vol. 39, no. 2, June 2013, p. 9, fig. 6, table 1. HHS Public Access.

23. Ibid., p 10.

24. Ibid., table 2.1.

25. CDC. "2014 Sexually Transmitted Disease Surveillance 2014." 2015, tables 10, 21, 35. The CDC data are the most reliable data available, although methodology and collection are imperfect due to state inconsistencies in collection. Given the size of *n*, however, CDC's conclusions should be considered generally reliable.

26. DSM-V, pp. 660–61, 764.

27. Foreman, Amanda. "The Heartbreaking History of Divorce." *Smithsonian Magazine*, Feb. 2014.

28. Wilcox, W. Bradford. "The Evolution of Divorce." *National Affairs*, 2009, p. 81.

29. US Census. *Statistical Abstract of the United States: 1998*, table no. 123 and subsequent years at comparable tables; see also US Census Bureau. "Number, Timing, and Duration of Marriages and Divorces: 2009." *Current Population Report: Household Economic Studies*, May 2011, pp. 7–10; Thomas, Susan Gregory. "The Divorce Generation." *Wall Street Journal*, 9 July 2011. Saturday Essay. Because divorce is politicized, not all states compile good data, federal funding for collection of data was restricted in the 1990s, and divorce data are notoriously hard to pin down, but the general *trend* in divorce can be discerned readily enough.

30. Kennedy, Sheela, and Steven Ruggles. "Breaking Up Is Hard to Count: The Rise of Divorce in the United States, 1980–2010." *Demography*, 8 Jan. 2014, p. 595, and cites associated with figures presented in this chapter for the rise in marital instability

after 1970. Boomers are now late middle-aged or senior, but their pattern of high marital instability continues. Subsequent generations do marry less frequently, and later, and their lower incidence of divorce is affected by those trends, since those who are not married cannot, by definition, get divorced.

31. Brown, Susan L., and I-Fen Lin. "The Gray Divorce Revolution: Rising Divorce Among Middle-Aged and Older Adults, 1990–2010." *Journals of Gerontology Series B*, vol. 67, no. 6, 2012, pp. 731–741; see generally Thomas, Susan Gregory. "The Gray Divorcés." *Wall Street Journal*, 3 Mar. 2012. Saturday Essay.

32. Brown, and Lin. "The Gray Divorce Revolution"; see generally Thomas, "The Gray Divorcés," and see also cites associated with figures presented herein.

33. Thomas (citing Strauss, William, and Neil Howe. *Generations: The History of America's Future, 1584 to 2069*. Quill, 30. Sept. 1992). I have my own doubts about *Generations* generally, but other literature supports its pithy summary.

34. Whitehead, Barbara Dafoe. *The Divorce Culture: Rethinking our Commitments to Marriage and Family*. Vintage, 3 Feb. 1998.

35. "Number, Timing, and Duration of Marriages and Divorces: 2009." US Census Bureau, 2009, table 4, www.census.gov/prod/2011pubs/p70-125.pdf; author's calculations.

36. For a good summary, see Arkowitz, Hal, and Scott O. Lilienfield. "Is Divorce Bad for Children? The Breakup May Be Painful, but Most Kids Adjust Well over Time." *Scientific American*, 1 Mar. 2013; see also Amato, Paul R., and Jacob Cheadle, "The Long Reach of Divorce: Divorce and Child Well-Being Across Three Generations." *Journal of Marriage and Family*, vol. 67, no. 1, Feb. 2005, pp. 192–193 et seq. and works cited therein.

37. Brown, p. 731.

38. DSM-V, p. 660.

39. Federal Reserve Bank of St. Louis. PSAVERT (BEA). The personal savings rate is the rate for individuals, nonprofit institutions, pensions, and assorted entities, but it's the best proxy on a longitudinal basis for individual savings as a percent of disposable income. For a further discussion of savings, see Chapter 12.

40. Ibid.

41. CDC. "Prevalence of Obesity Among Adults," and "Prevalence of Overweight, Obesity, and Extreme Obesity Among Adults: United States, Trends, 1960–1962 Through 2009–2010." CDC, National Center for Health Statistics. "Health, United States, 2015: With Special Feature on Racial and Ethnic Health Disparities." 2016, table 58, www.cdc.gov/nchs/data/hus/hus15.pdf#053.

42. World Health Organization, Global Health Observatory Data Repository, apps .who.int/gho/data/node.main.A900A?lang=en (data for 2010 and 2014).

43. CDC. "Prevalence of Overweight and Obesity among Children and Adolescents: United States, 1963–1965 through 2011–2012." Sept. 2014.

44. See notes 41–43; see also Leveille, Suzanne G. "Trends in Obesity and Arthritis Among Baby Boomers and Their Predecessors, 1971–2002." *American Journal of Public Health*, vol. 95, no. 9, Sept. 2005, p. 1607 et seq.; compare Reuters. "Obesity Rates for Elderly, Middle Aged on the Rise." *Huffington Post*, 25 Oct. 2012, www.huffingtonpost.com/2012/10/25/obesity-rates-elderly-middle-aged-rise_n _2017221.html.

45. See note 44.

46. Wang, Claire, et al. "Health and Economic Burden of the Projected Obesity Trends in the USA and the UK." *Lancet* 378, no. 9793, 27 Aug. 2011, pp. 812–825. The excess health-care costs are estimated to be on the order of tens of billions, possibly offset if obese people simply die earlier.

47. Wolfe, Tom. "Reports on America's New Great Awakening: The 'Me' Decade." *New York*, 23 Aug. 1976; see also Lasch, Christopher. *The Culture of Narcissism, American Life in an Age of Diminishing Expectations.* W. W. Norton, 1979; and Lasch's essays from the 1970s.

48. Hutchinson, Lydia. "The Rolling Stones' 'I Can't Get No Satisfaction.'" *Performing Songwriter.* 26 July 2013, performingsongwriter.com/rolling-stones-satisfaction/.

49. Twenge, Jean M., et al. "Changes in Pronoun Use in American Books and the Rise of Individualism, 1960–1980." *Journal of Cross-Cultural Psychology*, vol. 43, no. 3, 2012, p. 408, and generally pp. 406–415.

50. Ibid.

51. Ibid.; see also Google gram.

52. DSM-V, p. 660.

53. Bradley, Stefan M. *Harlem vs. Columbia University: Black Student Power in the Late 1960s.* University of Illinois Press. 2009, pp. 74–85; see also Fraser, Ronald. *1968: A Student Generation in Revolt.* Pantheon, 12 Apr. 1988, pp. 195–199; Martin, Douglas. "Henry S. Coleman, 79, Dies; Hostage at Columbia in '68." *New York Times*, 4 Feb. 2006. There have been self-serving assertions by students that Coleman had been ordered to stay in his office by the administration.

54. Anderson, p. 108.

55. Cf. Adler, Margot. "1968 Columbia Protests Still Stir Passion." NPR. 23 Apr. 2008 (statement of Allen Silver).

56. Twenge, Jean M., et al. "Changes in American Adults' Sexual Behavior and Attitudes 1972–2012," *Archives of Sexual Behavior*, vol. 44, no. 8, Nov. 2015, and various, esp. 9.

57. "Distracted by Technology at Mealtimes—It's Not Who You Think." Nielsen, 11 Nov. 2015, nielsen.com/us/en/insights/news/2015/distracted-by-technology-at-mealtimes-its-not-who-you-may-think.html.

Chapter 5: Science and Sentimentality

1. Pearce, Matt. "U.S. Rep. Paul Broun: Evolution a Lie from 'the Pit of Hell,'" *Los Angeles Times*, 7 Oct. 2012.

2. Berlin, Isaiah. *Against the Current.* 2nd ed., Princeton University Press. 2013, p. 205. Berlin describes the position of the French-influenced Enlightenment and then discusses its German romantic opposite. I do not use "empirical" in the philosophical sense of the divide, between empirical Anglophone and non-empirical Continental philosophy.

3. Declaration of Independence.

4. Constitution of the United States, art. I, sec. 8.

5. Saenz, Arlette. "Sen. Jim Inhofe Throws Snowball on Senate Floor in Attempt to Debunk Climate Change." ABC News. 26 Feb. 2015, abcnews.go.com/Politics/sen-jim-inhofe-throws-snowball-senate-floor-attempt/story?id=29255635 (embedded video of Inhofe and the snowball).

6. De Tocqueville, Alexis. *Democracy in America.* Edited and translated by Harvey C. Mansfield and Delba Winthrop. University of Chicago Press, 2000, ch. 10.

7. United States Congress. *Congressional Globe*, vol. 27, p. 1693; 7 USC § 304.

8. American Association for the Advancement of Science. "Historical Trends in Federal R&D." Federal R&D as a share of discretionary and total budget, 1962–2016, www.aaas.org/page/historical-trends-federal-rd, and see also and compare with the citations provided for the figure in this chapter.

9. White House, Council of Economic Advisers. "The 2016 Economic Report of the President." In *Economic Report of the President*, Feb. 2016, p. 220 (internal citations omitted).

10. Ibid., sec. 5.

11. National Science Foundation. "R&D Recognized as Investment in U.S. GDP Statistics: GDP Increase Slightly Lowers R&D-to-GDP Ratio." InfoBriefs, NSF 15-315, 30 Mar. 2015, www.nsf.gov/statistics/2015/nsf15315/. The American Association for the Advancement of Science and the BEA compile similar statistics showing the same trends.

12. Pion, Georgine M., and Mark W. Lipsey. "Public Attitudes Toward Science and Technology: What Have the Surveys Told Us?" *Public Opinion Quarterly*, vol. 45, no. 3, 1981, pp. 303–316 and table 1.

13. Ibid., table 1.

14. Ibid., table 2. The wording on the survey changed over the years, and data are provided for the 1972–1976 surveys as worded. However, the overwhelmingly positive prior response to a (less nuanced) question, in combination with the rest of the data in this chapter, suggests that things took a turn in the early 1970s.

15. Ibid., tables 3 and 309 (re: confidence in scientific establishment, support for basic research between the 1960s and 1970s); La Porte, Todd R., and Daniel Metlay. "Technology Observed: Attitudes of a Wary Public." *Science*, 11 Apr. 1975, tables 3–4 (re: science's ability to solve problems, from 1972 to 1974; sample based on California residents only).

16. La Porte and Metlay, secs. 3–4.

17. Ibid.

18. Handler, Phillip. "Public Doubts About Science." *Science*, vol. 208, no. 4448, 6 June 1980.

19. Pew Research Center. "Americans, Politics and Science Issues." 1 July 2015 (noting contemporary attitudes by cohort).

20. National Science Foundation. "Science and Engineering Indicators, National Science Foundation 2014." Appendix, tables 7–8 and ch. 7, generally, www.nsf.gov/statistics/2016/nsb20161/#/data. NSF decomposes the raw data, which can be found from the University of Chicago's GSS, using indicators SOLARREV, EARTHSUN, etc. Only respondents who answered the heliocentric question correctly were asked the year-revolution question; those who answered the former incorrectly were coded as being wrong about the latter.

21. Ibid.

22. Ibid., ch. 7.

23. Ibid., appendix, tables 2–17, 2–23, 2–33.

24. Epstein, Jennifer. "Graduation Gaps for Science Majors." *Inside Higher Ed*. 17 Feb. 2010, www.insidehighered.com/news/2010/02/17/stem; "Undergraduate Education, Enrollment, and Degrees in the United States." *Science and Engineering Indicators 2012*, ch. 2, www.nsf.gov/statistics/seind12/c2/c2s2.htm; Anderson, Stuart. "The

Importance of International Students to America." National Foundation for American Policy. NEAP Policy Brief, July 2013, www.nfap.com/pdf/New%20NFAP%20Policy%20Brief%20The%20Importance%20of%20International%20Students%20to%20America,%20July%202013.pdf (compiling data from NSF); National Science Foundation. "Science and Engineering Indicators, National Science Foundation 2014." Appendix, table 2-33 (available as download document).

25. Google Ngram Viewer searches for "feel," "how I feel," and "I feel that."

26. Google Ngram Viewer search for "true."

27. Pew Research Center. "Public Trust in Government: 1958–2014." 13 Nov. 2014, www.people-press.org/2014/11/13/public-trust-in-government/.

28. Ibid.

29. Burke, Edmund. "A Letter from Mr. Burke to a Member of the National Assembly; In Answer to Some Objections to his Book on French Affairs." 19 Jan. 1791, metaphors.iath.virginia.edu/metaphors/20164 (excerpted); original available at books.google.com/books?id=L1wPAAAAQAAJ&printsec=frontcover&source=gbs_ge_summary_r&cad=0#v=onepage&q=chain&f=false, pp. 68–69.

30. Reagan, Ronald. 12 Aug. 1986, available in the Public Papers of the Presidents of the United States (June 28–Dec. 31, 1986) at 1081.

31. Clymer, Adam. "M'Govern Asks Stand Against Tax-Cut Tide." *New York Times*, 18 Jun. 1978.

32. "Dietary Goals for the United States." Prepared by the Staff of the Select Committee on Nutrition and Human Needs (known as the "McGovern Commission"), Feb. 1977, pp. 1–2. Ninety-Fifth United States Congress, 1st Session.

33. "Vice President Spiro Agnew Speech." The Pacifica Radio/UC Berkeley. Social Activism Sound Recording Project. Houston, Texas, 22 May 1970, lib.berkeley.edu/MRC/pacificaviet/agnewtranscript.html.

34. Novak, Michael. "Reconsidering Vatican II." *CatholiCity*. 20 Apr. 2010.

35. Newport, Frank. "Catholics Similar to Mainstream on Abortion, Stem-Cells." Gallup. 30 Mar. 2009, www.gallup.com/poll/117154/catholics-similar-mainstream-abortion-stem-cells.aspx. Catholics who regularly attend church are more orthodox, but substantial minorities still hold more liberal, heterodox views on many matters.

36. "Pontifical Council for Legislative Text" (approved by Benedict XVI). 13 Mar. 2006, www.vatican.va/roman_curia/pontifical_councils/intrptxt/documents/rc_pc_intrptxt_doc_20060313_actus-formalis_en.html.

37. "A Church Divided: Ruling Ends Va.'s Episcopal Battle." NPR. All Things Considered. 10 Apr. 2012, www.npr.org/2012/04/10/150351713/a-church-divided-ruling-ends-va-s-episcopal-battle.

38. Montague, John. "The Law and Financial Transparency in Churches: Reconsidering the form 990 Exemption." *Cardozo Law Review*, vol. 35, no. 203, 2013, www.cardozolawreview.com/content/35-1/MONTAGUE.35.1.pdf.

39. "Do All Dogs Really Go To Heaven?" CBN. www1.cbn.com/700club/do-all-dogs-really-go-heaven.

40. Malachi 3:10 (King James Version).

Chapter 6: Disco and the Roots of Neoliberalism

1. Roosevelt, Franklin D. Second Inaugural Address. 20 Jan. 1937, http://avalon.law.yale.edu/20th_century/froos2.asp.

2. Von Mises, Ludwig. *Human Action: A Treatise on Economics.* The Ludwig von Mises Institute, 1998, at 874. The German edition appeared in 1940, the English edition, in 1949.

3. Von Mises, Ludwig. *Liberalism: In the Classical Tradition,* ch. 11, Mises Institute, mises.org/library/liberalism-classical-tradition/html/p/30.

4. Say, Jean-Baptiste. *A Treatise on Political Economy.* See also Smith, Adam. *The Wealth of Nations* (note, however, that Smith, while favoring a limited role for government and emphasizing the market's superior ability to organize itself, did endorse certain specific roles for the government, like the post, and the encouragement of certain industries—these specifics have now been lost to the generality of Smith's Invisible Hand).

5. Harris, Ethan S. *Ben Bernanke's Fed: The Federal Reserve After Greenspan.* Harvard Business Review Press. 15 July 2008, ch. 12. There are several similar, but slightly different versions of this quote floating around, but the substance is always the same.

6. "Statement of Aims." The Mont Pelerin Society. www.montpelerin.org/statement-of-aims/.

7. "Mont Pelerin Society Directory 2010." Re-created by DeSmogBlog. www.desmogblog.com/sites/beta.desmogblog.com/files/Mont%20Pelerin%20Society%20Directory%202010.pdf.

8. "'Goldwater Girl': Putting Context to a Resurfaced Hillary Clinton Interview." NPR. 26 Mar. 2016, www.npr.org/2016/03/26/471958017/-goldwater-girl-putting-context-to-a-resurfaced-hillary-clinton-interview?version=meter+at+7&module=meterLinks&pgtype=article&contentId=&mediaId=&referrer=https%3A%2F%2Fwww.google.com%2F&priority=true&action=click&contentCollection=meter-links-click.

9. Goldwater, Barry. *The Conscience of a Conservative.* E-book ed., Start Publishing, 2012, ch. 2, generally, and pp. 85–86.

10. Ibid., pp. 86–87.

11. Ibid., p. 88.

12. Ibid., p. 98.

13. Ibid., p.100.

14. Chomsky, Noam. "Richard Nixon Was 'Last Liberal President.'" *Huffington Post.* 21 Feb. 2014, www.huffingtonpost.com/2014/02/21/noam-chomsky-richard-nixon_n_4832847.html.

15. Bachman, Helena. "Global First? Every Swiss Could Be Guaranteed $2,600 a Month Tax-Free." *USA Today,* 6 May 2016, www.usatoday.com/story/news/world/2016/05/05/switzerland-referendum-monthly-income-tax-free/83940610/; "Switzerland's Voters Reject Basic Income Plan." BBC. 5 June 2016, www.bbc.com/news/world-europe-36454060.

16. Parker, Richard. *John Kenneth Galbraith: His Life, His Politics, His Economics.* 1st ed., University of Chicago Press, 1 Aug. 2006, p. 501; Perlman, Rick. *Nixonland: The Rise of a President and the Fracturing of America.* Scribner, 14 Apr. 2009, p. 710.

17. FRED, UNRATE.

18. Mayer, Gerald. "Union Membership Trends in the United States." *CRS Report for Congress.* 31 Aug. 2004, digitalcommons.ilr.cornell.edu/cgi/viewcontent.cgi?article=1176&context=key_workplace generally and at Appendix A (referring to "employed" workers; the same trends are true based on other subcategories with

minor differences in absolute levels); US Department of Labor, Bureau of Labor Statistics (hereinafter "BLS"). "Union members—2015." Press Release. 28 Jan. 2016, www.bls.gov/news.release/pdf/union2.pdf.

19. FRED, UNRATE, FPCPITOTLZGUSA (World Bank); CPI (BEA).

20. US Census, Income and Poverty Reports (various years); BEA, inflation indicators; author's calculations. See also "Trends in the Distribution of Household Income between 1979 and 2007," Congressional Budget Office, October 2011. The BLS also decomposes average hourly earnings overall and by sector and these show the same trends.

21. "President Gerald R. Ford's Address to a Joint Session of Congress on the Economy." Gerald R. Ford Presidential Library & Museum. www.fordlibrarymuseum .gov/library/speeches/740121.asp.

22. Mieczkowski, Yanek. *Gerald Ford and the Challenges of the 1970s.* University Press of Kentucky, 22 Apr. 2005, p. 131; see also Birnbaum, Jeffrey H. "Ford's Economic Record Belies His Reputation." *Washington Post.* 28 Dec. 2006, www.washingtonpost .com/wp-dyn/content/article/2006/12/27/AR2006122701580.html.

23. White House, Office of Management and Budget. "Historical Tables." Table 1.2, www.whitehouse.gov/omb/budget/Historicals. (2014–2016).

24. Carter, Jimmy. "'Crisis of Confidence' Speech." Miller Center. Transcript. 15 July 1979, millercenter.org/president/speeches/speech-3402.

Chapter 7: The Boomer Ascendancy

1. Hamilton, Alexander, James Madison, John Jay, Ian Shapiro (ed.). *The Federalist Papers.* No. 47 at 245. New Haven, CT: 2009. Madison was talking about separation of institutional powers. Asking whether Madison would have viewed institutional dominance by Boomers as being more parallel to his thinking in the *Federalist Papers* or *A Candid State of Parties* is probably too pedantic for an epigraph (or even an endnote); suffice it to say, I doubt he would have been thrilled by the Boomers.

2. US Census. "Historical National Population, Intercensal Estimates from 2000 to 2010, Population Estimates Program for 2013"; CDC, "Death Rates, CDC-NCHS Live Births from 1909 to 2003"; author's calculations; supra chapter 1, note 4.

3. US Department of Health and Human Services, CDC, Population Statistics, "Resident population, by age, sex, race, and Hispanic origin: United States, selected years 1950–2013", www.cdc.gov/nchs/hus/hispanic.htm#population (accessed for 2013 data); supra note 2.

4. Neale, Thomas H. "The Eighteen Year Old Vote: The Twenty-Sixth Amendment and Subsequent Voting Rates of Newly Enfranchised Age Groups." Report No. 83-103. Library of Congress, Congressional Research Service, 20 May 1983, digital.library .unt.edu/ark:/67531/metacrs8805/m1/1/high_res_d/83-103GOV_1983May20.pdf. The four states with sub-twenty-one voting ages were Georgia, Kentucky, Alaska (nineteen-year-old vote), and Hawaii (twenty-year-old vote)—and only two of these states had substantial electorates.

5. US Census, "Current Estimates Data" Population Estimates, 2015, www.census .gov/popest/data/index.html; CDC. "Live Births, Birth Rates, and Fertility Rates, by Race: 1909–2003." Vital Statistics of the United States, Table 1-1, www.cdc .gov/nchs/data/statab/natfinal2003.annvol1_01.pdf; US Census. "Death Rates by Age, Sex, and Race: 1950 to 2008." *Statistical Abstract of the United States: 2011,*

table 110, 2012, census.gov/library/publications/2011/compendia/statab/131ed/
tables/12s0110.pdf; author's calculations.

6. Kennedy, Edward M. "Voting Age to 18 Testimony Before the Senate Subcommittee on Constitutional Amendments." 9 Mar. 1970, tedkennedy.org/ownwords/event/voting_age.

7. I'm synthesizing the results of two surveys here, which is not best practice, but given the vast gulf between popular and political knowledge, a gap that's appeared repeatedly across many polls, the point stands. University of Pennsylvania, Annenberg Public Policy Center. "Americans Know Surprisingly Little About Their Government, Survey Finds." 17 Sept. 2014, cdn.annenbergpublicpolicycenter.org/wp-content/uploads/Civics-survey-press-release-09-17-2014-for-PR-Newswire.pdf; Pew Research Center. "What Americans Know: 1989–2007: Public Knowledge of Current Affairs Little Changed by News and Information Revolutions." 15 Apr. 2007, www.people-press.org/files/legacy-pdf/319.pdf.

8. Supra notes 2–3.

9. Ibid.

10. Nixon, Richard. "Letter to House Leaders Supporting a Constitutional Amendment to Lower the Voting Age." The American Presidency Project. 27 Apr. 1970, www.presidency.ucsb.edu/ws/index.php?pid=2487; Berman, Ari. "What the Supreme Court Doesn't Understand about the Voting Rights Act." *Nation.* 25 June 2013, www.thenation.com/article/what-supreme-court-doesnt-understand-about-voting-rights-act/.

11. US House of Representatives, History, Art & Archives. "The 26th Amendment." 1 July 1971, history.house.gov/Historical-Highlights/1951-2000/The-26th-Amendment/; Senate. Journal of the Senate. 92nd Congress, 1st session, 1971. S. S.J. Res. 7/ 65 Stat. 710, 1971.

12. "Ratification of Constitutional Amendments." U.S. Constitution Online, usconstitution.net/constamrat.html.

13. Fish, Eric S. "The Twenty-Sixth Amendment Enforcement Power." *Yale Law Journal,* vol. 121 no. 5 (Mar. 2012), pp. 1222–1224.

14. Ghitza, Yair, and Andrew Gelman. "The Great Society, Reagan's Revolution and Generations of Presidential Voting." Working Paper. 7 July 2014, p. 17; and Gallup. "Election Polls—Vote By Groups, 1968–1972." See also infra note 21.

15. Balz, Dan. "Karl Rove—The Strategist." *Washington Post.* 23 July 1999, www.washingtonpost.com/wp-srv/politics/campaigns/wh2000/stories/rove072399.htm.

16. Ghitza and Gelman. "The Great Society, Reagan's Revolution and Generations of Presidential Voting" (working paper); see infra note 21 for a discussion of this work.

17. Toomey, Traci L., et al. "The Age-21 Minimum Legal Drinking Age: A Case Study Linking Past and Current Debates." *Addiction,* vol. 104, no. 12, Dec. 2009, pp. 1958–1965 (the last state to lower its drinking age, Oklahoma, hewed an odd course: it allowed for the sale of "non-intoxicating" beer of under 3.2 percent alcohol content to women under twenty-one but not men; the Supreme Court found this constituted gender discrimination and banned the practice); *Craig v. Boren,* 429 US at 190–191 (1976).

18. 23 USC 158 (1984).

19. See infra note 23.

20. Based on author's calculations using an API pull from www.govtrack.us and comparison to Congress.gov, https://www.congress.gov/search?q=%7B%22source%22%3A%22members%22%7D. The chart's underlying data, from the API pull, calculates membership based on election results and the start of a Congressional term. Small variances are produced by resignations, deaths, and other changes to the House intraterm, but these are minor and often tended to increase the number of Boomers, as in 2008 where the replacements added to the net Boomer count. Excluded from these calculations are non-voting members of the House representing the District of Columbia and the territories. See also the footnote to this paragraph regarding my treatment of term dates of a given Congress. In general, Boomer shares of government cited in this book derive from the sources and methods noted here, usually the API pulls.

21. Ghitza and Gelman. See also the interactive tool available on the *NY Times* website, using the same data at: http://www.nytimes.com/interactive/2014/07/08/upshot/how-the-year-you-were-born-influences-your-politics.html. Ghitza and Gelman use presidential approval ratings as a proxy for party affiliation, and model cumulative preferences, and how a person born in a given year might vote in an "average" election. The Democratic sub-cohort of 1947–1954 is only about a third of the Boomer population and the rest of the Boomers drift Republican, pushing the whole generation into Republican territory. Exit polling data is another way to break out political preferences, but these surveys tend to clump age groups (e.g., 30–44) in large buckets that make it difficult to perform a continuous analysis. In general, the Boomers tended to favor the winning candidate (who won in large part due to Boomer electoral strength). From 1988–2008, presidential elections for Boomer cohorts either trended Republican or where a Democrat had a plurality, they tended to favor the Democrat somewhat more weakly than younger groups, and in very close elections like 2000, Boomer deviations had a significant impact. The exit poll data are for all people in the age bracket; stripping out the decisively Democratic vote of certain groups (like blacks) tends to push white Boomers into even greater deviation from younger groups in a Rightward tilt. Best, Samuel J., Brian S. Krueger, *Exit Polls: Surveying the American Electorate, 1972–2010.* Sage/CQ Press, Los Angeles (2012); author's calculations. The data for House elections is highly varied, though Boomers appeared to be the most Republican groups in certain critical House elections, like those of 1994 and 2010. Again, the absence of continuous and granular data over long periods, and the limited number of elections and often vivid comparisons between candidates (which Ghitza and Gelman tried to factor out), make it harder to draw robust inferences from exit polls. There does seem to be a tilt, and many authors do believe it is significant. In the end, the actual party affiliation matters less than the policies pursued by a given politician, which is the subject of the next chapters. The fact of a secret ballot (a definite social good) means that it will always be impossible to really *know* how anyone voted, and this may be a particular problem in self-reported data like exit polls from sociopaths prone to deception.

Chapter 8: Taxes

1. US Congress, Congressional Budget Office. "The Distribution of Household Income and Federal Taxes, 2013." 8 June 2016, pp. 3, 18–19.
2. *Oxford English Dictionary.* Online edition.

3. US Department of the Treasury, Internal Revenue Service. "IRS Proposes New Registration, Testing and Continuing Education Requirements for Tax Return Preparers Not Already Subject to Oversight." 3 Nov. 2014, www.irs.gov/uac/IRS-Proposes-New-Registration,-Testing-and-Continuing-Education-Requirements-for-Tax-Return-Preparers-Not-Already-Subject-to-Oversight.

4. Grieder, William. "Rolling Back the 20th Century: The Right-Wing Ideologues Are Dead Serious About Dismantling Government." *Nation*. 24 Apr. 2003, www.thenation.com/article/rolling-back-20th-century/.

5. Good, Chris. "Norquist's Tax Pledge: What It Is and How It Started." ABC News. 26 Nov. 2012, abcnews.go.com/blogs/politics/2012/11/norquists-tax-pledge-what-it-is-and-how-it-started/; "Federal Taxpayer Protection Pledge Questions and Answers." Americans for Tax Reform. 1 June 2011, www.atr.org/federal-taxpayer-protection-questions-answers-a6204.

6. Constitution of the United States. art. I, sec. 2.

7. "Fact Sheet, 100-Year Tax History: The Length and Legacy of Tax Law." CCH. www.cch.com/wbot2013/factsheet.pdf (a summary by a major publisher of the tax codes); *The Bible: Authorized King James Version*. Edited by Robert Carroll and Stephen Prickett. Oxford University Press. 15 May 2008; Amazon. www.amazon.com/Bible-Authorized-Version-Oxford-Classics/dp/0199535949/ref=sr_1_1?ie=UTF8&qid=1452610777&sr=8-1&keywords=oxford+king+james+bible.

8. Fraser, C. Gerald. "Writers and Editors to Defy Tax in War Protest." *New York Times*, 31 Jan. 1968, p. 2.

9. Writers and Editors War Tax Protest, http://jfk.hood.edu/Collection/Weisberg%20Subject%20Index%20Files/W%20Disk/Writers%20and%20Editors%20Protest/Item%2002.pdf (the "pledge").

10. "Joan Baez Declares War on IRS." *Desert Sun*, no. 282, 30 June 1964, cdnc.ucr.edu/cgi-bin/cdnc?a=d&d=DS19640630.2.32.

11. Schulz, Kathryn. "Pond Scum." *New Yorker*, 19 Oct. 2015, www.newyorker.com/magazine/2015/10/19/pond-scum; Brooks, Rebecca Beatrice. "Henry David Thoreau Arrested for Nonpayment of Poll Tax." History of Massachusetts, 14 July 2012, historyofmassachusetts.org/henry-david-thoreau-arrested-for-nonpayment-of-poll-tax/.

12. Internal Revenue Service. "U.S. Individual Income Tax." Statistics of Income Tax, Historical Table 23, May 2016, www.irs.gov/uac/soi-tax-stats-historical-table-23. For an Excel-ready summary, see Tax Foundation. "Federal Individual Income Tax Rates History: Nominal Dollar: Income Years 1913–2013." taxfoundation.org/sites/default/files/docs/fed_individual_rate_history_nominal.pdf (a tabular presentation of tax brackets without editorial gloss).

13. Jacobson, Darien B., Brian G. Raub, and Barry W. Johnson. "The Estate Tax: Ninety Years and Counting." Statistics of Income Bulletin 27.1 (2007): 118-28, https://www.irs.gov/pub/irs-soi/07sumbul.pdf.

14. Social Security Administration. "Research Note #12: Taxation of Social Security Benefits." Agency History. www.ssa.gov/history/taxationofbenefits.html. See also Social Security Amendments of 1983, Pub Law 98-21, enacted 20 April 1983 (applying to the first tax year after 1983—i.e., 1984).

15. Internal Revenue Service. "U.S. Individual Income Tax." Statistics of Income Tax, Historical Table 23, May 2016, www.irs.gov/uac/soi-tax-stats-historical-table-23.

16. Ventry, Dennis J. Jr. "The Accidental Deduction: A History and Critique of the Tax Subsidy for Mortgage Interest." *Duke Law Review*, vol. 73, no. 1, 2010, p. 275.
17. Ippolito, Dennis S. *Deficits, Debt and the New Politics of Tax Policy*. Cambridge University Press, Nov. 2012, p. 167. For a general discussion of Bush I's tax policies, see Brownlee, W. Elliot, *Federal Taxation in America: A History*, 3d ed., Cambridge University Press, 2016, pp. 210–220.
18. Ippolito, p. 167. (internal cites and quotes omitted).
19. Ibid.
20. Schmalz, Jeffrey, "The 1992 Election: The Nation's Voters: Clinton Carves a Wide Path Deep into Reagan Country." *New York Times*, 4 Nov. 1992, www.nytimes.com/1992/11/04/nyregion/1992-election-nation-s-voters-clinton-carves-wide-path-deep-into-reagan-country.html.
21. Omnibus Reconciliation Act of 1993, PL 103-66; Brownlee, at ch. 8. See also for a more readable history of rates: Tax Foundation. "U.S. Federal Individual Income Tax Rates History, 1862–2013." taxfoundation.org/sites/default/files/docs/fed_individual_rate_history_nominal.pdf.
22. Ippolito, p. 171.
23. Purdum, Todd S. "Clinton Angers Friend and Foe in Tax Remark." *New York Times*, 19 Oct. 1995, www.nytimes.com/1995/10/19/us/clinton-angers-friend-and-foe-in-tax-remark.html; Richter, Paul. "Clinton Apologies May Not Be Sorry Move, Analysts Say: Politics: Official Washington Is Reacting Negatively to the President's Statements, but the Tactic Has Worked in the Past, Observers Note." *Los Angeles Times*, 4 Nov. 1995, articles.latimes.com/1995-11-04/news/mn-64654_1_official-washington.
24. Taxpayer Relief Act of 1997, PL 105–34.
25. Ibid.
26. Economic Growth and Tax Reconciliation Relief Act of 2001, PL 107–16.
27. Jobs and Growth Tax Relief Reconciliation Act of 2003, PL 108–27.
28. Ibid.
29. Tax Relief, Unemployment Insurance Reauthorization, and Job Creation Act of 2010, PL 111-312.
30. American Taxpayer Relief Act of 2012, PL 112–140.
31. Ibid.
32. Ibid.
33. Ibid. See also for a summary, Sullivan, Paul. "The End of a Decade of Uncertainty over Gift and Estate Taxes." *New York Times*, 4 Jan. 2013, www.nytimes.com/2013/01/05/your-money/fiscal-deal-ends-decade-of-uncertainty-over-gift-and-estate-taxes.html.
34. The property-tax limiting Proposition 13 entered the California Constitution as Art. 13A.
35. "How Proposition 13 Changed California Politics." *Contra Consta Bee*. contracostabee.com/proposition-13-california-politics/; "Governor's Budget Summary—2016-2017"; California Budget. www.ebudget.ca.gov/2016-17/pdf/BudgetSummary/Introduction.pdf; Steinhauer, Jennifer. "In Budget Deal, California Shuts $41 Billion Gap." *New York Times*, 19 Feb. 2009, www.nytimes.com/2009/02/20/us/20california.html; "Two Steps Back: Should California Cut Its Way to a Balanced Budget?" The California

Budget Project. Feb. 2008. www.sdgrantmakers.org/Portals/0/PastPrograms/CBP
TwoStepsBack.pdf.

36. Office of Management and Budget. "Corporate Income Taxes." Budget of the U.S.
Government: Historical Tables, table 2.2, www.whitehouse.gov/sites/default/files/
omb/budget/fy2017/assets/hist.pdf.; FRED, CP (BEA); author's calculations.

37. Marr, Chuck, and Cecile Murray. "IRS Funding Cuts Compromise Taxpayer Service and Weaken Enforcement," updated 4 April 2016. Center on Budget and Policy
Priorities, http://www.cbpp.org/sites/default/files/atoms/files/6-25-14tax.pdf; Letter
from former IRS commissioners to the Senate and House Committees on Appropriations, 2015, taxprof.typepad.com/files/former-irs-comissioners-letter-on-agency
-budget.pdf; Johnston, David Cay. "Honey, They Shrunk the IRS." Reuters, 17 Jan.
2012, blogs.reuters.com/david-cay-johnston/2012/01/17/honey-they-shrunk-the-irs
(noting that the "likelihood of a big company being audited has plummeted 50 percentage points from 72 percent in 1990 to 22 percent in 2010"); Bischoff, Bill,
MarketWatch. "Worried about being audited by the IRS? Here are your chances."
MarketWatch, 29 Jan. 2016 (part of a series from MarketWatch on this subject,
including a prior article dated December 15, 2015).

38. Rubin, Richard. "IRS to Hire Up to 700 Enforcement Workers." *Wall Street Journal*, 3 May 2016, www.wsj.com/articles/irs-to-hire-up-to-700-enforcement-workers
-1462302623.

39. "Tax Gap Estimates for Tax Years 2008–2010." Internal Revenue Service, April
2016.

40. Quoted in Bartlett, Bruce. "The New Republican Tax Policy." *New York Times*,
Economix (blog), 20 Nov. 2012, economix.blogs.nytimes.com/2012/11/20/the-new
-republican-tax-policy/.

41. Dreyfuss, Bob. "Grover Norquist: 'Field Marshal' of the Bush Plan." *Nation*, 26 Apr.
2001, www.thenation.com/article/grover-norquist-field-marshal-bush-plan/.

42. Federal Reserve Bank of St. Louis, Economic Synopses, No. 24 (2011).

43. E.g., supra note 1 at 22.

44. "Total Government Receipts in Absolute Amounts and as Percentages of GDP:
1948–2015." Office of Management and Budget, 2016, https://www.whitehouse.gov/
omb/budget/Historicals.

45. Ibid.; author's calculations.

46. Ibid.

Chapter 9: Debt and Deficits

1. US Government Accountability Office. "Bureau of the Fiscal Service's Fiscal Years
2015 and 2014 Schedules of Federal Debts." GAO, Report to the Secretary of the
Treasury, Nov. 2015, www.treasurydirect.gov/govt/reports/pd/feddebt/feddebt
_ann2015.pdf.

2. Smith, Robert. "When the U.S. Paid Off the Entire National Debt (And Why It Didn't
Last)." NPR, 15 Apr. 2011, www.npr.org/sections/money/2011/04/15/135423586/
when-the-u-s-paid-off-the-entire-national-debt-and-why-it-didnt-last; Faber, Harold. "There Was a Surplus, Once." *New York Times*, 6 Feb. 1986, www.nytimes
.com/1986/02/06/us/there-was-a-surplus-once.html; Meacham, Jon. *American Lion:
Andrew Jackson in the White House*, reprinted ed., Random House Trade Paperbacks,
30 Apr. 2009, ch. 28, p. 298.

3. US Department of the Treasury, Treasury Direct. "Historical Debt Outstanding—Annual 1790–1849," www.treasurydirect.gov/govt/reports/pd/histdebt/histdebt_histo1.htm.

4. FRED, GFDEGQ188S (original sources: FRED and OMB). An overview can be found from the CBO, infra note 5.

5. US Congress, Congressional Budget Office. "The Budget and Economic Outlook 2016–2026." Jan. 2016, p. 1; US Congress, Congressional Budget Office. "The 2016 Budget Outlook"; Presentation by Keith Hall at the Peter G. Peterson Foundation's 2016 Fiscal Summit, 11 May 2016, p. 15; US Congress, Congressional Budget Office. "2015 Long-Term Budget Outlook." June 2015, pp. 11 and 79–80, www.cbo.gov/sites/default/files/114th-congress-2015-2016/reports/50250-LongTermBudgetOutlook-4.pdf. The first two cites show that the point when the war debt threshold will be surpassed has advanced from 2040 into the 2030s (based on changes in projections from 2015 to 2016).

6. Jefferson, Thomas. "Letter to James Madison." 1789, Memorial ed. 7:455; Jefferson, Thomas. "Letter to A. L. C. Destutt de Tracy." 1820, Ford ed. 10:175.

7. Hamilton, Alexander. "Letter to Robert Morris." 30 Apr. 1781, Founders Online, National Archives, last modified October 5, 2016, http://founders.archives.gov/documents/Hamilton/01-02-02-1167. (Original source: The Papers of Alexander Hamilton, vol. 2, 1779–1781, ed. Harold C. Syrett. New York: Columbia University Press, 1961, pp. 604–635.) Hamilton, Alexander. "Report on Public Credit." Reports of the Secretary of the Treasury of the United States, vol. 1, Blair & Rives, 1837, p. 27 (original statement made January 1790).

8. Nietzsche, Friedrich. "On The Genealogy of Morality." Second Essay.

9. Schama, Simon. Citizens: A Chronicle of the French Revolution. Vintage Books, Mar. 1990, p. 65.

10. Ibid., p. 66.

11. Organisation for Economic Co-operation and Development (hereinafter "OECD"), OECD Data. "General Government Debt." data.oecd.org/gga/general-government-debt.htm. It's impossible to precisely know or compare China's debt-to-GDP ratio because of government manipulations and government ownership of industries, but Chinese debt levels were and are high.

12. US Government Accountability Office. "Bureau of the Fiscal Service's Fiscal Years 2015 and 2014 Schedules of Federal Debts." Report to the Secretary of the Treasury, Nov. 2015, www.treasurydirect.gov/govt/reports/pd/feddebt/feddebt_ann2015.pdf (for fiscal years 2014–2015).

13. Constitution of the United States, art. I, sec. 10, and Tenth Amendment. States cannot abrogate their obligations, and declaring federal bankruptcy would put states under the jurisdiction of a federal judge, violating the sovereignty provisions of the Tenth Amendment.

14. Detrixhe, John. "U.S. Loses AAA Rating at S&P on Concern Debt Cuts Deficient." Bloomberg, 6 Aug. 2011, www.bloomberg.com/news/articles/2011-08-06/u-s-credit-rating-cut-by-s-p-for-first-time-on-deficit-reduction-accord.

15. Office of Management and Budget. "Federal Debt at the End of the Year: 1940–2021." 2016, www.whitehouse.gov/omb/budget/Historicals.

16. Bartlett, Bruce. "Starve the Beast." Independent Review, vol. 12, no. 1, Summer 2007, www.independent.org/pdf/tir/tir_12_01_01_bartlett.pdf. Bartlett was first

an assistant to Jack Kemp (one of the co-sponsors of the major 1981 cut) and then a Treasury Department official.

17. Blustein, Paul. "Recent Budget Battles Leave the Basic Tenets of Welfare State Intact." *Wall Street Journal*, 21 Oct. 1985.

18. US Congress, Congressional Budget Office. "The Budget and Economic Outlook: Fiscal Years 2002–2011." Jan. 2001, xiii, summary table 1, et seq.

19. Ibid.; and US Congress, Congressional Budget Office. "The Budget and Economic Outlook: 2014–2024." Table H-1; author's calculations.

20. US Congress, Congressional Budget Office. "Updated Budget Projections: 2016–2026." Mar. 2016, table 2.

21. White House, Office of Management and Budget. Historical Debt Tables, table 7.1, www.whitehouse.gov/omb/budget/Historicals (for fiscal 2015).

22. Ibid.; see also US Government Accountability Office. "Bureau of the Fiscal Service's Fiscal Years 2015 and 2014 Schedules of Federal Debts."

23. White House, Office of Management and Budget. Historical Debt Tables; see also US Department of the Treasury, Treasury Direct. "Historical Debt Outstanding—Annual 2000–2005," www.treasurydirect.gov/govt/reports/pd/histdebt/histdebt_histo5.htm.

24. Library of Congress, Congressional Research Service. Debt Ceiling History; see also US Government Accountability Office. "Bureau of the Fiscal Service's Fiscal Years 2015 and 2014 Schedules of Federal Debts."

25. Social Security Administration. "Frequently Asked Questions About the Social Security Trust Funds." Questions 4 and 7 (noting that the "cash exchanged for the securities [of the Trust Fund] goes into the general fund of the Treasury and is indistinguishable from other cash in the general fund"), www.ssa.gov/OACT/ProgData/fundFAQ.html#&a0=6.

26. Ibid.; and Social Security Administration. "Social Security Board of Trustees: Trust Fund Reserve Gains One Year for Projected Depletion Date." Press release, 22 July 2015, www.ssa.gov/news/#/post/7-2015-1.

27. Social Security Administration. "Frequently Asked Questions About the Social Security Trust Funds."

28. US Government Accountability Office. "Bureau of the Fiscal Service's Fiscal Years 2015 and 2014 Schedules of Federal Debts."

29. The Board of Trustees, Federal Hospital Insurance and Federal Supplementary Medical Insurance Trust Funds. *The 2015 Annual Report of the Boards of Trustees of the Federal Hospital Insurance and Federal Supplementary Medical Insurance Trust Funds 2015* (hereinafter "*Medicare Trustees Report 2015*"), p. 26, Centers for Medicare & Medicaid Services, www.cms.gov/Research-Statistics-Data-and-Systems/Statistics-Trends-and-Reports/ReportsTrustFunds/Downloads/TR2015.pdf. See the discussion in Chapters 12 and 13.

30. US Federal Reserve System, Board of Governors. "Federal Reserve Banks Combined Financial Statements: As of and for the Years Ended December 31, 2015 and 2014 and Independent Auditors' Report," www.federalreserve.gov/monetary policy/files/combinedfinstmt2015.pdf.

31. US Federal Reserve System, Board of Governors. "Financial Accounts of the United States." 10 Mar. 2016, table D3.

32. US Department of the Treasury. "Recovery Act," www.treasury.gov/initiatives/recovery/Pages/babs.aspx.

33. US Department of the Treasury. "Treasury Analysis of Build America Bonds Insurance and Savings," p. 3, www.treasury.gov/initiatives/recovery/Documents/BABs%20Report.pdf.

34. Federal Reserve. "Debt Outstanding by Sector." Financial Accounts of the United States, table D3, September 2016. www.federalreserve.gov/releases/z1/current/z1.pdf.; US Treasury. "Federal Debt." Treasury Bulletin, Table FD-1, September 2016. www.fiscal.treasury.gov/fsreports/rpt/treasBulletin/current.htm.; author's calculations. See also Chapter 12. The speculative items are all important, but they are contingent and will be paid over different time horizons, so I've excluded them—though they, and the additional ~2–3 percent of GDP added to the debt annually (via the deficit)—will all have to paid by the young.

35. US Department of the Treasury. *Fiscal Year 2015 Financial Report of the United States Government*, 2016, p. 19.

36. Wessel, David, and Thomas T. Vogel Jr. "Arcane World of Bonds Is Guide and Beacon to a Populist President." *Wall Street Journal*, 25 Feb 1993, A1.

37. US Federal Reserve System, Board of Governors. Selected Interest Rates (Daily)—H.15; US Department of Labor. Bureau of Labor Statistics. "Consumer Price Index."

38. US Department of the Treasury, Treasury Direct. "Interest Expense on the Debt Outstanding," treasurydirect.gov/govt/reports/ir/ir_expense.htm.

39. US Department of the Treasury, Office of Debt Management. "Treasury Presentation to TBAC," www.treasury.gov/resource-center/data-chart-center/quarterly-refunding/Documents/November%202014%20QRCombined%20Charges%20for%20Archives.pdf.

40. See supra notes 38–40; author's calculations (based on Treasury data and ten-year yields).

41. Appelbaum, Binyamin. "Donald Trump's Idea to Cut National Debt: Get Creditors to Accept Less." *New York Times*, 6 May 2016, www.nytimes.com/2016/05/07/us/politics/donald-trumps-idea-to-cut-national-debt-get-creditors-to-accept-less.html?_r=0.

42. US Federal Reserve System, Board of Governors "Financial Accounts of the United States," 10 Mar. 2016, table D3; Federal Reserve Statistical Release, G.19, Consumer Credit, released 6 May 2016.

43. US Federal Reserve Statistical Release. "Financial Accounts of the United States," 10 Mar. 2016, table D3.

44. Federal Judicial Center. "Bankruptcy Cases." www.fjc.gov/history/caseload.nsf/page/caseloads_bankruptcy; US Census. *Statistical Abstract of the United States: 1965*, part II, no. 3 (defines adults by excluding population nineteen and under).

45. Federal Judicial Center. "Bankruptcy Cases"; US Census. *Statistical Abstract of the United States: 1999*, sec. 1, no. 14 (defines adults by excluding population nineteen and under).

46. Eder, Steve, and Michael Barbaro. "Marco Rubio's Career Bedeviled by Financial Struggles." *New York Times*, 9 June 2015, www.nytimes.com/2015/06/10/us/politics/marco-rubio-finances-debt-loans-credit.html.

47. Rubin, Richard, and John McCormick. "Even 40,000 Scott Walkers Aren't as Wealthy as Donald Trump." *Bloomberg*, 3 Aug. 2015, www.bloomberg.com/politics/articles/2015-08-03/even-40-000-scott-walkers-aren-t-as-wealthy-as-donald-trump; Jacobs, Harrison. "Scott Walker has tens of thousands of dollars'

worth of credit-card debt." *Business Insider*, 3 Aug. 2015, www.businessinsider .com/scott-walker-has-tens-of-thousands-of-dollars-worth-of-credit-card-debt -2015-8.

48. Topaz, Jonathan, and Kristen East. "Bernie Sanders' Wife Accounts for All His Reported Assets." *Politico*, 16 July 2015, www.politico.com/story/2015/07/bernie -sanders-wife-accounts-for-reported-assets-120261; Gaudiano, Nicole. "Credit Card Debt a Regular Feature on Sanders' Finance Reports." *USA Today*, 12 June 2015.

49. McIntire, Mike. "Ted Cruz Didn't Report Goldman Sachs Loan in a Senate Race." *New York Times*, 13 Jan. 2016, www.nytimes.com/2016/01/14/us/politics/ted-cruz -wall-street-loan-senate-bid-2012.html.

50. "A Chance to Reset the Republican Race." Editorial. *New York Times*, 30 Jan. 2016, www .nytimes.com/2016/01/31/opinion/sunday/a-chance-to-reset-the-republican-race .html?action=click&pgtype=Homepage&clickSource=story-heading& module=opinion-c-col-top-region&region=opinion-c-col-top-region&W T.nav=opinion-c-col-top-region&_r=1; Niquette, Mark. "John Kasich's Lehman Days Create Rorshach Test for Viewing His Career." *Bloomberg*, 9 July 2015, www .bloomberg.com/politics/articles/2015-07-09/john-kasich-s-lehman-days-create -rorshach-test-for-viewing-his-career; Lee, MJ. "John Kasich's Wall Street Ties Could Haunt 2016 Bid." CNN, 8 June 2015, www.cnn.com/2015/06/08/politics/ john-kasich-2016-lehman-brothers-wall-street/index.html.

Chapter 10: Indefinitely Deferred Maintenance

1. DSM-V, pp. 659–61.

2. *Oxford English Dictionary*. Online edition.

3. BEA. NIPA tables, 2014, sec. 1, 5. Other countries have different accounting mechanisms, but the general point remains and is reinforced by a drive down any European or Japanese freeway.

4. Ibid. (text); Wessel, David. "Spending on Our Crumbling Infrastructure." *Wall Street Journal*. 10 Mar. 2015. http://blogs.wsj.com/washwire/2015/03/10/spending-on-our-crumbling-infrastructure/ (footnote). See also note 12 regarding Summers.

5. Bowe, Rebecca, and Lisa Pickoff-White. "Five Years after Deadly San Bruno Explosion: Are We Safer?" KQED News. The California Report, 8 Sept. 2015, ww2.kqed .org/news/2015/09/08/five-years-after-deadly-san-bruno-explosion-are-we-safer; Rawlings, Nate. "Joe Biden Says NYC Airport Like 'Some 3rd-World Country.'" *Time*, 7 Feb. 2014.

6. American Society of Civil Engineers. Infrastructure Report Card, 2013, pp. 11–12. Like all rigorous analyses, ASCE's methodology and assessments have changed somewhat over time, but the grades across time are clearly designed to be comparative.

7. Ibid., p. 67.

8. Ibid.

9. Ibid.; see also "About the Report Card: Methodology." www.infrastructurereportcard .org/a/#p/about-the-report-card/methodology.

10. American Society of Civil Engineers. Infrastructure Report Card, pp. 65–67; author's calculations.

11. Bivens, Josh. "The Short- and Long-Term Impacts of Infrastructure Investments on U.S. Employment and Economic Activity." Economic Policy Institute. Briefing paper,

374, 1 July 2014, p. 19 et seq. (citing CBO, CEA, Moody's, and its own research); International Monetary Fund. *World Economic Outlook*. Oct. 2014, ch. 3, p. 82.

12. Summers, Lawrence H. "The Age of Secular Stagnation: What It Is and What to Do About It." *Foreign Affairs*, March–April 2016, www.foreignaffairs.com/articles/united-states/2016-02-15/age-secular-stagnation.

13. US Department of Transportation, Federal Highway Administration. "Highway Statistics 2014." tables VM-1, MF-2, www.fhwa.dot.gov/policyinformation/statistics/2014/. (Though the report's title says 2014, the data are from 2015.)

14. Author's calculations based on, for example, US Department of Energy (DOE), Energy Efficiency and Renewable Energy (EERE), Transportation Energy Data Book (TEDB), June 2011, table 1.12. "2015 Urban Mobility Score Card." Texas A&M Transportation Institute, Aug. 2015, Ex. 1 et seq., d2dtl5nnlpfr0r.cloudfront.net/tti.tamu.edu/documents/mobility-scorecard-2015-wappx.pdf. The congestion costs alone are about $160 billion in fuel and time, with accidents and other effects adding even more.

15. Federation of Tax Administrators. "State Motor Fuel Taxes: Gasoline." Apr. 2016, (figures obtained by subtracting noted state delta of 5 cpg 2015–2016). Gas taxes include smaller, transport-related items like a contribution to mass transit, funding for leaking containers, etc.

16. Auxier, Richard. "Reforming State Gas Taxes." Tax Policy Center, 6 Nov. 2014, taxpolicycenter.org/UploadedPDF/413286-reforming-state-gas-tax.pdf.

17. US Department of Transportation, Federal Highway Administration. "Office of Highway Policy Information," tables 4.2.1 and 8.2.1, www.fhwa.dot.gov/policyin formation/statistics/2014/; US Department of Transportation, Federal Highway Administration. "Ask the Rambler." www.fhwa.dot.gov/infrastructure/gastax.cfm (gas taxes); BLS. CPI Inflation calculator.

18. Kearney, Melissa S., et al. "Racing Ahead or Falling Behind: Six Economic Facts About Transportation Infrastructure in the United States?" The Hamilton Project, May 2015, sec. 5, www.hamiltonproject.org/assets/files/six_econ_facts_transporta tion_infrastructure_united_states_final.pdf.

19. University of Massachusetts Amherst/WBZ. "Crosstabs: U Mass Amherst/WBZ Poll of Massachusetts Registered Voters." Ballot Question 1, cbsboston.files.wordpress .com/2014/09/crosstabs_september29_final.pdf.

20. Lehman, Chris. "Oregon to Test Switching to Mileage-Based Gas Tax." NPR, 1 June 2015, www.npr.org/2015/06/01/411138483/oregon-to-test-switching-to-mileage-based -gas-tax.

21. Public Law 114-41; US Department of Transportation, Federal Highway Administration. "Highway Trust Fund Ticker: Highway Account By Month," www.trans portation.gov/highway-trust-fund-ticker.

22. Broder, John M. "Democrats Divided over Gas Tax." *New York Times*, 29 Apr. 2008, www.nytimes.com/2008/04/29/us/politics/29campaign.html?partner=rssuserland &emc=rss&pagewanted=all&_r=0; Luhby, Tami. "U.S. Highway Fund Crushed by Cutback in Driving." CNN Money, 5 Sept. 2008.

23. US Department of Transportation, Federal Highway Administration. "Financial Federal-Aid Highways: The Highway Trust Fund." www.fhwa.dot.gov/reports/fifahiwy/fifahi05.htm.

24. Supra note 14, "2015 Urban Mobility Score Card." Ex. 1.

25. BLS. "American Time Use," 2014, table A-1.

26. See American Society of Civil Engineers. Infrastructure Report Card, 2013, generally; see also US Public Interest Research Group. Madsen, Travis, et al. "Road Work Ahead: Holding Government Accountable for Fixing America's Crumbling Roads and Bridges," Apr. 2010, p. 15 et seq.

27. TRIP. "Bumpy Roads Ahead: America's Roughest Rides and Strategies to Make Our Road Smoother," July 2015, Appendix A.

28. Tuss, Adam. "New Report: D.C. Area Really Does Have the Worst Traffic in the U.S." NBC 4, 5 Feb. 2013, www.nbcwashington.com/news/local/New-Report-DC -Really-Does-Have-the-Worst-Traffic-in-the-US-189744731.html; *USA Today*, and Scott Broom, WUSA. "Report: DC Traffic Is the Worst in the U.S." 26 Aug. 2015, www.wusa9.com/story/news/2015/08/26/report-dc-traffic-worst-us/32440837/.

29. US Department of Transportation, Federal Highway Administration. "Highway Bridges by State and Highway System." 31 Dec 2015, www.fhwa.dot.gov/bridge/nbi/ no10/defbr15.cfm#a, and see infra note 31.

30. Ibid.; see also American Society of Civil Engineers, Infrastructure Report Card 2013, Bridges Subsection.

31. Nixon, Ron. "$11 Billion Later, High-Speed Rail Is Inching Along." *New York Times*, 6 Aug. 2014, www.nytimes.com/2014/08/07/us/delays-persist-for-us-high -speedrail.html?emc=edit_th_20140807&nl=todaysheadlines&nlid=45299538& _r=0; 49 USC §26105.2.A. (defining "high-speed rail").

32. Nussbaum, Paul. "Amtrak's High-Speed Northeast Corridor Plan at $151 Billion." *Inquirer*, 10 July 2012, posted on Philly.com, articles.philly.com/2012-07-10/ news/32602302_1_amtrak-president-joseph-boardman-acela-express-northeast -corridor; Amtrak. "Amtrak Vision for the Northeast Corridor: 2012 Update Report," 2012, p. 28.

33. E.g., "World Speed Survey 2007: New Lines Boost Rail's High Speed Performance." *Railway Gazette*, 4 Sept. 2007, www.railwaygazette.com/news/single-view/view/ world-speed-survey-new-lines-boost-rails-high-speed-performance.html; "Top Ten Fastest Trains in the World." Railway-technology.com, 29 Aug. 2013, www.railway -technology.com/features/feature-top-ten-fastest-trains-in-the-world.

34. American Society of Civil Engineers. Infrastructure Report Card, 2013, p. 67.

35. Fandos, Nicholas. "Lengthy Shutdowns in Washington, D.C. Metro System Are Possible." *New York Times*, 30 Mar. 2016, www.nytimes.com/2016/03/31/us/lengthy -shutdowns-in-washington-dc-metro-system-are-possible.html.

36. American Society of Civil Engineers. Infrastructure Report Card, 2013, p. 67.

37. US Government Accountability Office. "Commercial Nuclear Waste: Effects of a Termination of the Yucca Mountain Repository Program and Lessons Learned." GAO-11-1129, released on 10 May 2011, www.gao.gov/assets/320/317634.html; see also US Government Accountability Office. GAO Testimony, GAO-13-532T, 11 Apr. 2013, introduction and generally.

38. American Society of Civil Engineers. Infrastructure Report Card, 2013, p. 15.

39. US Army Corp of Engineers. "National Inventory of Dams." June 2016; Association of State Dam Safety Officials. "2014 Statistics on State Dam Safety Regulation," Aug. 2015; see also Poindexter, Gregory B. "Alabama Remains Only U.S. State Lacking a State Dam Safety Program." HydroWorld.com, 23 Dec. 2015, www.hydroworld

.com/articles/2015/12/alabama-remains-only-u-s-state-lacking-a-state-dam-safety
-program.html.

40. US Army Corp of Engineers. "National Inventory of Dams," June 2016; Association of State Dam Safety Officials. "2014 Statistics on State Dam Safety Regulation," Aug. 2015.

41. Ibid.; author's calculations.

42. New York City, Department of Environmental Protection. "City Water Tunnel No. 3," www.nyc.gov/html/dep/html/dep_projects/cp_city_water_tunnel3.shtml.

43. Ibid.

44. In 2013, for example, the DoD requested about $150 billion for compensation expenses, including benefits and health care for present and former personnel, out of a total budget of about $470 billion, or roughly 1/3rd. US Congress, Congressional Budget Office. "Costs of Military Pay and Benefits in the Defense Budget," 14 Nov. 14, 2012. In a very substantial way, the military is and for some time has been, a *jobs* program.

45. Constitution of the United States, article I, sec. 8.

46. 45 USC §5501 and Public Law 101–427 (1990).

47. US Congress, Congressional Budget Office. "Updated Budget Projections: 2016 to 2026," 24 Mar. 2016, fig 4.

48. White House, Office of Management and Budget. "Outlays by Function and Superfunction—National Defense." Historical Tables, table 3.2, www.whitehouse.gov/omb/budget/Historicals. The sequester was based on legislation passed in 2011 and 2013 and was triggered in 2014 and 2015. If spending falls below legislated caps, there is no sequestration per se, although the budgets submitted to Congress are clearly drafted with the sequester in mind, and therefore the sequester has similar effects whether or not it is explicitly triggered.

49. US Department of Defense. *Quadrennial Defense Review 2014*, p. viii.

50. Ibid., p. 22.

51. National Defense Panel. "Ensuring a Strong U.S. Defense for the Future: The National Defense Panel Review of the 2014 Quadrennial Defense Review." Advance copy, 31 July 2014, p. 29.

52. Ibid.

53. Ibid., p. 30.

54. Ibid.

55. US Marine Corps. "Opening Statement to the Defense Subcommittee—House Appropriations Committee on Posture of the United States Marine Corps." Presented by Joseph F. Dunford Jr., 26 Feb. 2015.

56. Heritage Foundation. "2016 Index of U.S. Military Strength," pp. 228, 234; O'Hanlon, Michael E. "The Future of the U.S. Army." Brookings, 18 Sept. 2015 (noting that the present army is "fairly small by most relevant measures," that the author "would oppose" future reductions—which were contemplated, and that certain parts of the QDR were "mistaken").

57. "Houston Police Department Operational Staffing Model." Police Executive Research Forum, May 2014, p. 150, www.houstontx.gov/police/department_reports/operational_staffing/Houston_Police_Department_Operational_Staffing_Model_May_2014.pdf; Estonian Defense Forces, www.mil.ee/en/defence-forces. Bendavid, Naftali.

"Just Five of 28 NATO Members Meet Defense Spending Goal, Report Says." 22 June 2015; North Atlantic Treaty Organization. "Defense Expenditures of NATO Countries (2008–2015)," 28 Jan. 2016, p. 2; North Atlantic Treaty Organization. "Readiness Action Plan." 23 June 2016 (the "Wales Summit 2014").

58. White House, Office of Management and Budget. Historical Debt Tables, table 14.5, www.whitehouse.gov/omb/budget/Historicals.

59. Petroski, Henry. *The Road Taken: The History and Future of America's Infrastructure.* Bloomsbury, 16 Feb. 2016, p. 85; BLS. CPI Inflation calculator; Van Derbeken, Jaxon. "Bay Bridge Fix in Place, $25 Million Later." *SF Gate,* 19 Dec. 2013, www .sfgate.com/default/article/Bay-Bridge-fix-in-place-25-million-later-5076643.php.

60. Fitzsimmons, Emma G. "$2.4 Billion Subway Stop Was Leaking Before It Opened." *New York Times,* 29 Mar. 2016, mobile.nytimes.com/2016/03/30/nyregion/documents -reveal-early-concerns-about-leaks-at-hudson-yards-subway-station.html.

Chapter 11: Boomer Finance: The Vicious Cycle of Risk and Deceit

1. DSM-V, p. 660.

2. Courtauld, George. *England's Best Loved Poems: The Enchantment of England.* Random House eBooks, sec. 5.

3. Hitchens, Christopher. *And Yet...Essays,* e-books ed., p. 468 (first printed in *Slate,* "The Case Against Hillary." 14 Jan. 2008); see also Purdum, Todd. "Hillary Clinton Meets Man Who Gave Her 2 L's." *New York Times,* 3 Apr. 1995 (repeating improbable story by Clinton); see also "Edmund Hillary." Biography.com.

4. E.g., Securities Act of 1933; Securities Exchange Act of 1934; Investment Company Act of 1940; Investment Advisers Act of 1940; Banking Act of 1933 (Glass-Steagall; established FDIC); Commodity Exchange Act of 1936; Commodity Futures Trading Commission Act of 1974.

5. Brandeis, Louis D. *Other People's Money—And How the Bankers Use It.* Martino ed., 2009, p. 92.

6. Leeds, Jeff. "Andersen Auditor Details Shredding of Enron Papers." *Los Angeles Times,* 14 May 2002, articles.latimes.com/2002/may/14/business/fi-andersen14; Associated Press. "In Depositions, Arthur Andersen Staffers Detail 'Shred Room.'" Fox News, 15 Mar. 2002, www.foxnews.com/story/2002/03/15/in-depositions -arthur-andersen-staffers-detail-shred-room.html.

7. US Department of the Treasury, Bureau of the Fiscal Service. "Financial Report of the United States Government—2015," 25 Feb. 2016, pp. 18, 82 et seq.

8. Ibid., pp. 138–165. Pagination is based on the overall document's pagination appearing at the top left; subparts have their own pagination.

9. Ibid., "Statement of the Comptroller General," pp. 11, 37–38.

10. Ibid., p. 40.

11. No one really knows how large OBS liabilities are. Sometimes people cite some truly extraordinary figures—no less than the world's economic product and often *vastly* more—but these are often based on face/notional values, rather than probable exposure or cash paid, and many of these liabilities net (Bank A may lose $1 million on an OBS item, while Bank B gains $1 million and this may say nothing about the system as a whole). Nevertheless, it's clear that the total outstanding is quite large; e.g., US Federal Reserve, "Financial Accounts of the United States," table L.111 (Q2 2016) (noting about $40 trillion in "other" derivatives, $14 trillion

in interest derivatives, and assorted trillions, for just "Depository Institutions: Off-Balance Sheet Items"). The net, real exposure is probably an order of magnitude smaller—which is still a lot.

12. Rogin, Joshn. "Fiorina's HP Earned Millions from Sales in Iran." *Bloomberg*, 14 Sept. 2015, www.bloombergview.com/articles/2015-09-14/under-fiorina-hp-earned-millions-from-sales-in-iran.

13. Riegle-Neal Interstate Banking and Branching Efficiency Act, sec. 101.

14. Federal Deposit Insurance Corporation. "History of the Eighties—Lessons for the Future," vol. 1, 1997, p. 240.

15. Brooker, Katrina. "Citi's Creator, Alone with His Regrets." *New York Times*, 2 Jan 2010, www.nytimes.com/2010/01/03/business/economy/03weill.html?pagewanted=1&_r=0.

16. Labaton, Stephen. "Agency's '04 Rule Let Banks Pile Up New Debt." *New York Times*, 2 Oct. 2008, www.nytimes.com/2008/10/03/business/03sec.html.

17. For an interesting narrative history, see "Money, Power and Wall Street." PBS. *Frontline*, www.pbs.org/wgbh/frontline/film/money-power-wall-street/transcript/.

18. Labaton.

19. Nakamoto, Michiyo, and David Wighton. "Citigroup Chief Stays Bullish on Buyouts." *Financial Times*, 9 July 2007.

20. US Securities and Exchange Commission. "SEC Halts Short Selling of Financial Stocks to Protect Investors and Markets," 19 Sept. 2008, www.sec.gov/news/press/2008/2008-211.htm.

21. Ibid.

22. United States Census. *Statistical Abstract of the United States: 2012*. Internet preamble, www.census.gov/library/publications/2011/compendia/statab/131ed.html; Samuelson, Robert J. "Don't Kill America's Databook." *Washington Post*, 21 Aug. 2011.

23. Labaton.

24. Financial Accounting Standards Board. Statement No. 157, *generally* p. 15 (regarding "Level 3 inputs"); Financial Accounting Standards Board of the Financial Accounting Foundation. "Fair Value Measurement (Topic 820): Amendments to Achieve Common Fair Value Measurement and Disclosure Requirements in U.S. GAAP and IFRSs." Financial Accounting Series. Accounting Standards Update, No. 2011-04, May 2011; US Securities and Exchange Commission. "SEC Office of the Chief Accountant and FASB Staff Clarifications on Fair Value Accounting." Release 2008-234, 30 Sept. 2008; US Securities and Exchange Commission. "Investment Company Act of 1940— Section 2(a) (41) and Rules 2a-4 and 22c-1: Investment Company Institute Designated NRSROs." 19 Aug. 2010.

25. The Federal Reserve Act (1977 amendments); Federal Reserve Bank of Chicago. "The Federal Reserve's Dual Mandate." www.chicagofed.org/publications/speeches/our-dual-mandate.

26. US Federal Reserve System, Board of Governors. "Credit and Liquidity Programs and the Balance Sheet." www.federalreserve.gov/monetarypolicy/bst_recenttrends.htm, Aug. 2007–Dec. 2015.

27. Sanders, Bernie. "Transcript: Bernie Sanders Meets with the Daily News Editorial Board." New York *Daily News*, 4 Apr. 2016, www.nydailynews.com/opinion/transcript-bernie-sanders-meets-news-editorial-board-article-1.2588306.

28. US Federal Reserve System, Board of Governors. Statistical table 8. "Table 8. Initial margin requirements Under Regulations T, U, and X" (as percentage of market value).

29. New York Stock Exchange, "FRB Initial margin requirements—percent of total value required to purchase stock," http://www.nyxdata.com/nysedata/asp/factbook/viewer_edition.asp?mode=table&key=52&category=8.

30. Fortune, Peter. "Margin Requirements, Margin Loans, and Margin Rates: Practice and Principles." *New England Economic Review*, Sept.–Oct. 2000, pp. 43–44, www.bostonfed.org/economic/neer/neer2000/neer500b.pdf. Fortune began his article by positioning it at something of a direct response to Shiller's lament about margin requirements. To be fair, Fortune made some technical distinctions between initial, maintenance, and other margins, but missed the main point, as the crash showed.

31. Lahart, Justin. "S&P 500 Earnings: Far Worse Than Advertised." *Wall Street Journal*, 24 Feb. 2016.

32. Case-Schiller Cyclically Adjusted P/E Ratio, available via yCharts (series: I:SP500CAP). This cyclically adjusted ratio is not without its controversies, but is the best data set offering perspective over the long, long term. The raw S&P 500 P/E ratio was 11.7 in Q4 1988, 18.1 in Q4 1995, 30.5 in Q4 1999, and was around 23–25 in the first half of 2016. The story, in other words, is the same. The case could be made that things are somewhat better or somewhat worse—somewhat better because models digest interest rates, and interest rates are low, "justifying" higher valuations; somewhat worse, because of survivorship bias, the rise of ultra-high P/E ratios in private equity (if there's any "E" at all), etc. My view is that things are probably somewhat worse.

33. Holland, A. Steven. "Real Interest Rates: What Accounts for Their Rise?" Federal Reserve Bank of St. Louis, Dec. 1984, pp. 1–3 (online pagination), research.stlouisfed.org/publications/review/84/12/Rates_Dec1984.pdf. Note that Holland was measuring Treasury rates, not consumer rates, but the one drove the other; e.g., FRED MORTG vs. CPI (suggesting that real thirty-year mortgage rates verged toward 0 percent at times).

34. Ibid. The FRED database provides a number of consumer credit interest rates for everything from mortgages to credit cards, which can be usefully compared and show the same pattern.

Chapter 12: The Brief Triumph of Long Retirement

1. Banerjee, Sudipto. "Change in Household Spending after Retirement: Results from a Longitudinal Sample." Employee Benefit Research Institute (hereinafter "EBRI"). No. 420, Nov. 2015, www.ebri.org/pdf/briefspdf/EBRI_IB_420.Nov15.HH-Exp.pdf. I've adjusted to include changes in payments to mortgage spending—if mortgages are included, the average numbers rise further, while the median remains unaffected, so I have presented the lowest bound for the median, and the lowest bound for the average to be conservative; see also Butrica, Barbara, et al., "Understanding Expenditure Patterns in Retirement," Urban Institute, 18 Jan. 2005, www.urban.org/sites/default/files/alfresco/publication_pdfs/411130-Understanding-Expenditure-Patterns-in-Retirement.pdf. Note that different studies use different numbers, cohorts, processes, etc., but all come to the same general conclusion—retirement spending is ~80 percent of preretirement spending, at least in the early years. Spending in later years may decline as fewer trips are taken, though medical expenses grow.

2. FRED, PSAVERT; author's calculations. For the estimate of savings necessary on a "cash basis," I've assumed all savings are invested in very low-risk securities with a 2 percent real yield, a constant income and constant savings rate, that gains on retirement savings are continuous and not taxed until retirement, and that no additional sources of income are available. Every variable can be easily debated, but with the significant exception of the assumed rate of return, that method tends to be unduly generous to the savings rate. The point is that the savings rate can and should have been much higher, even if returns were closer to 5–6% in real terms.

3. Library of Congress, Congressional Research Service. Topoleski, John J. "U.S. Household Savings for Retirement in 2010," 23 July 2013, fas.org/sgp/crs/misc/R43057.pdf; Morrissey, Monique. "The State of American Retirement: How 401(k)s Have Failed Most American Workers," Mar. 2016, table 3 et seq., Economic Policy Institute, www.epi.org/publication/retirement-in-america/.

4. FRED, PSAVERT.

5. Ibid.

6. OECD. "Household Savings: Total % of Household Disposable Income, 2000–2015," data.oecd.org/hha/household-savings.htm#indicator-chart. It's important to emphasize the methodological differences between how the United States calculates savings and how the rest of the OECD does (since the rest of the OECD has substantial pension plans); and changes in plan values are important and included. To the extent changes in the US plans are included, as we will see, they would most likely further *reduce* American rates, quite substantially.

7. Helman, Ruth, et al. "The 2015 Retirement Confidence Survey." EBRI. No. 413, Apr. 2015, pp. 13, 16–23, www.ebri.org/pdf/briefspdf/EBRI_IB_413_Apr15_RCS-2015.pdf.

8. Roosevelt, Franklin D. "FDR's Statements on Social Security." Presidential Statements. Message to Congress Reviewing the Broad Objectives and Accomplishments of the Administration, 8 June 1934. Social Security Administration, www.ssa.gov/history/fdrstmts.html.

9. US Department of Housing and Urban Development. "FHA Reverse Mortgages (HECMs) for Seniors." portal.hud.gov/hudportal/HUD?src=/program_offices/housing/sfh/hecm/hecmabou.

10. Butrica, Barbara A. "The Disappearing Defined Benefit Pension and Its Potential Impact on the Retirement Incomes of Baby Boomers." *Social Security Bulletin*, vol. 69, no. 3, 2009, p. 1, www.ssa.gov/policy/docs/ssb/v69n3/v69n3p1.pdf.

11. Norris, Floyd. "Private Pension Plans, Even at Big Companies, May Be Underfunded." *New York Times*, 20 July 2012, nytimes.com/2012/07/21/business/pension-plans-increasingly-underfunded-at-largest-companies.html?_r=0 (citing $355 billion as of 2012 for just the S&P 500 companies).

12. Novy-Marx, Robert, and Joshua Ruah. "The Intergenerational Transfer of Public Pension Promises." National Bureau of Economic Research. Working Paper No. 14343, Sept. 2008; Novy-Marx, Robert, and Joshua D. Ruah, "The Revenue Demands of Public Employee Pension Promises." National Bureau of Economic Research. Working Paper No. 18489, Oct. 2012, p. 31.

13. Walsh, Mary Williams. "A Sour Surprise for Pensions: Two Sets of Books." *New York Times*, 17 Sept. 2016, http://www.nytimes.com/2016/09/18/business/dealbook/a-sour-surprise-for-public-pensions-two-sets-of-books.html?_r=0.

14. Martin, Timothy W. "Treasury Department Rejects Teamsters' Central States Proposal to Cut Retiree Benefits." *Wall Street Journal*, 6 May 2016, www.wsj.com/articles/treasury-department-rejects-teamsters-central-states-proposal-to-cut-retiree-benefits-1462558028.
15. Pension Benefit Guaranty Corporation. "2015 Annual Report: Preserving and Protecting Pensions." 2015, pp. 23–28, www.pbgc.gov/Documents/2015-annual-report.pdf.
16. Ibid., pp. 24, 28, 36.
17. Office of Inspector General. Semiannual Report to Congress, Apr. 2015, pp. 6, 9–10, available at Office of Inspector General, Pension Benefit Guaranty Corporation Audit Report. Prior and subsequent reports found essentially the same things; e.g., Office of Inspector General, Pension Benefit Guaranty Corporation Audit Report, Nov. 2015.
18. Roosevelt, Franklin. "Message to Congress Reviewing the Broad Objectives and Accomplishments of the Administration." 8 June 1934.
19. CDC. Life Tables, table A, 2011, www.cdc.gov/nchs/data/nvsr/nvsr64/nvsr64_11.pdf; CDC. Life Tables, table 6-A, 1982, www.cdc.gov/nchs/data/lifetables/life82_2acc.pdf.
20. Center for Retirement Research at Boston College (summarizing and interpreting Census information). "Frequently Requested Data." Mar. 2013. Retirement Period of Males, 1962–2050, crr.bc.edu/wp-content/uploads/1012/01/figure-101.pdf, and Average Retirement Age for Men, 1962–2012, crr.bc.edu/wp-content/uploads/1012/01/Avg_ret_age_men1.pdf. The age of average retirement reached a low in the 1990s and has since risen, but so has longevity, with the result that the total length of nonworking years has increased.
21. Author's calculations; see also Helman, Ruth, et al. "The 2016 Retirement Confidence Survey: Worker Confidence Stable, Retiree Confidence Continues to increase." EBRI. No. 422, Mar. 2016, p. 26 (noting that 48 percent think they need at least $500,000 and up to over $1.5 million to retire).
22. Helman, "The 2016 Retirement Confidence Survey," p. 5. Retirees become somewhat more confident, but people presently retired also have the greatest likelihood of collecting pension benefits and entitlements, which are evaporating for present workers.
23. FRED. CPIMEDSL vs. CPIAUSCL (BLS).
24. *Medicare Trustees Report 2015*, p. 41 and Appendix J (Statement of Actuarial Opinion), at 258.
25. Center for Retirement Research at Boston College, National Association of State Retirement Administrators. "Issue Brief: Public Pension Plan Investment Return Assumptions." Feb. 2016, p. 3; see also Public Plans Data. "National Data," publicplansdata.org/quick-facts/national/.
26. Ibid.; see also Martin, Timothy. "Public Pensions Roll Back Return Targets." *Wall Street Journal*, 4 Sept. 2015, www.wsj.com/articles/taxpayers-more-pension-burdens-headed-your-way-1441388090#:U_KmuhxfW4eYXA.
27. Social Security Administration. "Social Security History, Supreme Court Case: *Fleming vs. Nestor*." Social Security Online, www.ssa.gov/history/nestor.html.
28. 363 US 603 (1960).
29. Library of Congress, Congressional Research Service. Meyerson, Noah P. "Social Security: What Would Happen If the Trust Funds Ran Out?" 28 Aug. 2014, p. 6, www.fas.org/sgp/crs/misc/RL33514.pdf. Meyerson is a little cursory in his description,

but he seems to take the idea of legal entitlement a little more seriously than, say, the Supreme Court does.

30. 42 USC 1303.

31. Mettler, Suzanne, and Julianna Koch. "Who Says They Have Ever Used a Government Social Program? The Role of Policy Visibility." Cornell University, Department of Government. 28 Feb. 2012, p. 36, government.arts.cornell.edu/assets/faculty/docs/mettler/PerceptionGovt-KochMettler-022812.pdf.

32. Ventura, Elbert. "The Tea Party Paradox." *Columbia Journalism Review*, Jan.–Feb. 2012; see generally Williamson, Vanessa, et al. "The Tea Party and the Remaking of Republican Conservatism." *Perspective on Politics*, vol. 9, no. 1, Mar. 2011, p. 33.

33. Steuerle, C. Eugene, and Caleb Quakenbush. "Social Security and Medicare Lifetime Benefits and Taxes." Urban Institute. Sept. 2015, table 15. Measurements in 2015 dollars, both earning "average" wages, presented as present values. See their discussion for important assumptions about payouts, earnings histories, and discount rates (which seem reasonable).

34. E.g., The Board of Trustees, Federal Old-Age and Survivors Insurance and Federal Disability Insurance Trust Fund. *The 2015 Annual Report of the Board of Trustees of the Federal Old-Age and Survivors Insurance and Federal Disability Insurance Trust Funds*, 2015 (hereinafter *"2015 SSA Annual Report"*), pp. 6, 25, et seq., https://www.ssa.gov/oact/tr/2015/tr2015.pdf; *Medicare Trustees Report 2015*.

35. Clingman, Michael, et al. "Internal Real Rates of Return under the OASDI Program for Hypothetical Workers." *Actuarial Note*, no. 2015.5, Mar. 2016, table 1 et seq. (noting that internal rates of return fall toward 2.5 percent annually for average groups and under 1 percent for the youngest and richest, should cuts or benefits be enacted post-2033).

36. Kaiser Foundation. "Overview of Medicare Spending." kff.org/medicare/fact-sheet/medicare-spending-and-financing-fact-sheet/; see also *Medicare Trustees Report 2015*, pp. 23, 34, 38–40.

37. Levin, Josh. "The Welfare Queen." *Slate*, 19 Dec. 2013, www.slate.com/articles/news_and_politics/history/2013/12/linda_taylor_welfare_queen_ronald_reagan_made_her_a_notorious_american_villain.html.

38. Medicare. "Medicare's Wheelchair & Scooter Benefit." Revised Apr. 2014, www.medicare.gov/Pubs/pdf/11046.pdf.

39. Koltikoff, Laurence J., et al. *Get What's Yours: The Secrets to Maxing Out Your Social Security*. Simon & Schuster, 17 Feb. 2015, p. 5.

40. Ibid.

41. Ibid., p. 113.

42. Ibid., back cover.

43. *2015 SSA Annual Report*, table IV.B3, 2015, p. 61. https://www.ssa.gov/oact/tr/2015/tr2015.pdf.

44. Public Law 113-270, (2014; "No Social Security for Nazis Act").

45. *2015 SSA Annual Report*, table IV.B.3. Note that projections are for SSA's "intermediate" scenario and include the much smaller population of disabled persons as beneficiaries, per SSA methodology.

46. US Congress, Congressional Budget Office. "A Detailed Description of CBO's Cost Estimate for the Medicare Prescription Drug Benefit." July 2014, p. viii, www.cbo

.gov/sites/default/files/108th-congress-2003-2004/reports/07-21-medicare.pdf. *Medicare Trustees Report 2015*, table IV.B10. There would have been immaterial reductions due to technical changes of certain provisions, with the lowest net cost to federal spending being $395 billion.

47. Ramey, Corinne, "Insurers Probed on Hepatitis C Drug Coverage." *Wall Street Journal*, 2 Mar. 2016, www.wsj.com/articles/insurers-probed-on-hepatitis-c-drug -coverage-1456965087.

48. New York State Department of Health. "State Health Department Urges Hepatitis C Testing," May 15, 2014, https://www.health.ny.gov/press/releases/2014/2014-05-14 _may_hepatitis_awareness_month.htm; Ramey.

49. *Medicare Trustees Report 2015*, p. 198. See also note 51.

50. Certain groups of non-seniors, like the permanently disabled, may qualify for Medicare benefits. Most non-seniors do not.

51. National Institute for Health Care Management. "The Concentration of Health Care Spending." July 2012.

52. Osborn, Robin, et al. "International Survey of Older Adults Finds Shortcomings in Access, Coordination and Patient-Centered Care." *Health Affairs*, vol. 33, no. 12, 2014, pp. 2247–2255; United Health Foundation. America's Health Rankings, 2016, p. 21; "America's Health Rankings: Senior Report," 2016, United Health Foundation. https://assets.americashealthrankings/org/app/uploads/final-report-seniors -edition-1.pdf.

53. Social Security Administration. "Social Security History, ch. 4: The Fourth Round: 1957 to 1965," www.ssa.gov/history/corningchap4.html.

54. *Medicare Trustees Report 2015*, p. 198 (intermediate assumptions); US Census. "Person Income in 2015." Current Population Survey, 26 Aug. 2016; Kirby G. Posey. "Household Income: 2015." US Census, 16 Sept. 2016; author's calculations. There are certain differences in how Medicare accounts for costs, but these are immaterial. The larger question is whether, as Medicare itself suspects, costs will be *much higher.*

55. *Medicare Trustees Report 2015*, p. 198.

56. Ibid., pp. 69–71. Under "infinite horizon" scenarios, the number is higher, but these estimates are uncertain.

57. Ibid., p. 70.

58. Ibid., Appendix V.C.

59. Ibid., p. 194.

60. US Department of Health and Human Services, Centers for Medicare and Medicaid Services, Office of the Actuary. "Projected Medicare Expenditures Under Current Law, the Projected Baseline, and an Illustrative Alternative Scenario." 28 Aug. 2014, pp. 1, 14–16, www.cms.gov/Research-Statistics-Data-and-Systems/ Statistics-Trends-and-Reports/ReportsTrustFunds/Downloads/2014TRAlternativ eScenario.pdf.

61. Munnell, Alicia H., et al. "Are Retirees Falling Short? Reconciling the Conflicting Evidence," pp. 5, 22. Center for Retirement Research at Boston College, crr.bc.edu/ working-papers/are-retirees-falling-short-reconciling-the-conflicting-evidence/. The paper attempt to reconcile more and less optimistic scenarios, but trends toward the less optimistic.

Chapter 13: Preparing for the Future

1. DSM-V, pp. 659–660.
2. Winthrop, John. "A Model of Christian Charity" (1630). Collections of the Massachusetts Historical Society. 3rd series, 7:31–48, 1838, history.hanover.edu/texts/winthmod.html.
3. US Department of the Interior, National Parks Service. "Theodore Roosevelt and Conservation." www.nps.gov/thro/learn/historyculture/theodore-roosevelt-and-conservation.htm; US Department of Agriculture. "Major Uses of Land in the United States." 2002, p. 1, www.ers.usda.gov/media/250091/eib14_1_.pdf.
4. Public Law 88-206; amended by Public Laws 90-148, 91-604, 95-95, and 101-549; see also US Environmental Protection Agency. "Clean Air Act Overview." www.epa.gov/clean-air-act-overview/clean-air-act-text.
5. Ibid.
6. *Chevron USA v. NRDC*, 467 US 837 (1984); *Auer v. Robbins*, 519 US 452 (1997). Three justices abstained in *Chevron* for various reasons, but the remainder were unanimous; *Auer* was also unanimous. Justice Scalia delivered the *Auer* opinion, and then subsequently seemed to try to walk it back; he died, but the war against *Chevron/Auer* deference seems to be taking on new life.
7. *Michigan v. Environmental Protection Agency* (2015), slip opinion available at www.supremecourt.gov/opinions/14pdf/14-46_10n2.pdf. Whether the Supreme Court ever really took its own rulings seriously, lower courts were certainly bound by them. For a general discussion, see Saxman, Seth P. "The State of *Chevron*: 15 Years After *Mead*." *Administrative Law Review Accord*, vol. 68, 24 Mar. 2016, and also the writings of Bill Eskridge.
8. Turque, Bill. *"Inventing Al Gore: A Biography."* Houghton Mifflin, 2000, p. 133.
9. Ibid., pp. 105–106.
10. Ibid.; Morrison, Micah. "Al Gore, Environmentalist and Zinc Miner." *Wall Street Journal*, Commentary, 29 June 2000, www.wsj.com/articles/SB96224176442047890; Theobald, Bill. "Environmentalist Gore Allowed Zinc Mine." *USA Today*, 18 Mar. 2007, usatoday30.usatoday.com/news/nation/2007-03-18-goremine_N.htm; Hennenberger, Melinda. "Al Gore's Petrodollars Once Again Make Him a Chip off the Old Block." *Washington Post*, 8 Jan. 2013, www.washingtonpost.com/blogs/she-the-people/wp/2013/01/08/al-gores-petrodollars-once-again-make-him-a-chip-off-the-old-block/; Douglas, Frantz. "The 2000 Campaign: The Vice President; Gore Family's Ties to Oil Company Magnate Reap Big Rewards, and a Few Problems." *New York Times*, 19 Mar. 2000; Center for Public Integrity. "How the Gores, Father and Son, Helped Their Patron Occidental Petroleum," 11 Jan. 2000, www.publicintegrity.org/2000/01/11/3315/how-gores-father-and-son-helped-their-patron-occidental-petroleum.
11. Nussbaum, Bruce. "Al Gore's Carbon Footprint Is Big." *Bloomberg*, 27 Feb. 2007, www.bloomberg.com/news/articles/2007-02-26/al-gores-carbon-footprint-is-big-dot.
12. "Worldwide Effort Is Proposed to Study Climate and Its Impact." Special Contribution. *New York Times*, 13 Feb. 1979, C3; see also World Meteorological Organization. "World Climate Programme (WCP)." www.wmo.int/pages/prog/wcp/wcp.html; Bierly, Eugene W. "The World Climate Program: Collaboration and Communication on a Global Scale." *Annals of the American Academy of Political and Social Science*, vol. 495, Jan. 1988, pp. 113–114.

13. Infra note 14–15; and Betts, Richard A., et al. "When Could Global Warming Reach 4°C?" *Philosophical Transactions of the Royal Society*, vol. 369, no. 1934, 2011, pp. 67–84.

14. IPCC. Climate Change 2013: The Physical Science Basis. Contribution of Working Group I to the Fifth Assessment Report of the Intergovernmental Panel on Climate Change. Cambridge: Cambridge University Press, 2013, www.ipcc.ch/pdf/assessment-report/ar5/wg1/WG1AR5_Chapter01_FINAL.pdf (hereinafter "IPCC"), chapter 1 generally, figure 1.9, chapter 13 (separate contribution), and author's calculations. For more recent and dire predictions, see DeConto, Robert M., and David Pollard. "Contribution of Antarctica to Past and Future Sea-Level Rise." *Nature*. vol. 531, 31 Mar. 2016, p. 591; Hansen, James, et al. "Ice Melt, Sea Level Rise and Superstorms: Evidence From Paleoclimate Data, Climate Modeling, and Modern Observations that 2°C Global Warming Could Be Dangerous." *Atmospheric Chemistry and Physics*, vol. 16, no. 6, 22 Mar. 2016.

15. E.g., Fox, Douglas. "Scientists Are Watching In Horror as Ice Collapses." *National Geographic*, 12 Apr. 2016.

16. Pew Research Center. "Americans, Politics, and Science Issues." p. 38, 42, www.pewinternet.org/files/2015/07/2015-07-01_science-and-politics_FINAL.pdf. (A popup appears saying this file is an embargoed draft, but it's posted in several places on Pew, marked as final, and cited in Pew's press releases; it appears final). The effects of age appear somewhat more important even than the effects of education, but more research is required to detangle the variables.

17. Doran, Peter T., Maggie Kendall Zimmerman. "Examining the Scientific Consensus on Climate Change." Eos, Transactions American Geophysical Union. *AGU Publications*, vol. 90, no. 3, pp. 22–33; Cook, John, et al. "Quantifying the Consensus on Anthropogenic Global Warming in the Scientific Literature." IOPscience, Environmental Research Letters. 15 May 2013 (suggesting >97 percent consensus among those *expressing an opinion*).

18. Supra note 16, p. 52 et seq.

19. Ibid., p. 37.

20. Stokes, Bruce, et al. "Global Concern About Climate Change, Broad Support for Limiting Emissions." Pew Research Center, 5 Nov. 2015, p. 20. Younger people are substantially more likely to believe climate change will affect them personally, but are still unrealistic.

21. US Environmental Protection Agency. "US Greenhouse Gas Emissions by Gas Inventory Report: 1990–2014." www3.epa.gov/climatechange/ghgemissions/usinventoryreport.html; and US Environmental Protection Agency. "Inventory of U.S. Greenhouse Gas Emissions and Sinks: 1990–2014." 15 Apr. 2016, at ES-1. On a per capita basis, there has been some improvement, but per capita is not the most relevant metric for this issue.

22. Ibid., sec. 8 (noting US calculation exclusion of "Other"); IPCC, sec. 5.4; OECD. "Carbon Dioxide Emissions Embodied in International Trade." Sept. 2015, www.oecd.org/industry/ind/carbondioxideemissionsembodiedininternationaltrade.htm and associated spreadsheets and author's calculations. The Obama administration's plan for cuts is a reduction by 2025 of 26 to 28 percent below 2005 levels, or about 2.5 percent annually as a crude average. "U.S. Cover Note, INDC and Accompanying Information." It remains to be seen how the late 2016 acceptance

by Obama of the Paris Accords changes this target. United States of America, "Submission," 31 Mar. 2015, www4.unfccc.int/Submissions/INDC/Published%20 Documents/United%20States%20of%20America/1/U.S.%20Cover%20Note%20 INDC%20and%20Accompanying%20Information.pdf.

23. US Energy Information Administration. "Total Petroleum and Other Liquids Production, 2014," www.eia.gov/beta/international/rankings/#?prodact=53-1&cy=2014 and author's calculations. See also EIA at www.eia.gov/beta/international.

24. Ibid.

25. Cook, Lynn, and Erin Ailworth. "First Tanker of U.S. Crude Oil for Export Sails From Texas." *Wall Street Journal*, 31 Dec. 2015.

26. US Dept. of Transportation. "Summary of Fuel Economy Performance." 2013, pp. 3–4.

27. Ibid.

28. Author's calculations. The delta in range estimates is a product of differences between linear vs. compound growth.

29. IPCC. Annex II, table A.II, pp.18–19 et seq.

30. US Department of Defense. "National Security Implications of Climate-Related Risks and a Changing Climate," 23 July 2015, pp. 1, 14.

31. Vidal, John, and David Adam. "China Overtakes US as World's Biggest CO_2 Emitter." *Guardian*, 19 June 2007.

32. Cushman Jr., John H. "U.S. Signs a Pact to Reduce Gases Tied to Warming." *New York Times*, 13 Nov. 1998; 105th Congress, 1st Session, S. Res. 98 and Record Vote No. 205 (1997).

33. Ibid. (Congressional vote).

34. House Permanent Select Committee on Intelligence, House Select Committee on Energy Independence and Global Warming. "National Intelligence Assessment on the National Security Implications of Global Climate Change to 2030. Statement for the Record of Dr. Thomas Fingar," 25 June 2008, fas.org/irp/congress/2008 _hr/062508fingar.pdf.

35. 102nd Congress, Senate Consideration of Treaty Document 102-38, 1992, www .congress.gov/treaty-document/102nd-congress/38 (aka the "Rio Treaty").

36. US Energy Information Administration. "Nuclear Reactor Operational Status Tables," 2011.

37. International Atomic Energy Agency. Power Reactor Information System, France, 2015.

38. Sullivan, Peter. "Panel Members Clash over Fetal Tissue Subpoenas." *Hill*, 2 Mar. 2016, thehill.com/policy/healthcare/271474-panel-members-clash-over-fetal-tissue -subpoenas.

39. Phillips, Erica. "Massive Robots Keep Docks Shipshape." *Wall Street Journal*, 27 Mar. 2016, www.wsj.com/articles/massive-robots-keep-docks-shipshape-1459104327.

Chapter 14: Detention, After-School and Otherwise

1. Attributed. Certainly, it's consistent with Hugo's general sentiments.

2. Bureau of Justice Statistics. "Annual Probation Survey, Annual Parole Survey, Annual Survey of Jails, Census of Jail Inmates, and National Prisoner Statistics Program, 1980–2014," appendix 1 and data file; US Census. "Table 1. Annual Estimates

of the Resident Population for the United States, Regions, States, and Puerto Rico: April 1, 2010 to July 1, 2014." NST-EST2014-01.

3. Wirtz, Willard, et al. "On Further Examination: Report of the Advisory Panel on the Scholastic Aptitude Test Score Decline," College Entrance Examination Board, 1977, table 2, research.collegeboard.org/sites/default/files/publications/2012/7/misc1977-1-report-sat-score-decline.pdf. See also US Department of Education, National Center for Education Statistics, *Digest of Education Statistics*, 2014 (NCES 2016-006), chapter 2 and prior editions (hereinafter "NCES *Digest*" with relevant data specified).

4. Wirtz, pp. 45–46.

5. Ibid., sec. "Pervasive Change."

6. Ibid., sec. "Through Other Looking Glasses."

7. Ibid.

8. Ibid., sec. "As It Was in the Beginning."

9. Ibid., sec. 8 and Part IV.

10. Wirtz, table 2; "Scholastic Aptitude Test score averages for college-bound high school seniors, by sex: 1966–67 to 1993–94." National Center for Education Statistics, 1995, nces.ed.gov/programs/digest/d95/dtab124.asp. The College Board has subsequently recentered and rescored the SAT, but during the period covered the scale remained the same.

11. Reagan, Ronald. "State of the Union." 25 Jan. 1984; National Commission on Excellence in Education. David Pierpont Gardner. "*A Nation at Risk*" and "Letter of Transmittal." Apr. 1983.

12. Gardner, "*A Nation at Risk*" and "Letter of Transmittal"; National Commission on Excellence in Education. Apr. 1983, sec. "Findings Regarding Expectations."

13. Ibid.

14. Ibid.; Wirtz, p. 29.

15. Seelye, Katharine Q. "Relentless Moral Crusader Is Relentless Gambler, Too." *New York Times*, 3 May 2003, www.nytimes.com/2003/05/03/national/03GAMB.html. Bennett admitted to gambling, but said he also won; nevertheless, given how casinos make money, even if he'd just wagered $8 million he almost certainly lost a lot.

16. Ravitch, Diane. "*The Death and Life of the Great American School System: How Testing and Choice Are Undermining Education*." Basic Books, 2010, pp. 132–144 (citing multiple studies of all ideologies from public and private institutions).

17. Ibid., pp. 266–267 (summarizing—correctly—the results of Matthew G. Springer, et al. "Teacher Pay for Performance." National Center on Performance Incentives. Led by Vanderbilt Peabody College, 2010, pp. 43–49).

18. US Department of Education. National Assessment of Education Progress. Table 221.30 (assessing 1984 to 2012; homework for the oldest students remained highly stable; some younger students are receiving somewhat less).

19. Bromberg, Marni, and Christina Theokas. "Meandering Toward Graduation: Transcript Outcomes of High School Graduates." *Education Trust*, Apr. 2016, p. 1.

20. Ibid., pp. 4, 7.

21. UC Berkeley, Office of Undergraduate Admissions. "Student Profile" for 2015 freshmen, admissions.berkeley.edu/studentprofile; *U.S. News and World Report*. "National Universities Rankings." 2016 College Rankings, colleges.usnews.rankingsandreviews.com/best-colleges/rankings/national-universities/page+2.

22. American Society of Civil Engineers. Infrastructure Report Card, 2013, pp. 7–8, 59, 67.
23. Ibid., p. 7.
24. OECD. "Programme for International Student Assessment (PISA) Results from PISA 2012," p. 1 et seq., www.oecd.org/unitedstates/PISA-2012-results-US.pdf.
25. Duncan, Arne. "The Vison of Education Reform in the United States." Speech to UNESCO, 4 Nov. 2010, unesco.usmission.gov/duncan-remarks.html.
26. US Department of Education, Office of Inspector General. "The Office of Innovation and Improvement's Oversight and Monitoring of the Charter Schools Program's Planning and Implementation Grants." p. 9, www2.ed.gov/about/offices/list/oig/auditreports/fy2012/a02l0002.pdf.
27. NCES *Digest*. Table 208, Pupil/Teacher Ratio, 1955–2024.
28. Ibid.
29. National Assessment of Educational Progress. "Trends in Academic Progress: Reading 1971–2012, Mathematics 1973–2012." The Nation's Report Card, pp. 7 and 29.
30. Ibid., p. 16.
31. Ravitch, p. 31.
32. Desilver, Drew. "U.S. Students Improving—Slowly—in Math and Science, but Still Lagging Internationally." Pew Research Center, 2 Feb. 2015, www.pewresearch.org/fact-tank/2015/02/02/u-s-students-improving-slowly-in-math-and-science-but-still-lagging-internationally; National Center for Education Statistics. "Public High School Graduation Rates," nces.ed.gov/programs/coe/indicator_coi.asp.
33. E.g., Public Law 107-110 generally and at §§1117.a.5.i, 1119.a.3, 1501.a.2.A (2002).
34. Hirschfeld Davis, Julie. "President Obama Signs into Law a Rewrite of No Child Left Behind." *New York Times*, 10 Dec. 2015, nytimes.com/2015/12/11/us/politics/president-obama-signs-into-law-a-rewrite-of-no-child-left-behind.html?_r=0; PL 114-95.
35. Almasy, Steve. "Atlanta Schools Cheating Scandal: 11 of 12 Defendants Convicted." CNN, 14 Apr. 2015; Chandler, Michael Alison. "Six D.C. Schools Had 'Critical' Testing Violations, 11 Others Had Irregularities." *Washington Post*, 21 Sept. 2015; Bichao, Sergio. "How The Testing Craze Scandalized Woodbridge Schools and Cheated Kids Out Of Learning." MyCentralJersey.com; Martinez, Aaron, and Lindsey Anderson. "5 Educators Arrested in EPISD Scheme." *El Paso Times*, 27 Apr. 2016.
36. White House. "Remarks of President Barack Obama—Address to Joint Session of Congress," 24 Feb. 2009, www.whitehouse.gov/video/EVR022409/#transcript.
37. Ibid.
38. US Department of Labor, Bureau of Labor Statistics. "Median Weekly Earnings in 2014 Dollars of People 25 Years and Older, by Educational Attainment and Gender, 1979–2014" (noting for those with "some college or associate degree," wages fell from a peak of $1,000 median weekly to $872 by 2014, and for women from a high of $723 in 2004 to $661 by 2014 in adjusted dollars).
39. Author's calculations based on data from NCES *Digest*, on-line edition, Table 303.70, various years (total undergrad fall enrollment in degree-granting postsecondary institutions).
40. Ibid.
41. US Senate, Health, Education, Labor, and Pensions Committee. "Emerging Risk?" An Overview of Growth, Spending, Student Debt and Unanswered Questions in For-Profit Higher Education," 24 June 2010, p. 1, www.help.senate.gov/imo/media/doc/For-Profit%20Emerging%20Risk%20Report1.pdf.

42. Ibid., p. 3 (citing Dept. of Education Analysis); see also for a comprehensive list of reports on the subject, all reaching similar conclusions, National Conference of State Legislatures. "For-Profit Colleges and Universities." July 2013, www.ncsl.org/research/education/for-profit-colleges-and-universities.aspx.

43. Dayen, David. "This is America's Worst College: Screwed-Over Corinthian College Students Get Screwed Again by So-Called Debt Relief." *Salon*, 9 June 2015, www.salon.com/2015/06/09/this_is_americas_worst_college_screwed_over_corinthian_college_students_get_screwed_again_by_so_called_debt_relief/.

44. See supra notes 43–44 (noting that 18,256 were enrolled in for-profit colleges in 1970, and 106,397 in 1980, with the vast increase coming in 1990–2010).

45. University of California. "UC Merced Freshman Admission Profile," admission.universityofcalifornia.edu/campuses/merced/freshman-profile/index.html; University of California, Berkeley, Office of Undergraduate Admissions. "Student Profile," admissions.berkeley.edu/studentprofile; UCLA, Office of Analysis and Information Management, www.aim.ucla.edu/admissions.aspx.

46. National Assessment of Educational Progress, Institute of Education Sciences, National Center for Education Statistics. "First-Year Undergraduate Remedial Coursetaking: 1999–2000, 2003–04, 2007–08," Jan. 2013, pp. 1–2, nces.ed.gov/pubs2013/2013013.pdf. Students requiring remedial education are taken as "unprepared" for our purposes.

47. National Center for Education Statistics. "Characteristics of Postsecondary Faculty," nces.ed.gov/programs/coe/pdf/Indicator_CSC/COE_csc_2013_04.pdf; American Association of University Professors. "Background Facts on Contingent Faculty," www.aaup.org/issues/contingency/background-facts; see also www.aaup.org/sites/default/files/files/2013%20Salary%20Survey%20Tables%20and%20Figures/Figure%201.pdf (for historical data through 2011).

48. French, Laurie. "The Forever Professors: Academics Who Don't Retire Are Greedy, Selfish and Bad for Students." *Chronicle of Higher Education*, 14 Nov. 2014, chronicle.com/article/Retire-Already-/149965/?cid=at&utm_source=at&utm_medium=en; Williams June, Audrey. "Aging Professors Create a Faculty Bottleneck," *Chronicle of Higher Education*, 18 Mar. 2012, chronicle.com/article/Professors-Are-Graying-and/131226/ (noting a doubling of faculty aged sixty-five or older between 2000 and 2011).

49. US Federal Reserve System, Board of Governors. "Consumer Credit—G.19," www.federalreserve.gov/releases/g19/Current/.

50. FRED, SLOAS; Board of Governors of the Federal Reserve System. "Consumer Credit—G.19." Statistical Releases and Historical Data, August 2016, www.federalreserve.gov/releases/g19/current/.

51. Roeder, Oliver, et al. "What Caused the Crime Decline?" Brennan Center for Justice at New York University of Law, 2015, p. 3, www.brennancenter.org/sites/default/files/publications/What_Caused_The_Crime_Decline.pdf. The Brennan Center refers to "consumer confidence," which is highly correlated with economic growth, or at least its perception.

52. Ibid., p. 1.

53. Ibid., table 3.

54. Bureau of Justice Statistics. "Estimated number of persons under correctional supervision in the United States, 1980–2014." Total Correctional Population, 2016,

www.bjs.gov/index.cfm?ty=kfdetail&iid=487; US Census. "Annual Estimates of the Population for the United States, Regions, States, and Puerto Rico: April 1, 2000 to July 1, 2007 (NST-EST2007-01)." National Table, 2007, www.census.gov/popest/data/historical/2000s/vintage_2007/; author's calculations.

55. Vargas, Ricardo. "The anti-drug policy, aerial spraying of illicit crops and their social, environmental and political impacts in Colombia." *Journal of Drug Issues*, vol. 32, no. 1 (2002): 11–60. The Clinton program was known as "Plan Colombia" and well reported at the time.

56. Langton, Lynn, and Donald Farole, Jr. "State Public Defender Programs, 2007"; US Department of Justice, Office of Justice Programs, Bureau of Justice Statistics. Special Report. Sept. 2010, www.bjs.gov/content/pub/pdf/spdp07.pdf; US Department of Justice, Office of Justice Programs. "Public Defender Offices Nationwide Received Nearly 5.6 Million Indigent Defense Cases in 2007," 16 Sept. 2010, ojp.gov/newsroom/pressreleases/2010/BJS10122.htm. Contractors and pro bono attorneys provide additional services, but they cannot be relied on as the core of public defense. For a good overview, see Justice Policy Institute. "System Overload: The Costs of Under-Resourcing Public Defense." July 2011, www.justicepolicy.org/uploads/justicepolicy/documents/system_overload_final.pdf.

57. Constitution of the United States. Sixth and Fourteenth Amendments; *Gideon v. Wainwright*, 372 US 335 (1963).

58. Roeder, p. 56 et seq.

59. Infra note 62 and the prison and associated note for this chapter; Institute for Criminal Policy Research. "World Prison Brief"; CIA World Factbook.

60. US Department of Justice, Office of Justice Programs, Bureau of Justice Statistics. "Correctional Populations in the United States, 2014," table 1, www.bjs.gov/content/pub/pdf/cpus14.pdf (rev. Jan. 21, 2016); US Census, Population Division, Dec. 2015, https://factfinder.census.gov/faces/tableservices/jsf/productview.xhtml.

61. Ibid., p. 5 (DoJ).

62. US Department of Justice, Office of Justice Programs, Bureau of Justice Statistics. "Prisoners in 2014," Sept. 2015, table 8; see also US Government Accountability Office. "Growing Inmate Crowding Negatively Affects Inmates, Staff, and Infrastructure," Sept. 2012 (for historical data).

63. Henrichson, Christian and Ruth Delaney. "The Price of Prisons: What Incarceration Costs Taxpayers." Vera Institute for Justice. Updated 20 July 2012, pp. 7–8, www.vera.org/sites/default/files/resources/downloads/price-of-prisons-updated-version-021914.pdf.

64. California State Legislature, Legislative Analyst's Office. "How Much Does It Cost to Incarcerate an Inmate?" www.lao.ca.gov/PolicyAreas/CJ/6_cj_inmatecost (citing figures for 2008–2009).

65. Federal Register. "Annual Determination of Average Cost of Incarceration" (in 2014), 9 Sept. 2015, www.federalregister.gov/articles/2015/03/09/2015-05437/annual-determination-of-average-cost-of-incarceration.

66. FRED, G160121A027NBEA. FRED's original source is BEA, NIPA table 3.15.

67. University of California, "Budget for Current Operations 2015–16," appendix 1 (Nov. 2014); State of California, "California State Budget 2015–16," pp. 22, 33 (2015).

68. Ollove, Michael. "Ex-Felons Are About to Get Health Coverage." The Pew Charitable Trusts, 5 Apr. 2013, www.pewtrusts.org/en/research-and-analysis/blogs/stateline/2013/04/05/exfelons-are-about-to-get-health-coverage.
69. US Department of Justice, Office of Justice Programs, Bureau of Justice Statistics. "Prisoners in 2014," p. 15; see also National Association for the Advancement of Colored People. "Criminal Justice Fact Sheet," www.naacp.org/pages/criminal-justice-fact-sheet.

Chapter 15: The Wages of Sin

1. US Congress, Congressional Budget Office. "Trends in Family Wealth, 1989–2013," 18 Aug. 2016, p. 2.
2. Hughes, Robert. "Brideshead Redecorated." *Time*, 11 Nov. 1985.
3. Appelbaum, Binyamin. "Outspoken Fed Official Frets About Following Japan's Path." *New York Times*, 4 May 2016, www.nytimes.com/2016/05/05/upshot/outspoken-fed-official-frets-about-following-japans-path.html?mabReward=A3&action=click&pgtype=Homepage&_r=0.
4. US Department of Commerce, Bureau of Economic Analysis. National Income and Product Accounts Gross Domestic Product: Second Quarter 2016. Current releases available at: http://bea.gov/newsreleases/national/GDP/GDPnewsrelease.htm (accessed here October 10, 2016).
5. FRED, A939RX0Q048SBEA (BEA); author's calculations.
6. Iritani, Evelyn. "Great Idea but Don't Quote Him." *Los Angeles Times*, 9 Sept. 2004, articles.latimes.com/2004/sep/09/business/fi-deng9/2; Bao Tong. "How Deng Xiaoping Helped Create a Corrupt China." *New York Times*, 3 June 2015, www.nytimes.com/2015/06/04/opinion/bao-tong-how-deng-xiaoping-helped-create-a-corrupt-china.html?_r=0.
7. Iritani.
8. Congressional Budget Office. "Trends in Family Wealth, 1989 to 2013." 2016, www.cbo.gov/publication/51846, underlying tables; author's calculations.
9. "Intergenerational Justice in Aging Societies: A Cross-National Comparison of 29 OECD Countries." Bertelsmann Stiftung. Sustainable Governance Indicators. p. 6 et seq., news.sgi-network.org/uploads/tx_amsgistudies/Intergenerational_Justice_OECD.pdf.
10. US Census. Current Population Survey, 2014. Historical Poverty table 3 and p. 12.
11. Ibid.
12. Congressional Budget Office. "Trends in Family Wealth, 1989 to 2013."
13. BLS, table A-15, U-3 measure, http://www.bls.gov/news.release/empsit.t15.htm; Bureau of Labor Statistics. "How the Government Measures Unemployment," www.bls.gov/cps/cps_htgm.htm.
14. "About." Bernie Sanders's Senate website, www.sanders.senate.gov/about; Ronayne, Kathleen. "Sanders Declares as Democrat in NH Primary." *Burlington Free Press*, 5 Nov. 2015, www.burlingtonfreepress.com/story/news/local/2015/11/05/sanders-declares-democrat-nh-primary/75242938/. Sanders may ultimately change his registration to Democrat on a permanent basis, but his homepage as of the first half of 2016 continued to mention his status as an independent.
15. BLS, table A-15, U-6 definition, www.bls.gov/news.release/empsit.t15.htm.
16. FRED, UNRATE, UEMPMEAN, U6RATE (BEA); author's calculations.

17. Katz, Lawrence F., and Alan B. Krueger. "The Rise and Nature of Alternative Work Arrangements in the United States, 1995–2015." Working Paper. 29 Mar. 2016, p. 7, revised September 13, 2016.
18. With apologies to Robert Hughes on this.
19. Bauerlein, David. "Automakers' Drive into Southeast Misses Florida: Car Companies, Attracted by Incentives, Invest $6 Billion to Build Plants in Other Southeast States." Jacksonville.com, 8 Nov. 2011, jacksonville.com/news/florida/2011-11-08/story/automakers-drive-southeast-misses-florida#.
20. Costa, Daniel. "The Immigration Innovation (I²) Act of 2013." Economic Policy Institute. 27 Feb. 2013, www.epi.org/publication/immigration-innovation-i2-act-2013/; US Citizenship and Immigration Services. "H-1B Fiscal Year (FY) 2017 Cap Season." www.uscis.gov/working-united-states/temporary-workers/h-1b-specialty-occupations-and-fashion-models/h-1b-fiscal-year-fy-2017-cap-season#count.
21. "The Lesson of Zoe Baird." New York Times, Opinion, 23 Jan. 1993, www.nytimes.com/1993/01/23/opinion/the-lesson-of-zoe-baird.html; "Addressing Nannygate." New York Times, Opinion, 30 Mar. 1994, www.nytimes.com/1994/03/30/opinion/addressing-nannygate.html; Johnston, David. "Clinton's Choice for Justice Dept. Hired Illegal Aliens for Household." New York Times, 14 Jan. 1993, www.nytimes.com/1993/01/14/us/clinton-s-choice-for-justice-dept-hired-illegal-aliens-for-household.html; Wingert, Pat. "Nannygate II: A Women's Backlash?" Newsweek, 14 Feb. 1993, www.newsweek.com/nannygate-ii-womens-backlash-195214.
22. The CEA provides a good overview of market concentration and its effects. Council of Economic Advisors. CEA. "Benefits of Competition and Indicators of Market Power." Apr. 2016.
23. Trainer, David. "How Stock Buybacks Destroy Shareholder Value." Forbes, 24 Feb. 2016; see also Lazonick, William. "Profits Without Prosperity." Harvard Business Review, Sept. 2014.
24. Rosenbaum, Aliza, and Rob Cox. "Big Money: Is Big Beer Begging for an Anti-Trust Probe?" The Washington Post, 6 Sept. 2009, www.washingtonpost.com/wp-dyn/content/article/2009/09/04/AR2009090404236.html. Leeb, Stephen. "Wal-Mart Fattens Up on Poor America With 25% of U.S. Grocery Sales." Forbes. www.forbes.com/sites/greatspeculations/2013/05/20/wal-mart-cleans-up-on-poor-america-with-25-of-u-s-grocery-sales/#31fa4f262bea (alternative metrics have 90 percent of Americans living within 10 miles of a Wal-Mart; the effect is the same).
25. Sanders, Bernie, and Daily News Editorial Board. "Transcript: Bernie Sanders meets with News Editorial Board." New York Daily News, Opinion, 4 Apr. 2016, www.nydailynews.com/opinion/transcript-bernie-sanders-meets-news-editorial-board-article-1.2588306.
26. Fuglie, Keith, et al. "Rising Concentration in Agricultural Input Industries Influences New Farm Technologies." US Department of Agriculture, 3 Dec. 2012, www.ers.usda.gov/amber-waves/2012-december/rising-concentration-in-agricultural-input-industries-influences-new-technologies.aspx#.Vxf2yzArKM8.

Chapter 16: The Myth of Boomer Goodness

1. Mamet, David. *The Secret Knowledge: On the Dismantling of American Culture.* Penguin, e-books edition, 2001, pp. 281–282.

2. Bradner, Eric. "Bill Clinton Spars with Black Lives Matter Protesters." CNN, 8 Apr. 2016, www.cnn.com/2016/04/07/politics/bill-clinton-black-lives-matter-protesters/index.html.

3. Ibid.

4. Ibid.

5. 570 U.S. __ 2013, Docket No. 12–96.

6. Serwer, Adam. "Chief Justice Roberts' Long War Against the Voting Rights Act." *Mother Jones*, 27 Feb. 2013, www.motherjones.com/politics/2013/02/john-roberts-long-war-against-voting-rights-act; see also Rutenberg, Jim. "A Dream Undone." *New York Times Magazine*, 29 July 2015, www.nytimes.com/2015/07/29/magazine/voting-rights-act-dream-undone.html.

7. Howard, Cory H. "A Return to Dred Scott? How Recent Supreme Court Jurisprudence Reflects Dred Scott's Legal Reasoning and Fails to Protect the Most Vulnerable in Today's Society." *Faulkner Law Review*, vol. 6, no. 2, 2014–2015, part V. It's not that *Shelby* was a recapitulation of *Dred Scott* so much as the triumph of state's rights over individual civil rights in a similar context and with similar reasoning, with what some might see as not dissimilar implications.

8. "The Formula behind the Voting Rights Act." *New York Times*, 22 Jun. 2013, www.nytimes.com/interactive/2013/06/23/us/voting-rights-act-map.html; *Shelby v. Holder*, 570 US (2013) pp. 4–6.

9. US Census. Census of 1980, vol. 1, May 1983, title page.

10. *City of Mobile v. Borden*, 446 US 55 (1980).

11. For a general history with pro-VRA leanings, see Leadership Conference. "History of the VRA." www.civilrights.org/voting-rights/vra/history.html.

12. Santos, Fernanda. "Angry Arizona Voters Demand: Why Such Long Lines at Polling Stations?" *New York Times*, 24 Mar. 2016, www.nytimes.com/2016/03/25/us/angry-arizona-voters-demand-why-such-long-lines-at-polling-sites.html; see also for associated other questionable practices: Wigel, David. "Two Polling Places, Both Inside Police Stations." See also *Slate*, 18 Mar. 2014, www.slate.com/blogs/weigel/2014/03/18/_two_polling_places_both_inside_police_stations.html; National Association for the Advancement of Colored People. "Defending Democracy: Confronting Modern Barriers to Voting Rights in America," www.naacp.org/pages/defending-democracy.

13. Gay Stolberg, Sheryl, and Erik Eckholm. "Virginia Governor Restores Voting Rights to Felons." *New York Times*, 23 Apr. 2016, www.nytimes.com/2016/04/23/us/governor-terry-mcauliffe-virginia-voting-rights-convicted-felons.html?_r=0.

14. Chung, Jean. "Felony Disenfranchisement: A Primer." Sentencing Project, 10 May 2016, fig. B, www.sentencingproject.org/publications/felony-disenfranchisement-a-primer/.

15. Public Law 92–225 (1972).

16. Federal Election Commission. "About the FEC," www.fec.gov/about.sthml.

17. *Buckley v. Valeo*, 424 US 1 (1976).

18. *First National Bank of Boston v. Bellotti*, 435 US 735, pp. 826–28 (1978) (Rehnquist, J., dissenting).

19. Helderman, Rosalind S. "Donor Gave McDonnell and Family a Lake-House Vacation." *Washington Post*, 18 Apr. 2013, www.washingtonpost.com/local/va-politics/donor

-gave-mcdonnell-and-family-a-lake-house-vacation/2013/04/18/7573321c-a76f-11e2
-8302-3c7e0ea97057_story.html.

20. *Planned Parenthood v. Casey*, 505 US 833 (1992), pp. 874–77. *Whole Woman's Health v. Hellerstedt* kept the "undue burdens" test but drew a *modest* line toward a more permissive interpretation thereof. 579 US (2016).

21. Deprez, Esmé E. "Abortion Clinics Close at Record Pace After States Tighten Rules." *Bloomberg*, 3 Sept. 2013, www.bloomberg.com/news/articles/2013-09-03/abortion-clinics-close-at-record-pace-after-states-tighten-rules. For a particularly bizarre example of the renewed debate over abortion, there is, of course, the example of Trump. Krieg, Gregory. "Donald Trump's 3 Positions on Abortion in 3 Hours." CNN, 31 Mar. 2016, www.cnn.com/2016/03/30/politics/donald-trump-abortion-positions/index.html.

22. White House, Council of Economic Advisors. Issue Brief. "Gender Pay Gap: Recent Trends and Explanations," April 2015, p. 1, www.whitehouse.gov/sites/default/files/docs/equal_pay_issue_brief_final.pdf.

23. Cooper, Rob. "Inside Apple's Chinese 'Sweatshop' Factory Where Workers Are Paid Just £1.12 Per Hour to Produce iPhones and iPads for the West." *Daily Mail*, 25 Jan. 2013, http://www.dailymail.co.uk/news/article-2103798/Revealed-Inside-Apples-Chinese-sweatshop-factory-workers-paid-just-1-12-hour.html (based on reporting originally conducted by *Nightline*).

24. Hillenbrand. *2015 Annual Report*, p. 3, s1.q4cdn.com/966021326/files/doc_financials/annual/hillenbrand-ar-2015.pdf.

25. *Obergefell v. Hodges*, 135 S. Ct. 2584 (2015); Wang, Wendy. "The Rise of Intermarriage: Rates, Characteristics Vary by Race and Gender." Pew Research Center, 16 Feb. 2012, pp. 33–40, www.pewsocialtrends.org/files/2012/02/SDT-Intermarriage-II.pdf; *Loving v. Virginia*, 388 U.S. 1 (1967).

26. "Changing Attitudes on Gay Marriage." Pew Research Center, 12 May 2016, sec. 1; "Support for Same-Sex Marriage at Record High, but Key Segments Remain Opposed." Pew Research Center, 8 June 2015, p. 3.

27. Crabtree, Steve. "Gallup Brain: Strom Thurmond and the 1948 Election." Gallup, 17 Dec. 2002, www.gallup.com/poll/7444/gallup-brain-strom-thurmond-1948-election.aspx; National Defense Research Institute. "Sexual Orientation and U.S. Military Personnel Policy: Options and Assessment." Rand Corporation, 1993, p. 191 et seq.

28. Public Law 103-160, subtitle G, §654(a).15 (1993).

29. Goldwater, Barry M. "Ban on Gays Is Senseless Attempt to Stall the Inevitable." Carnegie Mellon University, www.cs.cmu.edu/afs/cs/usr/scotts/bulgarians/barry-goldwater.html (selections from Goldwater's commentary in the *New York Times* and the *Washington Post*); "Goldwater Backs Gay Troops." *New York Times*, 11 June 1993.

30. "More Support for Gun Rights, Gay Marriage Than in 2004, 2008." Pew Research Center for the People & the Press, 25 Apr. 2012, p. 5, www.people-press.org/files/legacy-pdf/4-25-12%20Social%20Issues.pdf.

31. Americans with Disabilities Act Amendments Act of 2008. 42 USC §§ 12102.1-2(A) (2009).

32. For an exemplar ad for Rascal reimbursement, see e.g., www.localcommunities.org/servlet/lc_procserv/dbpage=page&mode=display&gid=01331001151093379080423861

33. California Constitution, art. 1, sec. 1.

34. *Olmstead v. United States*, 277 U.S. 438 (1928) (Brandeis, J., dissenting).
35. Ibid.
36. Gellman, Barton, and Ashton Soltani. "NSA Infiltrates Links to Yahoo, Google Data Centers Worldwide, Snowden Documents Says." *Washington Post*, 30 Oct. 2013, washingtonpost.com/world/national-security/nsa-infiltrates-links-to-yahoo-google -data-centers-worldwide-snowden-documents-say/2013/10/30/e51d661e -4166-11e3-8b74-d89d714ca4dd_story.html.
37. Gugliotta Guy, and Juliet Eilperin. "Tough Response Appeals to Clinton Critics." *Washington Post*, 21 Aug. 1998, A17, www.washingtonpost.com/wp-srv/politics/ special/clinton/stories/react082198.htm. Most senators did not question Clinton's timing, but some did, and I do—at least in context with the tardiness of his other interventions.
38. Goldberg, Jeffrey. "The Obama Doctrine: The U.S. President Talks Through His Hardest Decisions About America's Role in the World." *Atlantic*, Apr. 2016, www .theatlantic.com/magazine/archive/2016/04/the-obama-doctrine/471525/.

Chapter 17: Price Tags and Prescriptions

1. Psalm 51:5 (King James Bible).
2. Puentes, Robert. et al. "A New Alignment: Strengthening America's Commitment to Passenger Rail." Metropolitan Policy Program at Brookings. 1 Mar. 2013, pp. 7–11, www.brookings.edu/wp-content/uploads/2016/06/passenger-rail-puentes-tomer .pdf. The Northeast Corridor receives almost no state support, unlike less intensively used lines, and runs a net operating profit (discounting depreciation).
3. Consumer Financial Protection Bureau. "Private Student Loans," 29 Aug. 2012, files.consumerfinance.gov/f/201207_cfpb_Reports_Private-Student-Loans.pdf.
4. US Department of Education. Federal Student Aid, "Interest Rates for New Direct Loans," studentaid.ed.gov/sa/about/announcements/interest-rate.
5. Psalm 90:10 (King James Bible). "Fourscore," by the way, is very close to the actual American life expectancy.
6. OECD. "How Does Sweden Compare?" Health Statistics 2014, www.oecd.org/els/ health-systems/Briefing-Note-SWEDEN-2014.pdf.
7. Pew Research Center. "Most Say Government Policies Since Recession Have Done Little to Help Middle Class, Poor: 'Partial' Recovery Seen in Jobs, Household Incomes," 4 Mar. 2015, www.people-press.org/files/2015/03/03-04-15-Economy -release.pdf.
8. US Department of the Treasury, Internal Revenue Service. "2014 Data Book." 1 Oct. 2013 to 30 Sept. 2014, table 9.b, www.irs.gov/pub/irs-soi/14databk.pdf.
9. Entin, Stephen J. "President Obama's Capital Gains Tax Proposals: Bad for the Economy and the Budget." Tax Foundation, 21 Jan 2015, taxfoundation.org/blog/ president-obama-s-capital-gains-tax-proposals-bad-economy-and-budget. The Tax Foundation has its own axes to grind, but is almost certainly correct on this point based on IRS data.
10. Congressional Budget Office, "The Distribution of Household Income and Federal Taxes, 2013." June 2016. See the supplementary data associated with this report and Chapter 9 of this book. There was a meaningful change in federal tax regimes for the richest Americans from 2012 to 2013, and some filers responded by accelerating income into 2012, which may understate the skew for 2013. Nevertheless, 2013 is

the latest tax data available and the general distribution of income and taxes over the recent past shows the same dynamic.

11. US Department of the Treasury, "FY 2015 Gift Contributions to Reduce Debt Held by the Public." http://www.treasurydirect.gov/govt/reports/pd/gift/gift_2015.htm.

12. US Department of the Treasury, Internal Revenue Service. "Tax Gap Estimates for Tax Years 2008–2010," Apr. 2016, www.irs.gov/PUP/newsroom/tax%20gap%20estimates%20for%202008%20through%202010.pdf. The IRS does not conduct "tax gap" analyses on a regular basis; these were the most recent figures—current figures are probably higher due to a slightly larger economy and inflation.

13. Myles, Udland. "US Companies Don't Pay What They're Supposed To in Taxes—And It's Getting Worse." *Business Insider*, 18 Oct. 2015, www.businessinsider.com/us-company-effective-tax-rate-below-statutory-rate-2015-10.

14. Pearson, Rich, and Kim Geiger. "Illinois Supreme Court Rules Landmark Pension Law Unconstitutional." *Chicago Tribune*, www.chicagotribune.com/ct-illinois-pension-law-court-ruling-20150508-story.html.

15. Freeland, Will. "Nonpayers of Federal Taxes and Net Beneficiaries of Federal Spending." Tax Foundation, taxfoundation.org/blog/nonpayers-federal-taxes-and-net-beneficiaries-federal-spending; author's own calculations regarding rebates and social consumption based on CBO analyses from the series "Distribution of Major Tax Expenditures" and "Distribution of Household Income and Federal Tax" series from various years.

16. Taylor, Paul, et al. "Once Again, the Future Ain't What It Used to Be." Pew Research Center, 2 May 2006, p. 2, www.pewsocialtrends.org/files/2010/10/BetterOff.pdf. Half of adults think children generally will do worse, though a declining majority think *their* children will do better—another instance of wishful thinking.

Afterword

1. Ortega y Gasset, Juan. *The Revolt of the Masses.* W. W. Norton, New York: 1993 (3d ed.) at 93. The philosopher believed that a generation lasted about thirty years, the first half practicing revolution and the second half preserving its legacy. The Boomers are still upending the system forty years on, distinct from both their predecessors and their eventual successors, and in this sense are still pretty revolutionary. Ibid. at fn. 1.

2. Schmitt, Carl. *The Concept of the Political.* University of Chicago Press, 15 May 2007 (generally).

3. Gabler, Neal. "The Secret Shame of the Middle-Class Americans: Nearly Half of Americans Would Have Trouble Finding $400 to Pay for an Emergency. I'm One of Them." *Atlantic*, May 2016. The *Atlantic* article serves as the source for most of the material quoted about Gabler, with some exceptions including his education and age (he was born 1950), facts reported in several profiles including one in the *Great Lakes Review.* E.g., Root, Robert L., "GLR Interview: Neal Gabler," *Great Lakes Review*, vol. 11, no. 11 (Spring 1985), pp. 32–38.

4. US Department of the Treasury, Internal Revenue Service. "Social Security Benefits Eligible for the Federal Payment Levy Program," www.irs.gov/individuals/social-security-benefits-eligible-for-the-federal-payment-levy-program.

INDEX

Page numbers in italics refer to charts and graphs in the text.

INDEX